INTERNATIONAL TRADE FROM ECONOMIC AND POLICY PERSPECTIVE

Edited by **Vito Bobek**

International Trade from Economic and Policy Perspective
http://dx.doi.org/10.5772/2726
Edited by Vito Bobek

Contributors

Maria Hamideh Ramjerdi, Carlos Brito, Ricardo Correia, Sujinda Chemsripong, Jesús López-Rodríguez, Cosmin Bolea-Gabriel, Taufik Abdul Hakim, Imbarine Bujang, Anita Maček, Andrés Cartín-Rojas, Mercy Mpinganjira, Mauro Silva Ruiz, Alexandre de Oliveira e Aguiar, Pedro Luiz Cortez, Cláudia Echevenguá Teixeira, Gustavo Silveira Graudenz, Mosè Gallo, Elpidio Romano, Liberatina Carmela Santillo, Romana Korez-Vide

Published by InTech

Janeza Trdine 9, 51000 Rijeka, Croatia

Copyright © 2012 InTech

Notice

Publishing Process Manager Martina Durovic
Technical Editor InTech Prepress, Novi Sad
Cover InTech Design team

Additional hard copies can be obtained from orders@intechopen.com

International Trade from Economic and Policy Perspective, Edited by Vito Bobek
p. cm.
ISBN 978-953-51-0708-8

For EU product safety concerns:
IN TECH d.o.o., Prolaz Marije Krucifikse Kozulić 3, 51000 Rijeka, Croatia,
info@intechopen.com or visit our website at intechopen.com.

Meet the editor

Professor Vito Bobek currently works as a Professor of International Management at the University of Applied Sciences FH Joanneum (Graz, Austria) and at the University of Maribor (Slovenia). He is also a manager and owner of Palemid – Consulting, Research, Education LLC. His other positions are: Member of supervisory board at KBM Infond (Investment company, Maribor, Slovenia), Regional editor for Central and Eastern Europe at "European Journal of International Management", Member of editorial board at "International Journal of Trade and Global Markets", Member of editorial board at "Imago Europae" (Florence, Italy), Member of "Team Europe Slovenia". His research interests are related to International Business, Strategic Management, Regional Economic Integration, Cross-Cultural Management and Management of Cities and Regions.

Contents

Preface

Today's international trade is radically more complex. The revolution in information and communication technologies fostered an internationalisation of supply chains which created a nexus between trade, investment, and services which is at the heart of so much of today's international commerce.

Fundamental changes in recent decades have heightened the need for new and viable solutions to the problems of international trade. In the new climate of internationalisation an expanding number of firms are engaged in international trade, barriers have been coming down, and trading blocs, whose members may share the advantage of lower tariffs and the absence of quotas, are beginning to predominate. The degree of recent change has created an uncertainty that now demands new global trade systems - a new set of rules for the new environment. This book tackles some of the unresolved issues in international trade that will continue to press into the next decades. Covering an array of topics critical to today's scholar, economic policy designer and business leader, the book *International Trade from Economic and Policy Perspective* is comprised of four sections:

Section on international trade theories starts from the fact that due to different factor endowments and production possibilities, national economies produce a variety of goods at different relative costs. The exchange of these goods can be beneficial to both of the participating economies (trade advantage). Furthermore, economies can also specialise in the production of the goods for which they have a comparative production advantage (specialisation advantage). Theoretical critiques of international trade based on comparative advantage and imperfect competition analyze the impact of multi-national corporations and transfer of technology on patterns of trade. This section explores different theories of international trade and their impacts on domestic and global production and welfare.

Section on trade patterns is focused on regions. Regions interact with multiple actors, and industrial companies are one of the most important players in this interaction. Due to their strategic actions and relationships, companies are simultaneously present in different regions and influence a territory's dynamics and structure. Moreover, territorial characteristics are also a condition that can shape a company's action. This reciprocal influence is recognized by an emerging theoretical background of relational geography. Interest in this phenomenon is also increasing within the industrial network approach. However, the interactions between companies and regions have not been sufficiently explained. There are also two cases presented in this context: (1) One chapter focuses on the analysis of the different regional dynamics followed by Romanian counties over the period 1995-2008 and the link between them and the economic geography of the country. The analysis of the growth dynamics is carried out for the 42 counties in which Romania is divided using different time spans. (2) The second case explains the extent of intra-industry trade in Thailand's foreign trade, especially its main trading partner, the ASEAN Economic Community. The results show that, parallel to Thailand's trade with the world, its trade with the AEC is moving towards intra-industry type trading. Moreover, the growth of intra-industry trade between Thailand and the AEC shows that Thailand's industrial base is dramatically changing from low-technology products to high-technology industries, especially since the ASEAN Free Trade Area agreement with AEC was put into effect in 1993.

Section on government policies and international trade starts from the fact that trade policy continues to be at the centre of the international economic policy agenda. It is an arena of conflict between governments, multinational companies and non-governmental organizations. It is a major source of tension between the United States and the European Union. Trade policy has been criticized for operating in a way that damages hopes for economic development in the Global South. Economic analysis has provided a systematic framework for examining the underlying issues of international trade. Economics provides a way of distinguishing the self-interested claims that trade is harmful to some groups from other arguments that certain trade policies might benefit the nation as a whole. Although economists have consistently stressed the overall gains from international trade, and in recent years have stressed the measurement of those gains, the debate over trade policy is a never ending one.

Section on business perspective of international trade consists of two chapters. The current situation about the exploitation of natural resources and the increasing pollution deriving from many human activities and, in particular, from all technological products during their lifecycle is pushing toward a redefinition of products' design. Actually, this requires also a more radical change in consumers' habits and, hence, in the underlying business models. A possible answer to these needs could be recovery activities of products at the final phase of their lifecycle. There are many recovery options for end-of-life products, remanufacturing shows to be a very interesting one. In the following chapter it is explored how can a specific form of diagonal cumulation of origin affect the transaction costs of company's global value chain activities if it is introduced at supranational level and properly perceived by managers. Companies can optimize their global value chain activities through proactive management of Rules of Origin.

I'd really like to thank InTech publishing company for providing me with the opportunity to become the editor for this book. I appreciate that they believed in me to provide the knowledge and technical assistance to make this book a reality. We collaborated to find great authors that helped us create this book. In the end, I believe that the team of authors that was chosen provides the perfect blend of knowledge and skills that went into authoring this book. I thank each of the authors for devoting their time and effort towards this book; I think that it will be a great asset to the community! I also wish to thank all of our technical reviewers. Their efforts helped to make this book complete and we couldn't have done it without them.

Prof Vito Bobek
University of Applied Sciences FH Joanneum, Graz,
Austria
University of Maribor
Slovenia

Section 1

International Trade Theories

Chapter 1

A Survey of Effects of International Trade on Growth

Maria Hamideh Ramjerdi

Additional information is available at the end of the chapter

http://dx.doi.org/10.5772/50097

1. Introduction

For many centuries economist simply upgrades Riccardian models and argued that free trade based on comparative advantage and according to geographical distribution of factors of production and specialization leads to efficient use of resources and increases world production frontier a "win-win" situation. While according to liberal economist trade liberalization creates faster growth there are economists who proclaimed that countries become more dependent on foreign resources which control process domestic growth and development. Recent models incorporate economies of scale, imperfect competition, R&D and assume that trade liberalization determine the geographical location of industries therefore gain from trade (Helpman and Krugman, 1985). This paper will review and contrast literatures on Old Trade theories, Post Keynesian, Endogenous Growth Models and International Trade, The New Trade Theory, Economic Geography and Theories of National Competitive Advantage.

2. Comparative advantage

Smith (1776) international trade makes it possible to increase extend of the market and specialization due to division of labor increases the productivity therefore economic growth. The international trade generates a dynamic force by intensifying the specialization of labor, encouraging technical innovations and the accumulation of capital, making it possible to achieve economic growth. A Laissez-faire Laissez-passer policy allowed markets to flourish encouraged division of labor, specialization, and technological development, thereby encouraging growth.

Ricardo (1817) theory of comparative advantage is based on the labor theory of value and present a dynamic model of economic growth and characterized it by high savings, capital accumulation, increased production and productivity which increases demand for labor forcing wages to increase and growth. But, resources especially land are subject to diminishing returns, the production is immersed by wages in an increasing proportion, this will reduce incentive to investments, and economy will eventually reach the "stationary state." Young (1928) in Smith tradition examined how international trade increases the dimension of the market and limitation of the division of labor therefore productivity. He further studied the inter-relation between industries and creation of new industries and technological progress in the process of economic growth.

3. The post Keynesian

The post Keynesian growth accounting the determinants of growth and business cycle, the first model goes back to Kalecki (1935) with many similarities to Keynesian model and develops a consumption function and assumes capitalists save all their income and labor consumes all their income therefore capital formation depends on income distribution can be expanded to a growth model. Domar's (1957) growth model productive capacity and potential output is treated as a constant multiple of stock of capital a "razor's-edge" growth path at which any deviation from exogenously fixed rate of capital output ratio, growth path would diverge from natural growth path and become unstable. The growth rate of GDP was equal to the ratio investment to GDP lagged by one year divided by the ratio of "required" investment to desired growth, the Incremental Capital Output Ratio. Harrod's (1953) fundamental equation the warranted rate of growth is a function of saving and optimal capital output ratio which is different from actual capital output ratio. Capital output ratio was treated exogenously. Harrod-Domar growth model closed economy model was path breaking in the sense they treated growth as an endogenous variable. Domar treats high unemployment rate as a given, therefore the surplus of labor will be absorbed by any additional capital formation. Domar claimed investment had two effects, adds to demand by purchase of new goods also adds to capacity, supply, but the problem was balancing aggregate demand and supply. Domar indicated that these two effects would not necessarily be equal which could cause economy to spiral off into either to prolonged overproduction or prolonged underproduction. If actual capital output ratio does not grow at the same rate as optimal capital output ratio the gap between actual growth and optimal growth will widen and economy will never return to optimal growth path, this financial gap according to World Bank report (1993) countries will require significant amount of foreign capital inflows ... "to provide sufficient resources to sustain economic growth" (p. 32.)

The literature on international trade and growth are built using absolute and comparative advantage and the Hecksher-Ohlin model, the Two by Two by Two model (two countries, two commodities, two factors). Their model makes a clear distinction between domestic and external factor mobility. Factor mobility is within the same country between domestic industries and assumed no international factor immobility takes place. Each country for each good has the same constant returns to scale production function but their capital and labor endowments are different. In the absence of trade, the more labor abundant countries would produce labor intensive goods as would be relatively cheaper than capital intensive goods and the more capital abundant countries would produce capital intensive goods as would be relatively cheaper than labor intensive goods. After trade, countries export goods intensive in the use of their more abundant factor, and import goods intensive in the use of their scarce factor. In long run trade will equate relative prices in different countries, and relative factor prices, assuming no transportation costs, relative price and factor price will be equal. The Heckscher-Ohlin trade model is focused on the idea that a major source of comparative advantage is international differences in factor endowments, the relative factor abundance and intensity is what drives trade patterns between countries.

Leontief (1953) used United States trade data from 1947 and performed the first empirical test of the Heckscher-Ohlin theorem. The United States was capital abundant relative to the rest of the world should have been importing labor intensive goods and exporting capital intensive goods but results showed the contrary which in literature is called "Leontief's paradox." Leontief's paradox has inspired a large body of research in international trade theory, for example Romalis (2004) developed an comprehensive version of the Heckscher-Ohlin model to be consistent with empirical data by taking into account variables such as multiple countries, technology, production variation, and human capital.

The Stolper-Samuelson theorem or so called Hecksher-Ohlin-Samuelson model examines the effects of international trade on employment and income, and concludes that under free trade the scarce factors of trading nations due to price equalization are to lose under free trade under, therefore in the United States since labor is considered as the scarce factor of production will not benefit from free trade. Rybczynski (1955) (Rybczynski theorem) builds on the Stolper-Samuelson theorem and "allows predictions about the resulting changes in a country's equilibrium trade volume and terms of trade. As the stock of capital grows, desired trade at given terms of trade will increase (decrease) if the country is capital-abundant (labor-abundant) relative to its trading partners. An expansion of the capital stock will thus lead to deterioration (improvement) in the country's terms of trade. Corresponding results hold for an expansion of labor with capital held constant." (Rybczynski, 1955)

The quasi-Heckscher-Ohlin prediction is that "countries capture larger shares of world production and trade in commodities that more intensively use their abundant factor."The quasi-Rybczynski effect is "countries that accumulate a factor faster than the rest of the world will see their production and export structure move towards commodities that more intensively use that factor." (Romalis, 2004)

Feder (1982) developed a framework to show the impact of international trade on economic growth by presenting a dualistic growth model by dividing the economy into two productive sectors, export sector and non-export sector, and concluded that the rate grow of investment, labor and exports explains the rate of growth of economy. Further the allocation of one unit of capital to the export sector would create higher marginal value for the economy than what would be have been generated by a non-export sector.

Ram (1987) expanded Feder's model using of time-series to data for 88 countries for the years 1960-1982 and concluded there was a positive correlation between exports and economic growth for more than 80% of the countries. Coe and Helpman (1993) examined the important role of domestic R&D as well as imported sum of R&D of a country's trade partner on the path of total productivity factor (TPF). They used accumulated R&D stock as a proxy for each countries stock of knowledge by using data from 22 industrialized economies for the period 1971-1990, the results showed both domestic and foreign R&D have a positive relation effect on a country's TPF. Further the more open the economy the greater the effect of the stock of external R&D on the domestic TPF and that the less developed countries benefited the most from the stocks of external R&D. Keller (1996) questioned Coe and Helpman's results and since he was also able to estimate foreign R&D spillover effects using bilateral trade share rather than the actual trade shares as a country does not have to directly trade with another country such as country A to benefit from the R&D spillover as long as one of its trade partners is engaged in with trade with country A will benefit from spillover.

4. Endogenous growth models and international trade

Endogenous growth theories treat growth as endogenous and as a result of scale and accumulation there is a positive relation between scale and productivity which outweigh the impact of accumulation which in the neoclassical model leads to diminishing returns. Schumpeter (1942) coined the seemingly paradoxical term "creative destruction," as primary source of economic growth:

"The opening up of new markets, foreign or domestic, and the organizational development from the craft shop to such concerns as U.S. Steel illustrate the same process of industrial mutation—if I may use that biological term—that incessantly revolutionizes the economic structure from within, incessantly destroying the old one, incessantly creating a new one. This process of Creative Destruction is the essential fact about capitalism." (p. 83). Schumpeter, coined the phrase "technological unemployment" the evolutionary process of growth is entrepreneurship and competition which fuel "creative destruction"

"The fundamental impulse that sets and keeps the capitalist engine in motion comes from the new consumers' goods, the new methods of production or transportation, the new markets, the new forms of industrial organization that capitalist enterprise creates." (p. 83)

Schumpeter (1942), recognized and analyzed the fluctuations in economic activity under capitalism although accepts the Say's Law, that the economy is self-correcting, in long-run equilibrium cannot be at less than full employment. He clearly distinguished between "'invention," the advancement knowledge and the "innovation," the economic activities of using that knowledge as well as capital accumulation as the cause of economic growth. Schumpeter by outlining the trajectories of creativity in five industries steel, automobiles, textiles, electric power and railroads in three countries US, UK and Germany demonstrate the significance of economies of scale and that creative destruction is the engine of capitalism which can be simplified into two terms:

1. The contribution from entry and exit.
2. The contribution of economies of scale

International trade creates specialization and economies of scales therefore economic growth.

Kenneth Arrow (1962) coined the term "learning by doing" and viewed the level of the "learning" coefficient is a function of collective investment. Learning was treated as a function of the absolute level of knowledge already accumulated in. "Learning by doing " of human capital just like physical capital accumulates and is a function of the accumulated knowledge, the aggregate human capital or "technical knowledge" . There is a positive spillover of accumulation of inputs on productivity which offsets diminishing return. Arrow assumed that A_i, the technical augmentation factor, is specific to the firm as well as the total "knowledge" in the economy which arises from past cumulative investment of all firms and is easily available to all forms in the process of "learning-by-doing," therefore is a public good and is a free good.

Therefore, the "economy-wide" aggregate production function is:

$$Y = A\,K^{a+z}L^{1-a}$$

Where z is accumulates of capital. Arrow (1962) assumed that $a + z < 1$, which implies increase of capital or labor does not lead to increasing returns, rather increasing returns arise because new knowledge is discovered in the process of investment and production and such knowledge became publicly known, external to individual firms.

Barro and Sala -i-Martin (1995) assume "learning-by-doing" is through each firm's investment, therefore there is a direct relation between a firm's capital stock and stock of knowledge. Further assume knowledge is a public good therefore all firm could access knowledge at zero cost once discovered, a portion of knowledge spills over instantly across the whole economy. Further the existence of increasing returns to scale does not alter the distribution of the output among the factors of production, the payment of marginal products of each input as in a competitive market, there is not such a mechanism that leads to a socially optimal equilibrium the distribution of knowledge, which implies the social rate of return is greater than the private rate of return of investment. To remedy Barro and Sala-i-Marin suggest subsidizing purchase of capital good or subsidizing production to reach optimum level of investment in the economy.

Paul Romer (1986) uses Arrow's "learning by doing" and argues that the rate of growth of capital alone may yield increasing returns, that $a + z > 1$ was possible. Romer presented an endogenous growth model in which "technological change in which long-run growth is driven primarily by the accumulation of knowledge by forward-looking, profit-maximizing agents." (1003) He further assumes "new knowledge is assumed to be the product of a research technology' that exhibits diminishing returns, this assumption implies that the long run rate of growth is independent of saving-investment quota. That is, given the stock of knowledge at a point in time, doubling the inputs into research will not double the amount of new knowledge produced. In addition, investment in knowledge suggests a natural externality. The creation of new knowledge by one firm is assumed to have a positive external effect on the production possibilities of other firms because knowledge cannot be perfectly patented or kept secret." (1003) and "knowledge is a capital good with an increasing marginal product." (1005) Further "Given increasing marginal productivity of knowledge, increasing marginal productivity of a composite k would still be possible if the increasing marginal productivity of knowledge were sufficient to outweigh the decreasing marginal productivity associated with the physical capital." (1020)

Romer (1990) proposed the technological progress appears with new knowledge formation, the knowledge via human capital can serve as an important production tools that like other forms of capitals which leads to increase in the national income of the advanced countries. In contrast, the developing countries with abundant manpower and capital have not reached a sustainable economic development. "The growth rate is increasing in the stock of human capital, but it does not depend on the total size of the labor force or the population. In a limiting case that may be relevant for historical analysis and for the poorest countries today, if the stock of human capital is too low, growth may not take place at all." (77) In this model Romer treats" knowledge as nonrival good makes it possible to talk sensibly about knowledge spillovers, that is, incomplete excludability." (79)

Romer (1990) model assumes there are four inputs labor, human capital, capital and an index of the level of the technology. Human capital is captured by such factors as education and on the job training, and final output is a function of these inputs. Under the specification of the model the economies with a larger total stock of human capital will experience faster growth and further put forward that free international trade can accelerate growth. Finally the model suggests the low growth rate in underdeveloped economies with large population can be explained by the low levels of human capital.

Spencer and Brander (1983) (1985) papers analyze the role of R&D policy on trade and conclude that R&D could play a significant role in trade. Both papers assume an international duopoly and use Cournot oligopoly model wherein a domestic firm and a foreign firm compete in a third-country market. Spencer and Brander (1983) use game theory in which a mixture of an export subsidy and R&D can increase domestic welfare by diverting profits from the foreign to the domestic firm, further R&D subsidy gives incentive to the domestic firm to increase the level of R&D, causing the foreign firm to reduce its R&D and exports, therefor home government can effectively subsidize or tax the home firm and influence the outcome of the game between firms.

The significance of the linkage between R&D activities, trade and growth has been highlighted intensely in the R&D based open economy growth models of Grossman and Helpman (1990, 1991). Trade leads to an increase in productivity and growth by providing a wider range of intermediate inputs. The analysis mostly focuses on the rate of innovation, which is the main source of sustained growth and how the outcomes of international trade affect innovations.

Models developed by Rivera-Batiz and Romer (1991) and Young (1991) centered on the effects of knowledge spillovers and international trade on the R&D activities that stem within domestic economies. Baldwin and Forslid (2000) also analyze R&D competition at international level and how this competition enhance growth by stimulating competition in the R&D sector at the global scale but they do not show how global competition of R&D affects either trade patterns or factor allocations.

Hausman, Hwang, and Rodrik (2007) maintain that "right" specialization permanently affects long-run growth which implies "leapfrogging" strategies aims to transfer the production of high technology products to developing economies. It is further argued that China's economic policies have led to **an** extensive leapfrogging in technology, and raise concern about its risk to U.S. security and commercial interests (Rodrik, 2006), (Choate and Miller, 2005) (Gomory and Baumol, 2000) and (Samuelson, 2004).

Gomory and Baumol (2000) and Samuelson (2004) use the comparative advantage equilibrium theory to examine how changing patterns of global production can affect the distribution of gains from trade. They conclude that advance of trade may not be the conventional "the win- win outcomes," rather trade expansion may generate winners and losers countries. The distribution of gains that regulates the terms of trade rest on the differences of supply and demand supply such as the relative prices of exports and imports, these factors can change therefore change the gains from trade.

Samuelson (2004) analysis the economic implications effects of increase in productivity of foreign trading partners due to technology catch-up that increase in productivity of foreign trading partners such as China, through domestic innovation or by transfer of technology through U.S. firms outsourcing of production to China, may weaken the United States' share of the gains from trade. China by catching up in the production of traditionally specialized export goods by United States will increase global supply and lowers price U.S. export, worsening the United States' terms of trade while the United States gains from trade but less than prior to China catching up.

Gomory and Baumol (2000) analyze the effects of transfer of industries and loss of the industrial base to other countries. Highlighting on the fact that comparative advantage in the 21th century is created and not endowed unlike the 18th century world when trade was based on endowments natural resource which determined the pattern of comparative advantage. In today's world, technology drives comparative advantage, and technology can be significantly influenced by human actions and policies which have enormous implications for the distribution of gains from trade among countries. Their models help international trade theory to integrate the new realities of globalization.

New endogenous growth models emphasize that international trade increases the rate of economic growth. Yet, less known is that if endogenous growth cans "permanently reduced rates of growth, as when trade pushes an economy to specialize in sectors with no dynamic scale or other benefits. The theoretical relationship between trade and growth is fundamentally ambiguous." (Rodrik, 1999, p.27).

5. The new trade theory

Grubel and Lloyd (1975) demonstrated that, a high percentage of trade took place within intra-industry rather than inter-industry. Balassa (1967) indicated that trade within intra-industry incurred with few costs of adjustment. These papers opened the way to new trade theory.

Krugman (1979 and 1981) in a Heckscher–Ohlin model of international trade model changes the traditional assumption of perfectly competitive market to monopolistically competitive market in which specialization occurs via intra-industry trade and large scale production with lower prices and a larger selections of products is the core of new trade theory. The New Trade Theory build on the principal of old trade theory of the factor price equalization and integrates factor markets internationally, the Rybczynski and Heckscher-Ohlin theorems, connecting factor endowments to production and patterns of trade, and the Stolper–Samuelson theorem, linking fluctuations in commodities prices to fluctuations in real factor payments.

Helpman (1987) used the monopolistically competitive model with manufacturing trade data between advanced economies, and showed that its main predictions were consistent. Hummels and Levinsohn (1995) showed that the monopolistically competitive model to work equally well for trade flows between non-OECD (Organization for Economic Co-operation and Development) countries, which one would expect comparative advantage to be overriding. On the contrary Evenett and Keller (2002) empirical work support the monopolistically competitive approach since the data for countries with a greater share of intra-industry trade are a better fit.

Krugman (1991) noted that the home-market effect "wholly dependent on increasing returns; in a world of diminishing returns, strong domestic demand for a good will tend to make it an import rather than an export" (p. 955). Davis and Weinstein (1999, 2002) industry production increases more than one to one with local demand for a good with convincing sign of increasing returns for manufacturing industries in both OECD countries and Japanese regions. Head and Ries (2001) find sign of similar to Davis and Weinstein for Canada and the United States. Both studies are consistent with home-market effects concluded that when technology and factor prices were similar, home-market effects were feasibly strongest.

6. Economic geography

The Home Market Effect is the main engine of the accumulation processes stressed by the new economic geography models. (Krugman, 1991) takes incomes as exogenous, but, in his paper titled "Increasing Returns and Economic Geography," published in the Journal of Political Economy in 1991 Krugman treats incomes as endogenous, because fully developed international factor mobility. Brander and Spencer (1985) and Krugman and Obstfeld (1992) formulate the notion of "strategic trade" assume two countries with different elasticities of demand, with national level internal economies of scale, when countries are historically ahead of other countries in producing a good, because of capacity to produce at a lower price due to economies of scale, then they have an advantage over others countries at the starting strategic point.

7. Theory of national competitive advantage

According to Stone and Ranchhod (2006), Porter's "focus on competition or 'rivalry' is a diversion from traditional economic thinking." (284) The primary contribution of Porter's

(1990) in The Competitive Advantage of Nations is to the analysis of investment and international trade, within the scope of the economic development of nations. Porter presents a model in which innovation is the focus of formation and sustainment of competitive advantage. Competitive advantage consists of strategies which matches a firm's resources to be successful in the market. Porter formulates a strategy in which firm's resource prospect is not only a function of its own previous investments, but also is a function of the positions of supply and formation of resources within its environment. Porter adopts a Schumpeterian concept of a process of dynamic change in which innovation and imitation constantly creates and destroys positions of competitive advantage. Change may be exogenous through the development of new technologies, change in demand, new industry, change in supply of resources, or changes in government regulations. On the other hand, change may be endogenous through innovation by firms, once created competitive advantage is subject to destruction.

Porter (1990) identifies four classes of a country's features the "National Diamond" land, labor and capital (including human capital), and distinguishes between skilled and unskilled labor, the underlying conditions for the determination the national competitive advantage of a nation and further emphases more on demand differences than on similarities to explain the international competitiveness of countries. In his model both the size of the home demand as well as the sophistication of home country buyers matters as is the configuration of home demand that shapes country's firms production, innovation to maintain their competitive positions to meet expectations of the home buyers. Explicitly, Porter (1990, 1998) regards sophisticated and demanding buyers as the main conditions for home demand to increase the market share of that industry, this maintain the competitive position of a firm and leads international demand.

However, dissimilar demand circumstances in different countries creates different demand structures therefore the geographical location economies of increasing returns, as explained by Economic Geography theories by Krugman & Obstfeld (2003) due to a specific set of demand conditions in a geographical location determines the location of an industry with economies of increasing returns, therefore comparative advantage is determined by demand conditions rather than differences in resource endowments. "Geographic concentrations of interconnected companies and Institutions in the particular field" (Porter, 1998) "Clusters are not seen as fixed flows of goods and services, but rather as dynamic arrangements based on knowledge creation, increasing returns and innovation in a broad sense" (Krugman, 1991)

8. Conclusion

The evolution of trade theory, from old trade doctrines Smith and Riccardo to the New Trade Theory, all seem to support of the free trade. In world of inadequate demand and unemployment, strategic policies to stimulate demand through such methods as subsidies and under-valued exchange rates, home industries that benefit from economies of scale, and increasing return, could results in gain from trade at the expense of expense of other countries. Never the less, these demand policies might increase demand for global production which stimulates the global economy.

Blinder discussed that "Although there are no reliable national data, fragmentary studies indicate that well under a million service-sector jobs in the United States have been lost to offshoring to date. (A million seems impressive, but in the gigantic and rapidly churning U.S. labor market, a million jobs is less than two weeks' worth of normal gross job losses.) However, constant improvements in technology and global communications virtually guarantee that the future will bring much more offshoring of "impersonal services" -- that is, services that can be delivered electronically over long distances with little or no degradation in quality." (2006). Which raise questions about the effects of international outsourcing and transfer of technology on domestic economies. Although companies earn foreign profits, outsourcing can weaken national income if it transfers technology that increases competition for domestic exports industries. On the other hand as corporations transfer the innovation and technology to a foreign production locations it contribute to progress of innovations and advancement of technology increases global production frontier and maximizes global profit but as Samuelson (2004) pointed this might not lead to maximize national gain, there will be winners and losers.

Author details

Maria Hamideh Ramjerdi
Montclair State University, William Paterson University, U.S.A.

9. References

[1] Arrow, K. J. The Economic Implication of Learning by Doing. The Review of Economic Studies, Vol. 29, No. 3 (Jun. 1962), pp. 155-173
[2] Balassa, B. Trade Liberalization among Industrial Countries, New York: McGraw-Hill. 1967
[3] Baldwin, R. E. and R. Forslid. Trade Liberalization and Endogenous Growth a Q-Theory Approach. Journal of International Economics. 2000 Vol. 50, pp. 497–517.
[4] Barro, R. J. and Sala-i-Martin, X. Economic Growth, McGraw-Hill, New York. 1995
[5] Blinder, Alan. Offshoring: The Next Industrial Revolution? Foreign Affairs, March/April 2006.
[6] Brander, J. A. and Spencer, B. J. Export Subsidies and International Market Share Rivalry. Journal of International Economics 1985, 18, 83–100.
[7] Choate, Pat, and Edward A. Miller. U.S.-China Advanced Technology Trade: An Analysis for U.S.-China Economic and Security Review Commission. Washington, Virginia: Manufacturing Policy Project, April 2005.
[8] Coe, D. and Helpman, E. International R&D spillovers. National Bureau of Economic Research (NBER) 1993 Working Paper no 4444.
[9] Domar, E. Essays in the Theory of Economic Growth. Oxford: Oxford University Press 1957

[10] Evenett, S. J. and Keller, W. On Theories Explaining the Success of the Gravity Equation. Journal of Political Economy 2002 110, 281–316.
[11] Feder, Gershon. On Export and Economic Growth. Journal of Development Economics, 1983 vol. 12, pp. 59-73. Economic Studies
[12] Davis, D. R. and Weinstein, D. E. Economic Geography and Regional Production Structure: An Empirical Investigation. European Economic Review 1999, 43, 379–407.
[13] Davis, D. R. and Weinstein, D. E. Bones, Bombs, and Break Points: The Geography of Economic Activity. American Economic Review 2002 92, 1269–1289.
[14] Hausman, Ricardo, Jason Hwang, and Dani Rodrik. What You Export Matters. Journal of Economic Growth 2007 12:1-25
[15] Harrod, R.F. Full Capacity vs. Employment Growth: Comment. Quarterly Journal of Economics, 1953 Vol. 67 (4), p.553-9.
[16] Helpman, E. Imperfect Competition and International Trade: Evidence from Fourteen Industrial Countries. Journal of the Japanese and International Economies 1987 1, 62–81.
[17] Hummels, D. and Levinsohn, J. Monopolistic Competition and International Trade:Reconsidering the Evidence. Quarterly Journal of Economics 1995 110, 799–836.
[18] Gomory, Ralph and William Baumol. Global Trade and Conflicting National Interest. Cambridge, MA: MIT Press, 2000
[19] Grossman, G. M. and E. Helpman. Trade, Innovation and Growth. American Economic Review, 1990 Vol. 80, pp. 86–91.
[20] Grossman, G. M. and E. Helpman (1991) Innovation and Growth in the Global Economy, Cambridge Mass.: MIT Press.
[21] Grubel, H. G. and Lloyd, P. J. Intra-industry Trade: The Theory and Measurement of International Trade in Differentiated Products, London: Macmillan. 1975
[22] Heckscher, Eli F and Bertil Ohlin, Hechscher-Ohlin Trade Theory, translated, edited and introduces by Harry Flam and M June Flanders Cambridge, Mass., MIT Press 1991
[23] Kalecki, Michael. A Macro-dynamic Theory of Business Cycle. Economica 1935 Vol 3 pp 327-344
[24] Keller, Wolfgang. Are international R&D spillovers trade-related?: Analyzing spillovers among randomly matched trade partners. European Economic Review, Elsevier, September 1998.vol. 42(8), pages 1469-1481
[25] Krugman, Paul. Increasing Returns, Monopolistic Competition, and International Trade. Journal of InternationalEconomics 1979
[26] Krugman Paul. Scale Economies, Product Differentiation, and the Pattern of Trade. American Economic Review paper December 1980, 70, 950–959
[27] Krugman, Paul. Import Protection as Export Promotion: International competition in the Presence of Oligopoly and Economies of Scale,. in Henryk Kierzkowski, ed., Monopolistic Competition in International Trade. Oxford University Press, 1984, 180-193.
[28] Krugman, Paul. Increasing Returns and Economic Geography. The Journal of Political Economy. June 1991 Vol. 99, No. 3. pp. 483-499.
[29] Krugman, Paul and Maurice Obstfeld. The Case Against EMU," The Economist, June 13, 1992.

[30] Krugman, Paul and Maurice Obstfeld. International Economics: Theory and Policy. 7th edition, (Pearson Addison-Wesley 2005) 1st edn. 1998, 7th edn. 2006.

[31] Leontief, Wassily. Domestic Production and Foreign Trade: The American Capital Position Re-examined. Proceedings of the American Philosophical Society September 1953 97, no. 4 pages 332–349.

[32] Porter, Michael E. The Competitive Advantage of Nations. New York: Free Press 1990

[33] Porter, Michael E. Clusters and the new economics of competition. Harvard Business Review, 1998 76(6), pp. 77–90.

[34] Ram, Rati. Exports and economic growth in developing countries: evidence from tim eseries and cross-section data. Economic Development and Cultural Change, 1987, Vol. 36, no 1, pp. 51-72.

[35] Rivera-Batiz, L. A. and P. M. Romer. Economic Integration and Endogenous Growth. Quarterly Journal of Economics, 1991Vol. 106, pp. 531–555.

[36] Rodrik, Dani. What's So Special About Chinese Exports? China and World Economy 2006

[37] Romalis, John. Factor Proportions and the Structure of Commodity Trade. American Economic Review March 2004, 95, no. 1, 70.

[38] Romer, Paul M. Increasing Returns and Long Run Growth. Journal of Political Economy, 1986 No 98, pp.1002-1037.

[39] Romer, Paul M. Endogenous Technological Change. Journal of Political Economy, 1990, Vol.98, N°5, pp.71-102.

[40] Rybczynski, T. M. Factor Endowment and Relative Commodity Prices. Economica 1955, 23 (88): 352–359.

[41] Samuelson, Paul. Where Ricardo and Mill Rebut and Confirm Arguments of Mainstream Economists Supporting Globalization. Journal of Economic Perspectives2004. 18, 3 page 135-46.

[42] Schumpeter, J. Capitalism, Socialism, and Democracy. New York, Harper Brothers Publishers 1942.

[43] Spencer, B. J. and Brander, J. A. International R&D Rivalry and Industrial Strategy. Review of Economic Studies. 1983, 50, 707–722.

[44] Stolper, Wolfgang, and Paul A. Samuelson. Protection and Real Wages. Review of Economic Studies Nomber 1941 IX pages 58–73

[45] Stone, H.B.J. & Ranchhod, A. Competitive advantage of a nation in the global arena: a quantitative advancement to Porter's diamond applied to the UK, USA and BRIC nations. Strategic Change, 2006 15: 283–294.

[46] World Bank. Guyana: From Economic Recovery to Sustained Growth 1993

[47] Young, Allyn A. Increasing Returns and Economic Progress. The Economic Journal, 1928 volume 38 , pp. 527-42.

[48] Young, A. Learning by Doing and the Dynamic Effects of International Trade. Quarterly Journal of Economics, 1991 Vol. 106, pp. 369–405.

Section 2

Trade Patterns

Chapter 2

Regions as Networks: Towards a Conceptual Framework of Territorial Dynamics

Carlos Brito and Ricardo Correia

Additional information is available at the end of the chapter

http://dx.doi.org/10.5772/46093

1. Introduction

Regions are frequently indentified as mere containers of activity that are confined to static territorial borders. Such an approach does not provide an accurate image of the specificities of territorial dynamics and gives rise to political management options which are exceedingly focused within territorial limits. The cluster concept defined by Porter [1, 2] is a clear example of such regional characterisation. According to this author, clusters are groups that are geographically near associated companies and institutions linked by similarities and complementarities in a certain domain [2]. The cluster is a strong organisational model, according to Porter, which provides efficiency, effectiveness and flexibility [1]. Along this line of thought, the regional or cluster development depends upon the co-localisation of competing and complementary enterprises supported by a good infrastructure network and support services [3]. Such a concept focuses inside the territory and is based upon a list of material resources that should be made available to the region and the companies located therein.

Underlying the success formula is conglomeration of companies within a close geographical space. Clusters are thus highly typical realities [1] and invariably show some characteristics which will develop the region where they are located. However, these analyses do not include the entire multiple and compounding elements which, with their diversity, may help enhance development. There is not a single mechanism to explain how a dynamic region eventuates [4]. Martin and Sunley [5] indicate a lack of clarity in the conceptualisation as well as empiric insufficiencies in the advantages attributed to clusters, defining them as "one-model-fits-all". Nevertheless, many policies on regional development follow this direction. Stimulus packages are handed out to regions to promote their take-off, normally in the form of subsidies, infrastructures and tax deductions. Whilst these measures have a positive impact "they are certainly problematical when they occur in a vacuum" [6,

p. 587], i.e., when they do not take into consideration the organisational and institutional basis of regional dynamism.

An institutional reference is clearly lacking in the explanation of spatial relationships in Porter's cluster concept [7]. Many regional developmental conditions are institutional and cultural, and are made up of "untraded forms of interdependency between economic agents, and hence they collectively constitute the relational assets of the regional economy (...) Relational assets of this sort are not freely reproducible from one place to another, and access to them is determined at least in part through network membership". This is often called the relational capital [8, 9] and is made up of social and economic relationships in a given geographical space [8]. The relational capital of a certain region is often one of its most important sources of success due to its inimitability characteristics [9].

Part of the advantages often attributed to clusters derives from the co-localisation of companies in a contiguous area and from the exchange of ideas and co-operation between them. A basic tenet for this approach shows more cooperation and interdependence between companies located near one another [10]. However, "the empirical evidence suggests that the prosperity and dynamics of clusters as compared to other locations may be unrelated to the co-location of firms from specific industries there, and that individual firms in clusters need not, on average, derive any unique advantages from their locations" [11, p. 450].

In a recent study on three winegrowing clusters located in Italy and in Chile, Giuliani [12] demonstrates that interaction and knowledge transfer in clusters surfaces in a selective manner for predetermined reasons and not randomly, whereas all can benefit and interact just by being there. When the cluster companies lack expertise and show low competences, the most advanced companies have no interest in linking with them and will cut off all internal interaction and connections in accordance with Coe and Bunnel [13, p. 439] when they state "innovation should not be considered in the context of an anarchic, placeless "space of flows" [14], but rather in terms of situated social relations between appropriate actors, in turn embedded in particular places".

Innovation and interaction cannot be explained by mere geographical proximity and company bundling [15, 16]. "Neighbours might ignore or even hate one another. Local firms can be rivals and refuse any cooperation" [17, p. 48]. The relational component is essential to generate a distinctive element. Companies do not cooperate and interact just because someone orders them to do so. The success of a region does not arise of nowhere in an automatic process, but derives from decades of interaction between different companies and organisations located in various regions [4]. In the cluster concept, there is also a clear tendency to focus on the internal analysis and on local elements, which results in neglected external factors [18]. Conversely, "clusters can rarely be viewed as regional systems (...) because regions are strongly dependent on national institutions and other external influences" [7, p. 204]. Local initiative and its interdependence and dependence on other regions are the conditions a region needs to prosper [19]. This is due to actors who are "capable of acting in real time in different places, which means that their registers of actions go far beyond their mere location" [17, p. 53]. In this manner, what is most relevant for the analysis is not defining where an actor is located, but to determine in what ways their actions can evolve simultaneously in various geographical directions.

Clusters cannot be conceived solely with regard to their internal linkages. It is imperious to recognise their external dimensions [4, 20, 21] since local economies reflect the policies and strategies of actors located in various regions [19]. The limitations associated to the traditional stand of economic geography and cluster theory have provided ground for a new trend within geography that reinforces the interactive and relational component. In fact "while regions (...) have been conceptualized intensively, less attention has been paid to their relations" [22, p. 540] and it is necessary to discover and research how interactions eventuate in different spaces [23]. This relational geography modifies the understanding of territorial dynamism and places the essence of regional economies within the dense interaction between all the various actors [24]. The industrial network approach is also characterising space relationally. The backdrop idea is that space and resources interact and affect each other [25]. The relevance of entrepreneurial interaction, irrespective of company localisation, is stressed in these approaches [4].

Due to their interactions, companies have become one of the most relevant actors in the shaping of territories. They create territorial characteristics in the way they train workers and in the way they introduce know-how into the region where they are implanted, and in their interacting they manage to bring about close contact between different territorial contexts [26, 27]. Although relationships and interactions established between companies and territories have become an important area of research "such relationships need clearer articulation and understanding." So far, "little attention has been paid to the precise nature of that relationship", and this has led to the fact that "the relationships between firms and territories are weakly conceptualized" [27, p. 346]. Equally neglected are the interactions between companies and other organisations creating economic value in the territory [28]. Indeed, classical systems of territorial management do not provide an accurate image of the mechanisms underlying relational and interactive dimensions of space, and thus the need to create knowledge in such a domain becomes obvious. Many territorial administrators "continue to maintain the reductionist assumption" and consider regions "as single, integrated, unitary, material objects to be addressed by planning instruments" [24, p. 624].

Because of (1) the obvious maladjustment between reality and the theories that assume regions as airtight entities, (2) and the theoretical insufficiencies in the explanation of the dynamic and interactive relationship between companies and regions, it is necessary to develop methodological tools that make it possible to approach space as a product of relationships and influences between various actors spreading far beyond their "artificial" physical boundaries. The objective of this chapter is to contribute to a better understanding of the dynamic and interactive relationship between companies and regions. Thus, we explore the contributions from relational geography concepts and the industrial network approach. We propose an analytical model that explains how companies' strategic action is reflected upon the territorial dynamics and structure and how such factors affect the companies' strategic action.

This chapter is divided into six sections. Firstly, we address territorial studies from the perspective of the relational geography approach that challenges the traditional vision of territorial management and economic geography. The second section outlines in some detail the process of companies' interactions from the perspective of the Industrial Networks analysis. With this strong theoretical contribution, it is possible to understand companies' interaction and strategic action that constitute one of the most important factors for territorial dynamics, highlighted but not sufficiently explained by the relational geography. In the third and fourth sections, we proceed to apply the recent industrial network approach contributions to spatial analysis and in this way reinforce the research deriving from relational geography. In the fifth section, based on the aforementioned theoretical approaches, we develop a theoretical model aimed at answering what has been detected as lacking and that can constitute a base to reinforce knowledge in this area which remains relatively unclear. The final section presents our conclusions and also suggestions for further research.

2. The relational geography contribution

The concept of territory has been evolving due to the inclusion of relational elements in its characterisation, and this has originated what is currently known as "relational geography" [9, 27-34]. Relational geography represents "a theoretical orientation where actors and the dynamic processes of change and development engendered by their relations are central units of analysis" [31, p. 109]. It came about because the traditional approaches of economic geography were unable to explain micro dynamics which support different means of economic coordination [31]. In traditional approaches, regions are considered as economic actors, and the real actors (people, companies and institutions) with the capacity to change and mould the region are often ignored. The factors explaining the decision-making process for localisation are physical distance and cost reduction.

The relational approach is based upon the interactions occurring at a micro level because of diverse territorial processes. Space is analysed in a continuous relationship with the economy and in sharp contrast with previous positions that take it as a separate entity which is truly independent of economic actions [27, 30, 33]. Thus, "economic actors and their action and interaction should be at the core of a theoretical framework of economic geography [30, p. 123-124] since the "economic action and interaction are the central object of knowledge in the analysis" [30, p. 125]. The conceptual basis for relational geography is based upon an institutional perspective [35, 36]. Here, actors' actions and objectives are not previously defined in order to conform to maximisation and rational logic. Instead, they are moulded by specific social contexts of the area where they are located at and which shape their actions. "We cannot understand economic geographies outside a set of formative, if perpetually changing and challenged, social relations" [37, p. 339].

There are three consequences of actions and economic interactions in the relational conceptualisation [28, 30]: (1) The relevance of the context – agents are considered to act within specific contexts of social, cultural and institutional relationships which create formal and informal relationships. On the other hand, theorists of relational geography try to frame the companies' actions within a specific space context and time framework [38]. (2) A *path-dependence* – a geographic place has "a memory which shapes the path of subsequent developments" [39, p. 603]. Past decisions influence future paths. (3) The contingency – notwithstanding the importance of the past, economic processes are not predetermined, as the individual and collective strategies are contingent and may alter the existing structures. These characteristics imply that there are no general laws of economic action and so the generic policies of territorial development cannot be developed as an ever-successful recipe that works every time the ingredients are available (as is postulated in the cluster theory). Instead they must be based upon an evolutionary and contextual understanding of economic action [28].

The relational view of territory does not assume local, national or global spheres as different components from the organisation and from social action. Indeed, it promotes a relational understanding of each of those as a "nexus of multiple and asymmetric interdependencies among and between local and wider fields of action, organisation and influence [40, p. 153]. This point of view makes the network perspective an excellent way to approach the relational space. The main advantage of a network approach is that it can transcend all those scales without falling into the conceptual trap of preferring any one of those [32]. Geographical lenses can be used to focus on specific localised representations of the economic processes [30] taking into consideration that any scale is co-maker of a dynamic and complex geographic reality in its entirety [41].

The network approach makes it possible to pinpoint various interactions between actors located in various territories but whose results show up in specific places [32]. "Space is bound into networks and any assessment of spatial qualities is simultaneously an assessment of network relations" [42, p. 332] given that most of the dynamics of a territory may lie in actors localised in other geographical spaces [32, 33, 43]. Reinforcing this point, Malecki [44] states that some territories or places are capable of creating and attracting economic activities just because they are able to establish links with other spaces.

Progressively, regions become part of a global network forming connections and influences from multiple actors afar [29]. It thus becomes harder to distinguish between local and global relationships since there is a growing interdependence between them [43]. These networks can be more localised when they mainly depend upon local or global competences or when the major actors are physically distant [32]. According to Murdoch [42] we should concentrate on the links, chains, networks and associations and not simply on dualistic geographical visions between local and global. Locales are places of meeting and intersections of dynamic influences and not closed or restricted spaces [37]. This local meeting of diverse fluxes and interactions is responsible for its heterogeneity [45], and consequently no two regions are exactly the same.

Within the context of relational approaches, companies are noteworthy territorial actors [5, 30, 46-48] because decision-making at company level moulds the territory and its development process [12]. Consequently, to understand the development trajectory and territorial dynamics, we need to focus on companies and their interactions. During their activity, companies instil characteristics in the regions that welcome them and contact is established between resources from various origins. Simultaneously, their activity is influenced by territorial configurations. Acknowledging this role played by the entrepreneurial actors, relational geography proposes an approach between spatial and economic management. Space and economy are interlinked and cannot be analysed separately [27, 30, 33].

The relationships between companies and the territory where they are located are obviously reciprocal [49]. Such reciprocal influence is well demonstrated in a paper by Schoenberger [48] "The Firm in the Region and the Region in the Firm". Such a relationship reflects the way in which companies' specific characteristics mingle with the specific characteristics of the territory. "While networks are embedded within territories, territories are, at the same time, embedded into networks" [32, p. 97], and that is the reason why such authors call companies "networks within networks". The dynamics and interactions associated with a region are referred to by the relational approach as essential for their development. "The tangible and intangible flows between the actors function as a blood circulation system in the region, enabling the system to meet the changing needs of the business environment" [50, p. 207]. The regions need their companies to have privileged links with internal or external actors capable of providing them with their dynamics. The external sources of knowledge are especially important to stimulate growth within that region [51].

A region must be linked to the outside world in what Owen-Smith and Powell [52] call *pipelines* to avoid declining due to entropy [53]. This concept is linked to knowledge originating in the outside world through a relationship between its diverse actors. However, when a region is linked to global production networks, such a fact does not automatically ensure a positive development since local actors may generate value in a manner that does not maximise the economic potential of that region. Local actors in a region may not be able to keep much of the value therein created [54].

Local companies must develop the capacity to assimilate the information and to efficiently apply it in order to create value. Cohen and Levinthal [55] use the term "*absorptive capacity*" to refer to the capacity of a company to identify, assimilate and exploit the knowledge deriving from its surroundings. To assimilate and benefit from new data, in a way that can create and develop new practices and activities, the companies must have the capacity to recognise, find and understand them. This acknowledgement demands the existence of previous knowledge. Territorial actors might not acknowledge this unless they have such previous knowledge. Accordingly, the benefit from this external knowledge depends upon local company actors' level of current knowledge, with the implication that any knowledge acquired in this manner is fully dependent on the existing knowledge base [56]. In larger companies, this knowledge derives from their research and development activities, but in smaller companies such knowledge is less formalised [57]. The capacity to absorb such knowledge in these smaller companies depends upon more tacit forms like learning by using and by doing, and it also depends upon their organisational configuration and the capacity to establish close relationships with various actors and the implementation of good practices in human resources [57-59].

Relational positioning emphasises the interdependent evolution between organisations and territories. However, it is crucial to possess a broader understanding of the processes which lie behind the interdependent actions that develop at a micro level [60]. There are many challenges to be faced in order to clarify the relationship between companies and the territorial dynamics. Namely, how to make theoretical connections between micro events at a company level and their spatial repercussions, normally only observable at a regional level [60]. The interactive relationship between companies and regions is not totally explained although the company is pinpointed as the key element in the relational space [30] since this approach does not entirely describe the company's organisation nor does it specify the basis for their interactions.

Authors of relational geography "are concerned with geographical space. Although they briefly refer to institutions, it is not made clear where (...) these fit in and how firms and institutions interact." [61, p. 5]. Existing publications reveal that research "has tended to have a naive view of the spatial character of firms and of the ways in which firms relate to territory" [27, p. 355]. Moreover, this gives birth to simplistic conceptions that are not in accordance with the interactive wealth of reality [27] and make it necessary to elaborate a broader analysis of the company and individual agents [31]. As far as the network approach is concerned, and notwithstanding numerous references and the relevance attributed to networks by the relational geography ideologues, seldom are such references made in an explicit manner [38, 62, 63]. "Much of the use of networks in economic geography has been rather selective, often metaphorical and little formalised" [49, p. 620]. The relevance of interlinking the local and outside worlds is stressed, but this process of connection and input of knowledge from outside is not described in its entirety.

Although there have been many current trends discussing the relational component of regions, there is not yet a robust conceptual corpus capable of making operational the conception of a socially constructed region based upon various dependencies. Indeed, one of the questions frequently asked and not yet properly answered, due to the limitations of relational geography, is: "how do firms interact with one another and what are the consequences for localised processes and structures?" [30, p. 138]. According to Waluszewski, "in order to investigate how companies co-evolve over time, including how local and non-local interaction contributes in this process, we have to use a tool that allows us to investigate the interactive features of industrial development" [4, p. 133].

The industrial network approach, a description of which follows, has, for the past thirty years, focused on the study of the interaction between companies. At the same time, it shows a notable adjustment with the characteristics conferred to the regions by relational geography and has made the interaction phenomena between companies and regions operational.

3. The IMP group perspective

This approach to industrial networking began to develop as "a tool to investigate relationships that connected dyadic counterparts not only to each other, but also to a larger structure": the network [64, p. 30]. This is characterised by the interactions that evolve from relationships established between the different actors who have access to resources and undertake activities [74]. These three variables appear together (actors, resources and activities) in structures which have a distinctive trace in the way in which they interact. Such structures are called relationship networks. *Lato sensu* this concept is used to mean the grouping of all relationships which are developing in a given economic sector, and in a strict sense when it refers to those relationships belonging to a given actor [65]. One of the most important research objects in industrial network research is the long-term relationship, its origins, characteristics and effects [66]. A clear-cut rupture between the positions that defined borders between organisations and their environment is also a common characteristic of this approach. Due to the links formed by these relationships the organisations do not consider the environment as unchanging, but as an element with which they interact in specific ways according to the context [67-69]. As a result of the interdependence between the units under study [70], the behaviour of a company should be understood in the global context of their relations with others [71].

Due to the breadth of the network, the actors only have a limited cognitive capacity of the networks they belong to. They are restricted to a horizon, which limits the reality they know. When the interacting companies have differentiated network horizons, the visualisation of new opportunities for interaction is vastly improved [72]. To overtake such limited knowledge of the network, the companies create diverse cognitive structures depending on the interactions occurring within the network that result from the interpretation of past experiences [73] which have the capacity to shape their future actions. These network theories are described by Mattsson [74, p. 417] as "the actor's set of systematic beliefs about market structure, processes and performance and the effects of its own and others' strategic actions". They not only affect the strategic action of the actor which formulates them, but also that of others, as they can be transmitted to counterparts [73, 75]. "Interaction with others is a major source and factor in the continuous adaptations in the cognitive structures guiding their behaviours" [76, p. 26].

Through these relationships actors exhibit to counterparts their theoretical formulations, and depending on their position have the capacity to influence them. Thus, changes in actor network theories, and consequently in the dynamism associated to the network, can occur, and result from the emergence of new relationships or from the interactions of already existing ones. Actors who interact with a company give it a position that depends on the set of relationships it has [73]. Any organisation occupies a position in the network. A company's network position is, however, a relative concept that is externally endorsed. Thus, there will not be two identical positions given by different actors to the same focal organisation [68].

A company's network position can be understood as a resource, an intangible asset that influences its action capacity and simultaneously, like any resource, supports and restricts its strategic action [77-79]. According to this perspective, Turnbull, Ford and Cunningham [78, p. 47] define position as "the company's relationships and the rights and obligations which go with them". Companies with a central position will have benefits resulting from the access to more information and opportunities in comparison to peripheral actors [80]. Network position also influences network theory as it is largely formed by the information resulting from relationships between actors [73]. The development of new relationships by the company changes the way its identity is perceptible in the network: i.e., its position. Due to relationships' dynamic character, a company's position is not definitive, and constantly changes with time [76, 81]. As all the companies are connected and the positions are relative and conferred by each individual actor, the change of a company's position will affect the position of other companies [82]. Thus, positions may be positively or negatively connected, and the strength of one actor's position may, according to the situation, lead to the strengthening or weakening of the position of other companies [73]. However, the company can influence its position but this is a task that requires relationship management, the choice of preferred counterparts and the development of ties between resources [82].

The industrial network approach is sceptical about the direct control over resources a company can obtain since a substantial part of the resources available to the firm are under the direct control of other actors and can only be accessed by interactions and relationships in the network [83, 84]. Araújo, Dubois and Gadde [85, p. 498] state that "no company controls all the resources they require," and the competitive advantage of the companies is not only inside the borders of what it has and controls, but in all the interfaces it develops with others [86]. Resources are used together and in interaction with other resources and their characteristics are created through these combinations [64]. Nevertheless, in order to act, companies need to know how to interact, connect and make their resources grow. Access to external competences is not automatic as it requires a specific range of competences and relational efforts [87].

Companies do not prosper only because of their individual effort. They also depend on the relationships they have with others and on the nature of the direct and indirect relationships others have with them [79]. An organisation's results largely depend on how and with whom it interacts [68, 84]. A company alone cannot build up its strategy [68, 83, 88] since such a strategy derives from interactions and it is indexed to relationships. In this manner, the interactions and the relationships become as important, or even more important, as management, in order to influence the company's strategy [68]. It is crucial to invest in creating and strengthening relationships so that companies are able to strategically perform and adapt most of their competitive advantages to the surrounding environment [89]. In this way of thinking, strategy is defined by the way "in which a firm achieves exchange effectiveness in relation to other firms in the surrounding network that is how a firm initiates and reacts to changes in the network in such a way that the firm keeps on being valuable to the network" [90, p. 409]. The strategy is, thus, the result of a joint process in which many companies take part [91]. Consequently, most strategic activity revolves around influencing others and managing relationships within a context built upon interaction.

4. The territorial side of industrial networks

The strength of conceptual research, by authors identified with the industrial network approach is currently so great that it surpasses the limits of industrial relationships that were at the centre of its origins. Indeed, valuable contributions to the understanding of the territorial dynamics appear from authors related with these approaches [4, 25, 26, 72, 92-96]. These approaches "instead of approaching place as a one-dimensional entity, as an object of analysis in itself, (...) allow us to investigate it as a multidimensional and embedded phenomenon interrelated with other variables" [94, p. 232]. The territory definition resulting from these studies is similar to those arising from the relational geography approaches: extremely dynamic, interactive and relational. Johnston and Araújo [95, p. 10] suggest that "territories are environments in which organisations are directly active and have a presence at a point in time, and are configured through relationships formed on the basis of activities and resources found within that specific environment". As a result of this vision, territory is no longer seen as, a simple container of economic activities is and is viewed rather as a structure of relations dependent upon specific resources.

Apart from attributing a dynamic character to regions, these authors also recognise the relevance of history for further development of any territory since they consider that regions should not be seen as individual entities merely linked with other geographical entities at a distance. Regions have different historical ancestries and dynamics which have diverse resource inflows and outflows that are capable of changing the spatial form and the relationships within the area [95]. This point of view is also shared by Waluszewski [4]. The author refers to territorial development as a process that is being built gradually and which does not happen overnight. More than looking into the current characteristics, it is essential to understand the historic patterns of the combination of resources available in the various regions.

Furthermore, Håkansson, Tunisini and Waluszewski [94] see space as a heterogeneous phenomenon; it is something simultaneously created and differently used by organisations with a significant dynamic component that changes with time. Accordingly, space is considered "as something that not only affects the individual company, but also the way the individual company interacts with other companies" because "the companies' interaction creates the place" [94, p. 231]. From the perspective of these authors, when territory is regarded as an organisation, each company inside it should be considered as a particular combination of resources that is part of a larger constellation. Thus, the characteristics of the social and institutional relationships that originate and develop in a territorial context are unique, inimitable, and affect the potential and attractiveness of the region where they are located.

Mota and Castro [96, p. 263] conceive industrial conglomerates as "territorially based networks" and state that "the dynamics in connections internal to those networks affect and are affected by local institutions as well as connections external to the territory". Territorial dynamics depend upon a network of connections resulting from the structure of relationships between companies since they are all involved in networks that outflow the regional boundaries. Hence, the dissemination of knowledge and network learning derives from a relational pattern and not only from physical proximity between actors [96]. Spatial proximity is just one factor that may be able to influence the relationships and network patterns. Other factors capable of influencing the relational pattern are social, technological and organisational proximity [97].

Baraldi [25] reinforces the interdependence between companies and territories previously recognised by relational geography by considering that "places are central to the life of every company, from the moment when it is born and throughout its various developmental stages". According to this author, this dependence is bidirectional: "companies interact constantly with various places, even without being fully conscious of doing so. Places affect companies' lives, but companies, alone or in interaction with others, also affect places" [25, p. 297]. Consequently, there are two levels (regional and industrial) in simultaneous and permanent interaction.

Regional interactions are based upon the interaction between the various actors belonging to those regions. Not all actors will become winners in the space interaction and some of them might even lose power, since such interaction exposes them to competition from other places and actors [26]. Multinationals are privileged actors in promoting the interaction of spaces and objects, and are defined by Baraldi, Hjalmar and Houltz [26] as place-connectors. In order to eventuate, interaction needs some form of relationship which becomes an important bridge to overcome spatial distances as well as cultural and competence distances [25]. These may overtake various places and create network configurations. In this manner, one space may be intimately dependent upon developments that are happening in another, and vice versa [92].

In short, the network approach proposes a vision that stresses the power of interaction and the gathering of resources in order to promote regional development. A company's horizon, position and interaction competences are more important than their mere localisation. The territorial dynamics are created according to the way in which companies value their resources, how they add/accumulate value and how they relate to each other (i.e., by what they do and how they do it) and not merely by existing. The potential for the interaction between space and companies' explanation revealed by the industrial network approach, is not yet sufficiently developed and focused on regions in a way that makes it possible to understand how such interaction occurs. Specifically, it is not explained how changes resulting from the company's strategic action reflect in the dynamics and territorial structure. Consequently, this gives rise to a research opportunity: to clarify the interaction between companies' action and territorial dynamics.

5. Conceptual framework

Literature about relational geography as well as about industrial network approaches question the generic and mechanical point of view that makes territorial development and the dynamics of replication one of the general factors of success. From the research conducted it is obvious that territories are entities each with their own history. As such they have their specificities, which make them heterogeneous and imply a continuous interaction with other organisations, namely, companies. This connection between companies and territories is a phenomenon which is both beguiling and complex and its study should be the central focus of research [27].

There are questions which are still unanswered relating to the influence and interaction between territories and companies and how they interact with, shape and mould each other [94]. Therefore, the central focus of the research model developed is to explain how companies' strategic action is reflected in the dynamics and territorial structure and how these territorial factors affect the companies' action. As a result of the theoretical approach followed, the answer to this question might be found not only in the company's dyadic relationships, but in the sum of its links enabling the company to belong to networks that are far beyond local scales. This implies that the model must be centred on three differentiated levels of analysis (Figure 1): the company, its relationship network and the territories where the company's network interacts.

The analytical model described in Figure 2 represents a structure which is both synoptic and integral showing the various levels of analysis being taken into consideration.

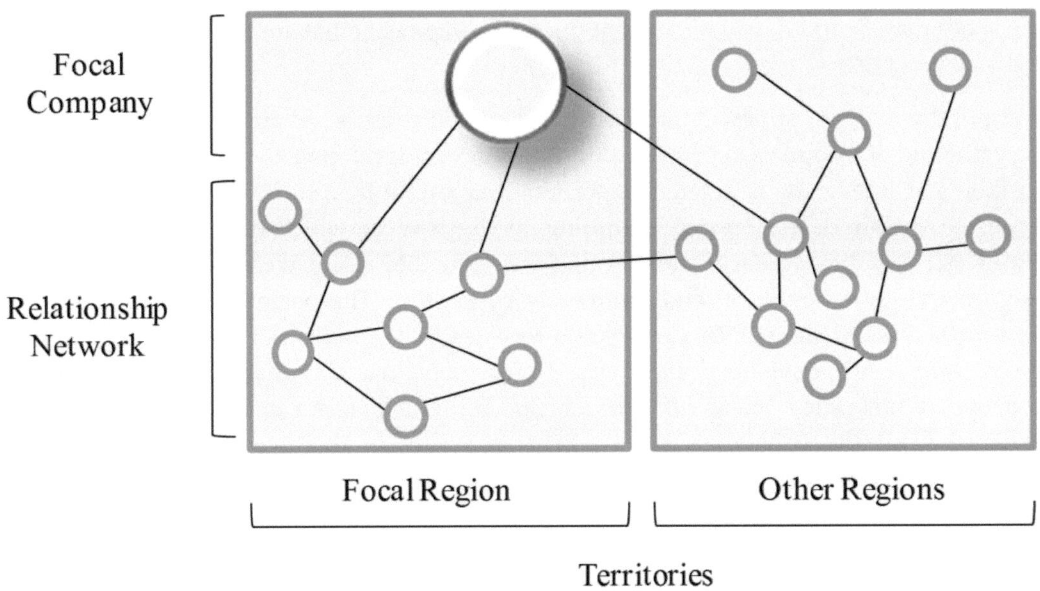

Figure 1. Levels of Analysis

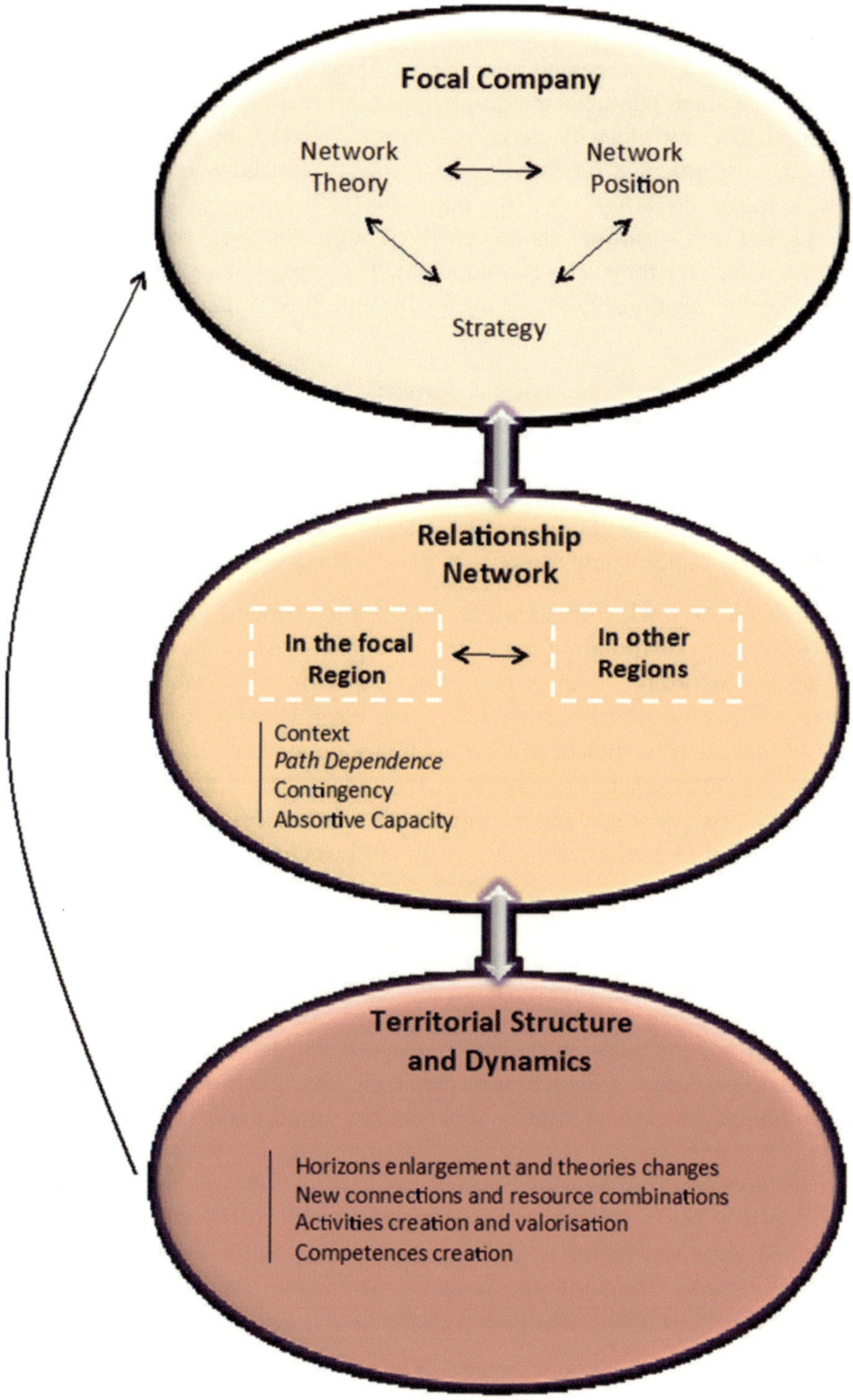

Figure 2. The Conceptual Framework

5.1. Companies

Whilst the relevance of companies and the entrepreneurial relationships for territorial dynamics is obvious, the relational geography approach neither clarifies the mechanisms in which it originates nor does it describe its motivational processes. The companies, considered an instrumental territorial actor, are superficially characterised which is undeniably a major limitation. Equally notorious is the lack of knowledge about the reasoning behind the strategic action of the companies and the relevance of their relationship structure for their own development. This omission is even more serious since the relevance of the relationship structure for the interlinking between various regions is well known.

The interaction and network approach characterises in detail the entrepreneurial actors, their interaction processes and the reasoning for their strategic actions, and helps shed light on one of the most obscure areas of relational geography. Thanks to the interaction and network approach the companies lose their homogenous and anonymous characteristics, and acquire their own personality which accords them specific characteristics [83, 98]. They are linked to the surrounding environment, depend upon it and influence it [68, 69].

Companies have a network theory, which guides their actions and the decoding of the behaviour of all actors surrounding them. They are positioned in the network of companies they are part of, according to their relevance and their relationship with counterparts. Access to resources from third parties, which are essential to add value to their internal resources and for the development of their activities, depends on the position they occupy. The theories and differentiated positions in the network lead the companies to specific strategic actions. Such strategic action undoubtedly influences the choice of counterparts they establish relationships with and the way in which such relationships occur.

5.2. Relationship network

With an approach based upon interaction and networks, we have been able to establish a great deal of knowledge on the concept of networks classified as vital in relational geography, but not sufficiently described. Networks are deconstructed into three major elements: actors, resources and activities [99, 100], and great relevance is given to the external component of each of those elements. The importance of the external analysis results from the connectivity of relationships. Relationships are connected since changes in any given relationship are likely to cause some kind of network effects [101, 102]. Any changes in the way the activities are coordinated and resources are used show up on a larger scale [64]. As a consequence, any change in a local network of relationships affects various other regions throughout the network. The same happens with the company's external links, which inevitably reflect upon the territory.

According to the company's strategic action, its relationships may be more localised or may spread outside the region. The pattern of a company's relationships with a region is also dependent upon the territorial characteristics. Here various factors have to be taken into consideration, such as the context, path dependence, contingency and the absorptive capacity that the territory reveals towards the company's actions.

5.3. Territorial structure and dynamics

Territorial dynamics are influenced by local connections and connections with external actors. Each organisation can be seen as a combination of resources from a constellation existing inside the territory [94]. This constellation is dynamic and can be influenced by interaction [103].

According to the focal network interaction with the region through the companies and installed organisations, various factors may occur which will have an impact on the territorial dynamics. These include horizons enlargement and a change of theories in the companies locally installed and, consequently, the awareness of new opportunities for interaction [72]. The development of new links between local companies can result in different combinations of resources. The creation of new activities, the valorisation of existing ones, and the creation of competences are also possible effects of the interaction between the company, its network and the region.

Changes in territorial structure and dynamics will impact on the focal company theory, and a readjustment of its strategy, which may affect its relationship network and, consequently, the whole of its relationship process with the territory.

6. Conclusion

Companies are fairly diverse. Even within the same economic sector their way of acting is different and this difference reflects upon the way their relationship network articulates in various regions. On the other hand, territories are also fairly heterogeneous and their particular development paths condition companies' activities. In this way, the relationship between companies and territories will always be specific and impossible to replicate. This specificity is not taken into account by the current literary trends which point to a generic thesis of development based upon the combination of various material factors inside a geographically delimited space.

The model based upon relational geography trends and the industrial network approach suggests that territorial dynamics are mostly dependent upon intangible factors and on interaction at various levels, and not on limited material components. From specific knowledge of a company based upon a particular relationship network, it is possible to focus on the interaction of this network with the characteristics of the territory. Some effects of this interaction result in changes to the territorial structure and dynamics.

Territorial configurations of company relationships may be more concentrated or dispersed in regional terms and create interaction in various spaces. It is not enough to have a substantial number of local links to create territorial dynamics. It is indeed essential that such links create competences that lead to the creation and rating of activities, which in turn originate new links and gather resources or contribute to a change in theories and a broader horizon for the interacting parts. Such effects largely depend upon the capacity of absorption by the territory. It is the interaction between the diverse organisational networks of the companies installed in a territory and the territorial characteristics that may create obstacles or advance the said effects.

The essential question challenging territorial administration is not subject to physical boundaries since all relationship networks may be connected to diverse spaces. In this manner, territorial managers must enhance the companies' internal links as well as develop the links to external networks where they will acquire dynamic factors. In order to do so, they must create a great deal of knowledge about companies' needs and strategies. This knowledge will allow the identification of companies which may be attractive and strategically compatible with organisational networks already established in the territory. The knowledge of entrepreneurial actors will enable territorial administrators to make efforts to reduce the relational distance.

Author details

Carlos Brito
University of Porto – School of Economics, Rua Roberto Frias, Porto, Portugal

Ricardo Correia
Polytechnic Institute of Bragança, Mirandela, Portugal

7. References

[1] Porter M. Clusters and the New Economics of Competition. Harvard Business Review. 1998;76(6):77-99.
[2] Porter M. Locations, clusters, and company strategy. In: Clark G, Feldman M, Gertler M, editors. The Oxford Handbook of Economic Geography. Oxford: Oxford University Press; 2000. p. 253-74.
[3] Porter M. On Competition. Boston: Harvard Business School; 1998.
[4] Waluszewski A. A competing or co-operating cluster or seven decades of combinatory resources? What's behind a prospering biotech valley? Scandinavian Journal of Management. 2004;20:125-50.
[5] Martin R, Sunley P. Deconstructing clusters: chaotic concept or policy panacea? Journal of Economic Geography. 2003;3:5-35.
[6] Scott A, Storper M. Regions, Globalization, Development. Regional Studies. 2003 August/October;37:579-93.
[7] Bathelt H. Geographies of production: growth regimes in spatial perspective (II) – knowledge creation and growth in clusters. Progress in Human Geography. 2005;29(2):204-16.
[8] Camagni R. On the concept of territorial competitiveness: sound or misleading? Urban Studies. 2002;39:2395-411.

[9] Storper M. Regional Economies as Relational Assets. In: Lee R, Wills J, editors. Geographies of Economics. London, New York, Sydney: Arnold; 1997. p. 248-58.
[10] Porter M. The Competitive Advantage of Nations. London: Macmillan; 1990.
[11] Håkansson L. Epistemic Communities and Cluster Dynamics: On the Role of Knowledge in Industrial Districts. Industry and Innovation. 2005;12(4):433-63.
[12] Giuliani E. The selective nature of knowledge networks in clusters: evidence from the wine industry. Journal of Economic Geography. 2007;7:139-68.
[13] Coe N, Bunnel T. ′Spatializing`Knowledge Communities: Towards a Conceptualization of Transnational Innovation Networks. Global Networks. 2003;3(4):437-56.
[14] Castells M. The Rise of the Network Society. Oxford: Blackwell; 1996.
[15] Boschma R. Proximity and innovation: a critical assessment. Regional Studies. 2005;39(1):61-74.
[16] Gertler M, Wolfe D. Local social management: Community actors, institutions and multilevel governance in regional foresight exercises. Futures. 2004;36:45-65.
[17] Torre A, Rallet A. Proximity and Localization. Regional Studies. 2005 February;39(1):47-59.
[18] Lazerson M, Lorenzoni G. The Firms that Feed Industrial Districts: A Return to the Italian Source. Industrial and Corporate Change. 1999;8:235-65.
[19] Sheppard E. Positionality and globalization in economic geography In: Giovanna V, editor. The Changing Economic Geography of Globalization: Reinventing Space: Taylor & Francis 2005. p. 45-72.
[20] Wolfe D, Gertler M. Clusters from the inside and out: local dynamics and global linkages. Urban Studies. 2004;41(5/6):1071-93.
[21] Bathelt H. Cluster Relations in the Media Industry: Exploring the 'Distanced Neighbour' Paradox in Leipzig. Regional Studies. 2005;39(1):105-27.
[22] Passi A. Place and region: looking through the prim of scale. Progress in Human Geography. 2004;28(4):536-46.
[23] Murdoch J. The Spaces of Actor-Network Theory. Geoforum. 1998;29(4):357-74.
[24] Graham S, Healey P. Relational Concepts of Space and Place: Issues for Planning Theory and Practice. European Planning Studies. 1999;7(5):623-46.
[25] Baraldi E. The Places of Ikea: Using Space in Handling Resource Networks. In: Baraldi E, Hjalmar F, Houltz A, editors. Taking Place: The Spatial Contexts of Science, Technology and Business. Sagamore Beach: Science History Publications/USA; 2006. p. 297-320.
[26] Baraldi E, Hjalmar F, Houltz A. Taking Place: The Spatial Contexts of Science, Technology and Business. Sagamore Beach: Science History Publications/USA; 2006.
[27] Dicken P, Malmberg A. Firms in Territories: A Relational Perspective. Economic Geography. 2001 October;77(4):345-63.
[28] Bathelt H. Geographies of production: growth regimes in spatial perspective 3 – toward a relational view of economic action and policy. Progress in Human Geography. 2006;30(2):223-36.

[29] Amin A. Regions Unbound: Towards a New Politics of Place. Geografiska Annaler. 2004;86(1):33-44.
[30] Bathelt H, Glückler J. Toward a relational economic geography. Journal of Economic Geography. 2003;3:117-44.
[31] Boggs J, Rantisi N. The 'relational turn' in economic geography. Journal of Economic Geography. 2003;3:109-16.
[32] Dicken P, Kelly PF, Olds K, Yeung HW-C. Chains and networks, territories and scales: towards a relational framework for analysing the global economy. Global Networks. 2001 2001;1(2):89-112.
[33] Yeung HW-c. Rethinking relational economic geography. Transactions of the Institute of British Geographers. 2005 March;30:37-51.
[34] Ettlinger N. Cultural economic geography and a relational and microspace approach to trusts, rationalities, networks, and change in collaborative workplaces. Journal of Economic Geography. 2003;3:145-71.
[35] Amin A. An Institutionalist Perspective on Regional Economic Development. International Journal of Urban and Regional Research. 1999;23:365-78.
[36] Amin A, Thrift N. Globalization, Institutions and Regional Development in Europe. Oxford: Oxford University Press; 1994.
[37] Lee R. 'Nice maps, shame about the theory'? Thinking geographically about the economic. Progress in Human Geography. 2002;26(3):333-55.
[38] Murphy J. Social space and industrial development in East Africa: deconstructing the logics of industry networks in Mwanza, Tanzania. Journal of Economic Geography. 2003;3:173-98.
[39] Maskell P, Malmberg A. Myopia, Knowledge Development and Cluster Evolution. Journal of Economic Geography. 2007;7:603-18.
[40] Amin A. Globalisation and Regional Development: A Relational Perspective. Competition & Change. 1998;3:145-65.
[41] Howit R. Scale. In: Agnew J, Mitchell K, Toal G, editors. A companion to political geography. Oxford: Blackwell; 2003. p. 138-57.
[42] Murdoch J. Towards a geography of heterogeneous associations. Progress in Human Geography. 1997;21(3):321-37.
[43] Amin A, Cohendet P. Geographies of Knowledge Formation in Firms. Industry and Innovation. 2005 December 2005;12(4):465-86.
[44] Malecki E. Knowledge and regional competitiveness. Erdkunde. 2000;54:334-51.
[45] Gibson-Graham J. Beyond global vs. local: economic politics outside the binary frame. In: Herod A, Wright M, editors. Geographies of Power: Placing Scale. Oxford: Blackwell; 2002.
[46] Taylor M, Asheim B. The concept of the firm in economic geography. Economic Geography. 2001;77(4):315-28.
[47] Yeung HW-C. The Firm as Social Networks: An Organisational Perspective. Growth & Change. 2005 Summer;36(3):307-28.

[48] Schoenberger E. The Firm in the Region and the Region in the Firm In: Barnes T, Gertler M, editors. The new industrial geography: Regions, regulation and institutions. London: Routledge; 1999. p. 205-24.
[49] Glückler J. Economic geography and the evolution of networks. Journal of Economic Geography. 2007;7:619-34.
[50] Smedlund A. The roles of intermediaries in a regional knowledge system. Journal of Intellectual Capital. 2006;7(2):204-20.
[51] Bathelt H, Malmberg A, Maskell P. Clusters and knowledge: local buzz, global pipelines and the process of knowledge creation. Progress in Human Geography. 2004 February;28(1):31-56.
[52] Owen-Smith J, Powell W, editors. Knowledge networks in the Boston Biotechnology community. Science as an Institution and the Institutions of Science; 2002; Siena.
[53] Camagni R. Local 'milieu', uncertainty and innovation networks: towards a new dynamic theory of economic space. In: Camagni R, editor. Innovation Networks: Spatial Perspectives. London: Belhaven; 1991. p. 121-44.
[54] Coe N, Hess M, Yeung HW-c, Dicken P, Henderson J. 'Globalizing' regional development: a global production networks perspective. Transactions of the Institute of British Geographers. 2004;29:468-84.
[55] Cohen W, Levinthal D. Innovation and Learning: the Two Faces of R&D. The Economic Journal. 1989;99:569-96.
[56] Cohen W, Levinthal D. Absortive capacity: A new perspective on learning and innovation. Administrative Science Quarterly. 1990;35:128-52.
[57] Muscio A. The Impact of Absorptive Capacity on SMEs' Collaboration. Economics of Innovation and New Technology. 2007;16(8):653-68.
[58] Vinding A. Human Resources: Absorptive Capacity and Innovative Performance. In: Christensen J, Lundvall B, editors. Product Innovation, Interactive Learning and Economic Performance. Oxford: Elsevier; 2004.
[59] Huselid M. The Impact of Human Resource Management on Turnover, Productivity and Corporate Financial Performance. Academy of Management Journal. 1995;38:635-60.
[60] Lee C-K, Saxenian A. Coevolution and coordination: a systemic analysis of the Taiwanese information technology industry. Journal of Economic Geography. 2008;8:157-80.
[61] Lane C. National Capitalisms, Global Production Networks: An Analysis of their interaction in two global industries. Socio-Economic Review 2008;6(2):227-60.
[62] Grabher G. Trading routes, bypasses, and risky intersections: mapping the travels of 'networks' between economic sociology and economic geography. Progress in Human Geography. 2006;30(2):163-89.
[63] Staber U. The Structure of Networks in Industrial Districts. International Journal of Urban and Regional Research. 2001;25:537-52.
[64] Håkansson H, Waluszewski A. Managing Technological Development. IKEA, the environment and technology. London: Routledge; 2002.

[65] Brito C. Estrutura e Dinâmica do Sector do Vinho do Porto. Porto: Instituto do Vinho do Porto; 1997.
[66] Henneberg S, Mouzas S. Network Pictures: Concepts and Representations. European Journal of Marketing. 2006;40(3/4):408-29.
[67] Astley W. Toward an Appreciation of Collective Strategy. Academy of Management Review. 1984;9(3):526-35.
[68] Håkansson H, Snehota I. No Business is an Island Scandinavian Journal of Management. 1989;5(3):187-200.
[69] Thorelli H. Networks: Between Markets and Hierarchies. Strategic Management Journal. 1986;7(1):37-51.
[70] Easton G, Håkansson H. Markets as Networks: Editorial Introduction. International Journal of Research in Marketing. 1996;13:407-13.
[71] Anderson J, Håkansson H, Johanson J. Dyadic Business Relationships Within a Business Network Context. Journal of Marketing. 1994;58(4):1-15.
[72] Lundberg H. Geographical Proximity Effects and Regional Strategic Networks. Doctoral Thesis, Department of Business Studies, Uppsala University. 2008.
[73] Johanson J, Mattsson L. Network Positions and Strategic Actions - An Analytical Framework. In: Axelsson B, Easton G, editors. Industrial Networks: A New View of Reality. London: Routledge; 1992. p. 205-17.
[74] Mattsson L-G. Reorganisation of Distribution in Globalisation of Markets: The Dynamic Context of Supply Chain Management. Supply Chain Management: An International Journal 2003;8(5):416-26.
[75] Brito C. Towards an institutional theory of the dynamics of industrial networks. Journal of Business & Industrial Marketing. 2001;16(3):150-66.
[76] Snehota I. Perspectives and theories of market. In: Håkansson H, Harrison D, Waluszewski A, editors. Rethinking Marketing: Developing a New Understanding of Markets. Chichester: Wiley 2004. p. 15-32.
[77] Duysters G, Man A-P, Wildeman L. A Network Approach to Alliance Management. European Management Journal. 1999;17(2):182-7.
[78] Turnbull P, Ford D, Cunningham M. Interaction, relationships and networks in business markets: an evolving perspective. Journal of Business & Industrial Marketing. 1996;11(3/4):44-62.
[79] Wilkinson I, Young L. On Cooperating: Firms, Relations and Networks. Journal of Business Research. 2002;55(2):123-32.
[80] Gulati R, Nohria N, Zaheer A. Strategic Networks. Strategic Management Journal. 2000;21:203-15.
[81] Henders B. Positions in Industrial Networks, Marketing Newsprint in the UK PhD thesis, Uppsala University, Department of Business Studies, Uppsala, Sweden; 1992
[82] Low B. Managing Business Relationships and Positions in Industrial Networks. Industrial Marketing Management. 1997;26(2):189-202.
[83] Ford D, Håkansson H. IMP - some things achieved: much more to do. European Journal of Marketing. 2006;40(3/4):248-58.

[84] Baraldi E, Brennan R, Harrison D, Tunisini A, Zolkiewski J. Strategic thinking and the IMP approach: A comparative analysis. Industrial Marketing Management. 2007;36(7):879-94.

[85] Araújo L, Dubois A, Gadde L-E. Managing Interfaces With Suppliers. Industrial Marketing Management. 1999;28(5):497-506.

[86] Gadde L-E, Huemer L, Håkansson H. Strategizing in Industrial Networks. Industrial Marketing Management. 2003;32(5):357-64.

[87] Araújo L, Dubois A, Gadde L-E. The Multiple Boundaries of the Firm. Journal of Management Studies. 2003;40(5):1255-77.

[88] Snehota I. Notes on a Theory of Business Enterprise: PhD Thesis, Uppsala University; 1990.

[89] Jüttner U, Schlange L. A network approach to strategy. International Journal of Research in Marketing. 1996;13:479-94.

[90] Holmen E, Pedersen A-C. Strategizing Through Analyzing and Influencing the Network Horizon. Industrial Marketing Management. 2003;32:409-18.

[91] Ford D, Håkansson H. The Idea of Business Interaction. IMP Journal. 2006;1(1):4-20.

[92] Baraldi E, Stromsten T. Combining Scientific Knowledge and Venture Capital Across Places and Networks of Resources. In: Houltz A, Hjalmar F, Baraldi E, editors. Taking Place: The Spatial Contexts of Science, Technology and Business. Sagamore Beach: Science History Publications/USA; 2006. p. 247-73.

[93] Cova B, Mazet F, Salle R. Milieu as a Pertinent Unit of Analysis in Project Marketing. International Business Review. 1996;5(6):647-64.

[94] Håkansson H, Tunisini A, Waluszewski A. Place as a Resource in Business Networks. In: Houltz A, Hjalmar F, Baraldi E, editors. Taking Place: The Spatial Contexts of Science, Technology and Business. Sagamore Beach: Science History Publications/USA; 2006. p. 223-46.

[95] Johnston B, Araújo L, editors. The Effects of Spatial Proximity on Inter-Organisational Relationships. 18th IMP Annual Conference; 2002.

[96] Mota J, Castro L. Industrial agglomerations as localised networks: the case of the Portuguese injection mould industry. Environment and Planning A. 2004;36:263-78.

[97] Ford D. The development of buyer-seller relationships in industrial markets. London: Thomson Learning; 2002.

[98] Huemer L, Becerra M, Lunnan R. Organizational Identity and Network Identification: Relating Within and Beyond Imaginary Boundaries. Scandinavian Journal of Management. 2004;20(1/2):53-73.

[99] Håkansson H, Johanson J. A Model of Industrial Networks. In: Axelsson B, Easton G, editors. Industrial Networks: A New View of Reality. London: Routledge; 1992. p. 28-34.

[100] Håkansson H, Snehota I. Developing Relationships in Business Networks. London: Routledge; 1995.

[101] Mattsson L-G. Industrial Marketing the Network Perspective. In: Backhaus K, Voeth M, editors. Handbuch Industriegüter Marketing: Gabler Verlag; 2004.

[102] Hadjikhani A, Thilenius P. The impact of horizontal and vertical connections on relationships' commitment and trust. Journal of Business & Industrial Marketing. 2005;20(3):136-47.

[103] Waluszewski A, Ford D, Håkansson H, Snehota I, Gadde L-E, editors. Analysing Business Interaction. 24th IMP Conference; 2008; Uppsala, Sweden.

Chapter 3

The Extent of Intra Industry Trade Between Thailand and ASEAN Economic Community (AEC)

Sujinda Chemsripong

Additional information is available at the end of the chapter

http://dx.doi.org/10.5772/47438

1. Introduction

At present, the Asian region has an increasingly important role in the global economy. Economic indicators show that region's GDP proportion (not including Japan) has increased from 9.7 per cent of world GDP in 1998 to 16.3 per cent in 2009. Therefore, the Asian region can be seen as the new engine to drive the new global economy. Many countries pay attention to increase investment and trading with Asian countries. Even though the ASEAN Economic Community (AEC) derived from the ASEAN leaders, the vision will still focus on transforming ASEAN into a single market and production base that is highly competitive and fully integrated into the global community by 2015. The economic integration goals will include, among others, the elimination of tariffs, free movement of professionals, freer movement of capital, and a streamlined customs clearance procedure [1]. The proportion of international trade between Thailand and the AEC shows that Thailand increased her exports to AEC countries from 19.34 percent in 2001 to 22.70 per cent in 2010. Imports from AEC to Thailand increased from 17.84 percent to 17.88 percent in the same period [2].

Intra-industry trade (IIT) involves the import and export of similar goods. While taking account of measurement limitations, it would appear that the IIT share of manufacture trade has increased significantly since the late 1980s across many AEC countries. This follows trend increases in IIT for all the major AEC countries between 1993 and 2010. Although various origins can be traced, the phenomenon of IIT as such first received attention in the 1960s in studies by Verdoon, P.J., [3] and Balassa, B., [4];[5];[6], on the increased trade flows among European countries. Grubel and Lloyd [7] provided the definitive empirical study on the importance of IIT and how to measure it. Concrete theoretical foundations for explaining IIT came later in the 1980s and 1990s with the new trade literature to a large extent based on a monopolistic competition framework.

Since that time numerous theoretical and empirical studies e.g. Globerman, S. and Dean, J. W. [8]; Duc, N. H. [9]; Glejser, H. [10]; Guell, R. C. and Richards, D. G. [11], have been conducted to measure the size and importance of IIT, and also to explore its determinants. In addition to the desirable welfare effects mentioned before, trade analysts also noted another positive aspect of IIT from the investigation of the ASEAN experience after the formation of the ASEAN, namely, the adjustment costs of economic integration.

It was shown from the actual experience of ASEAN in the late 1970s that IIT reduced the adjustment costs of an economy opening up to foreign trade as domestic industries could remain intact while moving to specialize only in a limited range of products. Intra-Industry Trade (IIT) is now widely accepted. The proposition of increasing IIT in developed nation's economies has found general support. Accordingly, the mass of empirical studies have focus on IIT of developed countries e.g. in Australia [12];[13]; in EEC [14]; in UK [15]; in EU [16] in Switzerland [17], etc. However, an increasing number of studies have also been done on developing countries e.g. in Turkey [18]; in Korea [19]; in APEC [20]; in ASEAN [21]; [22]; [23]; etc. Some of the studies in attempting to identify the determinants of IIT have focused on country-specific determinants while others have concentrated on industry-specific ones. However, there are some studies which focus on both types of determinants. IIT studies in recent times have also estimated the extent of horizontal and vertical IIT and identified their determinants.

Only a few studies have focused on Thailand's intra-industry trade, and on Thailand and the AEC in particular. This study tries to make a modest contribution to the relatively small stock of research on Thailand's IIT. Given that nearly half of Thailand's foreign trade is with the AEC and that a FTA between these two sides was introduced in 1993, this study pays particular attention to estimate the extent of Thailand's IIT, to identify the determinant's of its intra- industry pattern and test a number of country specific hypotheses concerning the determinants of intra industry trade between Thailand and the AEC.

The rest of the paper is organized as follows: Section II presents a brief discussion of the general performance of Thailand's foreign trade over the past three decades. Measurement alternatives of IIT are discussed in section III. The extent of intra-industry trade in Thailand's foreign trade is provided in section IV, and section V stresses the extent of intra-industry trade between Thailand and the AEC. The main findings are summarized in section VI.

2. General performance of international trade in Thailand

Thailand had trade deficits between 1970 and -1997 due to a dependency on raw material such as crude oil, machinery, raw material etc. Table 1 indicated that Thailand's total foreign merchandise trade (exports + imports) increased significantly from 0.40 billion baht in 1970 to 3.4 billion baht in 2000 and 5.5 billion in 2010, an increase of nearly 200 percent during this period. Owing to the far greater external orientation of the economy since the beginning of the 1980s, when Thailand embarked on a trade liberalization program, foreign trade has represented a much higher proportion of the national income in comparison to the pre-1980s period. As a percentage of GDP, total trade increased from 27.50 percent in 1970 to

121.55 percent in 2010. The increase in this ratio resulted from the increase in both export and import shares: the exports/GDP share rose from 9.62 percent in 1970 to 68.98 percent in 2010 while the corresponding imports/GDP share increased from 17.88 percent to 52.57 percent, respectively (Figure 1 and Table 1).

Year	Total trade (X+M) as Million of Baht	Exports (X) as % of GDP	Imports (M) as % of GDP	Total trade (X+M) as % of GDP
1970	40,784	9.62	17.88	27.50
1980	322,065	19.93	28.68	48.62
1990	1,421,548	26.71	38.39	65.10
1993	2,175,131	42.52	45.51	88.03
1994	2,487,346	44.59	47.78	92.36
1995	2,929,711	47.12	52.47	99.59
1996	2,843,789	42.03	49.25	91.28
1997	2,765,176	45.70	44.29	89.99
1998	2,586,313	55.28	38.78	94.06
1999	2,835,428	57.70	41.02	98.73
2000	3,444,753	64.72	49.78	114.50
2001	3,280,438	60.68	46.05	106.73
2002	3,698,033	64.53	49.71	114.24
2003	3,981,010	64.49	50.30	114.79
2004	4,429,093	66.46	53.63	120.09
2005	4,710,362	66.21	55.88	122.09
2006	5,015,762	68.76	54.94	123.71
2007	5,332,698	70.58	54.63	125.21
2008	5,692,016	72.38	58.03	130.41
2009	4,752,805	64.84	46.65	111.49
2010	5,586,669	68.98	52.57	121.55

Source: For 1970 -1990- data, S. Chemsripong (2004), pp. 210-211; For 1993 data, Bank of Thailand

Table 1. Thailand's External Trade, 1970-2010

Thailand's foreign trade gained momentum in the 1990s: in particular, since Thailand joined ASEAN to collaborate in trade integration. The key trade enhancing agreements, the ASEAN Trade in Goods Agreement (ATIGA) has been signed to consolidate and synergies various provisions on trade in goods into a single reference document. The ATIGA will supersede the 1993 Agreement on the Common Effective Preferential Tariff Scheme for the ASEAN Free Trade Area (CEPTAFTA). In 2010, nine ASEAN Member States (Brunei

Darussalam, Cambodia, Indonesia, Lao PDR, Malaysia, Myanmar, Philippines, Singapore and Viet Nam) have ratified the ATIGA. ASEAN continues to implement various trade facilitating measures such as the ASEAN Customs Declaration Document and the ASEAN Cargo Processing Model that relates to air freight services. Efforts are underway to activate the ASEAN Customs Transit System. Therefore, Thailand's exports increased from $56.72 billion in 1995 to $110.93 in 2005 and $195.31 billion in 2010. Imports rose from $70.71 billion in 1995 to $118.17 billion in 2005 and $182.41 billion in 2010, respectively.

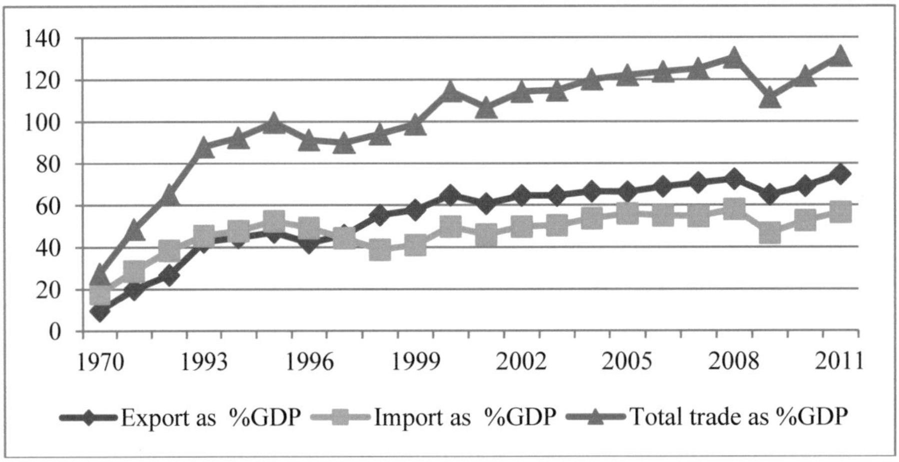

Source: data from Table A1

Figure 1. Thailand's External Trade, 1970-2010

Thailand showed great performances in exports in the year 2000, 2003, 2004 and 2010. Thailand's exports grew by 19.27, 17.43, 20.56, and 28.14 percent respectively. Although slowing down in relation to the previous years, export growth kept on rising, to 28.14 per cent in 2010. Imports in this period decreased first by 24.56 percent in 2000 due to the great contraction in the economy. However, when the economy recovered and grew again in the years between 2005 and 2010, imports also improved considerably, increasing 24.5 per cent in 2000, 25.67 per cent in 2005, 36.47 per cent in 2010. However, there has been a minor change in import structure in the last decade. Basically, the impact of intermediate goods has constituted an important part of total imports, with its share of 72.4 per cent in 1990 and 81.3 per cent in 2005. The other major components of imports showed slight changes: investment goods were 18.1 per cent in 1990 and 20.2 percent in 2005 while consumption goods were 9.5 per cent and 13.9 per cent during the same period.

Table 2 indicates that Thailand's international trade has been dominated by the United States and Japan for many decades. However trade with these countries has fallen from nearly 34.6 per cent of Thailand's trade in 1995 to 10 per cent in 2010. The trade with ASEAN countries has been relatively stable, increasing from 21.73 per cent in 1995 and 22.7 per cent in 2010. Trade within the AEC has constituted nearly 22 percent of both Thailand exports and imports. Among the country groups, therefore, the AEC with its geographical proximity and the level of economic development has been the most important group.

The share of Thailand's exports and imports with other groups namely EU (27 countries), NAFTA and the Middle East countries have been decreasing over time. As well, Thailand's share of exports and imports with countries such as the USA and Japan have been important, although they have diminished since 1995. However, the share of Thailand imports with the ASEAN has been striking over the last a couple of years.

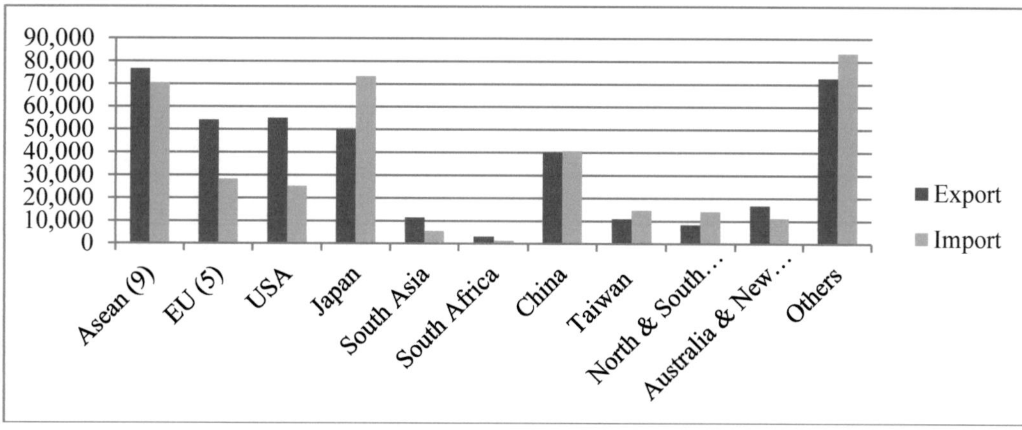

Figure 2. The share of Thailand's Export and Import in 2010

Region/countries	1995	2000	2005	2006	2007	2008	2009	2010
NAFTA	19.01	22.98	16.68	16.44	14.06	12.71	12.23	11.57
EU (27)	16.51	16.31	13.61	13.88	14.10	13.16	11.91	11.17
ASEAN	21.73	19.34	21.99	20.83	21.31	22.59	21.32	22.70
Middle East	4.50	3.03	4.03	4.41	4.86	5.34	5.74	4.93
USA	17.83	21.31	15.32	14.99	12.62	11.40	10.93	10.34
Japan	16.79	14.74	13.60	12.63	11.78	11.30	10.32	10.45
Hong Kong	5.18	5.04	5.56	5.52	5.65	5.65	6.22	6.72
China	2.91	4.07	8.26	9.04	9.65	9.11	10.58	10.99
Taiwan	2.40	3.50	2.45	2.59	2.16	1.52	1.48	1.65
South Korea	1.42	1.83	2.04	2.06	1.94	2.06	1.85	1.85
others	5.45	3.96	5.13	5.38	6.06	6.67	6.47	6.63
Total Export	100.00	100.00	100.00	100.00	100.00	100.00	100.00	100.00

Source: Bank of Thailand

Table 2. Thailand's Trade by Selected Export Destinations: (FoB : % Total Export)

Table 3 shows that Thailand's imports with NAFTA and EU decreased, while Thailand's trade with ASEAN and Middle East countries has increased. However, Thailand's import from individual countries decreased over time, as was the case with the USA and Japan, but the share of imports from China increased from 2.96 per cent to 13.29 per cent.

Region/countries	1995	2000	2005	2006	2007	2008	2009	2010
NAFTA	12.95	12.52	7.96	8.02	7.44	7.08	6.93	6.57
EU (27)	16.43	10.49	9.14	8.73	8.54	8.00	9.01	7.61
ASEAN 3/	13.32	16.64	18.30	18.33	17.91	16.82	18.48	16.63
Middle East	3.79	10.21	12.90	14.09	13.18	15.66	12.37	11.39
USA	12.01	11.77	7.35	7.45	6.78	6.37	6.26	5.85
Japan	30.55	24.73	22.03	19.93	20.28	18.71	18.72	20.75
China	2.96	5.45	9.44	10.56	11.59	11.25	12.74	13.29
Hong Kong	1.05	1.43	1.27	1.20	1.03	1.09	1.29	1.00
Taiwan	4.83	4.68	3.81	3.96	4.10	3.47	3.59	3.74
South Korea	3.50	3.50	3.29	3.98	3.78	3.83	4.06	4.42
Others	4.11	4.89	4.95	4.73	5.09	5.15	4.97	4.94
Total Imports	100.00	100.00	100.00	100.00	100.00	100.00	100.00	100.00

Source: Bank of Thailand

Table 3. Thailand's Trade by Selected Import Destinations: (CIF: % Total Import)

Thailand's total international trade (exports + imports) with ASEAN countries increased from 13 per cent ($8,578 million US) in 1991 to 20 per cent in 2009. Trade with non-ASEAN countries accounted to 87 per cent ($57,455 million US). The share of International Trade between Thailand and the AEC countries members indicated that Thailand's merchandise exports increased from 19.34 per cent in 2001 to 22.70 per cent in 2010, while Thailand's merchandise imports from the AEC countries remained unchanged (17.84 per cent in 2001 and 17.88 per cent in 2010) (see Table 5).

Year	Thailand Exports to AEC	%	Thailand Imports from AEC	%	Total Trade	%
1991	3,540.8	12.4	5,038.0	13.4	8,578.8	13.0
1992	4,490.2	13.8	5,541.4	13.6	10,031.5	13.7
1993	6,584.8	17.6	5,939.9	12.9	12,524.7	15.0
1994	9,058.4	19.9	7,450.4	13.7	16,508.9	16.5
1995	12,325.3	21.7	9,422.5	13.3	21,747.8	17.1
1996	12,113.4	21.7	9,639.6	13.3	21,753.0	17.0

Year	Thailand Exports to AEC	%	Thailand Imports from AEC	%	Total Trade	%
1997	12,734.2	21.8	8,127.6	12.9	20,861.8	17.2
1998	9,895.9	18.2	6,401.1	15.1	16,296.9	16.8
1999	10,871.6	18.6	7,906.4	15.8	18,778.0	17.3
2000	13,482.2	19.4	10,346.1	16.6	23,828.4	18.1
2001	12,599.1	19.3	10,012.7	16.2	22,611.8	17.8
2002	13,568.9	19.9	10,815.9	16.8	24,384.8	18.4
2003	16,486.0	20.6	12,489.2	16.6	28,975.2	18.7
2004	21,241.0	22.0	15,835.4	16.8	37,076.4	19.5
2005	23,892.0	21.7	21,608.7	18.5	45,500.6	20.1
2006	27,209.7	20.8	23,716.6	18.6	50,926.3	19.8
2007	32,488.6	19.9	25,066.9	16.7	57,555.5	18.4
2008	38,070.4	21.4	32,531.3	18.0	70,601.7	19.7
2009	32,491.1	21.3	24,699.9	18.5	57,191.0	20.0
2010	44,333,936	22.7	32,607,572	17.88	76,941,508	

Source: Information and Communication Technology Center, Office of the Permanent Secretary Ministry of Commerce with the Co-Operation of the Customs Department,

Table 4. Thailand Trade with AEC and its share in Thailand Trade (Million US Dollar)

YEAR	AEC	Non-AEC
1991	0.83	0.87
1993	0.95	0.87
1995	0.87	0.84
1997	0.78	0.91
1999	0.84	0.94
2001	0.94	0.98
2003	0.91	0.97
2005	0.98	0.96
2007	0.90	0.93
2009	0.90	0.99
2010	0.85	0.98

Note: Denote average for the period
Source: Calculated by author from the United Nations, *COMTRADE database*

Table 5. The IIT indexes for Thailand trading with AEC and Non-AEC member nations, 2000-2010

After becoming an AEC member, Thailand's exports increased with all member countries except Singapore. Table 6 shows that Malaysia Singapore and Indonesia are the top ranked countries for Thailand's exports and Brunei Darussalam takes the lowest rank. Malaysia, Singapore and Indonesia are the AEC member countries that comprise Thailand's highest import shares.

Countries	Before AFTA 1992		After AFTA 2003*		2009	
	Export	Import	Export	Import	Export	Import
World	**32,609.08**	**40,615.76**	**80,039.98**	**75,033.98**	**152,052.36**	**133,795.97**
Japan	5,710.43	11,885.22	11,356.20	18,074.36	15,732.00	25,024.00
USA	7,316.47	4,767.10	13,596.16	7,092.61	16,662.00	8,373.00
China	387.56	1,217.09	5,688.92	6,002.32	16,123.88	17,028.95
Others	8,401.05	11,982.98	26,853.87	29,874.12	103,984.48	83,370.02
Singapore	2,834.51	2,964.64	5,850.25	3,235.04	7,574.22	5,724.01
Malaysia	845.08	1,592.10	3,872.01	4,493.61	7,663.69	8,575.57
Indonesia	283.98	290.44	2,265.65	1,752.31	4,667.33	3,800.47
Vietnam	77.05	80.17	1,262.09	333.36	4,678.46	1,385.42
Philippins	155.35	121.07	1,616.26	1,337.75	3,022.05	1,783.17
Cambodia	66.13	92.99	685.35	12.25	1,580.61	77.73
Mynma	80.92	140.50	437.90	901.37	1,544.70	2,781.58
Lao	121.54	40.99	454.54	102.68	1,642.63	462.71
Brunei	25.59	218.47	41.98	320.83	117.39	109.19
ASEAN	**4,490.15**	**5,541.37**	**16,486.03**	**12,489.20**	**32,491.08**	**24,699.85**

Note: * 60% of inclusion list tax reduction = 0

Source: 1. Information and Communication Technology Center, Office of the Permanent Secretary Ministry of Commerce with the Co-Operation of the Customs Department,

2. Bank of Thailand

Table 6. Thailand export to ASEAN and import from ASEAN

3. Measurement of Intra-Industry Trade

Intra-industry trade (IIT) flows are conventionally defined as the two-way exchange of goods within standard industrial classifications. The extent of intra-industry trade is commonly measured by Grubel-Lloyd (G-L) indexes based on commodity group transactions. Thus, for any particular product class *i*, an index of the extent of intra-industry trade in the product class *i* between countries A and B is given by the following ratio:

$$IIT_{i,AB} = \left[\frac{(X_i + M_i) - \left[X_i - M_i \right]}{(X_i + M_i)} \right] * 100 \tag{1}$$

This index takes the minimum value of zero when there are no products in the same class that are both imported (represent by Mi) and exported (represent by Xi), and the maximum value of 100 when all trade is intra-industry (in this case Xi is equal to Mi). The indices reported in this section have been computed according to [1] for each pair of trading partners and for each two digit SITC revision 3 product class. Bilateral indices of intra-industry trade in the product class *i* between country A and all its trading partners are obtained as a weighted average of the bilateral indices [1] for each partner country B, using as weights the share of total trade of A accounted for by trade with B. Bilateral indices of intra industry trade between country A and country B for total manufacturing are the weighted average of the indexes in [1] for all product classes *i*, with weights given by the share of total trade of *i* over total manufacturing trade:

$$IIT_{AB} = \sum_i \left[\frac{(X_i + M_i) - \left[X_i - M_i \right]}{(X_i + M_i)} \right] * \left| \frac{(X_i + M_i)}{\sum_i (X_i + M_i)} \right| * 100 \tag{2}$$

A degree of caution must be used when comparing and interpreting intra-industry indices because their measurement crucially depends on the level of disaggregation chosen for the analysis. In the current context of assessing the importance of the division of the production process across countries, it should be recognized that, as well as measuring trade in intermediate goods at various stages of production, much intra-industry trade is trade in similar, but often highly differentiated, finished products.

4. The extent of Intra-Industry Trade in Thailand's foreign trade

As pointed out in section 3, this study centers on the G-L index measured by the ratio of difference between total trade and net trade expressed in terms of percentages. The estimated G-L indexes, IIT, are reported in Table 7. The G-L indexes, IIT, are calculated by aggregation across all products for Thailand with all AEC member nations and for Thailand with the rest of the world, hereafter referred to as non-AEC member nations. The estimation time span is 1991-2010.

About one-fourth of world trade consists of IIT, that is, two-way exchange of goods within standard industrial trade classification (SITC). For advanced industrial nations, IIT plays a large role in trade in manufactured goods which accounts for most of world trade. Industrial countries have become increasingly similar in their levels of technology and in the availability of capital and skilled labor. Since the major trading nations have become similar in technology and resources, there is often no clear comparative advantage within an industry, and much of international trade therefore takes the form of two- way exchanges within industries, probably driven by comparative advantage.

Apart from the quantitative increase in foreign trade, the most striking change that has occurred is in the sector share of Thailand exports since 1980. There has been a shift towards industrial goods, in contrast to the situation before 1980 when Thailand's agricultural exports typically accounted for about two-thirds of total exports. The share of manufactured products in total exports rose from 31.0 percent 1982 to 44.9 percent in 1986, while the share of exports of agricultural products fell from 70.3 percent in 1970 to 43.6 percent in 1985.

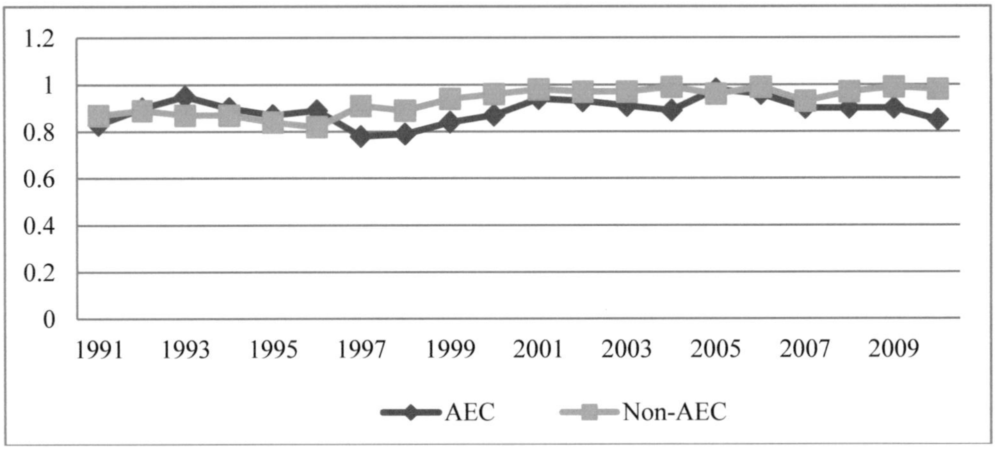

Source: data from Table A4

Figure 3. The IIT indexes for Thailand trading with AEC and Non-AEC member nations, 2000-2010

5. Industry composition for Thailand with individual AEC countries

5.1. Country analysis

In this section we turn our attention to the decomposition of bilateral trade by products. For each significant AEC nation with which Thailand has a trading relationship, the top ten products (ranked according to average IIT) are discussed. Table 7 points out that the top three products namely manmade filaments (54), articles of iron or steel (73), organic chemicals (29) have a highest level of IIT. Five from ten products are in SITC 5-9 and transform from low-technology products to high-technology industries.

The results of the highest average values of the IIT index during 2000-2010 show that within manufactures, certain resource-based labor intensive manufacturers and low technology manufactures occupy large shares of total trade. Common to both periods are the resource-based labor intensive manufactures. Post-AEC, the medium and high skill/technology intensive manufactures are footwear, gaiters and the like, parts thereof (64), soaps, lubricants, waxes, candles, and the low skill/technology manufactures of articles of iron or steel (73), aluminum and articles thereof (76), electrical, electronic equipment (85), plastics and articles thereof (39), aluminum and articles thereof (76). The trade environment for at least some of these products is changing. The quantitative restrictions in export markets and the reduction in domestic protection offered to the Thai textile and clothing industries have already been noted (BOT [24]).

ASEAN countries with high values of IIT, above 80 per cent are Malaysia, Singapore and Indonesia.

Rank	Code	Description	IIT (%)
1	54	Manmade filaments	90.75
2	73	Articles of iron or steel	90.26
3	29	Organic chemicals	87.87
4	85	Electrical, electronic equipment	86.76
5	36	Explosives, pyrotechnics, matches, pyrophorics, etc	86.59
6	64	Footwear, gaiters and the like, parts thereof	84.78
7	28	Inorganic chemicals, precious metal compound, isotopes	84.09
8	39	Plastics and articles thereof	82.11
9	76	Aluminums and articles thereof	82.84
10	48	Paper & paperboard, articles of pulp, paper and board	81.93

Source: Calculated by author from the United Nations, *COMTRADE database*

Table 7. Top 10 products ranked according to average IIT between Thailand and AEC, 2000-2010

The IIT index between Thailand and Malaysia, Singapore, Cambodia, Lao, Myanmar and Brunei Darussalam increased over time. The IIT indexes of Malaysia, Singapore, Myanmar are high and increasing IIT which means Thailand international trade structure with those countries are complementary rather than competitive. The IIT indexes of Indonesia and Philippines are high and decreasing IIT. In contrast the Lao People's Democratic Republic and Brunei Darussalam have low and increasing IIT. Viet Nam is low and decreasing IIT (see Table 8).

Countries	1995-1997	1998-2000	2001-2003	2004-2006	2007-2010	Change
ASEAN	0.84	0.83	0.88	0.91	0.85	0.01
Malaysia	0.76	0.91	0.92	0.90	0.97	0.21
Singapore	0.69	0.71	0.70	0.79	0.82	0.13
Indonesia	0.91	0.95	0.94	0.90	0.90	-0.01
Viet Nam	0.29	0.56	0.47	0.46	0.44	0.15
Philippines	0.89	0.94	0.93	0.92	0.75	-0.13
Cambodia	0.43	0.09	0.04	0.06	0.10	-0.32
Lao PDR	0.30	0.24	0.37	0.48	0.50	0.20
Myanmar	0.57	0.47	0.60	0.56	0.68	0.11
Brunei Darussalam	0.59	0.40	0.19	0.51	0.89	0.30

Note: 1.Countries are classified as having 'high' or 'low' level of intra-industry trade according to whether intra-industry trade is above or below 50 percent of total manufacturing trade on average over all periods shown and 'increasing' or 'stable' according to whether intra-industry trade increases by more than 5 percentage points between the first and last periods, as shown in the final column.
2. PDR denote People's Democratic Republic
Source: author calculations, based on International Trade Statistics.

Table 8. Determinant of IIT between Thailand and AEC, 1995-2010 (Million US)

Of particular interest when considering intra-industry trade and the internationalization of production are those countries where exports and imports account for a very high percentage of GDP. There are currently ten AEC economies (Thailand; Malaysia; Singapore; Indonesia; Viet Nam; Philippines; Cambodia; Lao People's Democratic Republic; Myanmar; Brunei Darussalam) where both imports and exports account for more than half of GDP. Although there is far from a perfect correspondence, these countries all tend to have relatively high intra-industry trade (Malaysia; Singapore; Myanmar); all but two (Vietnam and Cambodia) having measures of intra-industry trade that are below the average across all AEC countries and five of them (Malaysia, Singapore, Indonesia, Philippines and Brunei Darussalam) being in the top ten countries for the period 2007-2010.

Table 9 shows that Thailand's IIT with Indonesia increases from 1995 through to 2009. The basket of products in the top ten completely changes with no products in common in the top ten pre- and post- AEC. Despite this dramatic change, the overall industrial composition does not shift markedly with roughly 50 percent of products pre-and post-AEC being in the resource based labor intensive and low skill/technology manufactures (Table 9).

Rank	Code	Description	IIT
1	85	Electrical, electronic equipment	92.45
2	76	Aluminum and articles thereof	91.94
3	52	Cotton	90.84
4	61	Articles of apparel, accessories, knit or crochet	85.47
5	70	Glass and glassware	84.50
6	48	Paper & paperboard, articles of pulp, paper and board	80.20
7	34	Soaps, lubricants, waxes, candles, modeling pastes	79.82
8	57	Carpets and other textile floor coverings	79.61
9	29	Organic chemicals	76.22
10	68	Stone, plaster, cement, asbestos, mica, etc articles	75.77

Source: Calculated by author from the United Nations, *COMTRADE database*

Table 9. Top 10 products ranked according to average IIT between Thailand and Indonesia, 2000-10

Malaysia and Thailand have enjoyed a strong trade relationship with an increasing proportion of IIT. Of all the countries under review, Malaysia has the largest number of products common to both periods. Three of the four existing products from the top ten were drawn from the medium to high skill/technology manufactures, being Articles of iron or steel (73), stone, plaster, cement, asbestos, mica, etc articles (68), other made textile articles, sets, worn clothing, etc (63), machinery, nuclear reactors, boilers, etc (84). Thus, the striking feature of the industrial composition of the Malaysian basket is the relatively high proportion that falls into the medium to high skill products in both periods (five of the top ten in both time frames) (see Table 10).

Rank	Code	Description	IIT
1	96	Miscellaneous manufactured articles	93.83
2	39	Plastics and articles thereof	91.40
3	41	Raw hides and skins (other than fur skins) and leather	87.58
4	68	Stone, plaster, cement, asbestos, mica, etc articles	86.25
5	84	Machinery, nuclear reactors, boilers, etc	86.19
6	63	Other made textile articles, sets, worn clothing etc	82.44
7	29	Organic chemicals	82.10
8	15	Animal, vegetable fats and oils, cleavage products, etc	81.76
9	73	Articles of iron or steel	79.81
10	19	Cereal, flour, starch, milk preparations and products	78.53

Source: Calculated by author from the United Nations, *COMTRADE database*

Table 10. Top 10 products ranked according to average IIT between Thailand and Malaysia, 2000-2010

The pattern of IIT in manufactures between Thailand and the Philippines displays sizable variability over the period. Only four products are common and of these are in the medium skill/technology area. Four of the existing products come from the medium to high skill end of the spectrum, being electrical, electronic equipment (85), miscellaneous articles of base metal (83), machinery, nuclear reactors, boilers, etc (84), vehicles other than railway, tramway (87) and iron and steel (72). Similar to Malaysia, the overall Philippines industrial composition has a relatively high proportion that falls into the medium to high skill products in both periods (six and eight of the top ten pre- and post-AEC, respectively (Table 11).

Rank	Code	Description	IIT
1	85	Electrical, electronic equipment	91.48
2	83	Miscellaneous articles of base metal	86.64
3	19	Cereal, flour, starch, milk preparations and products	80.49
4	12	Oil seed, elegiac fruits, grain, seed, fruit, etc, nes	79.50
5	82	Tools, implements, cutlery, etc of base metal	75.80
6	84	Machinery, nuclear reactors, boilers, etc	74.47
7	90	Optical, photo, technical, medical, etc apparatus	70.64
8	87	Vehicles other than railway, tramway	70.60
9	08	Edible fruit, nuts, peel of citrus fruit, melons	62.76
10	72	Iron and steel	61.56

Source: Calculated by author from the United Nations, *COMTRADE database*

Table 11. Top 10 products ranked according to average IIT between Thailand and the Philippines, 2000-2010

Singapore, like Malaysia, has a high level of IIT with Thailand, though there is an indication of moderate decline in the late 1990s. Two products, both are at the medium skill/technology level, persist from the 1980s to the 1990s (85 and 96). Four of the products that are no longer in the top ten after 1990 are from the low skill/technology manufactures—A Ceramic products (69), manmade filaments (54), residues, wastes of food industry, animal fodder (23), come from the resources based labor intensive sector. However, four of new products on the list in the 1990s are also from these sectors- electrical, electronic equipment (85), optical, photo, technical, medical, etc apparatus (90), articles of iron or steel (73) and pharmaceutical products (30). Overall, one cannot deduce a shift in the industrial composition of IIT between Thailand and Singapore (Table 12).

Rank	Code	Description	IIT
1	85	Electrical, electronic equipment	93.26
2	96	Miscellaneous manufactured articles	88.27
3	21	Miscellaneous edible preparations	86.43
4	90	Optical, photo, technical, medical, etc apparatus	86.24
5	83	Miscellaneous articles of base metal	84.01
6	35	Albuminoidal, modified starches, glues, enzymes	82.97
7	59	Impregnated, coated or laminated textile fabric	81.94
8	69	Ceramic products	81.80
9	73	Articles of iron or steel	80.39
10	30	Pharmaceutical products	78.69

Source: Calculated by author from the United Nations, *COMTRADE database*

Table 12. Top 10 products ranked according to average IIT between Thailand and Singapore, 2000-2010

Myanmar has a low level of IIT with Thailand (below 50). Only two products, furniture, lighting, signs, prefabricated buildings (94) and manufactures of plaiting material, basketwork, etc. (46) have a high level. Many products still come from resources based labor intensive sector (see Table 13).

Rank	Code	Description	IIT
1	94	Furniture, lighting, signs, prefabricated buildings	73.22
2	46	Manufactures of plaiting material, basketwork, etc.	57.99
3	12	Oil seed, elegiac fruits, grain, seed, fruit, etc, nes	47.31
4	71	Pearls, precious stones, metals, coins, etc	46.47
5	23	Residues, wastes of food industry, animal fodder	37.23
6	09	Coffee, tea, mate and spices	35.38
7	08	Edible fruit, nuts, peel of citrus fruit, melons	34.31

Rank	Code	Description	IIT
8	41	Raw hides and skins (other than fur skin) and leather	30.85
9	92	Musical instruments, parts and accessories	28.36
10	24	Tobacco and manufactured tobacco substitutes	27.42

Source: Calculated by author from the United Nations, *COMTRADE database*

Table 13. Top 10 products ranked according to average IIT between Thailand and Myanmar, 2000-2010

Vietnam, like Myanmar has a low level of IIT with Thailand. All of the top ten products are above 50 percent of IIT level. A high proportion fell into the medium skill/technology area (see Table 14).

Rank	Code	Description	IIT
1	71	Pearls, precious stones, metals, coins, etc	85.16
2	62	Articles of apparel, accessories, not knit or crochet	75.07
3	85	Electrical, electronic equipment	70.66
4	61	Articles of apparel, accessories, knit or crochet	67.36
5	65	Headgear and parts thereof	66.61
6	54	Manmade filaments	64.87
7	12	Oil seed, elegiac fruits, grain, seed, fruit, etc, nes	59.90
8	69	Ceramic products	57.70
9	27	Mineral fuels, oils, distillation products, etc	56.79
10	07	Edible vegetables and certain roots and tubers	56.17

Source: Calculated by author from the United Nations, *COMTRADE database*

Table 14. Top 10 products ranked according to average IIT between Thailand and Vietnam, 2000-2010

Lao PDR, like Vietnam has a low level of IIT with Thailand. Five of the products are above 50 percent of IIT level. A high proportion fell into the resource based or low skill/technology area (see Table 15).

Rank	Code	Description	IIT
1	10	Cereals	61.35
2	62	Articles of pparel, accessories, not knit or crochet	58.71
3	09	Coffee, tea, mate and spices	57.89
4	41	Raw hides and skins (other than fur skins) and leather	56.60
5	36	Explosives, pyrotechnics, matches, pyrophorics, etc	50.76
6	49	Printed books, newspapers, pictures etc	48.44

Rank	Code	Description	IIT
7	42	Articles of leather, animal gut, harness, travel goods	38.15
8	50	Silk	37.06
9	27	Mineral fuels, oils, distillation products, etc	36.92
10	01	Live animals	33.72

Source: Calculated by author from the United Nations, *COMTRADE database*

Table 15. Top 10 products ranked according to average IIT between Thailand and Lao People's Democratic Republic, 2000- 2010

Brunei Darussalam is the only AEC member country that has a low level of IIT (below 50) for all products which means Thailand has no longer trade in terms of Intra-industry trade but Thailand will trade in term of international trade with other countries.

Rank	Code	Description	IIT
1	76	Aluminum and articles thereof	45.85
2	90	Optical, photo, technical, medical, etc apparatus	28.20
3	49	Printed books, newspapers, pictures etc	26.99
4	82	Tools, implements, cutlery, etc of base metal	26.44
5	83	Miscellaneous articles of base metal	19.40
6	74	Copper and articles thereof	15.80
7	44	Wood and articles of wood, wood charcoal	13.98
8	41	Raw hides and skins (other than fur skins) and leather	12.21
9	32	Tanning, dyeing extracts, tannins, derives, pigments etc	09.42
10	96	Miscellaneous manufactured articles	08.86

Source: Calculated by author from the United Nations, *COMTRADE database*, UN (2010)

Table 16. Top 10 products ranked according to average IIT between Thailand and Brunei Darussalam, 2000-2010

Cambodia, like Lao PDR has a low level of IIT with Thailand. Only three of the products are above 50 percents of IIT level. A high proportion fell into the resource based or low skill/technology area (see Table 17).

Rank	Code	Description	IIT
1	44	Wood and articles of wood, wood charcoal	63.86
2	09	Coffee, tea, mate and spices	56.17
3	03	Fish, crustaceans, mollusks, aquatic invertebrates, nes.	55.46
4	62	Articles of apparel, accessories, not knit or crochet	47.76

Rank	Code	Description	IIT
5	72	Iron and steel	46.90
6	76	Aluminum and articles thereof	45.21
7	10	Cereals	44.54
8	41	Raw hides and skins (other than fur skins) and leather	31.84
9	63	Other made textile articles, sets, worn clothing etc	31.06
10	61	Articles of apparel, accessories, knit or crochet	29.57

Source: Calculated by author from the United Nations, *COMTRADE database*

Table 17. Top 10 products ranked according to average IIT between Thailand and Cambodia, 2000-2010

5.2. Industry analysis

International trade can be investigated in terms of bilateral trade relationships between countries, in terms of product composition or in terms of bilateral trade decomposed by products. This section is concentrates on analysis by product composition.

Table 18 calculates the average annual IIT for all commodities within each specific product group and thus summarizes significant detail in its construction. The G-L indexes are calculated by aggregation a cross all classifications (SITC) at 1-digit level for Thailand with AEC member nations during 2001-2010. The results in Table 19 show that the share of IIT in SITC 3 is the highest IIT index while the share of IIT at SITC 5 and 6 have been increasing 2 times from 2001 to 2010. The share of IIT of SITC 3-9 is higher than 50 and SITC 0-2 is below 50.

SITC	2001	2003	2005	2007	2009	2010
0	40.74	42.14	43.54	40.69	37.52	44.71
1	34.60	30.81	35.93	37.80	40.92	41.69
2	40.94	41.03	39.19	43.88	42.98	49.40
3	61.02	67.03	67.56	72.69	68.03	66.41
4	59.38	55.66	50.09	56.85	59.45	53.93
5	31.81	43.81	48.94	41.99	53.26	53.66
6	35.96	48.05	53.98	54.11	56.47	56.15
7	59.90	54.21	65.98	57.05	62.89	56.02
8	51.76	57.97	57.82	63.34	54.23	52.78
9	50.79	61.76	45.75	45.79	42.06	56.70

Source: Calculated by author from the United Nations, *COMTRADE database*

Table 18. Average IIT according to SITC 0-9, 2001-2010

Table 19 indicates that from 2001 to 2010, the proportion of commodities with an IIT index of less than 30 fell from 36.45 to 24.98 percent, while the proportion with and IIT index greater than 50 percent rose from 42.70 to 57.10 percent.

SITC	2001	2003	2005	2007	2009	2010
0 and below 30 (%)	35 (36.45)	29 (27.84)	22 (22.90)	26 (27.08)	29 (30.19)	24 (24.98)
30 and below 50 (%)	20 (20.82)	20 (19.20)	24 (24.99)	25 (26.03)	20 (20.82)	17 (17.7)
50 and below 100 (%)	41 (42.7)	51 (48.96)	50 (52.08)	49 (51.04)	51 (53.12)	55 (57.28)
total sample (%)	96 (100.00)	96 (100.00)	96 (100.00)	96 (100.00)	96 (100.00)	96 (100.00)
Average IIT	46.69	50.25	50.88	51.42	51.78	53.15
all product	93.66	90.63	97.92	90.30	90.33	84.76

Source: Calculated by author from the United Nations, COMTRADE database
Note: a weighted by the trade share.

Table 19. Frequency distribution of IIT index at 3 digits SITC 0-9, 2001-2010

IIT for Thailand's trade with AEC countries changed from agricultural products (SITC 0-4) in 2001 to manufactured products (SITC 5-8) in 2010 for example soaps, lubricants, waxes, candles, modeling pastes (34), glass and glassware (70), coffee, tea, mate and spices (09), optical, photo, technical, medical, etc apparatus (90), organic chemicals (29) in 2001 to ceramic products (69), mineral fuels, oils, distillation products, etc. (27), (explosives, pyrotechnics, matches, pyrophorics, etc.(36), organic chemicals (29), works of art, collectors pieces and antiques (97).

At 3 digits SITC-0, the highest of IIT levels (above 80 percent) are coffee, tea, mate and spices (09), fish, crustaceans, mollusks, aquatic invertebrates, nes (03). In contrast, the lowest level IIT index are meat and edible meat offal (02), products of animal origin, nes (05), edible fruit, nuts, peel of citrus fruit, melons (08). Increasing IIT are dairy products, eggs, honey, edible animal product, nes (04), products of animal origin, nes (05), edible vegetables and certain roots and tubers (07), edible fruit, nuts, peel of citrus fruit, melons (08) (see Table 20).

Code	Description	2001	2003	2005	2007	2009	2010
TOL		93.66	90.63	97.92	90.30	90.33	84.76
01	Live animals	48.33	88.00	38.32	81.02	5.22	12.43
02	Meat and edible meat offal	4.22	2.57	60.08	6.14	1.32	0.50
03	Fish, crustaceans, molluscs, aquatic invertebrates nes	80.24	58.02	45.49	53.10	49.62	58.79
04	Dairy products, eggs, honey, edible animal product nes	28.46	33.68	35.46	46.88	63.61	67.53
05	Products of animal origin, nes	5.58	85.27	64.71	32.88	37.71	76.16
06	Live trees, plants, bulbs, roots, cut flowers etc	53.10	32.89	30.25	33.17	23.08	32.17

Code	Description	2001	2003	2005	2007	2009	2010
07	Edible vegetables and certain roots and tubers	45.63	59.90	78.25	52.28	77.91	91.88
08	Edible fruit, nuts, peel of citrus fruit, melons	3.07	7.54	29.33	39.71	35.44	48.05
09	Coffee, tea, mate and spices	98.03	11.40	10.00	21.08	43.74	14.87

Source: Calculated by author from the United Nations, *COMTRADE database*, UN (2010)

Table 20. Distribution of IIT index at 3 digit SITC 0, 2001-2010

Analysis at 3 digits SITC-1, indicated that the IIT index increased in cereals (10), oil seed, elegiac fruits, grain, seed, fruit, etc, nes (12), animal, vegetable fats and oils, cleavage products, etc (15), meat, fish and seafood food preparations, nes (16), sugars and sugar confectionery (17), cocoa and cocoa preparations (18), cereal, flour, starch, milk preparations and products (19). In contrast IIT decreased in milling products, malt, starches, insulin, wheat gluten (11), lac, gums, resins, vegetable saps and extracts, nes (13), vegetable plaiting materials, vegetable products, nes (14). The lowest IIT index at 3 digits SITC-1 is sugars and sugar confectionery (17). The highest IIT index at 3 digit SITC 1 are oil seed, oleagic fruits, grain, seed, fruit, etc, nes (12) and cereal, flour, starch, milk preparations and products (19) (see Table 21).

code	Description	2001	2003	2005	2007	2009	2010
TOL		93.66	90.63	97.92	90.30	90.33	84.76
10	Cereals	0.41	0.98	5.18	5.06	13.84	11.99
11	Milling products, malt, starches, insulin, wheat gluten	20.78	11.78	25.47	21.23	13.73	14.96
12	Oil seed, oleagic fruits, grain, seed, fruit, etc, nes	62.87	76.64	54.77	88.83	70.16	68.29
13	Lac, gums, resins, vegetable saps and extracts nes	48.80	24.65	36.99	24.79	32.71	45.82
14	Vegetable plaiting materials, vegetable products nes	24.18	11.87	10.61	4.97	0.61	0.72
15	Animal, vegetable fats and oils, cleavage products, etc	49.67	54.57	57.85	42.48	65.38	76.12
16	Meat, fish and seafood food preparations nes	12.84	12.48	29.75	27.39	54.02	48.06
17	Sugars and sugar confectionery	5.02	5.58	4.84	4.67	7.97	6.38
18	Cocoa and cocoa preparations	18.69	32.55	37.96	49.98	44.52	39.56
19	Cereal, flour, starch, milk preparations and products	68.55	47.17	65.16	75.83	79.14	75.33

Source: Calculated by author from the United Nations, *COMTRADE database*, UN (2010)

Table 21. Distribution of IIT index at 3 digits SITC 1, 2001-2010

At 3 digits SITC-2, the analysis indicated that the IIT index increased in vegetable, fruit, nut, etc food preparations (20), beverages, spirits and vinegar (22), residues, wastes of food industry, animal fodder (23), tobacco and manufactured tobacco substitutes (24), salt, sulphur, earth, stone, plaster, lime and cement (25), ores, slag and ash (26), mineral fuels, oils, distillation products, etc (27), organic chemicals (29). In contrast, IIT decreased in miscellaneous edible preparations (21), Inorganic chemicals, precious metal compound, isotopes (28). The highest IIT are mineral fuels, oils, distillation products, etc (27), inorganic chemicals, precious metal compound, isotopes (28), organic chemicals (29) (see Table 22).

code	Description	2001	2003	2005	2007	2009	2010
TOL		93.66	90.63	97.92	90.30	90.33	84.76
20	Vegetable, fruit, nut, etc food preparations	14.32	17.14	22.87	36.47	29.66	28.39
21	Miscellaneous edible preparations	43.70	41.69	37.59	38.83	29.59	29.86
22	Beverages, spirits and vinegar	8.69	37.63	33.52	23.34	12.87	11.24
23	Residues, wastes of food industry, animal fodder	20.88	15.13	20.70	21.10	22.03	28.06
24	Tobacco and manufactured tobacco substitutes	49.90	38.51	39.64	56.03	62.70	61.48
25	Salt, sulphur, earth, stone, plaster, lime and cement	9.79	11.44	9.96	10.85	7.73	11.50
26	Ores, slag and ash	4.19	6.47	1.54	22.41	4.46	50.56
27	Mineral fuels, oils, distillation products, etc	71.10	69.97	66.59	75.61	77.31	96.19
28	Inorganic chemicals, precious metal compound, isotopes	91.83	80.45	70.90	85.50	85.15	81.63
29	Organic chemicals	94.97	91.88	88.55	68.69	98.32	95.14

Source: Calculated by author from the United Nations, *COMTRADE database,* UN (2010)

Table 22. Distribution of IIT index at 3 digits SITC 2, 2001-2010

At 3 digits SITC-3, we found that the IIT level increased in fertilizers (31), tanning, dyeing extracts, tannins, derives, pigments etc (32), essential oils, perfumes, cosmetics, toiletries (33), explosives, pyrotechnics, matches, pyrophorics, etc (36), photographic or cinematographic goods (37), miscellaneous chemical products (38). IIT decreased in soaps, lubricants, waxes, candles, modeling pastes (34), albuminoids, modified starches, glues, enzymes (35). The highest IIT level are for explosives, pyrotechnics, matches, pyrophorics, etc (36). The lowest IIT levels are for albuminoids, modified starches, glues, enzymes (35) (see Table 23).

	Description	2001	2003	2005	2007	2009	2010
30	Pharmaceutical products	41.73	51.88	42.69	52.69	48.72	42.66
31	Fertilizers	30.08	40.10	57.63	56.17	61.57	53.18
32	Tanning, dyeing extracts, tannins, derivs, pigments etc	43.97	55.83	88.59	81.57	94.89	88.43
33	Essential oils, perfumes, cosmetics, toileteries	55.13	59.34	57.23	63.47	62.78	65.68
34	Soaps, lubricants, waxes, candles, modelling pastes	98.78	88.84	82.25	86.09	67.04	60.76
35	Albuminoids, modified starches, glues, enzymes	34.48	44.15	37.32	33.16	25.33	22.21
36	Explosives, pyrotechnics, matches, pyrophorics, etc	81.52	96.06	78.27	98.70	78.01	95.54
37	Photographic or cinematographic goods	61.20	74.07	85.63	97.74	81.14	70.73
38	Miscellaneous chemical products	74.16	71.31	66.96	79.14	86.14	87.29
39	Plastics and articles thereof	89.16	88.74	79.01	78.14	74.68	77.63

Source: Calculated by author from the United Nations, *COMTRADE database*, UN (2010)

Table 23. Distribution of IIT index at 3 digits SITC 3, 2001-2010

At 3 digits SITC-4, IIT increased in articles of leather, animal gut, harness, travel goods (42), wood and articles of wood, wood charcoal (44), cork and articles of cork (45), paper & paperboard, articles of pulp, paper and board (48). IIT decreased for rubber and articles thereof (40), raw hides and skins (other than fur skins) and leather (41), fur skins and artificial fur, manufactures thereof (43), manufactures of plaiting material, basketwork, etc. (46), pulp of wood, fibrous cellulosic material, waste etc (47), printed books, newspapers, pictures etc (49). The highest IIT index was for paper & paperboard, articles of pulp, paper and board (48), while the lowest IIT was for fur skins and artificial fur, manufactures thereof (43) (see Table 24).

	Description	2001	2003	2005	2007	2009	2010
40	Rubber and articles thereof	25.98	21.62	22.02	22.13	16.71	16.85
41	Raw hides and skins (other than furskins) and leather	94.97	71.51	42.21	43.73	45.95	37.71
42	Articles of leather, animal gut, harness, travel goods	65.46	51.37	64.76	63.64	76.04	75.13
43	Furskins and artificial fur, manufactures thereof	55.17	10.30	28.13	50.00	18.10	14.29
44	Wood and articles of wood, wood charcoal	15.52	23.45	32.44	71.01	77.25	81.90

	Description	2001	2003	2005	2007	2009	2010
45	Cork and articles of cork	11.32	50.00	9.22	16.35	91.20	54.96
46	Manufactures of plaiting material, basketwork, etc.	76.26	72.09	91.31	72.66	45.65	44.44
47	Pulp of wood, fibrous cellulosic material, waste etc	74.65	73.12	60.60	61.97	75.06	69.49
48	Paper & paperboard, articles of pulp, paper and board	81.58	88.17	90.33	76.12	75.24	83.23
49	Printed books, newspapers, pictures etc	92.86	94.97	59.92	90.84	73.26	61.30

Source: Calculated by author from the United Nations, *COMTRADE database*, UN (2010)

Table 24. Distribution of IIT index at 3 digits SITC 4, 2001-2010

At 3 digits SITC-5, IIT is increasing in silk (50), wool, animal hair, horsehair yarn and fabric thereof (51), vegetable textile fibres nes, paper yarn, woven fabric (53), wadding, felt, nonwovens, yarns, twine, cordage, etc (56), carpets and other textile floor coverings (57), special woven or tufted fabric, lace, tapestry etc (58), impregnated, coated or laminated textile fabric (59). IIT decreased in cotton (52), manmade filaments (54), manmade staple fibres (55). The highest IIT is for manmade filaments (54). The lowest IIT is for manmade staple fibres (55) (Table 25).

	Description	2001	2003	2005	2007	2009	2010
50	Silk	31.41	84.07	96.41	40.11	68.33	86.32
51	Wool, animal hair, horsehair yarn and fabric thereof	18.94	27.63	30.14	62.69	77.45	67.58
52	Cotton	35.86	33.97	30.02	15.30	15.99	29.62
53	Vegetable textile fibres nes, paper yarn, woven fabric	25.97	50.76	86.04	41.08	96.56	72.69
54	Manmade filaments	93.17	87.64	90.54	91.22	88.82	89.82
55	Manmade staple fibres	38.41	40.06	26.34	19.74	21.04	21.74
56	Wadding, felt, nonwovens, yarns, twine, cordage, etc	14.37	19.76	19.06	25.59	25.81	23.72
57	Carpets and other textile floor coverings	10.76	19.02	23.35	19.12	27.19	25.02
58	Special woven or tufted fabric, lace, tapestry etc	23.54	35.13	41.07	51.87	61.96	72.80
59	Impregnated, coated or laminated textile fabric	25.65	40.09	46.39	53.20	49.48	47.26

Source: Calculated by author from the United Nations, *COMTRADE database*, UN (2010)

Table 25. Distribution of IIT index at 3 digits SITC 5, 2001-2010

At 3 digits SITC-6, the analysis found that IIT increased in articles of apparel, accessories, knit or crochet (61), Articles of apparel, accessories, not knit or crochet (62), Other made textile articles, sets, worn clothing etc (63), footwear, gaiters and the like, parts thereof (64), headgear and parts thereof (65), umbrellas, walking-sticks, seat-sticks, whips, etc (66), ceramic products (69). IIT decreased in knitted or crocheted fabric (60), bird skin, feathers, artificial flowers, human hair (67), stone, plaster, cement, asbestos, mica, etc articles (68). The highest IIT is ceramic products (69), while the lowest IIT is stone, plaster, cement, asbestos, mica, etc articles (68) (Table 26).

	Description	2001	2003	2005	2007	2009	2010
60	Knitted or crocheted fabric	27.21	17.14	14.16	21.08	19.29	23.66
61	Articles of apparel, accessories, knit or crochet	13.95	24.66	34.04	51.34	46.62	49.65
62	Articles of apparel, accessories, not knit or crochet	26.46	22.90	31.80	52.96	57.69	51.40
63	Other made textile articles, sets, worn clothing etc	59.43	83.08	70.22	76.54	87.95	88.24
64	Footwear, gaiters and the like, parts thereof	52.98	85.64	74.76	88.51	96.34	93.13
65	Headgear and parts thereof	19.83	13.83	45.63	23.56	36.80	44.53
66	Umbrellas, walking-sticks, seat-sticks, whips, etc	16.62	37.80	40.63	22.75	17.90	34.29
67	Bird skin, feathers, artificial flowers, human hair	65.10	89.05	97.19	80.55	94.49	59.30
68	Stone, plaster, cement, asbestos, mica, etc articles	38.93	44.88	50.45	34.30	22.51	19.51
69	Ceramic products	39.10	61.56	80.91	89.47	85.05	97.80

Source: Calculated by author from the United Nations, *COMTRADE database*, UN (2010)

Table 26. Distribution of IIT index at 3 digits SITC 6, 2001-2010

At 3 digits SITC-7, we found that IIT increased in pearls, precious stones, metals, coins, etc (71), iron and steel (72), articles of iron or steel (73), aluminum and articles thereof (76), lead and articles thereof (78), IIT decreased in glass and glassware (70), copper and articles thereof (74), nickel and articles thereof (75), zinc and articles thereof (79). The highest IIT is lead and articles thereof (78), and the lowest IIT is pearls, precious stones, metals, coins, etc (27) (Table 27).

	Description	2001	2003	2005	2007	2009	2010
70	Glass and glassware	98.23	83.90	92.98	61.60	51.35	53.78
71	Pearls, precious stones, metals, coins, etc	11.86	30.87	62.01	47.03	20.31	27.01

	Description	2001	2003	2005	2007	2009	2010
72	Iron and steel	30.91	40.83	62.08	43.99	58.53	55.46
73	Articles of iron or steel	89.18	77.68	97.51	87.05	98.32	91.09
74	Copper and articles thereof	36.51	33.16	47.43	48.76	30.80	33.17
75	Nickel and articles thereof	84.98	24.73	22.48	10.30	87.25	35.33
76	Aluminium and articles thereof	62.55	75.99	72.15	94.92	98.53	84.25
78	Lead and articles thereof	68.97	95.28	99.08	71.79	86.15	91.34
79	Zinc and articles thereof	55.91	25.47	38.06	48.00	34.74	32.78

Source: Calculated by author from the United Nations, *COMTRADE database*, UN (2010)

Table 27. Distribution of IIT index at 3 digits SITC 7, 2001-2010

At 3 digits SITC-8, IIT increased in tools, implements, cutlery, etc, of base metal (82), ships, boats and other floating structures (89). IIT decreased in miscellaneous articles of base metal (83), machinery, nuclear reactors, boilers, etc (84), electrical, electronic equipment (85), railway, tramway locomotives, rolling stock, equipment (86), vehicles other than railway, tramway (87), aircraft, spacecraft, and parts thereof (88). IIT was stable in tin and articles thereof (80), other base metals, cermets, articles thereof (81). IIT was highest for tools, implements, cutlery, etc of base metal (82), and lowest for aircraft, spacecraft, and parts thereof (88) (Table 28).

	Description	2001	2003	2005	2007	2009	2010
80	Tin and articles thereof	24.08	41.16	10.50	70.08	73.67	23.76
81	Other base metals, cermets, articles thereof	34.84	59.80	82.63	84.70	52.96	35.44
82	Tools, implements, cutlery, etc of base metal	62.45	72.63	68.01	97.65	91.97	91.31
83	Miscellaneous articles of base metal	65.14	64.24	68.69	52.91	61.49	51.68
84	Machinery, nuclear reactors, boilers, etc	81.45	82.85	87.72	81.15	83.48	72.17
85	Electrical, electronic equipment	89.37	92.95	82.48	85.97	80.56	82.78
86	Railway, tramway locomotives, rolling stock, equipment	73.31	70.09	75.62	83.20	35.27	54.38
87	Vehicles other than railway, tramway	70.45	67.39	42.43	34.71	34.31	40.73
88	Aircraft, spacecraft, and parts thereof	13.94	5.10	1.09	1.75	7.03	3.18
89	Ships, boats and other floating structures	2.56	23.52	59.03	41.30	21.55	72.41

Source: Calculated by author from the United Nations, *COMTRADE database*,

Table 28. Distribution of IIT index at 3 digits SITC 8, 2001-2010

At 3 digits SITC-9, IIT increased in clocks and watches and parts thereof (91), arms and ammunition, parts and accessories thereof (93), furniture, lighting, signs, prefabricated buildings (94), miscellaneous manufactured articles (96), works of art, collectors pieces and antiques (97). IIT decreased in optical, photo, technical, medical, etc apparatus (90), musical instruments, parts and accessories (92), toys, games, sports requisites (95), commodities not elsewhere specified (99). The highest IIT is for works of art, collectors pieces and antiques (97), while the lowest IIT is for commodities not elsewhere specified (99) (Table 29).

code	Description	2001	2003	2005	2007	2009	2010
TOL		93.66	90.63	97.92	90.30	90.33	84.76
90	Optical, photo, technical, medical, etc apparatus	96.48	80.59	59.61	73.08	83.11	77.43
91	Clocks and watches and parts thereof	46.84	42.77	26.14	33.13	75.40	59.00
92	Musical instruments, parts and accessories	23.46	24.77	8.82	13.44	12.42	19.58
93	Arms and ammunition, parts and accessories thereof	4.07	18.17	6.79	56.84	49.65	55.30
94	Furniture, lighting, signs, prefabricated buildings	50.59	65.84	52.78	43.36	48.58	88.07
95	Toys, games, sports requisites	84.08	65.71	48.42	41.40	31.68	39.32
96	Miscellaneous manufactured articles	55.35	68.06	64.53	67.32	67.60	78.62
97	Works of art, collectors pieces and antiques	32.35	93.75	83.76	39.12	10.13	93.03
99	Commodities not elsewhere specified	63.87	96.15	60.89	44.40	0	0.00

Source: Calculated by author from the United Nations, *COMTRADE database*

Table 29. Distribution of IIT index at 3 digits SITC 9, 2001-2010

6. Conclusion

Since Verdoon, P.J., [25], Grubel and Lloyd [26] many studies stressed that there is strong empirical support for the hypothesis that countries that have common borders and have eliminated or lowered barriers on trade with each other will have relatively high levels of intra-industry trade. Moreover, the extent of intra-industry trade will be positively correlated with trade intensity. That is, as the trade volume with trade partners increases, there will be more opportunity for more differentiated products to be traded.

The results show that, Thailand's external trade with the AEC is significantly composed of the intra-industry type trading, especially so after the significant of the AFTA (ASEAN Free Trade Area) agreement with the ASEAN in 1993. The level of intra-industry trade is higher between Malaysia, Singapore and Indonesia compared to these countries and the rest of the world. However, the average level of intra-industry trade for AEC decreased from 93 percent in 2001 to 84 percent in 2010 as opposed to OECD countries over the same period: 36 percent and 48 percent, respectively. This result is, at the same time, parallel to Thailand's trade with the rest of the world. On the other hand, even though the AEC is Thailand's main trading partner, Thailand's share of IIT in total trade is lower with the AEC than with the rest of the world for the entire period. However, economic integration (AEC) with ASEAN countries has changed the production structure of Thailand toward the ASEAN industrial base. As stated by Lohrmann, A-M. [27], the production structure adjustment is an outcome of free trade. That is, the free trade between Thailand and the AEC led to adjustment of the production structure in the Thailand's economy. As a result of this, Thailand's IIT is increasingly changing from low-technology product to high-technology industries.

Author details

Sujinda Chemsripong
Naresuan University, Faculty of Management and Information Sciences, Department of Economics and Accountancy, Phitsanulok, Thailand

7. References

[1] WTO (2000), *Trade policy reviews: Thailand: December 1999,*1/23/2003 *icy reviews: Thailand: December 1999,*1/23/2003, http://www.wto.org/english/tratop_e/tpr_e/tp122_e.htm.

[2] BOT (various years), "Statistical", *Quarterly Bulletin Bank of Thailand,* Vol. various, pp. various.

[3] Verdoon, P.J.(1966), " The Intra-Bloc Trade of Benelux" In Intra-Industry Trade, (Eds, Lloyd, P.J. and Grubel, H.G.), Edward Elgar, Cheltenham, UK, pp.3-6.

[4] Balassa, B. (1966), "Tariff Reductions and Trade in Manufactures among the Industrial Countries", *American Economic Review,* Vol. LVI, pp. 466-473.

[5] Balassa, B. (1978), "Intra-Industry Trade and Integration of Developing Countries in the World Economy" In *On the Economics of Intra-Industry Trade* (Ed, Giersch, H.), pp. 245-270.

[6] Balassa, B. (1979), "Intra-Industry Trade and the Integration of Developing Countries in the world Economy", World Bank, Washington, D.C.USA., World Bank Reprint Series No. 113, 1979.

[7] Grubel, H. and Lloyd, P. J. (1975), *Intra Industry Trade: The Theory and Measurement of International Trade with Differentiated Products.* London: Macmillan.

[8] Globerman, S. and Dean, J. W. (1990), "Recent Trends in Intra-Industry Trade and Their Implications for Future Trade Liberalization", *Weltwirtschaftliches Archiv,* Vol. 126, pp. 25-49.

[9] Duc, N. H. (1994), "Intra-Industry trade among Asia-Pacific Economies: A case study in Econometric Analysis", Research School of Pacific and Asian Studies, Canberra Australia Economics Division Working Papers, 1994.

[10] Glejser, H. (1983), "Intra-industry Trade and Inter-industry Trade specialization: Trend and cycle in the EEC (1973-1979)" In *Intra-Industry Trade empirical & Methodological Aspects* (Ed, Tharakan, P. K. M.) Elsevier Science Publishers B.V., North-Holland, pp. 35-42.

[11] Guell, R. C. and Richards, D. G. (1998), "Regional Integration and Intra-Industry Trade in Latin America, 1980-90", *International Review of Applied Economics,* Vol. 12, pp. 283-301.

[12] Sharma,K. (1999), "Pattern and Determinants of Intra-Industry Trade in Australian Manufacturing", Economic Growth Center Yale University, Center Discussion Paper No. 813, Yale University and Charles Sturt University (Australia)

[13] Sharma, K. (2000), "The Pattern and Determinants of Intra-Industry Trade in Australian Manufacturing", *The Australian Economic Review,* Vol. 33, pp. 245-55.

[14] Glejser, H. (1983), "Intra-industry Trade and Inter-industry Trade specialization: Trend and cycle in the EEC (1973-1979)" In *Intra-Industry Trade empirical & Methodological Aspects* (Ed, Tharakan, P. K. M.) Elsevier Science Publishers B.V., North-Holland, pp. 35-42.

[15] Greenaway, D. (1983a) "Patterns of Intra-Industry Trade in the United Kingdom" In *Intra- Industry Trade Empirical and Methodological Aspects* (Ed, Tharakan, P. K. M.) Elsevier Science Publishers B.V., Holland, pp. 141-159.

[16] Lohrmann, A-M. (2002), "A Dynamic Analysis of Turkey's Trade with The European Union in The 1990s." *Russian and East European Finance and Trade,* vol. 38, no. 2, March–April 2002, pp. 44–58.

[17] Greenaway, D. (1983b) "Intra-Industry and Inter-Industry Trade in Switzerland", *Weltwirtschaftliches Archiv,* Vol. 119, pp. 109-121.

[18] Ali Koçyiğit and Ali Şen (2000), "The Extent of Intra-Industry Trade between Turkey and the European Union: The Impact of Customs Union", *Journal of Economic and Social Research* 9(2), 61-84

[19] Kim, C. and Choi, Y. C. (2001), "Intra-Industry Trade of Korea: Its Trends and Determinants", *Economic Papers,* Vol. 4, pp. 126-149.

[20] Chemsripong, S. (2004), "Economic Analysis of Intra-Industry Trade Between Thailand and Other Asia Pacific Economic Co-Operation (APEC) Countries", The University of Newcastle, New South Wales Australia.

[21] Thorpe, M. W. (1993), "Intra-Industry Trade and ASEAN- The Experience of Malaysia, The Philippines and Singapore", Department of Economics, The Florida State University College of Social Sciences, Florida USA Dissertation of Doctor of Philosophy

[22] Min, K. (1992), "Measurement and determinants of intra-industry trade in Asian countries", Economics, City University of New York, New York USA

[23] Menon, J. (1996), "Intra-Industry Trade and The ASEAN Free Trade Area", Australia-Japan Research Center, Melberun Australia Pacific Economic Paper, January 1996.

[24] BOT (various years), "Statistical", *Quarterly Bulletin Bank of Thailand,* Vol. various, pp. various.

[25] Verdoon, P.J.(1966), " The Intra-Bloc Trade of Benelux" In Intra-Industry Trade, (Eds, Lloyd, P.J. and Grubel, H.G.), Edward Elgar, Cheltenham, UK, pp.3-6.

[26] Grubel, H. and Lloyd, P. J. (1975), *Intra Industry Trade: The Theory and Measurement of International Trade with Differentiated Products.* London: Macmillan.

[27] Lohrmann, A-M. (2002), "A Dynamic Analysis of Turkey's Trade with The European Union in The 1990s." *Russian and East European Finance and Trade,* vol. 38, no. 2, March–April 2002, pp. 44–58.

Chapter 4

Regional Dynamics in Romanian Counties: Convergence and Trade

Jesús López-Rodríguez and Cosmin Bolea-Gabriel

Additional information is available at the end of the chapter

http://dx.doi.org/10.5772/48271

1. Introduction

The process of European integration beginning with the third stage of Economic and Monetary Union has intensified the coordination of the economic and sectoral policies of the EU Member States. The process of coordination has been done in order to harmonize national economic policy objectives to minimize the negative impact of economic policy measures taken by some EU member countries to other member countries and reduce the temptation for Member States to have an inadequate behaviour. In the case of Romania achieving real convergence was an essential goal for its integration into the European Union in 2007. The issue of convergence, both nominal and real, is very important not only from the policy perspective but also from the perspective of the theory of economic growth. From an economic policy point of view in the case of persistently large (or widening) gaps between poor and rich countries (regions) there could be a need for economic policy measures (domestic and international) to stimulate a catch-up process. The convergence issue is also relevant in the political context of European integration. The Article 2 of the Treaty of European Union stipulates itself that *"The Community shall have the task……to promote…… a high degree of convergence of economic performance……the raising of the standard of living and quality of life and economic and social cohesion and solidarity among Member States."* In a similar vein, article 130a stipulates that *"the Community shall aim at reducing disparities between the levels of development of the various regions including rural areas"*. Significant transfers have been provided for in the framework of the Structural and Cohesion Funds to support the process of economic convergence in the peripheral regions, i.e. regions with real per capita GDP significantly below the European Union average. From the perspective of the economic growth theory the reduction of existing gaps in developmental and income levels between countries and regions in other words the convergence of regional incomes is postulated by the neo-classical model of growth. The idea of a transitional growth path to a steady state income on which growth rates decline is the fundamental theoretical ingredient of convergence analyses.

In this chapter we analyzed the growth dynamics in the Romanian economic over the period 1995-2008 and the link between the observed growth dynamics and the economic geography of the country. The analysis of the growth dynamics is carried out at county level and using different time spans. Regarding the time spans we have first decided to perform the analysis for the whole period 1995-2008. However due to the fact that within this timeframe at least two periods with different growth dynamics can be distinguished we have broken down the whole period into three subperiods, 1995-2000 a period of recession in the Romanian economy, 2000-2004 and 2004-2008 two periods of expansion and high growth. The analysis of the growth dynamics is followed by an econometric exercise which first tries to check for the (non)existence of convergence and then we have studied to which extend the economic geography of the country is a key ingredient in the observed growth dynamics. The results on the one hand show that disparities across Romanian counties regardless of the time period under analysis have not been narrowing away. On the other hand when we look at the factors behind the observed growth dynamics, the economic geography of Romania emerges as one of the key factors behind this divergence phenomenon. Finally we have also analyzed the main patterns of trade in the Romanian economy over the period 2000-2007. The results show that trade deficit in Romania is growing over time.

The rest of the chapter is structured as follows: Section 2 briefly reviews the neo-classical growth model as it constitutes the theoretical framework on which the empirical section of the first part of the chapter is based. Section 3 offers a thorough analysis of the growth dynamics in Romania over the period 1995-2008. Section 4 carries out an econometric exercise to link the economic Geography of the country with is growth performance over the period 1995-2008. Section 5 gives a general overview of the Romanian trade after the transition. Section 6 looks at the specialization patterns of the Romanian trade. Section 7 studies the geographical orientation of the Romanian exports. Section 8 analyzes in more detail the international trade during the financial crisis of the years 2008-2010 and finally section 9 establishes the main conclusions of the chapter

2. Theoretical framework: The neo-classical model of growth

2.1. The neo-classical model of growth

For most of the period since the end of the Second World War the analysis of economic growth has been dominated by debates which have swirled around the neo-classical growth model. The concept of convergence has its roots in this model generally referred to as the Solow model of growth and whose origin were the works of [1,2]. The basic neo-classical model describes a one-sector closed economy with a composite single "Robinson Crusoe" agent (Household/producer) who owns the inputs and manages the production process.

The following discussion of this model is based on chapter one of [3] (1995) book titled *Economic Growth,* chapter one of [4] (2000) book titled *Apuntes de Crecimiento Económico* and [5]'s book titled Advanced in Macroeconomics.

In the simplest form of the neo-classical model output Y at time t is a function of the variables physical capital $K(t)$ and labour $L(t)$ and the level of technology which is exogenous:

$$Y(t) = F(A(t), K(t), L(t)) \tag{1}$$

The central characteristics of the neo-classical model are the assumptions that (i) The level of technology is exogenously determined. (ii) The production factors labour and capital each have diminishing marginal products and (iii) The production function shows constant returns to scale. The level of technology $A(t)$ is considered as given. It is exogenously determined. In the long term, only a rise in technological level enables an increase in the steady state output. The assumption of a given technology to which every economy has free access is a strong simplification, given that technological progress is largely the result of research activities; however, there is some justification for this assumption. On a world-wide scale certain technological standards have been reached to which an economy can find more and more easily access (for instance software that one can download from internet sites). In general, the argument of equal access to available technology or fast technology diffusion can be considered to be valid for highly open economies with a similar level of basic education of the population.

Technology is treated as labour augmenting: $Y = f(K, L * A(t))$. It raises output in the same way as an increase in labour. (In this sense an innovation is Harrod neutral. i.e. the relative inputs shares $K * F_K / L * F_L$ are unchanged for a given capital/output ratio[1].

In the neoclassical model of growth a key assumption is that the marginal product of capital is positive but it declines with raising capital. Hence, all other factors equal, any additional amount of capital yield a decreasing rate of return in the production function. Under this condition, capital accumulation does not make a constant contribution to income growth. The assumption of diminishing returns has been heavily challenged by new growth theory which believes for instance human capital accumulation to yield constant returns, if not increasing ones- a possibility when considering knowledge spill-overs.

The condition of constant returns to scale implies that we can rewrite the production function in per capita terms. in its intensive form as it is also called:

$$y = f(k) \equiv F\left(\frac{K}{AL}, 1\right) = k^{\alpha} \tag{2}$$

[1] An alternative assumption is that technological progress is Hicks neutral

2.2. Convergence in the neo-classical model of growth: Theoretical concept

The neo-classical model of growth postulates the convergence of regional incomes. Given the dynamics of this model of growth discussed in the previous section, one may expect that in a set of economies, which have the same steady state per capita income and which differ only in their initial capital endowment per person and per capita income, initially poor economies will grow faster than rich economies to converge finally to the same per capita income. In the literature, the phenomenon that poorer economies on average will grow faster than richer ones (over the long term) has been termed as *β- convergence*. Such differential growth is necessary to reduce the inter country variation of per capita income levels. A tendency for the dispersion of per capita incomes (as measured by their standard deviation) across a group of countries to fall over time has been labelled σ - convergence. Clearly, progress in *σ -convergence* is not only a function of the differential rates of growth between poorer and richer countries but also of the size of the initial income gap.

β -convergence is a necessary but not a sufficient condition for *σ -convergence*[2]. β - convergence implies the existence of a longer-term catch-up mechanism, i.e forces which work towards the narrowing of income differences across countries. These forces, however, can be offset by temporary shocks which adversely (or positively) affect short-run growth performance. This is why the existence of *β -convergence* may not be fully reflected in changes of the dispersion of income levels[3].

The basic kind of convergence to a common steady state is referred to *as absolute convergence* ([6, 3, 7, 8, 9, 10]). The assumption of a unique steady state will be only satisfied if all economies have the same fundamental parameters, i.e., saving rate, population growth, capital depreciation and above all the same level of technology. The view that economic growth is a complex function of a wide range of interrelated factors over and above traditional factor inputs has led some analysts to develop the idea of *conditional convergence.* This remains within the neo-classical framework but describes the tendency of countries to converge on their own long run equilibrium paths as a function of a number of preconditions or "conditioning variables", i.e richer economies converge towards a high level of income, whereas poor economies converge towards a lower level income level (see [11]). Differential growth rates then reflect the distance of countries from their own steady states[4]. This of course is a concept of convergence which has a completely different meaning from that of (absolute) *β -convergence.* In the case of groups of countries with broadly similar long-run equilibrium positions, there may be a tendency for (absolute) convergence within such groups (Convergence clubs) but not between them[5].

---

[2] For a discussion of these convergence concepts see [12].

[3] See [14] and [15].

[4] [16], p.284.

[5] [17] Comparing income levels in 1870 and 1979, identified a group of 16 advanced economies in such a convergence club. It is noteworthy that he found also some tentative evidence for club convergence among a group of the former

2.3. Methodologies of convergence analysis

Convergence studies can be placed in three broad categories: Cross-Section studies for absolute and conditional convergence, panel data analysis and Markov chain analysis. I sketch their main arguments and characteristics here.

2.3.1. Cross section estimation of absolute convergence

[13] in their prominent paper titled "Convergence" (Journal of Political Economy, Vol. 100(2), April 1992, pp.223-249) estimate the absolute β convergence on the basis of a univariate cross-country regression of per capita income growth between year t and $t+T$ ($\frac{1}{T}\log\left(\frac{y_{i,t+T}}{y_{i,t}}\right)$) on the initial level of per capita income ($y_{i,t}$). The steady state income per capita of an economy is y_i^* and x_i^* is the steady state growth rate of output corresponding to the labour augmenting technological progress. So the specified equation to test β convergence would be:

$$\frac{1}{T}*\log\left[\frac{y_{i,t+T}}{y_{i,t}}\right]=x+\frac{(1-e^{-\beta*T})}{T}*\log\left[\frac{y_i^*}{y_{i,t}}\right]+u_{it,t+T} \tag{3}$$

In practice, estimation is effected with the reduced form ([3, 4]):

$$\frac{1}{T}*\log\left[\frac{y_{i,t+T}}{y_{i,t}}\right]=a+\frac{(1-e^{-\beta*T})}{T}*\log\left[y_{i,t}\right]+u_{it,t+T} \tag{4}$$

In this specification one does not find the steady state y^* or the steady state growth rate x. Both are contained in the intercept a:

$$a=x+\frac{(1-e^{-\beta*T})}{T}*\log(y_i^*) \tag{5}$$

2.3.2. Cross Section estimation of conditional convergence

The available empirical evidence does not support the universal convergence hypothesis: there is no systematic tendency for poor economies to grow faster than richer ones. In fact, the dominant feature has been for diverging productivity levels and real per capita incomes between the group of advanced industrialized economies on the one hand and the developing countries on the other[6]. There are, of course, some significant exceptions, such as

centrally planned economies. A more restrictive form of the "club convergence" hypothesis is the requirement that countries are broadly similar both as regards their fundamental structural characteristics and their initial conditions [9].

[6] For this empirical evidence see [18, 19, 20, 4].

the East Asian growth rates. The general conclusion however, is that countries do not tend to converge to the same balanced growth path but rather settle on different ones. Such differences would lead to steady state differences. Conditional convergence is estimated on the basis of a multivariate regression analysis with initial income and a set of "conditioning variables" X_i as proxies for the determinants of the long-term balanced growth path of the individual economies.

The equation to estimate is the following one:

$$\frac{1}{T} * \log\left[\frac{y_{i,t+T}}{y_{i,t}} \right] = a + \frac{(1-e^{-\beta * T})}{T} * \log\left[y_{i,t} \right] + X_i + u_{it,t+T} \tag{6}$$

Conditional convergence exists if the coefficient on the initial income is negative. In other words, in case of conditional convergence there is a negative partial correlation between initial income per capita and subsequent growth.

2.3.3. *Panel data estimation of convergence*

Region-specific effects can be modelled by employing panel data estimation techniques. As a panel data estimation technique uses observations for several points in time it is built on a richer information set[7].

The general econometric specification of a panel data model is the following one:

$$\frac{1}{T} * \log\left[\frac{y_{i,t+T}}{y_{i,t}} \right] = a_i - \frac{1}{T}(1-e^{-\beta * t}) * \log\left[y_{i,t} \right] + \psi_{t,t+T} + u_{it,t+T} \tag{7}$$

However in order to use OLS in the estimation, the coefficient $\frac{1}{T}(1-e^{-\beta * t})$ is changed by a general coefficient b an the equation can be rewrite in the following way.

$$\frac{1}{T} * \log\left[\frac{y_{i,t+T}}{y_{i,t}} \right] = a_i - b * \log\left[y_{i,t} \right] + \psi_{t,t+T} + u_{it,t+T} \tag{8}$$

where the error term are composed of a_i an unobserved individual effect which is constant over time, a time-specific factor $\psi_{t,t+T}$ which equally effects all individuals and a random error $u_{it,t+T}$.

The average growth rate between t and $t+T$ should be negatively related to the initial logarithm of the per capita income level $\log(y_{i,t})$. This relationship is represented by the common coefficient b. The region-specific fixed effect present over the whole sample period is captured with a_i. The term $\psi_{t,t+T}$ represents the time-specific effect affecting all

[7] [23] show that cross-section analysis lead to a systematic downward bias of the convergence coefficient due this technique neglects unobservable factors and hence suffers an omitted variable bias.

individuals in period t, $t+T$. This specification of the model means that we estimate convergence through a two-way fixed effects model (see [21, 22]).

The region-specific fixed effect a_i determines the region's steady state income. This fixed effect is a concept similar to taking explanatory variables or country dummy variables in the conditional convergence analysis. The difference with the conditional convergence analysis is that panel data estimation allows for continuous individual conditional effects while the former assumes to identify groups of individual units.

3. Growth dynamics at the Romanian county level

This section analyses the growth dynamics across Romanian counties over the period 1995-2008. Figure 1 plots the 1995-2008 average real per capita GDP growth rate at county level. During this period we can see that 23 counties are growing below the national average per capita GDP growth rate and 19 counties are growing above the average. Map 1 shows that the poorest regions are in the East, South-East and South parts of the country and the richest counties are in the West and North-West parts of Romania. The county of Covasna located in the center of the country with its high mountainous geography can be considered an exception.

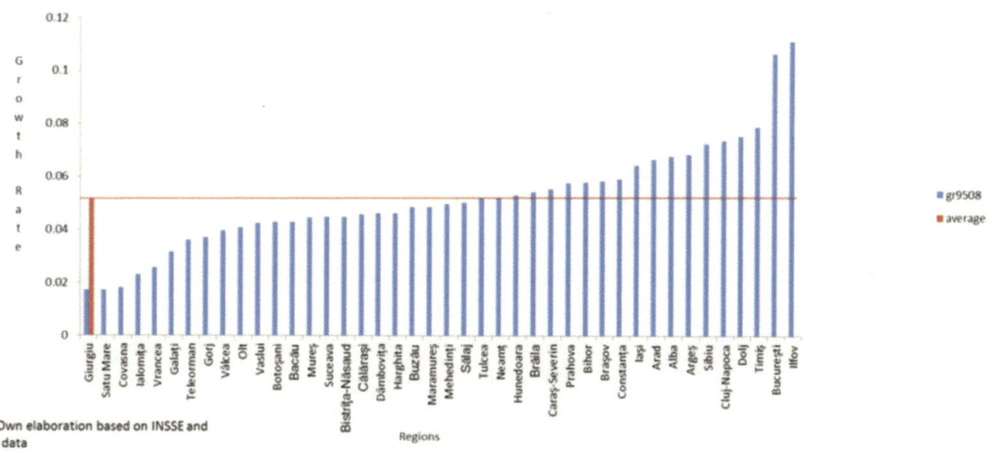

Figure 1. Average growth rate in Romanian counties: 1995-2008

Map 1 shows very clearly the different growth paths across Romanian counties. Giurgiu, Ialomita and Gorj at the lower end of the growth scale can be seen as isolated counties in the sense that they are not sorrounded by other counties wich feature the same growth path. Only Covasna and Vrancea are neighbors within this group. At the upper end of the scale. the best performing counties are situated in the West part of the country and Transilvanya with the exception of the capital Arges and Dolj. It is also worth to remark that the next group of counties which are above the lower end in terms of growth rates are place mainly in the North-East economic region with the exception of three counties from the Center economic region and another three counties from the South-Muntenia economic region.

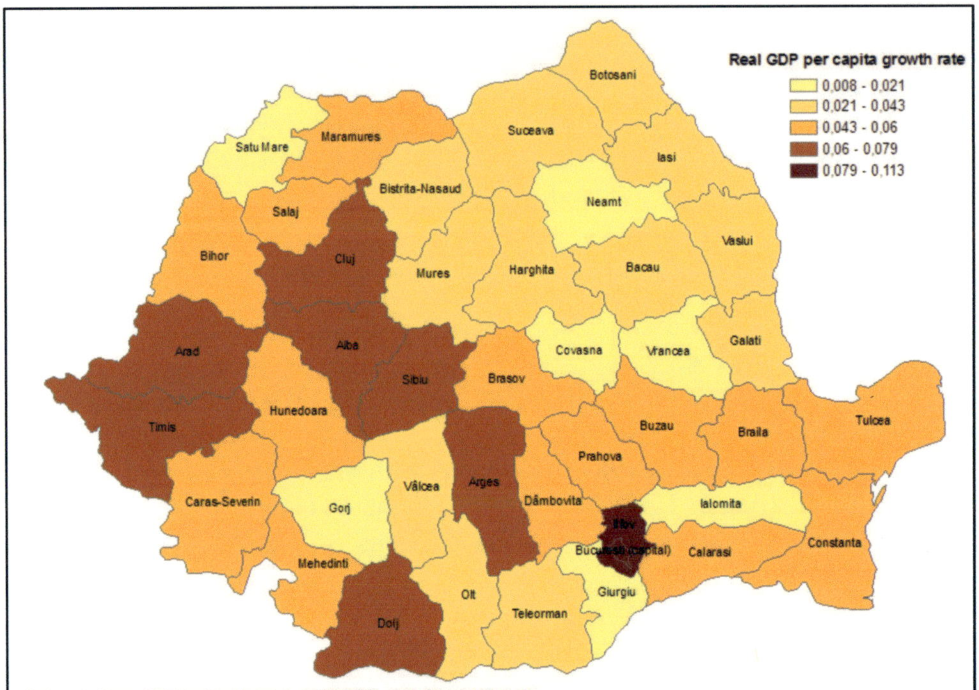

Source: Own elaboration based on INSSE and Eurostat data

Map 1. Growth rate of Romanian regions 1995-2008

If we standardized the value of the national average per capita GDP growth rate and compute each county´s relative ratio to the national average a much clearer picture about those counties which perform better and worse than the national average and how are they spatially distributed can be obtained. The results of this transformation can be seen in map 2. From the map it can be seen that 18 counties plus the capital are situated above the national average and 23 counties are below this average. Among the highest disparities between neighboring counties in a spatial sense are the cases of the Bucharest-Ilfov county and Giurgiu and Ialomita counties. Giurgiu and Ialomita ratio is 44% whereas the Bucharest-Ilfov region ratio with the national average is situated 163% above it. Again the map shows that the Western parts of the country are emerging among the best performers.

Figure 2 represents the average per capital GDP growth rate in Romanian regions in the years of the economic crisis of the 90s. 19 counties are situated below the national average per capita GDP growth rate, most of them from the Eastern and Southern parts of Romania. The most spectacular fall in growth was registered in the Neamt county (North-East) with almost a -20% per capita GDP growth rate. During this period only five counties have registered positive growth rates. Map 3 provides us with an image of the spatial distribution of counties according their respective growth rates.

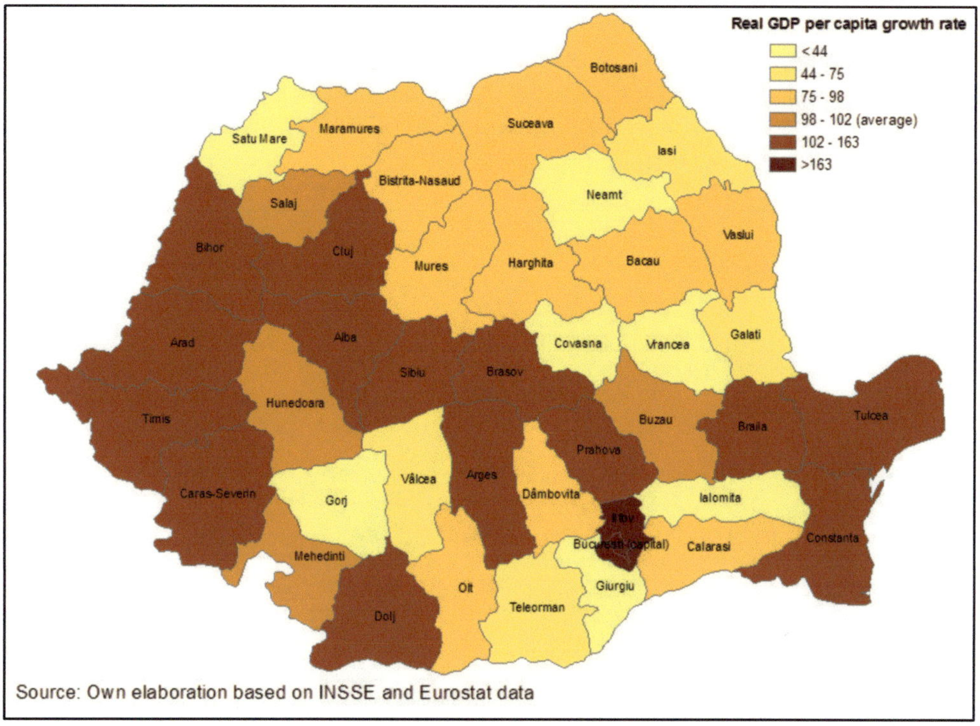

Map 2. Growth rate in Romanian regions 1995-2008 (average pcGDP growth=100, 1995)

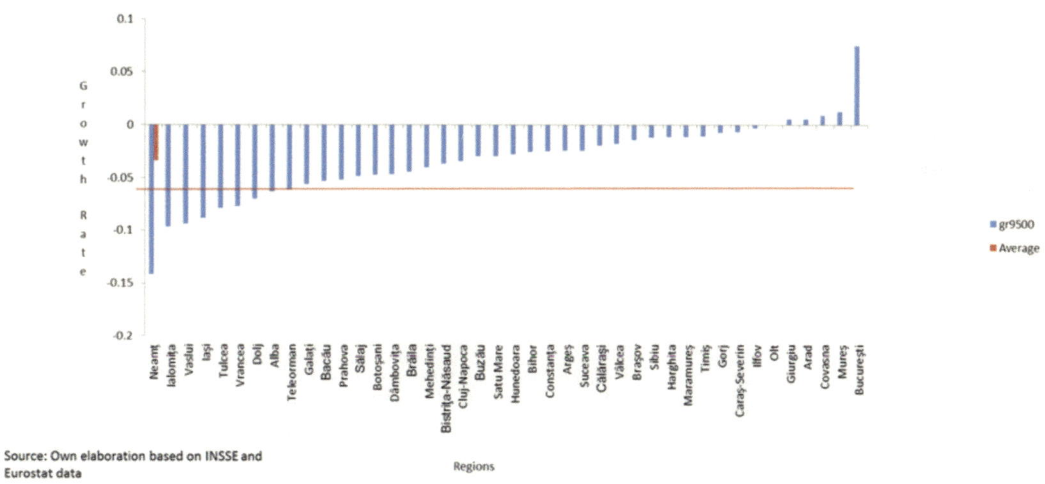

Figure 2. Average Growth Rate in Romanian counties: 1995-2000

After the economic crises in the last half of the nineties and the implementation of the economic reforms and new elections in 2000 a totally new economic landscape showed up for Romania. New economic activities were boosted and the growth rates in some counties reached values between 15 to 18%. This positive economic trend was in part helped by a European favorable economic climate. Under these circumstances during the period 2000-

2004 (figure 3) 19 Romanian counties experienced a rapid economic growth above the national average and just 2 counties from the South experienced a growth rate just below 5%. One of the most relevant cases is the Giurgiu county which continued in recession until 2004. In the period 2004-2008 this position was taken by the Covasna county. Both counties are the poorest counties in Romania.

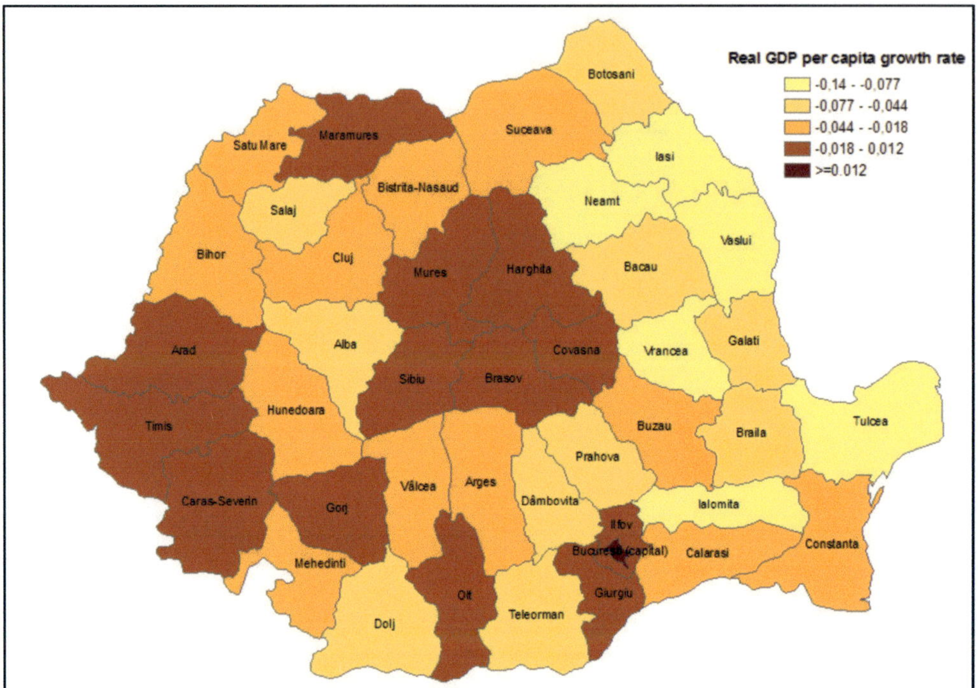

Source: Own elaboration based on INSSE and Eurostat data

Map 3. Growth rate in Romanian regions 1995-2000

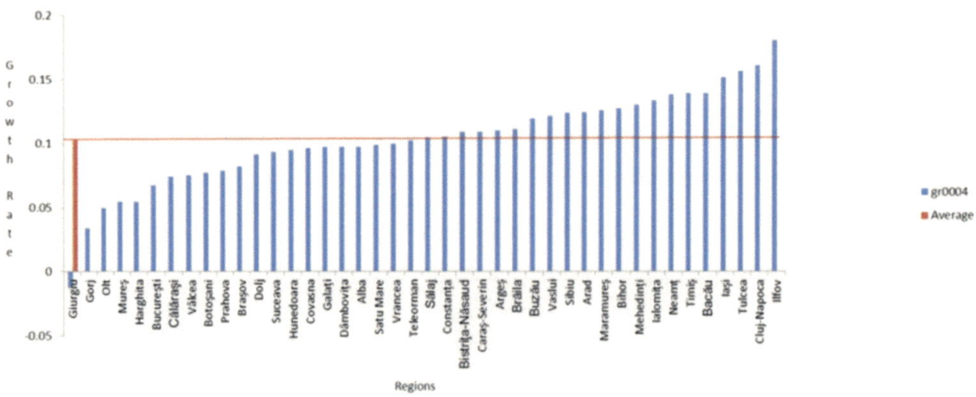

Source: Own elaboration based on INSSE and Eurostat data

Figure 3. Average Growth Rate in Romanian counties: 2000-2004

The economic boom in the first half of the 2000s continued in the period 2004-2008 (figure 4) although with a mild reduction in growth rates with respect to the previous period. However. even during this period some counties outperform their previous growth rate values such as Bucharest with a 20% growth rate two points above its average growth rate in 2000-2004. Again the countries from the West parts of Romania remain as the ones performing above the national average growing on the range 11-16% annualy.

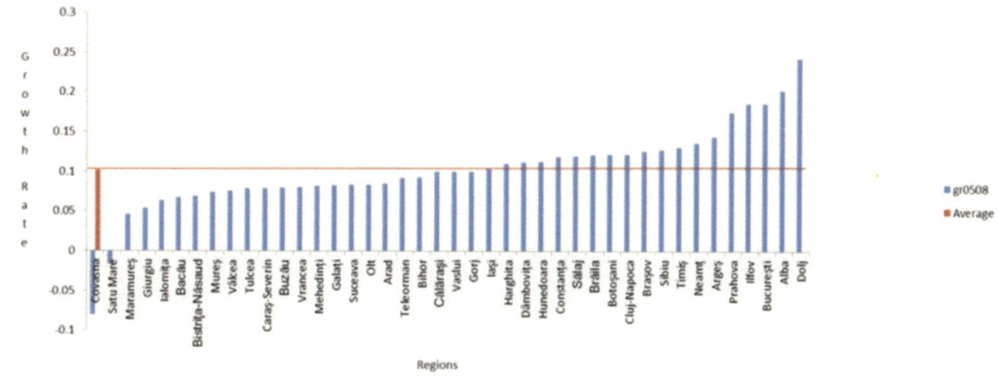

Source: Own elaboration based on INSSE and Eurostat data

Figure 4. Average Growth Rate in Romanian counties: 2004-2008

In order to wrap up some final conclusions on the economic boom from 2000 onwards we have merged in figure 5 the growth rates across Romanian counties for 2000-2008. It is worth remarking that many counties during this period have experienced growth rates well above the national average and the majority of the good performing counties are located in the West and Center parts of Romania (map 4). The capital once again highlights being the leader in terms of economic growth and the Covasna and Giurgiu counties experienced the lowest growth rates during this period.

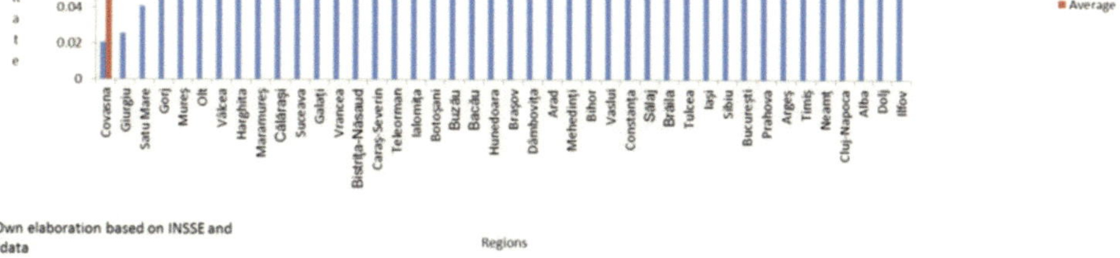

Source: Own elaboration based on INSSE and Eurostat data

Figure 5. Average Growth Rate in Romanian counties: 2000-2008

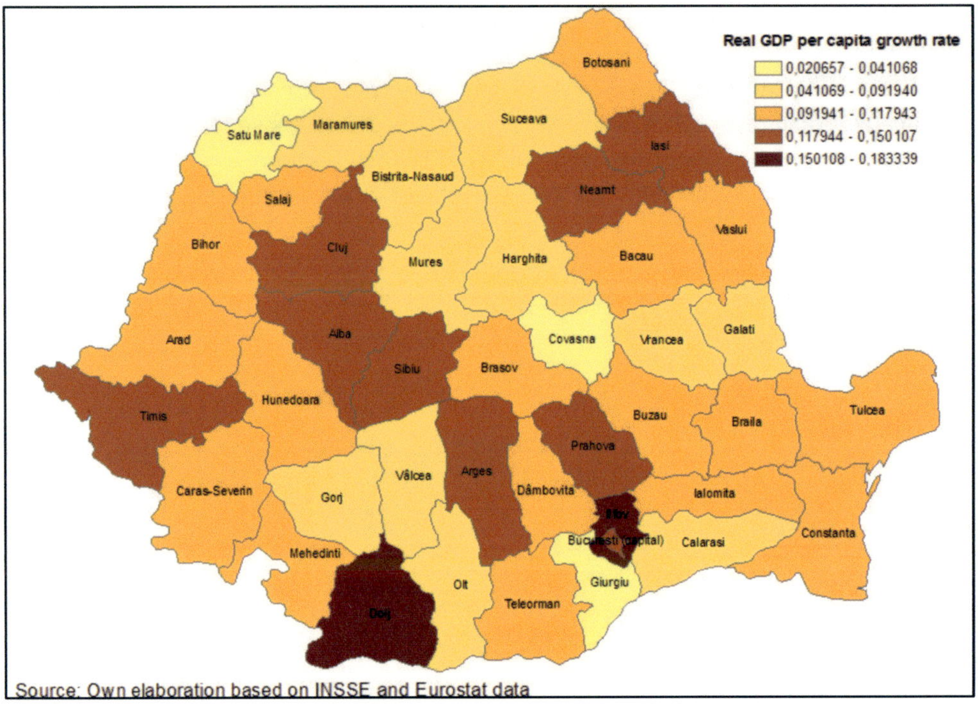

Map 4. Growth rate in Romanian regions 2000-2008

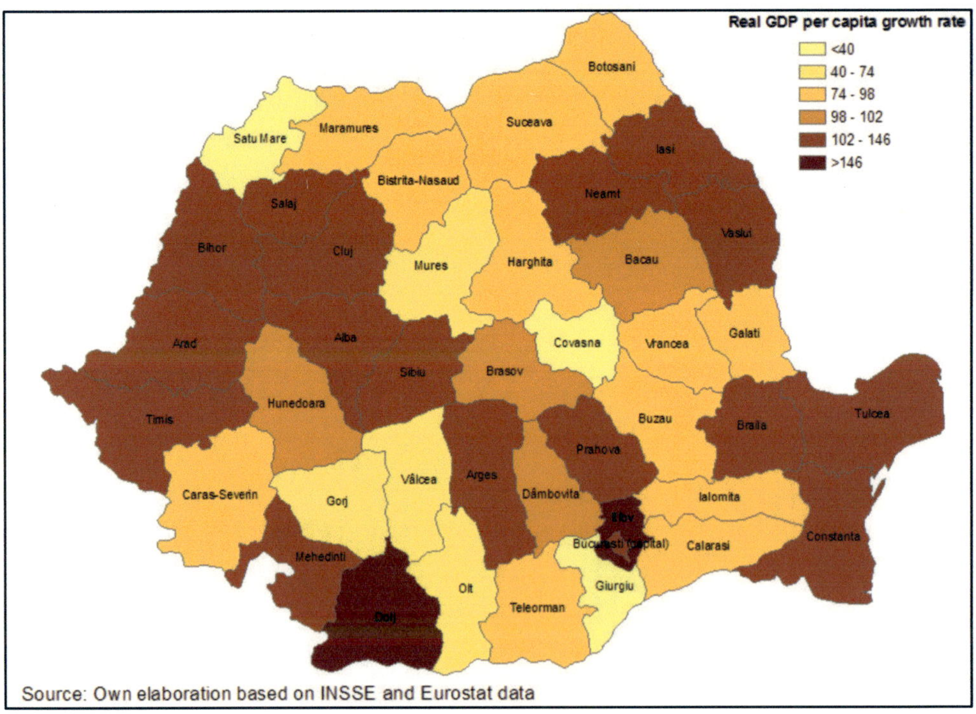

Map 5. Growth rate in Romanian regions 2000-2008 (Average pcGDP growth rate = 100, 2000)

Computing the county ratios of the per capita GDP growth rates with respect to the national average give a quite interesting picture (map 5). The Giurgiu, Covasna and Satu Mare counties are the counties located at the lower end of the index (below 40% with respect to the national average). On the upper end of the scale are Bucharest and Dolj county (above 146% of the national average). The West economic region jointly with North-West and Center economic regions were the leading regions that boost the Romanian economy during the 2000-2008 period due mainly to the high investments in the auto-motion electronic industry (Timis, Cluj, Sibiu and Bihor county).

4. Growth dynamics and economic geography in Romania: 1995-2008

In this section we will perform an econometric exercise to test for the pattern of divergence found in the analysis of the Romanian growth by typology of region. In this section we test to which extend variations in regional market access over time have an impact on the growth rates observed across the different periods under scrutiny. Therefore, we will carry out OLS estimations regressing growth rates for three periods, 1995-2008, 1995-2000 and 2000-2008 against the initial level of GDP per capita in 1995, 1995 and 2000 respectively and the increase in regional market potential observed over the period under analysis. The data for this analysis comes from the Romanian National Institute of Statistics located in Bucharest (INSSE) which offers data on nominal GDP per capita (GDP p.c.) in the Romanian currency "new leu" (RON) at different levels of desegregation Nuts 1, Nuts 2 and Nuts 3[8] and data on annual inflation rates at country level. In our case and following the vast majority of European regional convergence analysis, we will use data for the 42 counties in which Romania is divided at Nuts 2 level. The reason why we have chosen 1995 as our initial year is due to problems with data availability and comparability. The Romanian National Institute of Statistics does not have data on GDP per capita for the years 1990-1994 at Nuts 2 level. However we could resort to use Eurostat data which is available since 1993 but these data is not computed using the same methodology since the data for the period 1993-1997 are calculated according to the ESA 79 methodology and from 1995 onwards according to the ESA 95 methodology. Therefore we have decided to start with the year 1995 in order to avoid comparability problems. Before carried out our estimations we have transformed our nominal per capita GDP figures into real values by building up a GDP deflator using the information on the annual inflation rates from the INSSE database. Regarding the other key variable, the increase in the regional market access for the different periods of time, we have first computed the regional market potential for the years 1995, 2000 and 2008 by resorting to the well-known [24]′ (1954) market potential function. If we consider a world made up of n regions; i:1........n, the Harris′ (1954) market potential in the ith region can be obtained as a weighted sum of the volume of economic activity in the surrounding locations where the weighed scheme is the inverse of the distance between

[8] Nomenclature of Territorial Units for Statistics is a geographical division of the European Union′s territory that subdivides each Member State into a whole number of regions at NUTS 1 level. Each of them is then subdivided into a number of regions at NUTS 2 level and these again are subdivided into a number of regions at NUTS 3 level.

locations. Mathematically, [24]'s (1954) market potential in its simplest formulation obeys to the following expression:

$$MP_i = \sum_{j=1}^{n} Y_j g(d_{ij}) \tag{9}$$

where MPi is the market potential on location I, Y_j is an index of purchasing capacity of location j (usually gross value added, gross domestic product or population), d_{ij} is the distance between two generic locations i and j and g(·) is a decreasing function. The market potential function can be understood as a measure of how far a location is from its consumer markets and therefore it can be used as a proxy for the demand potential that the whole population exerts over every location in the space. Therefore the higher is the market potential index of a location; the higher is its attraction power on production activities.

In our case we will compute market potentials for the years 1995. 2000 and 2008 proxying the volume of economic activity by the real Gross valued Added. In a second step we will compute the increase in regional market potentials over the period on which we run the estimations. Regarding the calculation of bilateral distances in the market potential function it is made on the basis of the road distances expressed in kilometres between the capital cities of each Nuts 2 region in which Romania is divided. For the calculation of the internal distance within each Nuts 2 region, it is approximated by a function that is proportional to the square root of each regions' area. The expression used is $0.66\sqrt{\frac{Area}{\pi}}$ where area is each region area expressed in squared kilometres (km2). This expression gives the average distance between two points on a circular location (see [25, 26, 27]) for a discussion of this measure of internal distance).

Therefore the model adopts the following form:

$$\log\left[y_{i,t+T} \big/ y_{i,t} \right] = \alpha + \beta \log\left[y_{i,t} \right] + \gamma \log[\Delta MP_{i,t,t+T}] + u_{it,t+T} \tag{10}$$

The term on the left-hand side of the equation is the growth of per capita GDP from the base year *t* to the year *t*+T. Initial per capita GDP in region *i* is given by $y_{i,t}$. $\Delta MP_{i,t,t+T}$ represents the change in market potentials between the base year t and the year t+T and and $u_{i,t,t+T}$ is the disturbance term.

All data are nationally standardized in order to minimize spatial autocorrelation problems. Thus, our variables are indices of how well a county region is doing with respect to its national average or how much market potential a county has in relation to the national average. Results will tell us to which extend variations in market potentials are affecting counties 'performance. (see [xx]) [xx] Lopez-Rodriguez, J. Cosmin-Bolea, G. and A. Faiña (2011). Economic Remoteness and Wage Disparities in Romania, Tijdschrift voor economische en sociale geografie, Vol(102) 5, pp. 594–606.

Table 1 presents the results of estimating equation (10) on the sample of 42 regions in Romania for the periods 1995-2008. 1995-2000 and 2000-2008. In Columns 1 we regress the average per capita GDP growth rate in the period 1995-2008 on the 1995 per capita GDP level. In column 2 we regress the average per capita GDP growth rate in the period 1995-2000 on the 1995 per capita GDP level and in column 3 we regress the average per capita GDP growth rate in the period 2000-2008 on the 2000 per capita GDP level. The results of these first set of estimations show that the coefficient of the initial level of GDP per capita in each period is always positive and significant, signalling the process of regional divergence. Columns 3 to 6 introduce the effect of the variation in the market potentials over time. The results of these last set of estimations show once again that even after controlling for the effects of changes in regional market potentials over time the initial level of per capita GDP levels is positive and statistically significant. Moreover our results also point out to the fact that regional changes in market potentials positively affect Romanian cross-regional growth rates. This result is consistent with a pattern of divergence in income levels among Romanian regions, pattern we have already seem in the previous section of this chapter.

Dependent Variable	per Cápita GDP Growth					
	1995-2008	1995-2000	2000-2008	1995-2008	1995-2000	2000-2008
Regressors	(1)	(2)	(3)	(4)	(5)	(6)
Constant	0.69**	-0.25	0.94**	0.56**	-0.22	0.94**
	(0.06)	(0.25)	(0.04)	(0.09)	(0.26)	(0.095)
Log per cápita GDP 1995	0.29**	1.44**		0.52**	1.42**	
	(0.04)	(0.17)		(0.04)	(0.18)	
Log per cápita GDP 2000			0.026**			0.034**
			(0.009)			(0.01)
Log inc MPGDP1995-2008				0.11		
				(0.05)		
Log inc MPGDP1995-2000					0.020**	
					(0.009)	
Log inc MPGDP2000-2008						0.094
						(0.01)
Estimation	OLS	OLS	OLS	OLS	OLS	OLS
R2	0.55	0.69	0.51	0.59		0.57
Prob (F-statistic)	0.00	0.00	0.00	0.00	0.00	0.00
Number observations	42	42	42	42	42	42

Note: Table displays coefficients for OLS estimations and Huber-White heterocedasticity robust standard errors in parenthesis. The dependent variable is the log of per capita GDP growth in the years 1995-2008, 1995-2000 and 2000-2008 (Columns 1, 2, 3, 4 and 6) . Log per capita GDP1995 and 2000 is the logs of per capita gross domestic product in the years 1995 and 2000. Log inc MPGDP1995-2008, 1995-2000 and 2000-2008 are the increases in market potentials between 1995-2008, 1995-2000 and 2000-2008 respectively. For data sources see text. * and ** signify statistical significance at the 5% and 1% levels

Table 1. Regional Growth estimations

5. Romanian trade after the transition: General overview

After 1989 the volume of Romanian international trade was very much affected by the national economic crisis. the collapse of CAER and the cold relations with Yugoslavia (because of the war) and the conflicts in the Arab countries[9]. On top of these issues we have to add the imbalances of the Romanian economy characterized by an over dimensioned industrial structure, the lack of leading technology industries and a clear development strategy at national level. Moreover, for many Eastern European economies was very difficult to reconstruct flows based on market economy grounds. Technical standard differences between Eastern and Western Europe trade goods led to a reorientation of exports towards low value added ones.

During the mid-nineties Romania exports, following other former socialist countries in Central Europe, were mainly directed to EU countries. In 1997 Romanian exports to the EU represented 55% of total exports, being the most important trade partner. However, still nowadays Romanian international trade has a marginal position within the framework of world international trade flows.

Year	Export FOB	Import CIF	Balance (Export FOB-Import CIF)	Year	Export FOB	Import CIF	Balance (Export FOB-Import CIF)
1990	5.775	9.755	-3.980	1999	8.505	10.392	-1.887
1991	4.266	5.793	-1.527	2000	10.367	13.055	-2.688
1992	4.363	6.260	-1.897	2001	11.385	15.552	-4.167
1993	4.892	6.522	-1.630	2002	13.876	17.862	-3.986
1994	6.151	7.109	-958	2003	17.618	24.003	-6.385
1995	7.910	10.278	-2.368	2004	23.485	32.664	-9.179
1996	8.085	11.435	-3.350	2005	27.730	40.463	-12.733
1997	8.431	11.280	-2.849	2006	32.336	51.106	-18.770
1998	8.302	11.838	-3.536	2007	40.471	70.414	-29.943

Table 2. Commercial balance of Romania during 1990-2007 (billion dollars)
Source: Romanian Institute for National Statistics (INSSE)

Table 2 gathers data on the evolution of exports[10], imports and trade balance (figures expressed in billion US dollars) for Romania over the period 1990-2007. In a similar vein to the division carried out for the analysis of the growth dynamics across Romanian regions in the previous sections of the chapter, international trade flows can be broken down into three sub periods: a) 1990-1995 a period characterized by an increase in the volume of trade both in exports and imports. Regarding the exports they increase in this period from 4.2 billion US dollars to 7.9 billion of US dollars (an increase of 85% in the value of exports and from

[9] According to the WTO, Romania was ranked in 38 place in 1988 in terms of world exports, in 1996 was ranked 59 and in 2010 in 50 place.

[10] See Annex for methodology of trade data gathering

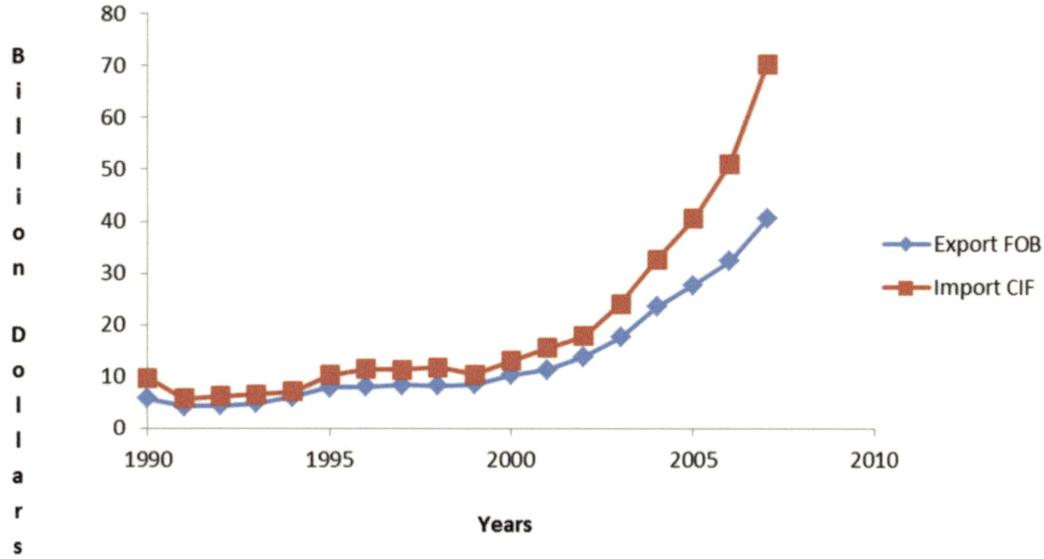

Figure 6. Comercial Balance of Romania: 1990-2007

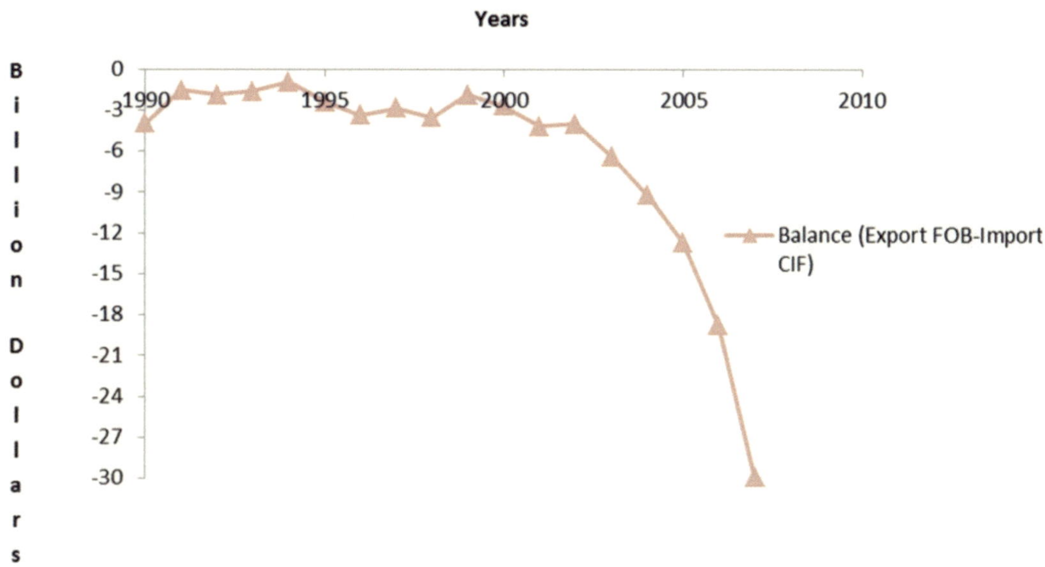

Figure 7. Trade deficit in Romania: 1990-2007
Source: Own elaboration based on INSSE figures

5.79 billion US dollars to 10.2 billion US dollars (77% increase in imports), b) 1996-1999 a period characterized by stagnation in the trade volumes. During this period the Romanian exports practically kept unchanged whereas the imports decrease by 1 billion of US dollars, c) 2000-2007 a period characterized by a boom in terms of the volume of trade between Romania and its trade partners, mainly due to the extraordinary growth of the Romanian economy over this period and also for the positive result of the reforms in the economic structure. The exports move up from 10 billion of US dollars to 40 billion of US dollars over this period and the imports form 13 billion of US dollars to 70 billion of US dollars, figures which expressed in percentage terms mean an increase of 290% the volume of exports over the course of this seven years and 439% increase in the volume of imports in the same period. As a result in this period the trade deficit increased substantially. from 3 billion US dollars to almost 30 billion of US dollars mainly as a consequence of a process of intensification in the integration of the Romanian economy into the European economy and the rest of the world.

6. Specialization patterns of Romanian trade: 2000-2007

As regards to the exports, Romania is specialized in sectors which are mainly labor intensive (clothing. footwear and furniture) and also in those which are intensive in the use of natural resources (steel products, wood and non-ferrous metals). On the import side, Romanian economy imports are from sectors which are capital intensive.

Tables 3 and 4 (see appendix) show the composition of the Romanian exports by groups of goods and the relative share each group represents in the total volume of exports over the period 2000-2007.

Table 3 breaks down Romanian exports into 10 groups over the period 2000-2007. The data show that the most dynamic groups both in terms of trade volumes and growth are the group of Machinery and transport equipment with an increase over the period 2000-2007 of 372%. This group is followed by the group of manufactured goods classified mainly by raw material with an increase of 194%, the group of mineral fuels, lubricants and materials derived with an increase of 176% and the group of Chemicals and related products not elsewhere with an increase of 157%. One important group of goods in terms of trade volumes but with a much lower dynamism in terms of growth is the second group miscellaneous manufactured articles with an increase of 59%.

A series of observations can be made from data collected in tables 3 and 4:

a. There is a change in the relative importance of the goods exported. In 2000 the group of goods with the highest share in total exports was miscellaneous manufactured articles (36.64%), followed by manufactured goods classified mainly by material: leather, rubber, wood, fabrics, iron, steel nonferrous metals, etc.(19.49%) and machinery and transport equipment (18.91%). By 2007 the group of goods with the highest share in total exports was machinery and transport equipment (34.06%), followed by manufactured different articles (22.31%) and manufactured goods classified mainly by raw material (21.87%)
b. The share of these three groups of goods in the total amount of goods exported increase from 2000 to 2007 representing in the year 2000 over 75% of total exports and in 2007 over 78% of total exports;
c. The lowest share of exported goods is represented by oils, fats, waxes of animals and plants, beverages and tobacco with a total percentage of 0.41% in the year 2000 and 0.87% in 2007.

Group number	Type of goods	2000	2001	2002	2003	2004	2005	2006	2007
1	Machinery and transport equipment	2.132	2.525	3.106	3.356	4.491	5.663	7.738	10.064
2	Miscellaneous manufactured articles	4.131	5.120	5.734	6.071	6.435	6.600	6.666	6.593
3	Manufactured goods classified mainly by raw material	2.197	2.400	2.756	3.019	4.024	4.654	5.234	6.462
4	Mineral fuels. lubricants and materials derived	809	794	1.160	1.023	1.282	2.378	2.597	2.238
5	Chemicals and related products not elsewhere	658	659	686	746	1.039	1.277	1.465	1.693
6	Raw materials inedible. excluding fuels	1.019	778	801	974	1.147	1.078	1.469	1.572
7	Food stuff and animals alive	268	358	359	344	404	489	563	658
8	Beverages and tabacco	25	38	46	37	31	31	46	195
9	Oils. fats and waxes of animal and plants	21	27	9	27	64	63	58	62
10	Goods and transactions not classified in another section of CSCI	13	23	18	17	18	22	14	12
	TOTAL EXPORT	**11.273**	**12.722**	**14.675**	**15.614**	**18.935**	**22.255**	**25.850**	**29.549**

Table 3. Romanian Exports by groups of goods (Billion euros)
Source: Own elaboration based on INSSE figures

With regard to Romanian imports, tables 5 and 6 (see appendix) show the total value of imports by category of goods and the relative share each category represents in the total amount of goods imported over the period 2000-2007. The increase in the volumes of import goods over the period 2000-2007 is bigger than the increase in the volumes of the export goods. The value of imports increase from 14.235 million euro in 2000 to 51.322 million euro in 2007 (360.53% increase) compared with an increase from 11.273 million euro in 2000 to 29.549 million euro in 2007 (262% increase) in the value of export goods.

Group number	Type of goods	2000	2001	2002	2003	2004	2005	2006	2007
1	Machinery and transport equipment	18.91	19.85	21.17	21.49	23.72	25.45	29.93	34.06
2	Miscellaneous manufactured articles	36.64	40.25	39.07	38.88	33.98	29.66	25.79	22.31
3	Manufactured godos classified mainly by raw material	19.49	18.86	18.78	19.34	21.25	20.91	20.25	21.87
4	Mineral fuels. lubricants and materials derived	7.18	6.24	7.90	6.55	6.77	10.69	10.05	7.57
5	Chemicals and related products not elsewhere	5.84	5.18	4.67	4.78	5.49	5.73	5.67	5.73
6	Raw materials inedible. excluding fuels	9.04	6.12	5.46	6.24	6.06	4.84	5.68	5.32
7	Foodstuff and animals alive	2.38	2.81	2.45	2.20	2.13	2.20	2.18	2.23
8	Beverages and tobacco	0.22	0.30	0.31	0.24	0.16	0.14	0.18	0.66
9	Oils. fats and waxes of animal and plants	0.19	0.21	0.06	0.17	0.34	0.28	0.22	0.21
10	Goods and transactions not classified in another section of CSCI	0.11	0.18	0.12	0.11	0.10	0.10	0.05	0.04
	TOTAL EXPORT	**100**	**100**	**100**	**100**	**100**	**100**	**100**	**100**

Table 4. Share of exports by groups of goods (%) Source: Own elaboration based on INSSE figures

With regard to the type of goods imported by the Romanian economy, the most relevant group both in terms of amounts, relative share and growth over the period is represented by machinery and transport equipment (group 1) with an increase from 4.1 billion euros in 2000 to almost 20 billion euros in 2007 followed by manufactured goods classified mainly by raw material (group 2) and mineral fuels, lubricants and materials (group 3) with an increase in the volume of imports from 3.8 and 1.7 billion euros in 2000 to 11.8 and 5.5 billion euros in 2007 respectively.

In terms of relative shares the following observations can be made:

a. Machinery and transport equipment is the type of goods with the highest share in total imports over the period: 29.27% in the year 2000 and 38.33 in the year 2007
b. Raw materials (group 2), mineral fuels, lubricants and materials (group 3) and miscellaneous manufactured articles (group 5) which are the second, third and fourth most important group of goods in terms of imports are losing importance over the period. In 2000 their relative shares were 26.70%, 12.08% and 10.88 whereas in 2007 they were 23.15, 10.73 and 8.91 respectively.
c. The share of the first three groups of goods in the total amount of goods imported increased slightly from 2000 to 2007 representing in the year 2000 around 68% of total imports and in 2007 around 72% of total imports;

Group number	Type of goods	2000	2001	2002	2003	2004	2005	2006	2007
1	Machinery and transport equipment	4.168	4.848	5.323	6.251	8.548	10.819	14.415	19.671
2	Manufactured goods classified mainly by raw material	3.801	4.861	5.496	5.942	6.908	7.955	9.514	11.879
3	Mineral fuels. lubricants and materials derived	1.720	2.195	2.103	2.312	3.114	4.548	5.517	5.509
4	Chemicals and related products not elsewhere section specified	1.417	1.721	2.032	2.186	2.727	3.324	4.315	5.238
5	Miscellaneous manufactured articles	1.550	1.892	2.171	2.415	2.581	3.100	3.683	4.574
6	Foodstuff and animals alive	774	1.060	905	1.204	1.297	1.528	1.833	2.664
7	Raw materials inedible. excluding fuels	610	578	597	631	778	903	1.013	1.326
8	Beverages and tobacco	158	185	176	199	260	308	363	312
9	Oils. fats and waxes of animal and plants	37	43	77	59	64	78	87	143
10	Goods and transactions not classified in another section of CSCI	0	0	1	2	4	5	6	6
	TOTAL	**14.235**	**17.383**	**18.881**	**21.201**	**26.281**	**32.568**	**40.746**	**51.322**

Table 5. Romanian Imports by groups of goods (Billion euros) Source: Own elaboration based on INSSE figures

Group number	Type of goods	2000	2001	2002	2003	2004	2005	2006	2007
1	Machinery and transport equipment	29.27	27.89	28.19	29.48	32.52	33.22	35.38	38.33
2	Manufactured goods classified mainly by raw material	26.70	27.96	29.11	28.03	26.29	24.42	23.35	23.15
3	Mineral fuels. lubricants and materials derived	12.08	12.63	11.14	10.90	11.85	13.96	13.54	10.73
4	Chemicals and related products not elsewhere section specified	9.95	9.90	10.76	10.31	10.38	10.21	10.59	10.21
5	Miscellaneous manufactured articles	10.88	10.88	11.50	11.39	9.82	9.52	9.04	8.91

Group number	Type of goods	2000	2001	2002	2003	2004	2005	2006	2007
6	Foodstuff and animals alive	5.44	6.10	4.79	5.68	4.93	4.69	4.50	5.19
7	Raw materials inedible. excluding fuels	4.28	3.33	3.16	2.98	2.96	2.77	2.49	2.58
8	Beverages and tobacco	1.10	1.06	0.93	0.94	0.99	0.95	0.89	0.61
9	Oils. fats and waxes of animal and plants	0.30	0.25	0.41	0.28	0.24	0.24	0.21	0.28
10	Goods and transactions not classified in another section of CSCI	0	0	0.01	0.01	0.02	0.02	0.01	0.01
TOTAL		**100**	**100**	**100**	**100**	**100**	**100**	**100**	**100**

Table 6. Share of Imports by groups of goods (%) Source: Own elaboration based on INSSE figures

7. Geographical orientation in exports and imports in Romania 2000-2007

Many political factors influenced the economic trade of Romania during the ´90s (Yugoslavia´s war, abolition of CAER, Arab conflicts). However, the transition of the Romanian economy towards a market economy meant also a new step in international trade basically with the reorientation of its trade to other partners which were not the usual ones.

Table 7 (see appendix) shows the international trade (exports and imports) in Romania by geographical area over the period 1995 and 2007:

Table 7 clearly shows that the European Union is the principal trade partner of Romania over the period 2000-2007 both in terms of imports and exports. The main Romanian export countries are Germany, Italy, France, UK, Belgium, Spain, Poland, Netherland, Turkey and Hungary whereas the main importing countries are Germany, Netherlands, Hungary, France, China, Russia, Austria, Poland and Turkey. The amount of exports directed to the EU countries were 8.2 billion euros in 2000 and 21.3 billion euro in 2007 which represented in both periods around 72% of the value of total Romanian exports. With regard to the imports from EU countries they increased from 9.33 billion euros in 2000 to 25.87 billion euros in 2007 however in relative terms the total share of imports from EU countries decrease from 66% to 63%. The second most important trade partner is made up of the other European countries which in 2000 represented 10.6% of total exports and by 2007 15.7%. With respect to the import shares from these countries the figures changed from 14.6 % in 2000 to 16.5%. Therefore, two important observations can be made to the trade flows to this second group; first there is an increase over time in the volumes of trade to these countries and there is also a tendency towards a more balance trade with these countries. Another important feature of the geography of the Romanian trade is the imbalance and changing pattern with respect to Asian countries. While the value of exports to Asian countries kept stable between 2000 and 2007 (3% of total) the amount of imports is much higher and increased from 9% in 2000 to 13% in 2006. South America and Australia/Oceania are the only trade partners whose shares both in imports (2%) and exports (1%) has kept stable between 2000 and 2007. The balance trade with US and Canada is very stable between 2000 and 2007 with a decrease in both exports and imports from 4% to 2%. With regards to the Romanian trade with Latin America the situation is pretty similar. There are no changes in the relative shares of trade balance between 2000 and 2007.

Geographical Area	E (Exports) I (Imports)	2000	2001	2002	2003	2004	2005	2006	2007
EU COUNTRIES	E	8.20	9.67	10.87	11.85	14.28	15.68	18.26	21.39
	I	9.33	11.67	12.87	14.45	17.33	20.56	25.87	
EUROPE non EU	E	1.20	0.97	1	1.36	2.14	2.99	3.76	4.64
	I	2.08	2.45	2.63	3.44	4.16	5.41	6.75	
ASIA	E	0.35	0.41	0.71	0.64	0.58	0.8	0.81	0.95
	I	1.22	1.25	1.86	1.89	2.76	4.13	5.25	
AFRICA	E	0.38	0.31	0.28	0.26	0.33	0.45	0.52	0.49
	I	0.06	0.11	0.10	0.10	0.12	0.15	0.21	
USA - CANADA	E	0.45	0.44	0.67	0.59	0.59	0.98	0.72	0.63
	I	0.48	0.61	0.62	0.60	0.89	1	1.11	
SOUTH AMERICA	E	0.08	0.1	0.07	0.05	0.05	0.1	0.15	0.28
	I	0.26	0.30	0.28	0.30	0.42	0.57	0.63	
ARAB COUNTRIES	E	0.35	0.46	0.65	0.51	0.60	0.79	1	0.98
	I	0.11	0.22	0.20	0.11	0.16	0.28	0.45	
AUSTRALIA	E	0.004	0.004	0.004	0.004	0.07	0.08	0.05	0.03
OCEANIA	I	0.10	0.009	0.002	0.004	0.004	0.005	0.008	

Table 7. Foreign Trade in Romania by geographical area (billion euros)
Source: Own elaboration based on INSSE figures

8. International trade during the financial crisis: 2008-2010

This last section of the chapter looks at the Romanian International trade over the course of the financial crisis. 2008-2010. Table 8 shows the data for this period. In 2009 Romanian trade flows were severely affected by the crisis initiated during the last quarter of 2007 and beginning of 2008. The decrease in the volume of exports in 2009 compared with the previous year was 13.8% but even more important was the sharp decrease in the value of goods imported. 31.9%. In 2010 the situation changed and both exports and imports had a good performance. Exports increase by 28.2% compared with 2009 in part due to higher foreign prices and a shift towards the export of capital goods. The share of exports in total GDP rose continuously even during the crisis, from 24.1% in 2008 to 30.6% in 2010. The amount of imports increase by 20.1% in 2010 with respect to 2009 but the share of imports in total GDP suffered a sharp decrease in 2009 with respect to 2008 from 37.8% to 31.0% and then a recovery in 2010 to 35.4%.

The coverage of imports trough exports has evolved in a positive way increasing from 63.8% in 2008 to 86.3% in 2010 and also the openness of the Romanian economy has moved in a good direction increasing from 61.9% in 2008 to 65.9%.

	2008	2009	2010*	Annual change 2009/2008	2010/2009
	EUR millions			%	
Exports (FOB)	33.725	29.084	37.294	-13.8	28.2
Imports (CIF)	57.240	38.953	46.802	-31.9	20.1
Trade balance (FOB-CIF)	-23.515	-9.869	-9.508	-58.0	-3.7
	%				
Share of exports in total GDP	24.1	25.1	30.6	1.0	5.5
Share of imports* in total GDP	37.8	31.0	35.4	-6.8	4.4
Share of trade balance* in GDP	-13.7	-5.9	-4.8	7.8	1.1
Coverage of imports* trough exports	63.8	80.9	86.3	17.1	5.4
Economy openness*	61.9	56.1	65.9	-5.8	9.8

Table 8. International Trade 2008-2010
Source: National Bank of Romania, National Institute of statistics and Romanian Center for Trade and Investment calculations.
Note: * provisional data

In relation to the type of goods exported (table 9), the most important items in terms of volume were machinery, equipment and transports means amounting more than 15.8 billion euros (these goods represent in 2010 a share of 40.6% on the total value of exports), followed by metal products, paper and wood products, mineral products and agri-foodstuff, beverages and tobacco products. The only types of goods in which the Romanian economy show a strong resistance in terms of exports during 2009 were agri-foodstuff, beverages and tobacco products and machinery, equipment and transport means with an increase in exports during the worst year of the recession by 3.6% and 2.9% respectively.

	2008	2009	2010*	Annual change 2009/2008	2010/2009
	EUR millions			%	
Exports-Total	33.725	29.084	37.294	-13.8	28.2
Agri-foodstuff. beverages and tobacco products	2.165	2.242	3.124	3.6	39.3
Mineral Products	3.142	1.784	3.124	-43.2	15.4
Chemical. rubber and plastic products	3.139	2.506	2.060	-20.2	41.4
Paper and wood products	1.112	1.084	3.545	-2.5	34.6
Textiles. apparel. footwear and leather goods	4.782	3.924	1.458	-17.9	9.7
Base metals and products thereof	4.941	2.922	4.304	-40.9	52.5
Machinery. equipment and transport means	12.200	12.553	15.890	2.9	26.6
Others	2.244	2.069	4.455	-7.8	18.8

Table 9. Export Product Structure 2008-2010
Source: National Bank of Romania, National Institute of statistics and Romanian Center for Trade and Investment calculations.
Note: * provisional data

As in the previous years, European countries were the most important trade partner in terms of exports for the Romanian economy accounting for more than 87% of total exports.

Asia was the second geographical area in relative importance (10%) followed at large distance by African countries (2%) and America (1%).

With regard to the imports (table 10), during this period the most relevant imports were made up of machinery, equipment and transport means (35.9% of the total volume of imports in 2010), chemical, rubber and plastic products (16.9%). mineral products (11%). metal products (10.9%) and agro-food products (8.4%). The imports of mineral products suffers the highest fall between 2009/2008 of about 50% followed by base metals and products thereof 41.6% but in 2010 these figures turn up to positive values and also representing the highest increases between 2009 and 2010, 33.1% and 34.9% respectively.

Regarding to the main importing partners, again Europe is rank number one with 84% of the total amount of imports and Asia (especially China) is the second geographical area with more than 13% of total imports. The imports from America reached 2% in 2010 and from African countries just 1%. Australia and Oceania represented less than 1% of total Romanian imports.

	2008	2009	2010*	Annual changes 2009/2008	2010/2009
	EUR millions			%	
Exports-Total	57.240	38.953	46.802	-31.9	20.1
Agri-foodstuff. beverages and tobacco products	4.347	3.823	3.915	-12.0	2.4
Mineral Products	7.850	3.883	5.169	-50.5	33.1
Chemical. rubber and plastic products	8.040	6.842	7.971	-14.9	15.7
Paper and wood products	1.566	1.274	1.360	-18.7	6.8
Textiles, apparel, footwear and leather goods	4.027	3.180	3.560	-21.0	11.9
Base metals and products thereof	6.501	3.794	5.116	-41.6	34.9
Machinery. equipment and transport means	20.846	13.429	16.792	-35.6	25.0
Others	4.063	2.728	2.973	-32.8	9.0

Table 10. Import Product Structure 2008-2010
Source: National Bank of Romania, National Institute of statistics and Romanian Center for Trade and Investment calculations.
Note: * provisional data

9. Conclusions

In this chapter the growth dynamics of the Romanian economic over the period 1995-2008 have been studied and them a link between the economic geography of Romania and the observed patterns of growth has been established. The analysis looks at the evolution of growth patterns at county level (42 counties). The time periods used in the analysis follow a natural classification based on the relative performance of the Romanian economy over them. Therefore we have distinguished for the Romanian economy a period of recession 1995-2000 and two periods of expansion 2000-2004 and 2004-2008.

The results of growth regressions carried out for the different periods show that the coefficient of the initial level of GDP per capita in each period is always positive and significant, signaling a process of regional divergence and therefore giving support to the fact that disparities across Romanian counties, regardless of the time period under analysis, have not been narrowing away. Moreover our results also point out to the fact that regional changes in market potentials positively affect Romanian cross-regional growth rates and therefore the economic geography of Romania emerges as one of the key factors behind this divergence phenomenon. Attenuation of the development gaps maintained between Romania and the EU cannot be achieved solely through the use of market forces. The Carpathian counties are among the poorest with few exceptions. There is also a clear undeveloped region in East of the country made up of Botosani, Vasluia and Tulcea and in the South taken in Olt, Calarasi, Ialomita and Gorj. Once with the integration of Romania in the European Union, the mission of the European funds will be to reduce the existing gaps within the regions in Romania and between Romanian regions and the rest of the European Union. In the second part of the chapter we have analyzed the main patterns of trade (volumes of trade, geographical area, and trade composition) followed by the Romanian economy over the period 2000-2010 in light of the growth dynamics seen in the first part of the chapter. The results show that during the years of the boom of the Romanian economy the trade deficit has increased very rapidly. We have also analyzed in more detail the period of the financial crisis, 2008-2010 and the results point out to an improvement in the terms of trade deficit. The geographical orientation of Romanian exports and imports over the whole period is mainly to European countries.

Author details

Jesús López-Rodríguez*
Jean Monnet Group on Competition and Development (C+D)
Department of Economic Analysis and business Administration, Faculty of Economics and Business, Universidad de A Coruña, Spain

Cosmin Bolea-Gabriel
Department of Economic Analysis and business Administration, Faculty of Economics and Business, Universidad de A Coruña, Spain

Acknowledgement

A significant part of this chapter has been finished while the first author was a Visiting Scholar in the department of economics at Harvard University during fall 2012. The first author also wants to thank very especially professors Pol Antràs and Nathan Nunn for sponsoring his visit to Harvard University. Part of this chapter has benefited from the very helpful comments of David Brasington, Olivier Parent, John Winters, Nick Willians, Debashis Pal and seminar participants during the presentation made at the University of Cincinnati economics department seminar series held on March 30th 2012.

---

* Corresponding Author

Financial support from the Spanish Ministry of Science and Innovation through Grant ECO2011-28632 is gratefully acknowledged. The usual disclaimer applies.

Appendix

Annex: Methodology of trade data gathering

1. Data sources:
Intra-community trade of goods details
Extra-community trade of goods details
National Custom Authority (NAC) until 2006 and NCA and NIS after 2007
d. For EXTRA-EU trade:

EXTRASTAT statistical customs declarations collected by the National Custom Authority (NCA) .

National Institute of Statistics (NIS) collects by statistical forms and process data for imports and exports of electricity and natural gas from importing/exporting companies through statistical forms. These data is subsequently submitted to NCA in order to be processed and to complete the data obtained from custom declarations.

e. For INTRA-EU trade:

INTRASTAT statistical declarations collected by NIS directly from the trade operators which achieved a value volume of intra-community dispatches of goods higher than lei 900 000 or a volume of intra-community arrivals of goods higher than lei 300 000.

2. Methodology:
Statistics of foreign trade with goods are compiled by cumulating the data from INTRASTAT and EXTRASTAT systems:
INTRASTAT system: for INTRA-EU trade (exchange of goods between Romania and other member states of European Union);
EXTRASTAT system: for EXTRA-EU trade (exchange of goods between Romania and states which are not member of European Union).
3. Definition

Export of goods include all goods which by onerous title or free of charge leave the economic territory of the country to the rest of the world destination.

Exports of goods include:

a. National goods (or nationalized) which leave the territory of the country for ever;
b. National goods (or nationalized) which leave the territory of the country in order to be processed and then re-imported;
c. Foreign goods re-exported after the processing for which they were imported;
d. Non-monetary gold (non-refined gold including ores and concentrates); semi-wrought gold whose gold value represents at least 80% of total value including founding and dust as primary form both coins and bars and alloys;

e. Exports of electric energy and natural gas;
f. Goods sent by postal package;
g. Art objects, collections, antiquities;
h. Ships and aircrafts;
i. Silver ores, concentrates, lingots, non-released pieces and silver wrought or semi-wrought;
j. Supply with fuel and food the foreign ships and aircrafts on the national territory;
k. Exported cinema and TV motion pictures;
l. Exports of goods under financial leasing;
m. Goods used as support for information and software, including floppy disks and CD-ROM with software for general use (not ordered);
n. Exchanges by programme title of civil and military aid, war compensation and military equipment;
o. Goods delivered under leasing or rent condition, which are not returned at deadlines or are purchased for ever;

Exports of goods do not include:

a. Goods leaving the territory of the country and entering the customs warehouses;
b. Dispatches of goods in transit;
c. Temporary exports, namely goods dispatched abroad for various works, repatriated afterwards;
d. Monetary gold;
e. Personal effects and items of passengers;
f. Silver and metal coins, treasury notes and titles in circulation;
g. Goods for national institutions (embassies or armed forces) abroad;
h. Animals temporarily leaving the territory, in order to take part in the races competitions or to be presented at the circus, zoo etc.;
i. Fish sold by Romanian ships, abroad or to the foreign ships;
j. Goods bought and sold abroad without transit of the country;
k. Machinery, equipment, installations and materials sent abroad, which are used by the specialists in construction and assembling works, drilling, prospections, explorations and repatriated afterwards;
l. Sales of goods, services and utilities paid in foreign currency to the joint companies with foreign firms having their headquarters in Romania;
m. Value of repairs for the ships, aircrafts, rolling stocks and cars;
n. Interests cashed from credit exports;
o. Currency contribution achieved abroad from construction and assembling works;
p. Order software;
q. Exports of goods under operational leasing
r. Value of technical assistance and provision of services for imported goods, granted by our national specialists on account of external suppliers.

Exports of goods are estimated at FOB value. corresponding to external market price of goods at the borders of exporting country. Free exports of goods are estimated at FOB value of similar goods.

10. References

[1] Solow RM (1956) A Contribution to the Theory of Economic Growth. Quarterly Journal of Economics. 70(1):65-94.

[2] Swan TW(1956) Economic Growth and Capital Acumulation. Economic Record.32:334-361.

[3] Barro R, Sala-i-Martin X (1995) Economic Growth. New York: McGraw Hill

[4] Sala-i-Martin X (2000) Apuntes de Crecimiento Economico. Antony Bosh Editor. 2ª Ediccion.

[5] Romer D (1996) Advanced in Macroeconomics

[6] Barro R, Sala-i-Martin X (1991) Convergence Across States and Regions. Brookings Papers on Economic Activity.1: 107-182.

[7] Sala-i-Martin X. (1996a) The Classical Approach to Convergence Analysis. The Economic Journal. 106: 1019-1036

[8] De la Fuente A (1995) The Empirics of Growth and Convergence. A Selective Review. CEPR Discussion Paper.1275.

[9] Galor O (1996) Convergence: Inferences from Theoretical Models. CEPR Discussion Paper. 1350

[10] Seidel H (1995) Wirtschaftswachstum und Konvergenz. Wifo-Monatsberichte.1: 48-62.

[11] Ben-David D (1994) Convergence Clubs and Diverging Economies. CEPR Discussion Paper. 922.

[12] Sala-i-Martin X (1996b) Regional Cohesion: Evidence and Theories of Regional Growth and Convergence. European Economic Review. 40: 1325-1352.

[13] Barro R, Sala-i-Martin X (1992) Convergence. Journal of Political Economy. 100(2):223-251.

[14] Barro R (1997) Determinants of Economic Growth (The Lionel Robbins Lectures) Cambridge. The MIT Press Second Printing.

[15] Henin P, Le Pen Y (1995) Les épisodes de la convergence européene. Revue Économique. 46 (3): 667-677.

[16] Mankiw G (1995) The growth of Nations. Brookings Papers on Economic Activity. 0(1):275-310.

[17] Baumol W (1986) Productivity Growth, Convergence and Welfare: What the Long Run Data Show.American Economic Review.76(5):1072-1085.

[18] Pritchett L (1997) Divergence, big time. Journal of Economic Perspectives. 11(3):3-17.

[19] Jones C (1997) On the Evolution of the World Income Distribution. Journal of Economic Perspectives. 11(3): 19-36.

[20] UNCTAD (1997) Trade and Development Report. United Nations publication. E.97.II.D.8: 69-86.

[21] Hsiao Ch (1986) Analysis of Panel Data. Cambridge University Press. Cambridge.

[22] Islam N (1995) Growth Empirics: A Panel Data Approach. Quarterly Journal of Economics.4: 1127-1170.

[23] Canova F, Marcet A (1995) The Poor Stay Poor: Non-Convergence Across Countries and Regions. CEPR. 1265

[24] Harris C (1954) The market as a factor in the localization of industry in the United States. Annals of the Association of American Geographers. 64: 315–348
[25] Crozet M (2004) Do Migrants Follow Market Potentials? An Estimation of a New Economic Geography Model. Journal of Economic Geography. 4: 439-458.
[26] Head K, Mayer T (2000) Non-Europe: The Magnitude and Causes of Market Fragmentation in the EU. Weltwirtschaftliches Archiv.136: 284-314.
[27] Nitsch V (2000) National borders and international trade: evidence from the European Union. Can J Econ. 22:1091–1105

Section 3

Government Policies and International Trade

Chapter 5

The Impact and Consequences of Tax Revenues' Components on Economic Indicators: Evidence from Panel Groups Data

Taufik Abdul Hakim and Imbarine Bujang

Additional information is available at the end of the chapter

http://dx.doi.org/10.5772/48415

1. Introduction

Taxes are one of the major revenue for a country in where taxes are collected from citizens, companies, investors and so on to generate economy. There have several impacts of taxes due to economic growth whether it is positive or negative impacts. According to Bofah (2003), taxes refer to the revenue that is collected by the government to provide services and finance themselves. According to the theory of tax competition, the government will reduce the taxes on mobile asset through the occurrence of globalization due to rise in economic growth in a country. Change in tax rate also will give the different impact to an open economy. According to Bretschger (2010), he found negative impacts of corporate taxes on openness and total tax revenue to the economic growth in 12 OECD countries. He also mentioned on the tax competition theory that argues that, when tax rate of capital is reduced, it will cause the capital inflow to a country. This is because; the tax rate is one of the cost for capital holder (Bucovetsky, 1991 and Wilson, 1991). These two researches were found that private return on investment is influenced by the changes in capital taxes.

There are more than 20 studies which look for evidence on tax rates and economic growth in the United States and internationally. In all of the studies, it was concluded that reduction of all marginal rates by 5% and average tax rates by 2.5% leads to increase 0.2% to 0.3% of long-term growth. Christina and David (2007) conducted study of the impact of changes in the level of taxation on economic growth in which they investigated the effects of tax on GDP in United State in the post-World War II period. The study found that a tax increase by 1% leads to reduced 2% to 3% of GDP in United State.

However, some of the studies give opposite results in term of the negative relationship between tax and economic growth. According to Uhliga and Yanagawa (1999), increased capital income taxes will generate the economy. This is because, the capital income accrues for the old, in which increase on the capital income taxes will burden tax for the young and increase their saving, if the interest elasticity of saving is low. The other study by Glomm and Ravikumar (1998), found that when the government reduces the capital income taxes, it will reduce the spending on education and the long-run growth. In this case, the capital income taxes have positive correlation with the economic growth. Besides that, Gober and Burns (1997) have done a study about the relationship between tax structure and economic indicators for the OECD countries. From their finding, total tax revenue has negative relationship with two economic indicators that are saving and investment. However, according to them, personal income tax, corporate income tax, sales tax (consumption tax) and other taxes are highly significant, in which there is positive relationship with economic growth (GDP or GNP).

This study also involves another variable that affects the collection of tax revenue in a country. The variable is inflation rates. Usually, if the country faces the economic crisis, the government will try to recover the problem using monetary or fiscal policy. In fiscal policy, the government will use either taxes or government spending based on the problem. High inflation rate in a country will force the government to increase the tax of goods and services due to increased the price and stabilize the consumption also aggregate expenditure. With that, excise tax on some products may be affected with the change in inflation rate (Tanzi, 1989).

2. Literature review

The previous empirical studies found that most of the tax structures were highly significant and related with the economic growth in a country. One of the earlier studies done by Marsden (1983) mentioned that change in tax policy will affect the economic planning. According to Gober and Burns (1997), a countries economy may be affect differently due to any changes in each tax components. Based on their finding, excise taxes as percentage of Ireland's total revenue was four times the level in U.S. Change in economic growth depends on each of tax structures (Gold, 1991).Mahdavi (2008) suggest that the effect of rises in total tax revenue will reduce the growth in developing countries. Due to by the fiscal crisis in the past several decades, several developing countries had to revive its economy by changing the level of taxes. Two of the early studies by Hinrisch (1966) and Musgrave (1969) examined the relationship between the ratio of tax revenue to GDP (TAX/GDP) and found it was relatively low in the developing countries.

One of the studies that focus on African countries by Leuthold (1991) was examined the effect of (TAX/GDP) from 1973 to 1981 which used the OLS estimation method. From his study, the share of agriculture will affect the level of taxation and robust the relationship of total tax revenue into direct and indirect taxes. The level of taxes will give the different effect to growth and other indicators caused by the macroeconomic variables such as extent of corruption and adversely affected by the inflation rate in nine African countries over the period 1985-1996 (Ghura, 1998). Agbeyegbe (2004) used the same geographical sample, which are 22 countries in sub-Saharan Africa from 1980 to 1996. The study examined the effect of tax revenue on trade liberalization or "openness". He focused on three components in total tax revenue (taxes on income, international trade and goods and services tax) which are as ratio of GDP and found the weak relation among these three tax types.

The potential variable that will change the amount of tax revenue is change in inflation rate in a country. High inflation rate in a country will force the government to increase the taxes on goods and services by increasing the price and stabilizing the consumption and aggregate expenditure. With that, excise tax on some products may be affected with the change in inflation rate (Tanzi, 1989). A study by Mahdavi (2008) mentioned the effect of income, profit and capital gain tax due to change in inflation rate and investment plans. Based on his study, when the inflation rates increase, the household will protect their assets by substituting it with the assets that less domestic tax such as jewelleries.

2.1. Effect on Foreign Direct Investment (FDI)

The other variable that included in this research is to study the effects of taxes on FDI. Usually, the tax rate on capital is measured by stock of capital or capital flows that related to the FDI. One of the earliest studies by Hartman (1984) was a study on the relationship between FDI, after-tax rate of return by foreign investors and capital in United State. From his study, he suggested that the tax has a strong relationship with FDI. The tax regime in Mexico and United State has responded to the U.S's FDI. Two of the previous studies give the direction about the impact of taxes on FDI which are study by Scholes and Wolfson (1992) and Hines (1999). Based on Scholes and Wolfson (1992), tax will affect the decision of foreign investors to invest in a country caused by the changing in rates of return on assets. They argue that higher in tax will reduce the rates of return and discourage the FDI in-flow to a country. Hines (1999) found that FDI is sensitive with the tax, in which high tax rates can change the foreign investment rapidly. He concludes that reduction of only 10% on tax rates will increase more than 10% in FDI.

3. Data and methodology

This study is based on studies by Gober and Burns (1997), Mahdavi (2008) and Gordon and Li (2009). The dependent variables change in GDP, ratio of gross saving to GDP (SAVING/GDP) and foreign direct investment as ratio to GDP (FDI/GDP) to relate it with all the component of taxes (independent variables) since 1960 to 2009.

3.1. Data on tax policy in low, middle, and high income countries

Table 2 shows the percentage of several important components of tax revenue among the countries based on the different level of income. Based on the Table, rich or high income countries collect total tax revenue as ratio of GDP (TTX) more than two times compared with the poor or low income countries, in which the rich countries collect revenue of 27.60% of GDP and poor countries only collected 11.89%. This is caused by the high per capita

Variable	Definition
GDP	Gross Domestic Product annual percentage change.
FDI	Foreign Direct Investment (inflow) divided by GDP.
SAV	Gross Saving divided by GDP.
IPCT	Taxes on income, profit and capital gain divided by total tax revenue.
GST	Taxes on goods and services divided by total tax revenue.
ITT	Taxes on international trade divided by total tax revenue.
ET	Taxes on export divided by total tax revenue.
TTR	Total tax rate divided by total profit.
TTX	Total tax revenue divided by GDP.
INF	Inflation rate (consumer price index).

Table 1. Definition and sources of variables.

Variable	**GNI per capita (US$)**			
	≤ 975 (%)	**976 – 3855 (%)**	**3856 – 11905(%)**	**≥ 11906 (%)**
TTX	11.89	15.75	20.80	27.60
IPCT	19.82	28.34	33.00	48.25
GST	26.53	31.86	34.87	22.50
ITT	18.78	18.21	7.79	1.89
ET	4.91	2.70	3.06	NA
TTR	49.08	40.56	51.26	41.39
SAV	15.78	19.87	20.18	25.13
FDI	2.31	3.54	2.94	3.97
INF	15.18	15.90	22.98	7.30

Notes: Authors' calculations based on available data between 1960 and 2009 from World Data Catalogue (World Bank, 2010). The ranges for GNI per capita follow the World Bank 2008 classification of low income, lower middle income, upper middle income and high income countries. Data within each cell are weighted averages. Tax revenue (% of GDP) is weighted by GDP, inflation rate, and the other components of taxes are weighted by the total tax revenue of each country.

Table 2. Sources of government revenue (1960 – 2009).

income and large amount of international companies in many rich countries that leads to high taxes on income, profit, and capital gain as fraction of total tax revenue (IPCT). Among the four different levels of income, taxes on goods and services (GST) is the main source of tax revenue for the low and middle income countries, in which 34.87% of total tax revenue was collected in upper middle income countries. Inflation rate (22.98%) also states the highest in the country.

3.2. Unit root test

This co-integration test is to test for the existence of unit root for these variables. For this study, Augmented Dickey – Fuller (ADF) test is used to test for the non-stationary and the regression function is:

$$\Delta X_t = \delta_0 + \delta_1 + \delta_2 \ X_{t-1} + {}_{t-i} + \mu_t$$

Where, Xt is the logarithm of the model for all variables at time t. For the variable that symbol is $\Delta Xt\text{-}1$ means that the first differences with lags of k. The coefficients of $\delta 0$, $\delta 1$, $\delta 2$ and αi are being estimated. Only taxes on export (ET) and taxes on income, profit and capital gain (IPCT) are stationary at first difference for while the other variables are stationary at level

3.3. Variance Inflation Factors (VIF)

This method can detect the multicollinearity problem in an ordinary least squares (OLS) regression that examines the value of variance in the model. Based on this method, the value of variance will increase due to collinearity. According to Wooldridge (2000), variance of the OLS can be shown as follows:

$$\text{VIF}\ ({\scriptstyle i}) = 1/\,(1 - R^2)$$

The higher VIF, the greater of finding $_i$ insignificant that will detect the problem of multicollinearity. The lower values of VIF (less than 10) indicate that all the models were not suffered from multicollinearity problem.

3.4. Breusch-Pagan-Godfrey test

This test will estimate the variance of the residuals from the model. Compared to the other methods of testing heteroscedasticity, this method is least general and most powerful. It is also useful to test in this study because more than one independent variable is involved.

$$\mu^2 = \beta_0 + \beta_1 X_{1i} + \beta_2 X_{2i} + \ldots + \beta_K X_{KI}$$

This method relates the observation R^2 and the value of chi-squared. If the result show observation R^2 is significant with chi-squared value, the null hypothesis of no heteroscedasticity will be rejected.

3.5. Glejser test

The absolute value of the residual will detect the problem of heteroscedasticity.

$$|\hat{u}_i| = \beta_0 + \beta_1 X_i + e_i$$

The $|\hat{u}_i|$ represent the residual and $\beta_1 X_i$ indicates the independent variables in the model of regression.

3.6. Harvey-Godfrey test

This method transforms the residual to log square ($\ln RESID^2$). The equation for Harvey test can be shown as follow:

$$\ln\mu^2 = \beta_0 + \beta_1 X_{1i} + \beta_2 X_{2i} + \ldots + \beta_K X_{KI}$$

The null hypothesis that states no heteroscedasticity will be rejected if the value of chi-squared test is significant. Overall results of the three tests for heteroscedasticity was shown in Table 3 below:

H_0 = There is no heteroscedasticity in the model regression.

H_1 = There is a heteroscedasticity in the model regression.

	GNI per capita (US$)				
	All	≤975	976-3855	3856 – 11905	≥11906
Breusch-Pagan	**Reject H_0**	Reject H_1	**Reject H_0**	**Reject H_0**	Reject H_1
Harvey	**Reject H_0**	**Reject H_0**	RejectH_1	Reject H_1	Reject H_1
Glejser	**Reject H_0**	**Reject H_0**	RejectH_1	Reject H_1	Reject H_1

Table 3. Result of Heteroscedasticity test

Model regression for all 120 countries, low, lower and upper middle income countries rejected the null hypothesis that states no heteroscedasticity. It means that the model was strongly suffered from heteroscedasticity. However, heteroscedasticity was not found in the high income countries.

Breusch-Godfrey Serial Correlation LM Test

This method is used to detect the model regression for serial or autocorrelation problem. According to Gujarati and Porter (2010), this test is more general than several tests for autocorrelation. The residual regression is shown below:

$$e_t = \beta_1 + \beta_2 X_{1t} + \beta_2 X_{2t} + C_1 e_{t-1} + C_2 e_{t-2} + \ldots.. + C_k e_{t-k} + \upsilon_t$$

The regression above also called by auxiliary regression that obtain the observation R^2 (obs*R^2) from the residuals regression (nR^2 ~). If the value of obs*R^2 are significant with the probability of chi-squared, the null hypothesis will be rejected. The result shows that, the model regression for high income countries is significant for this method. The value of nR^2 ~ 13.57 =, in which the value of probability for chi-squared as much as 13.57 or greater for 5 d.f is significant at 5% level.

4. Hypothesis

Hypothesis one

For the first hypothesis, the dependent variable is annual change of GDP and the independent variables are the component of taxes as ratio to total tax revenue, total tax rate, and total tax revenue as ratio to GDP. The first hypothesis stated in null form is:

- H0: There is no relationship between tax components and inflation rate on GDP for a given countries based on the level of income.
- H1: There is a relationship between tax components and inflation rate on GDP for a given countries based on the level of income.

All the variables were transformed to the log difference. Due to the problem of heteroscedasticity, models regression for all 120 countries, low, lower middle and upper middle income countries have to be transformed as the square root transformation. This remedial measure follows Gujarati and Porter (2010). According to them, the error variance $\upsilon_i = u_i/$ in the transformed regression is homoscedasticity. For high income countries, the model regression for error term μ_t was transformed to one-period lag that multiply with the ρ value was showed no serial correlation. The error term follow the AR (1) scheme:

$$\mu_t = \rho\mu_{t-1} + \upsilon_t \qquad -1 \leq \rho \leq 1$$

With that, the new equation for high income countries can be rewrite as:

$$(Y_t - \rho Y_{t-1}) = \beta_1 (1-\rho) + \beta_2 (X_t - \rho X_{t-1}) + \upsilon_t$$

The regression function for each models are:

All 120countries:

$$\ln_t = \beta_{0t} + \beta_1 \ln_t + \beta_2 \ln_t + \beta_3 \ln_t + \beta_4 \ln_t + \beta_5 \ln_t + \beta_6 \ln_t + \beta_7 \ln_t + \mu_t$$

High income countries:

$$\Delta \ln\rho GDP_{t-1} = \beta_0(1-\rho)_t + \beta_1 \Delta \ln\rho TTX_{t-1} + \beta_2 \Delta \ln_t\rho IPCT_{t-1} + \beta_3 \Delta \ln\rho GST_{t-1} + \beta_4 \Delta \ln\rho ET_{t-1} + \beta_5 \Delta \ln\rho ITT_{t-1} + \beta_6 \Delta \ln\rho TTR_{t-1} + \beta_7 \Delta \ln\rho INF_{t-1} + \mu_t$$

Lag one or two years and first or second difference for all variables are based on the stationary (unit root) test, means that value for each tax structures for the previous year(s) will affect the GDP for current year.

Hypothesis two

Hypothesis two estimates the ratio of gross saving to GDP as dependent variable due to the ratio of each components of tax revenue to total tax revenue and inflation rate. The null hypothesis is:

- H0: There is no relationship between tax components and inflation rate on saving for a given countries based on the level of income.
- H1: There is a relationship between tax components and inflation rate on saving for a given countries based on the level of income.

Change of the tax components such as goods and services tax, consumption tax, personal and income tax will also affect the gross saving in a country. It's based on the previous study by Gober and Burns (1997) that study about the relationship between tax structure and economic indicators using the cross sectional data of OECD's countries. However, the affect is not constant with the different level of income for the countries.

Hypothesis three

For this third hypothesis, the dependent variable is foreign direct investment (FDI) as ratio to GDP and the independent variables are the components of tax revenue as ratio to total tax revenue and inflation rate. The null hypothesis form is:

- H0: There is no relationship between tax components and inflation rate on FDI for a given countries based on the level of income.
- H1: There is a relationship between tax components and inflation rate on FDI for a given countries based on the level of income.

Based on the previous studies, inflow of FDI also is influenced by the change for each components of tax revenue in a country. Usually, the return that the investors will get is earning per share (EPS) or dividend per share (DPS) by the company. The investors will be attracted by higher EPS or DPS, in which both of this returns are influenced by inflation rate and tax rates. The formula of EPS can be shown as:

$$EPS =$$

With that equation, increase in rates of corporate income tax and taxes on profit will reduce the EPS and discourage investors to invest.

5. Findings

The square root transformation of ordinary least squared (OLS) is used to estimate the unknown parameters in regression model for the three hypotheses.

5.1. All countries

The null hypothesis states that there is no relationship between components of tax revenue and inflation rate on GDP, inflow of FDI, and gross saving for a given countries based on the level of income, is rejected. Based on the Table 4, the regression shows that there is a relationship between the ratios of components of tax revenue to total tax revenue and inflation rate on economic indicators. The null hypothesis is rejected based on the significant (0.1, 0.05 or 0.01 level), using P-value in OLS method.

	(1) Δln(GDP/())	(2) Δln(SAV/())	(3) Δln(FDI/())
ln(ET/())	0.052732	0.106424	-0.028067
	(0.048729)	(0.151287)	(0.039931)
ln(GST/())	0.140677***	0.329904***	0.044219*
	(0.024231)	(0.075228)	(0.025958)
ln(INF/())	-0.050570**	-0.018236	0.034902**
	(0.021850)	(0.067836)	(0.015281)
ln(IPCT/())	0.272917***	0.443273***	-0.000393
	(0.025914)	(0.080453)	(0.026812)
ln((ITT/())	0.216337***	0.408508***	-0.014601
	(0.026501)	(0.082275)	(0.027654)
ln()	0.449083***	-0.987863**	-0.113624
	(0.156441)	(0.485694)	(0.133659)
ln((TTR/())	0.089823***	0.050482	-0.021454
	(0.016281)	(0.050548)	(0.013351)
(1/( ))	-0.553458***	0.093488	0.105316*
	(0.074562)	(0.231488)	(0.052510
R-squared	0.992899	0.970843	0.257284
Adjusted R-squared	0.992455	0.969021	0.162064
F-statistic	2237.176	532.7575	2.701999
No. observations	120	12	120

Notes: Values in parentheses are standard error. ***, **, and * indicates significant at 0.01, 0.05, and 0.1 level.

Table 4. All countries

Column (1), (2), and (3) on the top of table represents the results for the three hypothesis based on the different three dependent variables (GDP, gross saving, and FDI-inflow). Total tax revenue (TTX) as ratio to GDP is highly significant with the two economic indicators, in which showed the negative relation to saving and FDI. These results are same results that found by Gober and Burns (1997), Marsden (1983) and Smith (1990). Surprisingly, total tax revenue has high positive significance to the change in GDP, in which four of the components of tax revenue (GST, IPCT, ITT, and TTR) showed the high positive and significance. However, the impacts of tax revenue on the three indicators are not consistent for all countries in the four level of income. The high R^2 for model (1) and (2) showed that the independent variables are highly correlated with the dependent variables.

The other potential variable that is involved in this study is inflation rate, in which indicates the negative sign to the GDP and gross saving, while showing significant positive effect to the FDI. This result suggests that inflation rate will affect directly to plans of FDI by increasing in inflation rate in a country will increase the taxes and generate the inflow of FDI in a country. This is based on Mahdavi (2008) that found increase in inflation rate will increase the tax revenue through the increase in sales tax. Additionally, the study by Scholes and Wolfson (1992) suggest, an increase in tax will also increase the FDI-inflow.

5.2. Low income countries

Only 11 percent of GDP contributed to the revenue each country in this level of income. Taxes on goods and services have the highest percentage among all components of tax, in which 27 percent are from total tax revenue.

	(1)	(2)	(3)
Δln(GDP/())	Δ^2ln(SAV/())	Δ^2ln(FDI/())	
Δ^2ln(ET/())	0.004116*	0.140740**	0.071701
	(0.002206)	(0.051837)	(0.079145)
Δln(GST/())	0.083729**	1.108370	2.828571**
	(0.033901)	(0.901270)	(1.220902)
Δ^2ln(INF/())	-0.006402	-0.340943*	0.452805**
	(0.007656)	(0.183899)	(0.174043)
Δ^2ln(IPCT/())	0.025607**	0.710050**	0.213314
	(0.012414)	(0.307536)	(0.478474)
Δ^2ln(ITT/())	-0.010491	-0.523789**	0.710989*
	(0.014244)	(0.245165)	(0.372067)
Δln()	0.086472***	0.973560**	-2.436644**
	(0.025902)	(0.451495)	(0.966585)
Δln(TTX/())	-0.075491**	-0.502112***	-4.719960*
	(0.028567)	(0.165618)	(2.280927)
(1/( ))	0.086768**	-1.364480	2.099512**
	(0.036923)	(0.915260)	(0.333206)
R-squared	0.761138	0.674075	0.632356
Adjusted R-squared	0.606580	0.391606	0.356624
F-statistic	4.924613	2.386369	2.293367
No. observations	30	30	30

Notes: Values in parentheses are standard error. ***, **, and * indicates significant at 0.01, 0.05, and 0.1 level.

Table 5. Low income countries

Based on Table 5, GST was positively significant to the GDP and FDI. This study found that increase in GST will generate the growth and inflow of FDI in a country. TTR also has the significant effect to the three indicators, has positive effect to GDP and SAV, but negative relationship with the inflow of FDI. This result show that rates of tax is the cost in investment, in which increase in rates of tax will increase the cost of investment and discourage investors to invest in a company. The SAV and FDI have highly significant with the taxes on international trade (ITT) on the second difference and lagged two years. However ITT does not have the same effect on both of the economic indicators, in which negative effect on gross saving but positive effect on FDI. Increase in ITT will increase the price of imported goods and relatively price of domestic goods are cheaper than imported good. This situation will lowers the taxes on domestic goods and services which are encourage consumption on domestic goods and reduce gross saving.

5.3. Lower middle income countries

All four components of tax revenue (ET, IPCT, ITT, and ET) were contributed 81 percent of total tax revenue. With that, the TTX was directly affected by these components of tax revenue and affect the three economic indicators.

	(1) Δln(GDP/())	(2) Δln(SAV/())	(3) Δln(FDI/())
Δln()	0.127092***	0.101162***	0.041029***
	(0.019778)	(0.003365)	(0.000300)
Δln(GST/())	-0.126540***	-0.199845	-0.009767
	(0.041591)	(0.254834)	(0.034629)
Δ^2ln(INF/())	-0.029079	0.977954***	-0.113493**
	(0.051961)	(0.319115)	(0.043264)
Δ^2ln(IPCT/())	-0.024651	0.793698**	0.095368*
	(0.086117)	(0.313223)	(0.050239)
Δ^2ln(ITT/())	-0.152141**	-0.635001*	-0.126333***
	(0.070476)	(0.296184)	(0.032095)
Δln(TTX/())	-0.295484***	-1.081111**	-0.058318
	(0.091906)	(0.419215)	(0.076522)
Δ^2ln(TTR/())	0.038275	-1.174050	-0.104859*
	(0.052312)	(1.038849)	(0.045704)
(1/( )	-0.093347**	0.527982	-0.181886***
	(0.048015)	(0.437581)	(0.046372)
R-squared	0.999739	0.991386	0.999692
Adjusted R-squared	0.999477	0.988213	0.999384
F-statistic	3823.683	312.3938	3246.214
No. observations	30	30	30

Notes: Values in parentheses are standard error. ***, **, and * indicates significant at 0.01, 0.05, and 0.1 level.

Table 6. Lower income countries

Table 6 examined the parameters of the equation for components of tax revenue in the lower middle income countries. Based on the Table, total tax revenue on the first difference has negative effect to the growth of GDP, in which reduce 0.30 percent for each 1 percent increase in TTX. The same effect also shows on the other two indicators. The ET in this group of countries is the lowest percentage among the other group of countries. That component of tax was highly significant and had positive effect to the GDP, SAV, and FDI, in which will generate the economic from 0.04 to 0.13 percent.

The most affected on the three indicators by IPCT was on gross saving to GDP-ratio that increase 1 point in IPCT will increase 0.79 percent to SAV. Gross saving was affected most by ITT, in which discourage 0.64 percent in SAV. The result was influenced by the consumption on domestic goods and services. Increase in ITT will increase the price of imported goods and is relatively expensive than domestic goods. This situation increased consumption of domestic goods while reduced the domestic saving in a country.

5.4. Upper middle income countries

The percentage of total tax revenue of GDP is more than 20 percent in this group. It means, the tax revenue was higher in the higher income countries. However, the inflation rate is the highest in this group (23%) compared with the other groups of countries. The expectation of this study that relate inflation rate and taxes by goods and services tax can be shown by higher in inflation rate which will generate more to GST. The taxes on goods and services have 35 percent of total tax revenue that contributed the highest percentage in this group. Table 7 shows the coefficient of parameter for each of the variables.

	(1) (2)	(3)	
	Δln(GDP/())	Δln(SAV/())	Δ^2ln(FDI/())
Δln(ET/())	0.080414	-0.005814	0.965147
	(0.315284)	(0.619843)	(5.111205)
Δln(GST/())	-0.111859	-0.261029***	-3.972020**
	(0.184919)	(0.036354)	(1.223192)
Δln(INF/())	-0.103090**	-0.013045	0.277478
	(0.047930)	(0.094230)	(0.788610)
Δln()	0.340124**	0.097691***	0.937624
	(0.102388)	(0.020129)	(1.656401)
Δln((ITT/())	0.144577	0.613801**	-2.459903**
	(0.121094)	(0.238068)	(1.114730)
Δln()	-0.082579*	0.070147**	-0.115269
	(0.038906)	(0.033425)	(0.645417)
Δln(TTX/())	-0.241508*	-0.096494	3.329078
	(0.135578)	(0.444352)	(3.938132)
Δ^2ln(TTX/())	-0.015812	0.014138	-1.425103*
	(0.038992)	(0.076659)	(0.720536)
(1/)	-0.315512***	0.234584*	0.350857**
	(0.058128)	(0.114279)	(0.239737)
R-squared	0.876603	0.565446	0.649214
Adjusted R-squared	0.784056	0.239531	0.348540
F-statistic	9.471929	9.441269	7.844066
No. observations	30	30	30

Notes: Values in parentheses are standard error. ***, **, and * indicates significant at 0.01, 0.05, and 0.1 level.

Table 7. Upper middle income countries

The taxes on goods and services (GST) that contributed the highest percentage of total tax revenue had negative and highly significant to the dependent variables. This result is not consistent with the low income countries, in which it had positive effect to the economic growth. From the findings, this study concludes the different effects of the tax components based on the different tax structures and different tax policy for each group of countries. The rates of inflation also influence these tax components. The second highest percentage of tax revenue is taxes on income, profit, and capital gain (IPCT) also shows the significant coefficient to the economic indicators. The parameter of coefficient of IPCT has positive correlation on GDP, gross saving, and inflow of FDI in a country. The significance of this variable indicates that IPCT as revenue to an upper middle or developing countries that will contribute to generate economy. Based on this study, high level of income in the countries will increase the IPCT.

5.5. High income countries

This level of countries has the highest income per capita. These countries also called as rich or developed countries. Total tax revenue in this group of countries contributed 28 percent of GDP, in which the highest component of tax revenue was taxes on income, profit and capital gain (IPCT). This group has the lowest inflation rate (7%) and the lowest percentage of GST among the groups of country. Based on these results, this study suggest that inflation rate affected the tax revenue on GST and the higher income per capita in a country will contribute higher IPCT.

	(1) ΔlnρGDP	(2) ΔlnρSAV	(3) ΔlnρFDI
ΔlnρGST	-0.000547	-0.440172**	0.188973*
	(0.042312)	(0.182018)	(0.106621)
ΔlnρINF	-0.020855	-0.098160	-0.074966
	(0.035559)	(0.152969)	(0.089605)
ΔlnρIPCT	0.060493***	-0.236123***	0.088073**
	(0.015169)	(0.065255)	(0.038224)
ΔlnρITT	0.056751	-1.542499*	0.670518*
	(0.200967)	(0.806938)	(0.363431)
ΔlnρTTR	-0.072165**	-0.278812*	-0.016070
	(0.034403)	(0.147994)	(0.086691)
ΔρlnTTX	0.033375***	0.481297***	-0.043469*
	(0.008764)	(0.037702)	(0.019591)
1 - ρ	0.003555	0.087138*	-0.015224
	(0.011677)	(0.047841)	(0.016530)
R-squared	0.853691	0.937180	0.329289
Adjusted R-squared	0.815523	0.920793	0.154321
F-statistic	22.36688	57.18804	2.763909
No. observations	30	30	30

Notes: Values in parentheses are standard error. ***, **, and * indicates significant at 0.01, 0.05, and 0.1 level.

Table 8. High income countries

Dependent Variable	Hypothesis tested	F1	F2
lnGDP	There is a unidirectional relationship between lnGST and lnGDP (lnGDP <= lnGST).	4.93467***	0.99348
	There is a unidirectional relationship between lnIPCT and lnGDP (lnGDP <= lnIPCT).	5.10761***	0.77747
	There is a unidirectional relationship between lnITT and lnGDP (lnGDP <= lnITT).	14.1273***	1.29654
	There is a unidirectional relationship between lnGST and lnINF (lnINF => lnGST).	1.82627	5.72733***
lnSAV	There is a unidirectional relationship between lnGST and lnSAV (lnSAV => lnGST).	0.26215	2.39471*
	There is a unidirectional relationship between lnINF and lnSAV (lnSAV <= lnINF).	2.35779*	1.28879
	There is a bilateral relationship between lnIPCT and lnSAV (lnSAV ◎ lnIPCT).	6.21313***	2.44256*
	There is a unidirectional relationship between lnITT and lnSAV (lnSAV => lnITT).	1.14057	3.41127**
	There is a bilateral relationship between lnTTR and lnSAV (lnSAV ◎ lnTTR).	4.87729***	2.27390*
	There is a unidirectional relationship between lnTTX and lnSAV (lnSAV <= lnTTX).	3.26684**	1.57568
	There is a unidirectional relationship between lnGST and lnINF (lnINF => lnGST).	2.00220	2.14039*
	There is a unidirectional relationship between lnTT and lnGST (lnGST => lnITT).	2.02530	2.46395*
lnFDI	There is a unidirectional relationship between lnINF and lnFDI (lnFDI => lnINF).	1.21026	4.26882**
	There is a unidirectional relationship between lnIPCT and lnFDI (lnFDI => lnIPCT).	0.60109	7.20832***
	There is a unidirectional relationship between lnITT and lnFDI (lnFDI => lnITT).	0.25346	3.07362*
	There is a bilateral relationship between lnTTR and lnFDI (lnFDI ◎ lnTTR).	4.48555**	10.2675***
	There is a unidirectional relationship between lnTTX and lnFDI (lnFDI <= lnTTX).	4.42107**	0.15690

Notes: ***, **, and * indicates significant at 0.01, 0.05, and 0.1 level.

Table 9. Granger causality tests

The parameter of coefficient for high income countries was shown in Table 8. Based on the Table, the coefficient for TTX shows the significant and different affect to all three economic indicators. Opposite result in TTX on the economic growth, in which TTX will generate the GDP compared with the low and middle income countries. This result was influenced by the different tax policy and lower inflation rate in a rich country. This is based on the study by Mahdavi (2008) that mentioned inflation rate is one of the potential variables that will influence the tax revenue and tax policy in a country. Increase in tax and tax policy was dramatically used by the low and middle income countries due to reducing the high inflation. With that, the effect of TTX on economic growth for the three levels of countries showed negative impact caused by TTX is generated by tax policy and forced the tax such as taxes on goods and services (GST) to increase. However, in high income countries that has low inflation rate, the countries did not increase the tax and tax policy dramatically, while the most important and highest percentage of tax revenue on high income countries was generated by taxes on income, profit, and capital gain. High in tax revenue was not forced by high inflation rate, but generated by high in per capita income and revenue or profit in many medium sized and large companies in a high income country.

Further analysis using Granger causality test

In order to test whether the time series data has causal relationship between all the variables, this study uses the Granger causality test. This test was also used by the previous study such as Anastassiou and Dritsaki (2005) by referring to the F statistic. Each of the variables is separate in function, in which the hypothesis of statistical significance for the F statistic in a group of variables to examine the relationship. The result shows that the independent variables have Granger causal relationship to the dependent variables. Table 9 shows the Granger causality test for all the variables that involves all 120 countries.

Based on Table 9, almost all the components of tax revenue in 120 countries, in which it involved four groups of country, have causal relationship with the annual change in GDP, gross saving to GDP-ratio, and FDI-inflow to GDP-ratio. It is based on the value of F-test that significant at 0.01, 0.05, and 0.01 levels. This results shows that the components of tax revenue that involve in this study were significant to relate it with the economic growth and other economic indicators. The potential variable, inflation rate also has causal relationship with the taxes such as GST. With that, it proves the inflation rate in a country will affect the GST to change. For the FDI-inflow, we can conclude that total tax rate (TTR) and FDI correlated with each other based on this method. The result supports the study of investment and tax rate by Palacios and Harischandra (2008) that mentioned, an investor's willing to invest is higher if the marginal tax rates are lower by increasing the returns on investment.

6. Conclusions

From the regression analysis, the main findings may be summarized as follows:

1. This study found statistical evidence suggesting that the total tax revenue to GDP ratio is higher in the high income countries compared with the low and middle countries.
2. The inflation rate in a country was significant and directly affect the components of tax revenue especially taxes on goods and services (GST). The higher inflation rate in low and middle income countries has the highest percentage of GST to total tax revenue ratio.
3. Taxes on income, profit, and capital gain (IPCT) will contribute more on total tax revenue in the higher income countries. Increase in IPCT was generated by increase in per capita income and many medium sized and large companies that has higher profit

to be taxed by the government in a country. Total tax rate (TTR) was highly significant on the FDI-inflow, in which corporate tax rate and marginal tax rate as the cost to investment. This result suggests that increase in TTR will reduce both profit of a company and rate of returns on investment (FDI).

4. Increase in total tax revenue (TTX) will encourage gross saving to increase in a country caused by increase in GST or sales tax that reduces consumption. However, taxes on international trade (ITT) has negative impact to gross saving, in which increase in ITT will increase the price of imported goods and relatively expensive than domestic goods that will encourage consumption and reduce gross saving.

Inconsistent impacts of TTX and the other components of tax revenue that involve in this study caused by the different levels of income in a country. Besides, the potential variable such as inflation rate will affect the tax reformed and tax policy that give different impacts to the economic growth, gross saving to GDP ratio and FDI-inflow to GDP ratio.

Author details

Taufik Abdul Hakim and Imbarine Bujang
Faculty of Business Management, Universiti Teknologi MARA, Sabah Malaysia

Appendix

Low income	Lower middle income	Upper middle income	High income
Afghanistan	Angola	Algeria	Andorra
Bangladesh	Belize	Argentina	Australia
Benin	Bolivia	Belarus	Bahrain
Cambodia	Cameroon	Bosnia and Herzegovina	Belgium
Comoros	China	Brazil	Brunei
Congo Dem Rep	Cote d'Ivoire	Bulgaria	Canada
Eritrea	Ecuador	Chile	Croatia
Ethiopia	Georgia	Colombia	Czech Republic
Ghana	Guyana	Costa Rica	Denmark
Guinea	Honduras	Cuba	Finland
Haiti	India	Dominica	France
Kenya	Indonesia	Fiji	Germany
Liberia	Iraq	Gabon	Greece
Malawi	Jordan	Jamaica	Hong Kong China
Mali	Kosovo	Kazakhstan	Italy
Mauritania	Maldives	Latvia	Japan
Mozambique	Moldova	Malaysia	Korea Rep
Myanmar	Mongolia	Mexico	Kuwait
Nepal	Paraguay	Namibia	Netherlands
Niger	Philippines	Palau	Norway

Rwanda	Samoa	Panama	Oman
Senegal	Sri Lanka	Peru	Portugal
Somalia	Sudan	Poland	Singapore
Tajikistan	Swaziland	Romania	Spain
Tanzania	Thailand	Serbia	Sweden
Togo	Timor-Leste	South Africa	Switzerland
Uganda	Tonga	Suriname	Trinidad and Tobago
Uzbekistan	Tunisia	Turkey	United Arab Emirates
Vietnam	Ukraine	Uruguay	United Kingdom
Zimbabwe	Vanuatu	Venezuela RB	United State

Table 10. Countries in the sample.

7. References

[1] Agbeyegbe, Terence, Stotsky J. G., and WoldeMariam A., (2004). Trade liberalization, exchange rate changes, and tax revenue in sub-Saharan Africa. *IMF Working Paper WP/04/178 Washington D.C.: International Monetary Fund* .

[2] Anastassiou T., and Dritsaki C., (2005). Tax Revenues and Economic Growth: An Empirical Investigation for Greece Using Causality Analysis. *Journal of Social Sciences, 1,* 99-104.

[3] Bofah K., (2003). The Impact of Tax on Investment and Business Decisions. htttp://www.ehow.com/facts_5910416_impact-tax-investment-business-decisions.html

[4] Bretschger L., (2010). Taxes, mobile capital, and economic dynamics in a globalizing world. *Journal of Macroeconomics 32,* 594–605.

[5] Bucovetsky S., (1991). Asymmetric tax competition. *Journal of Urban Economics 30,* 167–181.

[6] Christina and David R., (2007). The Macroeconomic Effects of Tax Changes: Estimates Based on New Measure of Fiscal Shocks, *NBER Working Paper 13264*

[7] Ghura H.,. (1998). Tax revenue in sub-Saharan Africa: Effects of economic policies and corruption. *WP/98/135 Washington D.C.: International Monetary Fund* .

[8] Glomm G., and Ravikumar B., (1998). Taxes government spending on education and growth. *Review of Economic Dynamics 1,* 306–325.

[9] Gober J.R., and Burns J.O., (1997). The Relationship Between Tax Structures and Economic Indicators. *Journal of International Accounting, Auditing & Taxation, 6,* 1-24.

[10] Gold S.D., (1991). Changes in state government finances in the 1980s. *National Tax Journal 44,* 1-19.

[11] Gordon R., and Li W., (2009). Tax structures in developing countries: Many puzzles and a possible explanation. *Journal of Public Economics 93,* 855–866.

[12] Gujarati D.M., and Porter D.C., (2010). *Essential of Econometrics.* New York: McGraw Hill.

[13] Hartman, D. G., (1984). Tax policy and foreign direct investment. *Journal of Public Economics 26,* 107–121.

[14] Hines J.R., (1999). Taxes and the location of foreign direct investment in America. *American Economic Review 86,* 1076–1094.

[15] Hinrisch H.H., (1966). A general theory of tax structure change during economic development. *Harvard Law School International Tax Program Development .*

[16] Leuthold J. H., (1991). Tax shares in developing economies: A panel study. *Journal of Development Economics, 35,* 173–185.

[17] Mahdavi S., (2008). The level and composition of tax revenue in developing countries:Evidence from unbalanced panel data. *International Review of Economics and Finance 17,* 607–617.

[18] Marsden K., (1983). Links between taxes and economic growth. *World Bank Staff Working Paper Number 605,* The World Bank, Washington, D.C.

[19] Musgrave R. A., (1969). Fiscal systems. : Yale University Press.

[20] Palacios M., and Harischandra K., (2008). The impact of taxes on economic behavior, *NBER Working Paper 13264.*

[21] Scholes M.S., and Wolfson M.A., (1992). Taxes and business strategy: A planning approach. *Prentice-Hall, Englewood Cliffs, NJ .*

[22] Smith R., (1990). Factors affecting saving, policy tools, and tax reform. *International Monetory Fund Stuff Papers 37,* 1-70.

[23] Tanzi V., (1989). The impact of macroeconomic policies on the level of taxation and the fiscal balance. *International Monetary Fund Stuff Papers 36,* 633-656.

[24] Uhliga H., and Yanagawa N., (1999). Increasing the capital income tax may lead to faster growth. *European Economic Review, 40,* 1521-1540 .

[25] Wilson J.D., (1991). Tax competition with interregional differences in factor endowments. *Regional Science and Urban Economics 21,* 423–451.

[26] Wooldridge J. M., (2000). *Introductory Econometrics: A Modern Approach.* South Western.

[27] World Bank. (2010). World Development Indicators. World Bank, Washington, D.C.

Chapter 6

A Comparative Analysis of the Economic Effects of Cross-Border Mergers and Acquisitions in European Countries

Anita Maček

Additional information is available at the end of the chapter

http://dx.doi.org/10.5772/48342

1. Introduction

International capital flows (ICF) moved very dynamically through time. Their volume changed due to different circumstances and the same applies to their forms.

Compared to the role of foreign direct investments (FDI) in international capital flows today, their role was supposedly much less prominent before the First World War. This can be attributed to differences in their evaluation then and now, while the pre-1914 concept of FDI (in today's sense) was not fully differentiated from other forms of investments in foreign companies that come from the private sector (Lipsey, 2001).

The First World War caused international confidence to plummet and the interventional policy of national governments to increase, while war debts and high reconstruction costs have caused growth of FDI inflows to overseas colonies. The main player in these processes at the time was the United States. After the Second World War, the USA also held the role of the main investor, the general climate was favourable to FDI and FDI into industry prevailed. A bigger increase of FDI volume within the framework of global ICF is evident after 1980. In the period 1983-1989, FDI increased by 29% annually. This is three times faster than global export growth (9.4% annually) and four times faster than global GDP growth (7.8% annually). The favourable climate that increased the volume of FDI was affected by the liberalisation of trade (the Uruguay Round) and on national level by privatisation and the liberalisation of investments. After 1980, the main source of outward FDI was Europe followed by the USA (UNCTAD, 1991; Lipsey, 1999). Figure 1 shows the development of FDI inflow and outflow and of cross-border mergers and acquisitions (C-B M&As) from 1990 to 2010.

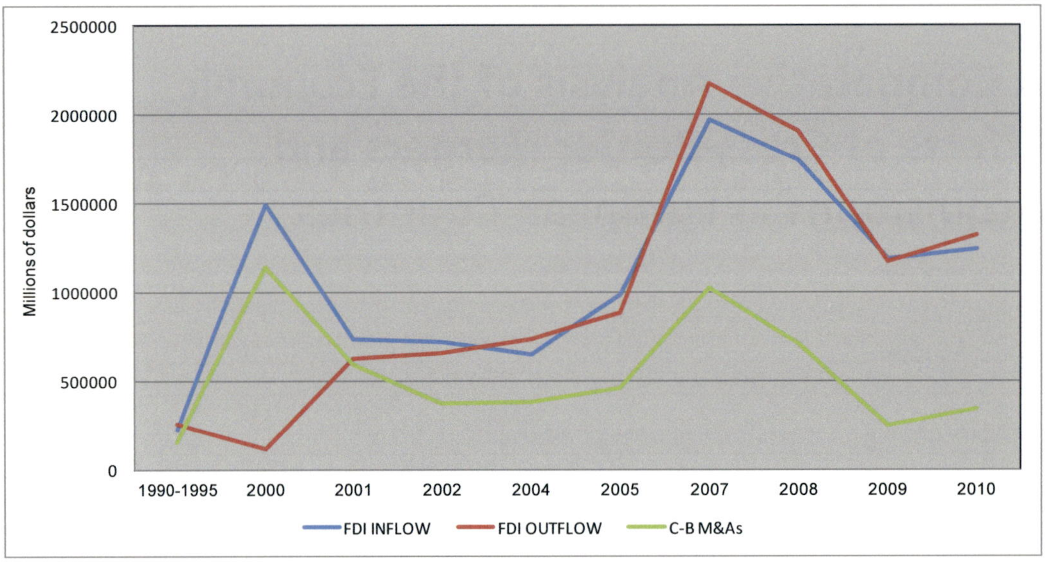

Figure 1. The development of FDI and C-B M&As from 1990 to 2010 (Adapted from UNCTAD 2000a, 2001, 2002, 2005, 2011).

Considering the shock caused by the WTC attack in 2001, we can see that compared to 1990 global FDI settled at a high level. This is the result of the favourable FDI policy in the form of liberalisation of trade (the completed Uruguay Round), the removal of capital movement restrictions with privatisation programmes on national level and the expansion of NAFTA and the EU. Also in this period, FDI were concentrated in the more economically developed countries in three global regions – the European Union, North America and South, Southeast and East Asia (UNCTAD 2000a, 2001, 2002, 2005, 2011).

In 2000, worldwide inward FDI reached record levels of $1,300 billion. The consequences of the 2001 terrorist attacks in the United States caused a decline in confidence and reduced the volume of FDI[1]. In 2003, FDI again stabilised and reached 1997 levels (about $600 billion). In 2005, FDI already reached $982 billion, while the main groups of economies, i.e. developed countries, developing countries and the transition economies already indicated growth trends. In 2007 (UNCTAD 2008, 3-9), global FDI already recorded $1,970 billion. In 2008, growth was interrupted due to the economic and financial crisis. In 2008 and 2009, the volume of global FDI thus reduced. In 2008, it was reduced by 12% compared to the previous year and in 2009 by 32% compared to 2008. In 2010, the volume of global FDI began increasing and thus increased by 5% compared to 2009 (to $1,200 billion) but was still by 37% lower than the highest volume of FDI that was recorded in 2007 ($1,970 billion).

Throughout the years, the highest volume of global FDI was recorded in developed countries, while in 2010 developing and transition economies for the first time together attracted more than half of global FDI flows. International production strongly increased

[1] The largest decrease in the volume of FDI in 2001 was especially evident in developed countries, when FDI decreased by almost 50% (UNCTAD, 2003).

and national multinational companies played an important role in the ICF market in 2010. According to UNCTAD (2011), there were at least 650 state-owned transnational corporations in 2010, with 8,500 foreign affiliates across the globe. While they represent less than 1 per cent of transnational corporations, their outward investment accounted for 11% of global FDI in 2010.

Figure 1 also shows the development of C-B M&As within FDI. Data for this type of FDI are available from only since 1987, when C-B M&As stood at $75 billion. In 2000, they grew to $1,144 billion and in 2007 the value of transactions already amounted to $1,022 billion. This value plummeted due to the economic and financial crisis and in 2010, the value of this transactions stood at $338 billion.

The ownership and management of state-owned transnational corporations undoubtedly puts some pressure on national economic objectives and thus the economic policy of host countries (Ovin, 2003), while an additional reason for concern is provided by the increase in volume of C-B M&As and thus their share in total FDI[2] and the changed structure of investments of C-B M&As. Investments of C-B M&As by sector in the period 1987-2010 are shown in Figure 2.

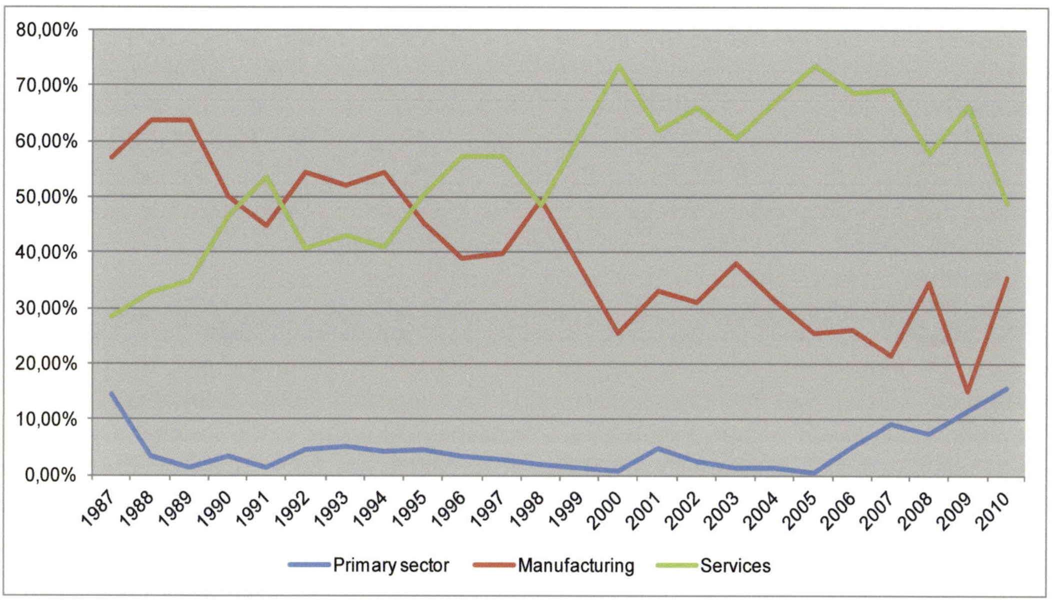

Figure 2. Investments of C-B M&As by sector, 1987-2010 (Adapted from UNCTAD 2002, 2005, 2011).

Figure 2 shows that until 1994 (with the exception of 1990 and 1991) the most important investments of C-B M&As were that in manufacturing, while since 1995 there is an increase in the importance of C-B M&As in the service sector (financial services, mobile telephony,

[2] In 2005, C-B M&As represented a 97% share in global FDI, in 2006 this share stood at 79% and in 2007 at 89% (UNCTAD, 2008).

real-estate). The share of investments of C-B M&As in the primary sector was relatively small in the period from 1989 to 2004, while after 2005 there is an increase of investments of C-B M&As in the primary sector, especially in the oil industry. In 2010, the share of investments of C-B M&As in services stood at 49%, in industry at 35% and in the primary sector at 16%.

Increased volume of C-B M&As, investment structure of these flows and the ownership of transnational corporations by individual states represent certain pressure on the economic policies in the receiving countries and this pressure recently caused reactions of economic policy known as economic nationalism.

The first part of the proposed chapter will bring a review of the research of factors influencing the flows of C-B M&As and their impact on the economy of the host country, while the second part of the chapter will provide stylised facts with C-B M&As in European receiving countries as shown in the research Maček (2009).

2. Characteristics of international capital flows

2.1. Factors influencing FDI flows and C-B M&As

Discussions on factors influencing exclusively C-B M&As flows are not as frequent in literature as studies of factors influencing total FDI flows. The reasons for this lie predominantly in poorer accessibility of C-B M&As data, the fact that these transactions usually expose participants to great business risks and the political risks that the national policy is exposed to, as C-B M&As usually deal with "releasing national sovereignty" over strategically important companies or sectors. Due to the share of C-B M&As in global FDI, factors influencing FDI flows can partially be considered also as factors influencing C-B M&As flows.

Literature often mentions political risk, investment environment, infrastructure, regulatory framework, bureaucratic hurdles and red tape, judicial transparency and the extent of corruption in the host country as factors influencing FDI flows (Mottaleb, 2007, 4). Commonly mentioned factors are also the size of the host country, the country risk rating, the availability of skilled labour (Nonnemberg & de Mendonça, 2004, 2), the openness of the market and labour costs (Taylor & Francis Group, 2004; Cheng & Kwan, 2000). Bevan & Saul (2000) add gravity factors and Chen (1996) additionally stresses transportation infrastructure and research and development capability in the host country.

The factors shown by these authors are derived from empirical analyses that the authors used to check the interdependence of FDI flows and the chosen factors. For this reason, individual authors show only a set of factors that influenced the increase of FDI in a country or a group of countries in a specific period of time. A complete set of factors influencing the development of FDI can be found in the World Investment Report 1998. According to this source, factors that determine FDI flows are classified in the group of microeconomic factors (factors related to acquiring new markets, extraction of natural resources and greater efficiency), economic and political factors (the privatisation policy, international FDI agreements, the trade policy, the fiscal policy, etc.) and factors that are related to business facilitation (investment incentives, promotion of FDI, location attractiveness, etc.) (UNCTAD, 1998, 91). The economic and political framework for FDI in the host country is an important determinant of FDI flows but liberalisation and globalisation have reduced its impact. Business facilitation has become more important and according to UNCTAD (1998), microeconomic factors hold the most important role.

As mentioned before, factors that determine FDI flows within different forms of FDI do not differ substantially, however, literature stresses two special factors in the foreign investor's decision on a "Greenfield" FDI or C-B M&As: speed and access to proprietary assets. In the sense of speed, C-B M&As represent the fastest means of building market presence, gaining market power, spreading risks or realising synergies. In order to increase proprietary assets, C-B M&As can further provide access to assets in the form of R&D, technical know-how, patents, brand names, etc. (UNCTAD, 2000a, 140).

2.2. Economic effects of FDI and C-B M&As

Literature usually does not differentiate the effects for the host country by FDI forms but shows them as part of total FDI effects. Although there is empirical evidence of a partial difference in the effects of »Greenfield« FDI and C-B M&As, it has also been proven that in the long run these effects are equalised (UNCTAD 2006, 2007, 2008).

2.2.1. Positive and negative effects of C-B M&As

There are several studies showing the effects of FDI in different host countries. Some relate to horizontal and other to vertical spillover effects of FDI. The findings of these studies differ. Some show positive effects (Barro, 1991; Barro & Sala-i-Martin, 1995; Lipsey, 2002; Baliamoune-Lutz, 2004), other neutral effects (Kokko et al., 1996) and there are also studies indicating negative effects of FDI on domestic companies (Aitken & Harrison, 1999; etc.).

The earliest statistical analyses of FDI relate to studies by Caves (1974) and Blomström & Persson (1983), who studied the existence of spillover effects by testing the effect of foreign ownership on productivity in a domestic firm. They concluded that the effects are positive, while the same conclusions were later also drawn by Nadiri (1991), Blomström & Wolf (1994), Chuang & Lin (1999), Liu et al. (2000), Driffield (2001) and Kolasa (2008). Other studies (Estrin et al. (1997), Ikiara (2003), Torlak (2004), Stephan (2005) and Perez (2008), Lin (2008) show that FDI affect the development potential of the economy as well as reduce unemployment, affect transfer of new technologies and knowledge, generate additional tax revenue for the state, support development strategies of individual sectors, affect the development of managerial knowledge, increase engagement of local companies in supplier and subcontractor networks and generate a better utilisation of the local infrastructure and service activities. According to Borensztein et al. (1995), Pain (2001) and Neuhaus (2006), inward FDI strongly contribute to economic growth in the host country, while Alfaro (2003) believes that FDI have a positive effect only if made in manufacturing, while the results of his study show that FDI in the primary sector tend to have a negative effect on growth. On the other hand, certain studies even prove negative effects of FDI on economic growth of the host country (Kawai, 1994; Mencinger, 2004).

The benefits of FDI are not self-evident and greatly differ among different countries. The results of Lin's study (2008, 31) show that the benefits from FDI are enhanced in an open investment environment with a democratic trade and investment regime, active competition policies, macroeconomic stability and privatisation and deregulation. The distribution of positive compared to the negative effects depends on the economic policy towards these processes and the entrepreneurial environment as well as other factors affecting their consequences. Reisen (1999) points out that positive effects of these transactions usually occur with a time lag. Cantwell (1989) and Perez (1998) believe that the occurrence and intensity of positive effects of ICF depends on the sector in which the foreign investment is entered.

It is important to know, that with unfavourable conditions, FDI can bring also negative effects. These are especially evident in the form of reducing productivity of the host country (Aitken & Harrison,1999; Kokko et al., 1996; Aslanoglu, 2000), reducing employment (Kokko, 2006), diminished R&D intensity (Hitt et al., 1991; Blonigen & Taylor, 2000), increased concentration in the domestic market and the closing of companies (UNCTAD, 2007), shrinking of the domestic stock market because shares are being transferred to a foreign stock market (Tsang & Hauck, 2007), anti-competitive reactions of the acquired firms (Haller 2005), abnormally low sales prices of companies (UNCTAD, 2000b, 2) or eliminated competition in the domestic market (UNCTAD, 2000a; UNCTAD, 2007, 123). In their studies, Maček & Ovin (2006, 2011) stress the crowding out of domestic firms, too low prices paid for domestic companies and anti-competitive behaviour of foreign affiliates as the most common threats of C-B M&As in European countries. In recent years, negative effects often include also threats to national sovereignty and autonomy of the host country and thus losing control of strategic industries (Lin, 2008), whereby the threat of losing economic independence is especially emphasised (Kamaraj, 2008).

2.2.2. Differences in effects of »Greenfield« FDI and C-B M&As

In studying differences in effects of »Greenfield« FDI and C-B M&As, literature provides studies (Li & Chen, 1998; Meyer & Nguyen, 2003; Jensen, 2003) that prove that among all forms of FDI, »Greenfield« FDI have the highest share of positive macroeconomic effects, especially as they relate to sectors where host countries do not hold sufficient growth capacities. However, it has generally been proven that the difference in effects of »Greenfield« FDI and C-B M&As is especially visible at the moment of entering the foreign market or in the short-term, while later these effects are unified (UNCTAD, 2000a, 196-198).

The differences in the effects of both forms of FDI are supposed to disappear in the long-term, as C-B M&As are often followed by additional investments of foreign bidders, which are especially substantial under the circumstances of privatisation. In the long run, C-B M&As – similar to »Greenfield« FDI – lead to increased investments and manufacturing. C-

B M&As may be followed by transfer of new or better knowledge (organisation and managerial skills), especially if wishing to improve the efficiency of the acquired company. In time, C-B M&As can also increase employment, especially if there are later additional investments made or the links to the acquired company are strengthened.

2.3. Real economic policy in the field of C-B M&As in the EU

Despite the EU's endeavours, it seems that the free movement of goods, services, persons and capital between countries will not happen for some time. Past reactions of individual governments show that they do not fully trust the market activity and thus wish to improve it with their measures. By intervening in ICF, governments wish to protect the domestic labour force from the foreign labour force, reduce the deficit in the state's balance of payments and protect developing sectors or sectors of strategic importance (Salvatore, 1998; Hill, 2005).

In the last years, the countries supposedly increased control of ICF due to the negative experiences from past financial crises. The protectionism against C-B M&As was greatly enhanced by the fact that state-owned firms or firms in which the state holds a share have increasingly become the subject of acquisitions (UNCTAD, 2008). The Global FDI Policy report (Marchick & Slaughter, 2008) lists Russia, Germany, Hungary, France and Greece as countries that stand out in terms of adopting legislation that regulates FDI or C-B M&As. They mostly focus on protection from the entry of foreign investors into companies that are part of strategic industries. On the other hand, there is the United Kingdom that has received the highest amount of inward FDI in the last twenty years since the strong revival of ICF. Its liberal regulation has advanced to such an extent that a foreigner may acquire control shares of the majority of British corporations.

The research report on protectionism with respect to FDI by CMS (2008) that surveyed concrete cases and policies in 17 European countries shows that – except for the United Kingdom and the Netherlands – rules exist which discriminate against foreign investors.

Especially in 2005, 2006 and later years, we witnessed high-attention cases of protectionism with regard to foreign investments in developed countries. In 2006 for example, German Chancellor Angela Merkel stopped Russia's Sistema holding company from acquiring a stake in Deutsche Telekom. In the same year, the Italian infrastructure minister blocked plans of the Spanish Abertis to acquire the Italian motorway toll operator Autostrade. The Spanish government repeatedly and successfully blocked E.ON's bid for Endesa. Former French Prime Minister de Villepin helped in the merger between Suez and Gaz de France in order to prevent a takeover of Suez by Italy's energy company ENEL. In 2007, the Italian Olimpia began negotiations with AT&T and the Mexican operator America Movil to sell them Olimpia's stake in Telecom Italia. However, political pressures of protection against foreign investments prevented the deal to succeed. In the same year, a much-noted case was also that of the French intervention when the French government, ensuing speculation that the French bank Societe Generale would be taken over, emphasised that the bank will remain in state ownership (CMS, 2008).

The obstacles placed by the economic policy to stop FDI affect the duration of the transaction, price and subsequent development of FDI. And in the long run, hindering FDI flows can also cause a reduced FDI flow (Marchick & Slaughter, 2008).

Even though governmental interventions in individual foreign bids have in the past proven to be negative, governments still favour the idea of "national champions", because it has the potential of benefiting them twice. Insisting on national ownership of important companies gives them positive publicity and once companies are in trouble, they provide help and appear as guardian angels (Heufers, 2008). They obviously count on the poor memory of the political market that forgets that these same companies lost their competitive edge precisely due to the extensive government support and dependence. From the economic viewpoint, the growing protectionism in the field of FDI is unfavourable, as it triggers a revolt of global capital with substantial consequences for the global economy. We must not forget that arbitration in terms of ICF is not made only on the basis of different marginal rates of return and investment security. Private investors are also searching for stable conditions that are predominantly characterised by the attitude of the real policy towards FDI and C-B M&As (Maček, 2008, 33).

3. Empirical study

3.1. The data, sample and method

Studies dealing exclusively with the effects of C-B M&As on the economy of the host country are not as common as studies on total FDI, especially due to problems with obtaining data. Furthermore, they mostly focus on the analysis of individual macroeconomic or financial consequences of such processes or relate to a group of companies or sectors. While the first group of studies are too broad to be able to recognise the differences among individual groups of countries, the latter are too narrow to be able to explain and establish stylised facts. Researchers and real economic policy undoubtedly find them interesting, as they provide insight into what actually occurs in the mentioned field.

In order to be able to recognise stylised facts and eventual differences among groups of countries, we used the total analysis (Walras) in our study. Empirical facts about the experiences of individual microeconomic units or countries were thus joined on the level of a group of countries. This methodological approach allowed us to gain relevant information and obtain robust results.

Studies employing a similar methodological approach replace the lack of data on C-B M&As with interviews of government officials or journalists from individual countries (Vaara et al., 2001; EGIP, 2005; GFC/Net, 2007), where authors rely on information obtained from editors and renown journalists. They are thus exposed to risks of either biased information or lacking knowledge of the subject matter. In order to avoid these risks to the highest possible extent, the sample in our total analysis comprises scientists, professors and experts employed at European business schools. The risk of bias was reduced as deans of schools invited their colleagues to participate, whose research or pedagogical work deals with the treated phenomenon. The respondents were to some extent included in C-B M&As or were at least very familiar with the professional and public debate in local circles and the media. When testing the size of the difference in the answers provided by professionals from the same country, there was no need to reject or exclude any of the answers from the sample used in the empirical analysis.

Our analysis was carried out with the help of a questionnaire consisting of 21 questions in the fields of effects of inward C-B M&As, government reactions and the media relation to these processes in European countries. The sample included experts from 104 business schools from the following 36 countries (the number of respondents is in parentheses): Austria (4), Belarus (2), Belgium (2), Bosnia and Herzegovina (2), Bulgaria (2), Croatia (4), Cyprus (2), Czech Republic (4), Denmark (2), Estonia (2), Finland (2), France (2), Germany (3), Georgia (2), Greece (2), Hungary (4), Ireland (2), Italy (3), Island (2), Latvia (3), Lithuania (6), Netherlands (2), Norway (2), Poland (4), Portugal (2), Romania (4), Russia (4), Slovakia (3), Slovenia (4), Spain (5), Serbia and Montenegro (2), Sweden (2), Switzerland (2), Turkey (4), UK (3) and Ukraine (4). In most parts of the research, we divided these countries into two groups: 19 developed countries and 17 transition countries. The criteria used for this separation were the nature of their systems and national policies before 1989.

For statistical analysis the program SPSS-X for Windows and Microsoft Excel were used. This chapter uses frequency distribution to present the obtained answers on the effects of C-B M&As and the reactions of governments to these processes. In individual questions, we used an independent sample t-test for analysing the existence of statistically significant differences between the answers provided by the respondents from developed and transition countries.

3.2. Analysis of effects of C-B M&As

Within the framework of effects of C-B M&As, we initially verified the positive expectations of the respondents for the upcoming C-B M&As in their country. The results are shown in Figure 3.

The results show that the respondents from developed countries expect C-B M&As to bring access to new markets, while the respondents from transition countries mostly stressed know-how transfer as expected benefits of C-B M&As. Globally speaking, almost all answers received higher scores from respondents from transition countries, who gave the average score of under 3.5 only to external and internal pressures of foreign investors on domestic economic policies in order to be able to act more efficiently and transparently in the field of investments. The only benefit that the respondents from developed countries evaluated higher than the respondents from transition countries was access to new markets. The respondents from developed countries graded the majority of other benefits under 3.5, which shows that in European developed countries positive evaluations of C-B M&As predominantly relate to factors of market expansion.

Relative to the expectations from developed countries, the anticipated positive effects of C-B M&As in transition countries are mostly the support to the transition process, external and internal pressure of foreign investors on domestic economic policies, the development of management skills and technology improvement. These expectations mirror the most important transition objectives, which allows us to conclude that the professional public in the countries from our sample sees C-B M&As as an important instrument of transition.

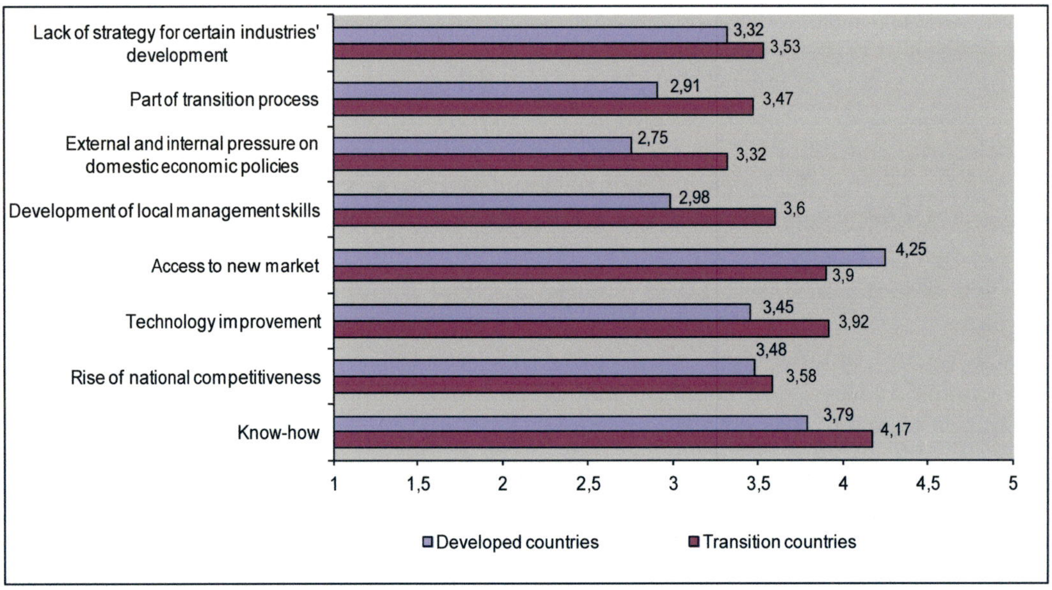

Figure 3. Positive expectations for the upcoming C-B M&As

Technology improvements in the form of anticipated benefits of C-B M&As are emphasised more in transition countries, which corresponds to Lall's (2002) findings, who stressed that technology improvement as a result of C-B M&As was especially evident in countries, where technology levels were low prior to the foreign investment. The difference in the role of technology improvement in transition countries compared to developed European countries also needs to be stressed. In the first, the function of closing the gap to the developed countries is stressed, while in the latter it mainly contributes to consolidating strategic industries[3]. Second to technology improvement, the respondents see the development of managerial skills, support for strategy of individual industries and rise of national competitiveness as benefits of C-B M&As. There are no significant differences in the answers on these benefits between the two groups of countries; however the respondents in transition countries do evaluate them slightly higher. Both groups of countries expect C-B M&As to bring benefits in the form of support to the transition process, which can be attributed to the fact that with dynamic growth, as a characteristic of transition, C-B M&As appear both in developed and transition countries. As the least important anticipated benefits of C-B M&As, the respondents state benefits in the form of external and internal pressures on domestic economic policies, which are more expected in transition than in developed countries due to the transition process. The results of questions on the

[3] A typical example is the consolidation of military vehicles industry in Europe (see Baumann, 2003).

anticipated benefits of C-B M&As in the future correspond to the results of numerous studies where authors proved benefits of C-B M&As. According to Davis et al. (1993), the reason for C-B M&As lies in market entry, while Bertrand & Zitouna (2006), Bertrand & Zuniga (2006) see the main contribution of C-B M&As to be in know-how transfer, increased productivity and development of R&D facilities. According to Finkelstein (1999), the positive effect of C-B M&As is noted especially in technology development to which Neto et al. (2008) added know-how transfer and Gallagher & Zarsky (2006) the development of managerial skills. A comparison of results provided by our empirical analysis with other often quoted studies thus shows realistic expectations of the professional public concerning the benefits that C-B M&As are supposed to bring.

The next segment shows answers to the question to what extent have C-B M&As influenced privatisation income in the host country. The results are shown in Figure 4.

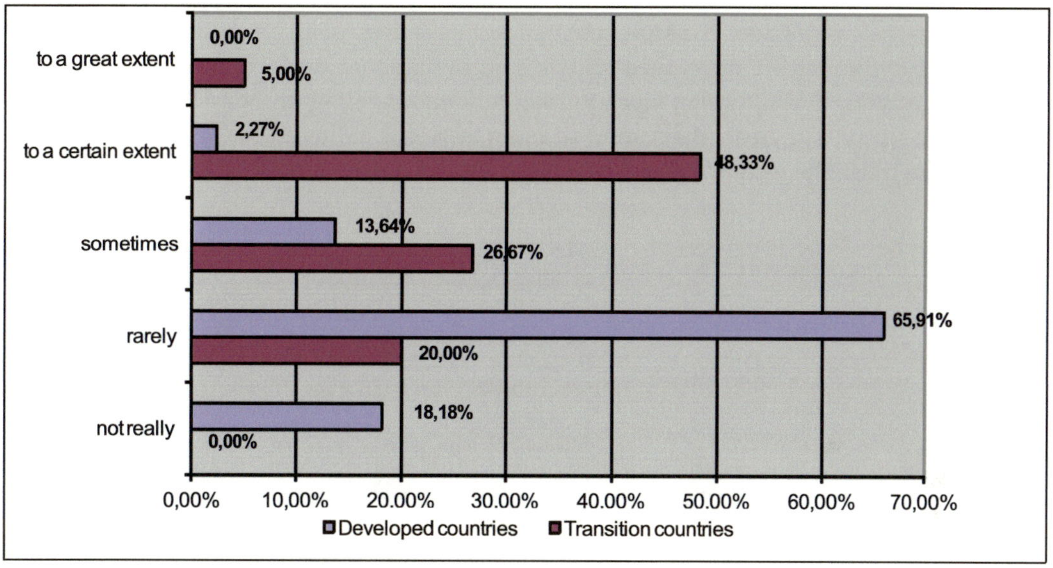

Figure 4. Contribution of C-B M&As to privatisation income

The Figure 4 shows that privatisation income increased more in transition countries. The distribution of answers in the two groups of countries shows some differences in answers. While approximately 84% of the respondents from developed countries believed that these processes did not contribute to the increase of privatisation income, only 2% believed that the contribution was substantial. On the other hand, the distribution of answers in transition countries shows a relation of approximately 20% to 53%. The result of testing the statistically significant difference in answers obtained from both groups of countries shows a statistically significant difference at the 0.000 significance level (t value = -9.328, 102 degrees of freedom).

We believe that the higher increase of privatisation income due to C-B M&As in transition countries is present, as these are countries with a prevailing privatisation model, where a substantial share of state property has been allocated to residents and mutual funds that did not produce any privatisation property. In this sense, the increase of privatisation income with limited domestic sales in these countries was understandably larger. The actual volume of the increase of income was also affected by the actual volume of C-B M&As in an individual country. The respondents in transition countries with a lower share of inward C-B M&As thus noted that the increase of privatisation income due to C-B M&As was small. The results of our empirical analysis are comparable to the study by Calderon et al. (2004) that empirically proved the increased volume of C-B M&As particularly in countries undertaking privatisation of public enterprises.

As mentioned in the previous chapter, C-B M&As can also bring threats or risks to the host country. Studies show (Hitt et al., 1991; Benacek 2000; Blonigen & Taylor, 2000; Tandon, 2000; Haller, 2005; Johnson, 2005; Tsang & Hauck, 2007; UNCTAD, 2007; Kamaraj, 2008) that typical risks of C-B M&As comprise anti-competitive behaviour of foreign affiliates, diminished R&D intensity, the closing of companies, diminished competition on the domestic market, reduction of employment, too low prices paid for domestic companies with regard to the market price, the shrinking of the national stock market because shares are being transferred to a foreign stock market and endangering economic objectives of an individual country. The treats that can most often be noted in literature were verified in our empirical analysis. The results are shown in Figure 5.

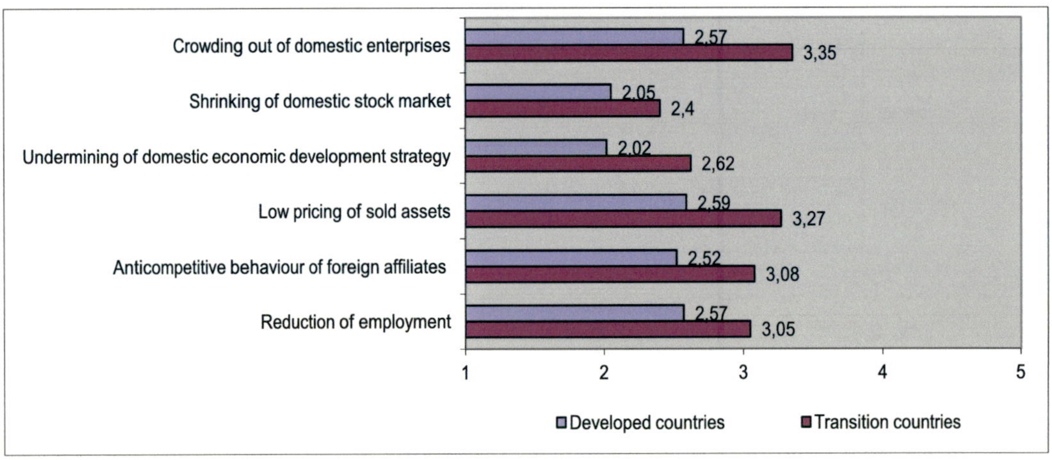

Figure 5. Realised threats of C-B M&As

With regard to the total average score, the greatest threat of C-B M&As represent the crowding out of domestic enterprises and too low prices paid for domestic companies. In these terms, the lowest threat is the shrinking of domestic stock market and undermining of the domestic economic development strategy.

There are individual differences in the classification of threats between developed and transition countries. The main difference is that in answers provided by respondents from developed countries all realised threats have been evaluated under the mean value (i.e. 3), which means that they were rarely present. In transition countries, only two out of six threats were below mean value. The respondents from transition countries gave an above the mean value to threats of the crowding out of domestic enterprises, too low prices, anti-competitive behaviour of foreign affiliates and reduction of employment. Even though the values did not substantially exceed mean values, they still indicate that the mentioned threats are more often realised in transition than in developed countries. On the other hand, the results shown in transition countries indicate the effect of globalisation and increased volume of C-B M&As on the professional public, which has started to accept these processes as a tool of privatisation and economic restructuring that as such have to happen.

The less exposed threats of C-B M&As in developed countries indicate that better developed financial markets and a favourable entrepreneurial environment in these countries enable a reduction of negative consequences of C-B M&As, however such deliberations of professionals on the other hand do not confirm the beliefs of governmental representatives which we can witness in real policies of preventing takeover bids, especially in developed European countries (see Subchapter 2.3).

Comparing the obtained results with the results of Available from studies, we can notice a larger perception of threats in terms of C-B M&As in transition countries, even in the study by Gallagher & Zarsky (2006). They proved that negative impacts of these processes are usually present in poorer and less developed countries. The results of the empirical analysis are also similar to the results of Lall's study (2002) that has proven that the threat of crowding out of domestic firms because of C-B M&As, which the respondents in our empirical analysis mostly ranked the highest, can happen in all countries regardless of the development level if the foreign firm has privileged access to local factors (capital and skills) relative to local competitors.

The respondents in our study did not especially stress the threat of reduction of employment because of C-B M&As, which is often the subject of discussion in literature (UNCTAD 2007). This allows us to conclude that the professional public is aware that the threat of reduction of employment can occur at the time of entering a foreign market, especially as C-B M&As do not open new production capacities. In the long run, once an acquired company strengthens its market position, C-B M&As can contribute to increased employment in the host country.

Within the framework of effects of C-B M&As, we also checked the frequency of the threat of asset stripping and closing of companies due to C-B M&As, which was especially stressed by Lall (2002, 7) as a consequence of these processes. The results are shown in Figures 6 and 7.

As seen in Figure 6, the threat of asset stripping and closing of firms due to C-B M&As was realised only in individual cases, which is also indicated by the total mean value that is close to the mean value standing at 3.12. The table shows that the answers substantially differ in both groups of countries. On the one hand, about 7% of the respondents from developed countries believe that this did not happen and approximately 32% believe that it happened often or even very often. Among the transition countries, the first result stands at approximately 3% and the second at 43%. The difference in the answers between both groups of countries is not statistically significant.

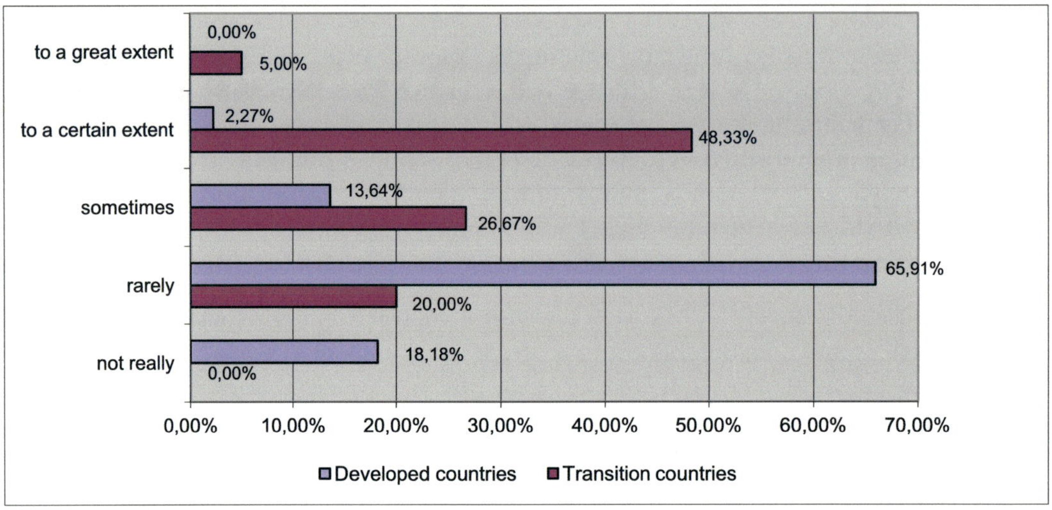

Figure 6. Have C-B M&As caused asset stripping and closing of firms?

The threat of closing R&D facilities because of C-B M&As was realised to an even smaller extent than the previous threat. Different authors have proven the effect of C-B M&As on R&D facilities in different ways. While Hitt et al. (1991) stressed the reduced volume or closing of R&D facilities as a highly likely consequence in the event of C-B M&As, Bae & Seungwook (2001), Cassiman et al. (2005) Bertrand & Zuniga (2006) have shown that the effect of C-B M&As on the R&D department is positive and a consequence of continual investments of foreign investors in these departments. The authors believe that in evaluating this effect, we need to consider that the foreign acquisition of a company changes the R&D department's function in such a company. It often happens that prior to the foreign acquisition the domestic company used the R&D department predominantly to support local products or to adapt its products to the market, while once a foreign owner enters, the R&D department is specialised to become a department for shaping knowledge and ideas. The extent to which C-B M&As have caused the closing or reduction of R&D facilities is shown in the figure below.

The figure shows that the mentioned threat was not a very often one in our sample of countries and it appeared more often in transition countries. In developed countries, 75% of the respondents said it happened rarely or very rarely, while respondents from transition countries gave different answers. 15% of the respondents believed that it happened often or very often and 40% believed that it rarely happened. The difference in the answers provided by the respondents from developed and from transition countries is statistically significant ($t = -3.165$, 102 degrees of freedom).

The presented results show that the professionals comprising our study sample predominantly hold a positive view of C-B M&As and also see these processes as a component part of opening and growth of host countries. On the other hand and as mentioned before, the reactions of the real economic policy on C-B M&As (some examples are presented in

Subchapter 3.2) show the anxiety of individual countries that as a consequence of successful acquisitions their influence in individual activities and the economy in general could diminish. Even though we can speak of a dominance of supply side economics in 2008, it is also clear that each opening results in a reduced influence of national politics. This also results in reduced control of politics over the realisation of economic objectives that the national politics are interested in, as their political term depends on their realisations.

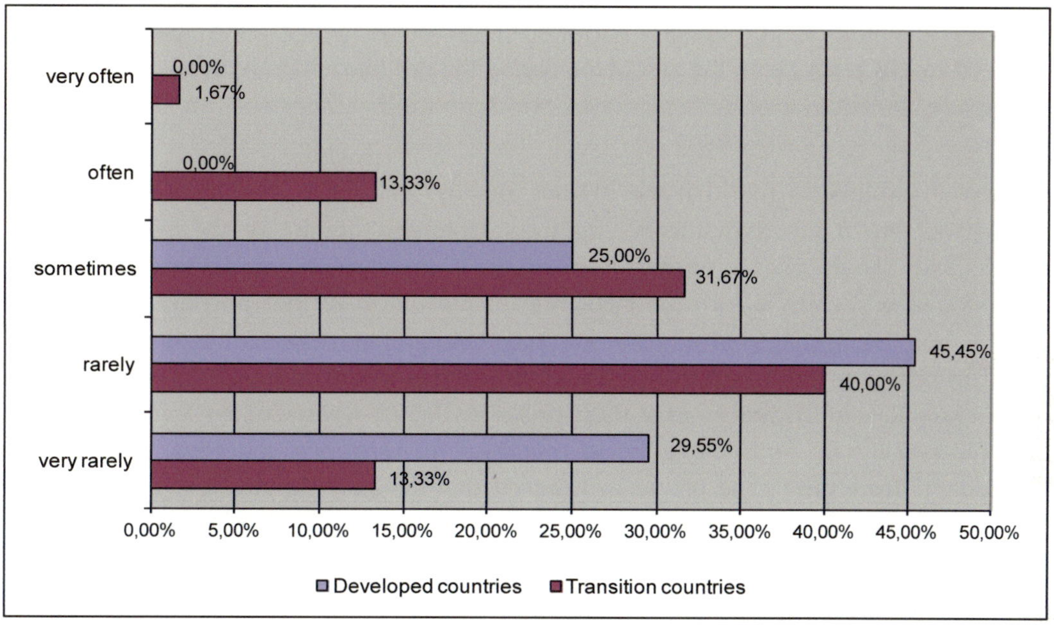

Figure 7. Have C-B M&As caused ceasing of R&D facilities?

Greater emphasis on economic effects and their consequences for the growth of the national economy that was placed by the professional public comprising our study sample shows that economic objectives – even those that are related to social balance (a high employment rate, dynamic growth of the number and size of national companies) – are not a priority of experts. This allows us to explain their more open attitude towards C-B M&As. However, we also need to consider the asymmetry of information Available from to professionals and to the politicians. While the industry is included in individual C-B M&As projects, especially in the role of advisors, members of supervisory boards or researchers that evaluate these processes on the basis of statistical data or as evaluators of practices that they learn about from the media, the politics on the other hand has access to inside information about the majority of C-B M&As but usually also possesses partially lacking knowledge about C-B M&As and their short-term and long-term effects.

3.3. Analysis of governmental attitudes towards C-B M&As

As noted previously, despite the increased trend of liberalisation of ICF, there have been numerous governmental interventions in recent years when dealing with C-B M&As.

Politicians usually justify these interventions with the argument that they are protecting a "national champion" (Kekic, 2006, 6) that a foreign company should not acquire because of strategic interests of the host country. However, we are dealing with the fear that a completely open market would result in loss of control over the country's strategic industries (Lin, 2008). Governmental interventions in ICF processes can take different forms. On the one hand, there are extreme interventions with governments publishing a list of sectors that are closed to foreigner investors, as was seen in France and Germany (Yased 2007). On the other hand, there are also mild interventions where governments are being included in C-B M&As with the aim of increasing the positive effects of these processes and a complete liberalisation of these processes, which means that they are left to the laws of the market.

In light of the notable role that the EU has already realised in the liberalisation of C-B M&As, we were in our study interested in the respondents' opinion on the role that the EU and the state should play in further liberalisation of these processes. The total mean score (3.65) shows a slightly more prominent role of the EU in further liberalisation of such process but the opinions of experts are split. Individual respondents from transition countries believe that this field should be fully regulated by the state (3.3%) or that the state needs to regulate individual cases of these processes (8.3%), while we cannot find advocates of a consistent state control over these processes in developed countries. 13.6% of the respondents from developed countries believed that the state should have a visible role. Literature and the media (Dixon, 2004; Gordon, 2006; Dempsey, 2006; Ahearn, 2006; Capron & Guillen, 2006; EUROMOVE, 2006) show that countries defend their "national interests", so we assume that in this case the respondents probably referred to the inclusion of an individual country in the field of protecting the country's firms from strategic industries. This is also shown by studies published by Wruuck (2006), OECD (2007) and Lin (2008), which stress fear of losing control over strategic industries due to C-B M&As.

It is interesting that the respondents in our empirical analysis expect a greater role to be played by the EU in overcoming obstacles of C-B M&As (the mean value of answers given by respondents from transition countries stands at 3.47 and of those from developed countries at 3.91). This shows the difference between the viewpoints held by the professional public on the one hand and the real governmental policy on the other. In order to corroborate this claim, we specifically analysed the difference between the viewpoints expressed by the professionals in our empirical analysis and the real policy of European governments in developed countries. The real policy of developed countries towards these processes was shown in Subchapter 3.2. We here considered not only the CMS (2008) study and the report by Marchick & Slaughter (2008) but also the Directive on Takeover Bids. The Directive on Takeover Bids was adopted only in 2004 following indecisive support of the member states and after more than 17 years of coordination and negotiations (Wymeersch, 2008). For it to be adopted, it was important to allow the member states that upon transferring this legislation into their national legal system, they are allowed to keep antitakeover defence mechanisms. The CMS (2008) study and the report by Marchick &

Slaughter (2008) relate to concrete cases on interventionism of individual countries and clearly show the defence policy of developed host countries when dealing with C-B M&As in strategic industries. From the viewpoint of the professional public, as our study has shown, we have their viewpoints on the role of the EU in overcoming obstacles to C-B M&As. The mean value of the importance of the EU in overcoming obstacles to ICF obtained from respondents from European developed countries was rather high (3.9), so we believe that this result clearly shows the difference between the viewpoints of the professional public on the one hand and the real economic policy of the same countries on the other. In transition countries however, there are not so many relevant cases of governmental interventions in these processes in terms of real policy. Comparing both groups of countries, the cases presented under 3.2 show a major difference between real economic policy towards these processes. On the other hand however, even though the difference in the answers provided by the professional public from transition countries is statistically significant ($t = 2.291$, 102 degrees of freedom), the previously stated allows us to claim that the difference is smaller on the level of the professional public than on the level of the real economic policy.

Our study verified the attitude of the government towards C-B M&As with three questions. We were interested in the frequency of governmental actions in order to increase positive effects of C-B M&As, the frequency of governmental interventions in C-B M&As in order to protect the national economy and shareholders and the opinion of the professionals on the need for governmental interventions in order to protect strategically important sectors.

Governmental activity in order to increase positive effects of C-B M&As turned out to be very rare according to our respondents. More detailed results are evident from the figure below.

As evident from Figure 8, average answers prevail together with answers depicting governments as being inactive. Comparing answers from both groups of countries, we can note that it was the governments of developed countries that more often intervened in C-B M&As in order to increase positive effects. In a sense, this is probably due to the dimension of effects of C-B M&As on the economic structure of developed countries, but 13% is still not a sufficient share with regard to all the respondents in order to be able to claim such a fact. The independent sample t-test did not show a statistically significant difference in the answers from both groups of countries.

Politicians justify numerous governmental interventions with protecting shareholders and domestic companies. FDI can positively affect shareholders when the acquired company and the acquiring company record large profits. Results of different studies (Hughes 1993; Alberts & Varaiya, 1989) however indicate that this rarely happens. A negative effect of C-B M&As on shareholders might be due to the fact that the management of the acquiring company pays a premium for protecting the acquisition, while in cases of dispersed ownership with numerous stockholders, control over the work of management is not possible. For these reasons, in his study published already in 1989, Caves proposed governmental interventions to protect shareholders in the event of C-B M&As (Caves, 1989). In our study, the provided answers on the frequency of governmental interventions in order to protect the national economy and shareholders have shown very different reactions of governments in this field. Limit values have a very similar distribution, which is especially evident in transition countries where approximately 18% of the respondents did not remember any such interventions, 22% remembered very few and 33% remembered many or a lot. The respondents from developed countries answered mainly in the direction of the government's inactivity in this field, but the shares of answers are again unevenly distributed along the Likert scale. 43% of the respondents stresses that there were no interventions or that they were very rare and 32% remembered such interventions. The independent sample t-test did not show a statistically significant difference in the answers from both groups of countries.

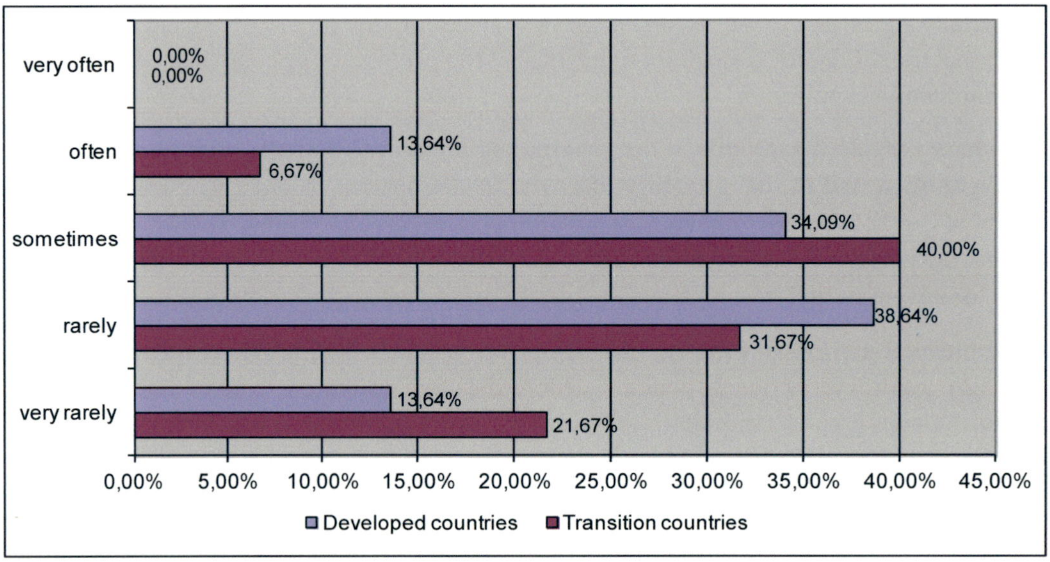

Figure 8. Specific policy measures

The last question in the set aiming to define governmental attitudes towards these processes looked into the opinion of the professional public about the needs for governmental interventions in host countries when C-B M&As occur in industries that are of great importance to the country.

As seen in Figure 9, the opinions of the professional public differ, however the prevailing consensus is that only chosen sectors have to be protected. 11% of the respondents from developed countries believe that the government should not control even the most important sectors. 29 % believes that the government can exercise control in the majority of cases. In transition countries, more precaution was shown and governmental interventions in C-B M&As were more stressed in cases where protection of important strategic sectors is concerned. The difference in the answers between both groups of countries is not statistically significant.

The absence of statistically significant differences in the answers between both groups of countries in verifying governmental reactions to C-B M&As again shows that the difference in how these processes are evaluated in the two groups of countries is smaller on the level of the professional public than on policy level.

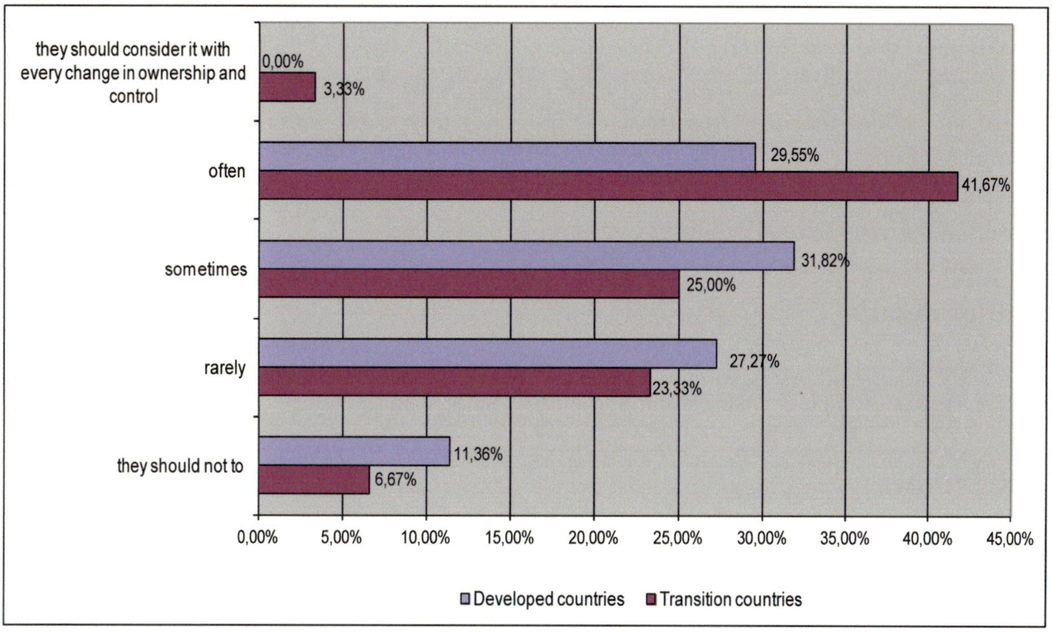

Figure 9. Should countries try to exercise policy measures so as to hinder changes in ownership and control in the most important sectors and companies?

4. Conclusion

The results of the empirical analysis stress the emphasis of positive effects of cross-border mergers and acquisition in European developed and transition countries. The professional public believes them to occur mostly in the form of access to new markets, technology improvements and know-how transfer. On the other hand, the professional public also points to certain threats of such processes, especially in the form of crowding out domestic firms, low pricing of sold assets and anti-competitive behaviour of foreign affiliates.

As the benefits have nevertheless been stressed more than threats, we can claim that the cases noted in real economic policy towards these processes show that there is a difference between the viewpoints of professionals and the measures of real economic policy. The viewpoints expressed by professionals do not show nearly as much guard as the reactions of the real economic policy when foreign bidders enter domestic industries and companies of strategic importance.

This difference between the professional public and politics is especially evident in European developed countries. They also stressed positive effects of C-B M&As over the negative ones. Such a result was however anticipated, as in the case of developed countries we are dealing with an economic environment and an infrastructure that is able to utilise more spillover effects with such investments. But when discussing the effects of international capital flows on national economic objectives, we can on the other hand see that the primary interest of the governments lies in protecting objectives such as full employment and maintaining the domestic economic competition. This is why developed countries are usually less inclined to foreign investments if they deal with increased foreign control in sectors that are important for the most important economic objectives. Actual examples of interventions in C-B M&As in the past allow us to conclude that the real economic policy is in contradiction with the rational evaluation of the effects of C-B M&As as seen in the professional public in our empirical analysis.

Author details

Anita Maček
DOBA Faculty of Applied Business and Social Studies Maribor, Slovenia

5. References

Ahearn, R. (2006). Europe: Rising Economic Nationalism? *CRS Report for Congress. Order Code RS22468.*

Aitken, B. & Harrison, A. (1999). Do domestic firms benefit from direct foreign investment? Evidence from Venezuela. *The American Economic Review,* Vol.89, No.3, pp. 605-618, ISSN 0002-8282.

Alberts, W.W. & Varayia, N.P. (1989). Assessing the Profitability of Growth by Acquisition: A Premium Recapture Approach. *International Journal of Industrial Organization,* No.7, pp. 136–55, ISSN 0167-7187.

Alfaro, L. (2003). *Foreign Direct Investment and Growth: Does the Sector Matter?* 02.04.2009, Available from: http://www.grips.ac.jp/teacher/oono/hp/docu01/paper14.pdf.

Aslanoglu, E. (2000). Spillover effects of foreign direct investments on Turkish manufacturing industry. *Journal of International Development,* No.12, pp. 1111-1130, ISSN 1099-1328.

Bae, S. C. & Seungwook, N. (2001). Multinational Corporations versus Domestic Corporations: A Comparative Study of R&D Investment Activities. *Journal of Multinational Financial Management,* No.11, pp. 89-104, ISSN 1042-444X.

Baliamoune-Lutz, M. N. (2004). Does FDI contribute to economic growth? Knowledge about the effects of FDI improves negotiating positions and reduces risk for firms investing in developing countries. *Business Economics,* Vol.39, No.2, pp. 49–56, ISSN: 0007-666X.

Barro, R. (1991). Economic Growth in a Cross Section of Countries. *Quarterly Journal of Economics,* Vol. CVI, No.2, pp. 407-444, ISSN 0033-5533.

Barro, R. & Sala, M. (1995). Economic Growth. New York: McGraw-Hill, Chap. 5.

Baumann, H. (2003). The consolidation of the military vehicles industry in Western Europe and the United States. *Background paper for the SIPRI Yearbook 2003.*

Benacek, V. (2000). Foreign Direct Investment in the Czech Economy. *Politicka ekonomie,* No.1, pp. 7–24, ISSN: 0032-3233.

Bertrand, O. & Zitouna, H. (2006). Trade liberalization and industrial restructuring: the role of cross-border mergers and acquisitions. *Journal of Economics and Management Strategy,* No.15, pp.479–515, ISSN: 1530-9134.

Bertrand, O., & Zuniga, P. (2006). R&D and M&A: Are cross-border M&A different? An investigation on OECD countries. *International Journal of Industrial Organization*, Vol.24, No.2, pp. 401–423, ISSN 0167-7187.

Bevan, A. A. & Saul, E. (2000). The Determinants of Foreign Direct Investment in Transition Economies, William Davidson Institute Working Paper 342.

Blomström, M. & Persson, H. (1983). Foreign Investment and Spillover Efficiency in an Underdeveloped Economy: Evidence from the Mexican Manufactoring Industry. *World Development,* Vol.11, No.6, pp.493–501, ISSN: 0305-750X.

Blomström, M. & Wolf, E. (1994). Multinational Corporations and Productivity Convergence in Mexico. In: *Convergence of Productivity: Cross – National Studies and Historical Evidence,* Baumol W., Nelson R. & Wolff E., (Ed.). Oxford: University Press.

Blonigen, B. & Taylor, C. (2000). R&D activity and acquisitions in High Technology Industries: Evidence from the US Electronics Industry. *Journal of Industrial Economics,* Vol.47, No.1, pp. 47-71, ISSN 0022-1821.

Borensztein, E., De Gregorio, J., & Lee, J-W. (1995). How Does Foreign Direct Investment Affect Economic Growth? *National Bureau of Economic Research Working Papers 5057*.

Calderon, C., Loayza, N. & Serven, L. (2004). Greenfield foreign direct investment and mergers and acquisitions - feedback and macroeconomic effects. *The World Bank Policy Research Working Paper 3192.*

Cantwell, J. (1989). *Technological Innovation and Multinational Corporations*, pp. 239, ISBN 0631138471, Basil Blackwell, Oxford.

Capron, L., & Guillen, M. (2006). *Fighting economic nationalism in deals,* 29.11.2008, Available from: http://www.fco.cat/files/imatges/Butlleti%2067/FT4.pdf.

Cassiman, B., Colombo, M.G., Garrone, P. & Veugelers, R. (2005). The Impact of M&A on the R&D Process: An Empirical Analysis of the Role of Technological- and Marketrelatedness. *Research Policy,* No. 34, pp. 195-220, ISSN: 0048- 7333.

Caves, R. E. (1974). Multinational firms, Competition and Productivity in Host-Country Markets. *Economica,* Vol. 41, No. 162, pp. 176–193.

Caves, R. E. (1989). Mergers, Takeovers and Economic Efficiency: Foresight vs. Insight. *International Journal of Industrial Organization,* No. 7, pp. 151-174, ISSN: 0167-7187.

Chen, C. (1996). Regional determinants of foreign direct investment in Mainland China. *Journal of Economic Studies,* No. 23, pp. 18-30, ISSN 0144-3585.

Cheng, L. K., & Kwan, Y. K. (2000). What are the determinants of the location of foreign direct investment? The Chinese experience. *Journal of International Economics,* No. 51, pp. 379-400, ISSN: 0022-1996.

CMS. (2008). *Fortress Europe. The risk of rising protectionism in Europe*, 07.01.2009. Available from: http://www.cmslegal.com/newsmedia/news/newsdetail/pages/default.aspx?PublicationGuid=64cb4272-74d7-436b-9956-055d1ffab1b7.

Davis, E., Shore, G. & Thompson, D. (1993). Continental Mergers Are Different. In European Mergers and Merger Policy Bishop, M.J., Kay, (Ed.). University Press, Cambridge.

Dempsey, J. (2006). New Polish Chief a Skeptic on Integrated Europe. *New York Times*, 9. 3. 2006, Accessed 18.01.2009. Available from: http://query.nytimes.com/gst/fullpage.html?res=9D0DEEDA1231F93AA35750C0A9609C8B63&sec=&spon=.

Dixon, C. (2004). Post-crisis restructuring: foreign ownership, corporate resistance and economic nationalism in Thailand. *Journal of Contemporary Southeast Asia*, No. 26, pp. 45–72.

Driffield, N. (2001). The Impact on Domestic Productivity of Inward Investment in the UK. Manshester School, Vol. 69, No. 1, pp. 103–119.

EGIP - European Group for investor protection (2005), 22.09.2007. Available from: http://www.egip.org/root/index.php?page_id=128.

Estrin, S., Hughes, K., & Todd, S. (1997). Foreign Direct Investment in Central and Eastern Europe. London: Royal Institute of International Affairs.

EUROMOVE - Euopean Movement UK (2006). *The EU and "Economic Nationalism"*, 29.11.2008. Available from: http://www.euromove.org.uk/index.php?id=6529.

Finkelstein, S. (1999). Safe ways to cross the merger minefield. Financial Times Mastering Global Business: The Complete MBA Companion in Global Business. London: Financial Times Pitman Publishing, pp. 199-123.

Gallagher, K. P. & Zarsky L. (2006). Rethinking Foreign Investment for Development. Post-autistic Economics review 37.

GFC/Net - Global Financial Communication Network (2007). *Economic Patriotism/Nationalism Likely to Intensify According to Business Journalists Worldwide. Business Wire*, 12.11.2007. Available from: http://www.allbusiness.com/trade-development/trade-development-finance/5420005-1.html.

Globerman, S. (1979). Foreign Direct Investment and Spillover Efficiency Benefits in Canadian Manufactoring Industries. *Canadian Journal of Economics*, No. 12, pp. 42–56, ISSN 1540-5982.

Gordon P. (2006). Cross-Border Acquisitions Facing Growing Interference From Tighter Security Reviews. In: *Global Finance*, 23.05.2007, Available from: http://www.allbusiness.com/government/4088375-1.html.

Haller, S. A. (2005). The Impact of Multinational Entry on Domestic Market Structure and R&D. *Economics Working Papers 16*. European University Institute.

Heufers, R. (2008). National champions - a waste of taxpayer's money, In: Fnst freiheit organization, 30.06.2008, Available from: http://www.fnst-freiheit.org/webcom/show_article.php/_c-705/_nr-149/printmode-true/i.html.

Hill, C. W. L. (2005). *International Business: competing in the global marketplace*. New York: McGraw-Hill Irvin.

Hitt, M. A., Hoskisson, R.E., Ireland, R.D. & Harrison, J.S. (1991). Effects of acquisitions on R&D inputs and outputs. *Academy of Management Journal,* Vol. 34, No. 3, pp. 693–706, ISSN: 0001-4273.

Hughes, A. (1993). Mergers and Economic Performance in the UK: A Survey of the Empirical Evidence 1950-90. In European Mergers and Merger Polic, M., Bishop & Kay J., (Ed.) Oxford: University Press.

Ikiara, M. M. (2003). Foreign Direct Investment (FDI), Technology Transfer, and Poverty Alleviation: Africa's Hopes and Dilemma. *ATPS special paper series 16*, 05.05.2008, Available from: http://www.atpsnet.org/pubs/specialpaper/SPS%2016.pdf.

Jensen, C. M. (2003). The Role of FDI in the Re-location of Industrial Activity. The Impact of Foreign Direct Investment on Regional Development in Poland. *Workpackage 4.*

Johnson, A. (2005). The effects of FDI inflows on host country economic growth. In: ETS, 22.02.2009, Available from: http://www.etsg.org/ETSG2005/papers/johnson.pdf.

Kamaraj, C. (2008). *Foreign Direct Investment*, 04.03.2009, Available from: http://www.indianmba.com/Occasional_Papers/OP203/op203.html.

Kawai, H. (1994). International Comparative Analysis of Economic Growth: Liberalization and Productivity. *Developing Economies*, No. 32, pp. 372-397, ISSN: 0012-1533.

Kekic, L. (2006). Trends in foreign direct investment and crossborder mergers and acquisitions. *The Economist Intelligence Unit 26.*

Kokko, A. (2006). The Home Country Effects of FDI In Developed Economies. *The European Institute of Japanese Studies Working Paper Series 225.*

Kokko, A., Tansini, R., & Zejan, M.C. (1996). Local technological capability and productivity spillovers from FDI in the Uruguayan manufacturing sector. *The Journal of Development Studies,* No. 32, pp. 602-611, ISSN 0022-0388.

Kolasa, M. (2008). How does FDI inflow affect productivity of domestic firms? The role of horizontal and vertical spillovers, absorptive capacity and competition. *The Journal of International Trade & Economic Development,* Vol. 17, No. 1, pp. 155 – 173, ISSN 0963-8199.

Lall, S. (2002). Implications of Cross-Border Mergers and Acquisitions by TNCs in Developing Countries: A Beginner's Guide. *QEH Working Paper Series 88.*

Li, D. D. & Chen, Q. (1998). *Why Aren't Foreign Direct Investments Always Welcome? – A Political Economy Analysis*. University of Michigan, mimeo.

Lin, C. H. (2008). Role of Foreign Direct Investment in Telecommunication Industries: A Developing Countries' Perspective. *Contemporary Management Research,* Vol. 4, No. 1, pp. 29–42.

Lipsey, R. E. (1999). The role of foreign direct investment in international capital flows. *National Bureau of Economic Research Working Paper 7094.*

Lipsey, R. E. (2001). Foreign Direct Investment and the Operations of Multinational Firms: Concepts, History and Data, *National Bureau of Economic Research Working Paper 8665.*

Lipsey, R. E. (2002). Home and Host Country Effects of FDI, *Paper for ISIT Conference on Challenges to Globalization.*

Liu, X., Siler, P., Wang, C. & Wei Y. (2000). Productivity Spillovers from Foreign Direct Investment: Evidence from UK Industry Level Panel Data. *Journal of International Business Studies,* Vol. 31, No. 3, pp. 407–425, ISSN 0047-2506.

Maček, A. (2008). Regulacija mednarodnih tokov kapitala – komu naj služi? *Bančni vestnik,* Vol. 57, No. 10, pp. 30-33, ISSN 0005-4631.

Maček, A. (2009). Čezmejne združitve in prevzemi kot dejavnik tranzicije v EU, *Doktorska disertacija.* Maribor: Ekonomsko-poslovna fakulteta.

Maček, A., & Ovin, R. (2006). Cross-border mergers and acquisitions - a cause for growing economic nationalism? *Global Business & Economic Anthotology.*

Marchick, D. M. & Slaughter, M.J. (2008). Global FDI policy: correcting a protectionist drift. In: CSR 32, 15.06.2008, Available from: http://www.cfr.org/content/publications/attachments/FDI_CSR34.pdf.

Mencinger, J. (2004). Tuje neposredne naložbe-mana z neba? *Gospodarska gibanja,* No. 362, pp. 25-44, ISSN 0351-0360.

Meyer, K., & Nguyen, V. H. (2003). Foreign Investor's Entry Strategies and Sub-national Institutions in Emerging Markets. *DRC Working Papers Foreign Direct Investment in Emerging Markets 14.* Centre for New and Emerging Markets, London Business School.

Mottaleb, K. A. (2007). Determinants of Foreign Direct Investment and Its Impact on Economic Growth in Developing Countries, 04.03.2009, Available from: http://mpra.ub.uni-muenchen.de/9457/1/MPRA_paper_9457.pdf.

Nadiri, M. I. (1991). Innovations and Technological Spillovers. *Working Paper 31.* New York University.

Neto, P., Brandao, A. & Cerqueira A. (2008). The impact of FDI, Cross-Border Mergers & Acquisitions and Greenfield Investment on Economic Growth. *FEP working paper 291.*

Neuhaus, M. (2006). The Impact of FDI on Economic Growth an Analysis for the Transition Countries of Central and Eastern Europe. Physica Verlag.

Nonnemberg. M. B. & de Mendonça M. J. C. (2004) The Determinants of Foreign Direct Investment in Developing Countries. In*: Anais do XXXII Encontro Nacional de Economia 61,* 02.02.2009, Available from: http://ideas.repec.org/p/anp/en2004/061.html.

OECD - Organization for Economic Co-operation and Development. (2007). Freedom of Invesment in a Changing World. *International Investment Perspectives.*

Ovin, R. (2003). Ekonomska politika Slovenije na poti v odprto gospodarstvo, *Economic and Business Review,* No. 5, pp. 63-73, ISSN 1580- 0466.

Pain, N. (2001). *Inward Investment, Technological Change and Growth. The impact of Multinational Corporations on the UK Economy*. Houndsmills: Pelgrave.

Perez, T. (1998). *Multinational Enterprises and Technological Spillovers*. The Netherlands: Harwood Academic Publishers.

Perez, R. P. (2008). A regional approach to study technology transfer through foreign direct investment: The electronics industry in two Mexican regions. *Research Policy,* Vol. 37, No. 5, pp. 849-860, ISSN 0048- 7333.

Reisen, H. (1999). After the Great Asian Slump: Towards a Coherent Approach to Global Capital Flows. *Policy Brief 16*. Paris: OECD Development Centre.

Salvatore, D. (1998). *International Economics*. New Yersey: Prentice Hall, ISBN: 0070549508.

Stephan, J. (2005). *Technology Transfer via Foreign Direct Investment in Central and Eastern Europe. Theory, Method of Research and Empirical Evidence.* England: Palgrave Macmillan.

Tandon, Y. (2000). M&A is takeover of firms in north, economies in south. Geneva. In: Third world network, 04.02.2005, Available from:
http://www.twnside.org.sg/title/firms.htm.

Taylor & Francis Group. (2004). *Determinants Of Foreign Direct Investment: Empirical Evidence From EU Accession Candidates,* 02.04.2009, Available from:
http://jobfunctions.bnet.com/abstract.aspx?docid=313929.

Torlak, E. (2004). *Foreign Direct Investment, Technology Transfer, and Productivity Growth in Transition Countries Empirical Evidence from Panel Data,* 05.04.2009. Available from: http://ideas.repec.org/p/got/cegedp/26.html.

Tsang, M. & Hauck, D. (2007) Stock Markets Contract as M&A Overtakes Equity Sales. In: Bloomberg.com, 05.06.2008, Available from:
http://www.bloomberg.com/apps/news?pid=20601087&sid=aOgjATE5e50s&refer=.

UNCTAD - United Nations Conference on Trade and Development. (1991). *World Investment Report 1991, The triad in foreign direct investment.* New York.

UNCTAD - United Nations Conference on Trade and Development. (1998). *World Investment Report 1998. Trends and Determinants.* New York.

UNCTAD - United Nations Conference on Trade and Development (2000a) World Investment Report 2000. *Cross-Border Mergers and Acquisitions and Developement.* New York and Geneva, ISBN 92-1-112490-5

UNCTAD - United Nations Conference on Trade and Development (2000b) Impact of cross-Border mergers and acquisitions on development and policy issues for consideration. In: Unctad.org., 21.03.2008, Available from:
http://www.unctad.org/en/docs/c2em7l1.en.pdf.

UNCTAD - United Nations Conference on Trade and Development (2001) *World Investment Report 2001, Promoting linkages.* ISBN 92-1-112523-5, New York and Geneva.

UNCTAD - United Nations Conference on Trade and Development. (2002). *World Investment Report 2002, Transnational Corporations and Export Competitiveness.* ISBN 92-1-112551-0, New York and Geneva.

UNCTAD - United Nations Conference on Trade and Development. (2003). *World Investment Report 2003, FDI policies for Development: National and International perspectives.* ISBN 92-1-112580-4, New York and Geneva.

UNCTAD - United Nations Conference on Trade and Development. (2005). *World Investment Report 2005, Ttransnational Corporations and the internationalization of R&D.* ISBN 92-1-112667-3, New York and Geneva,

UNCTAD - United Nations Conference on Trade and Development (2006) World Investment Report 2006, FDI from Developing and Transition Economies, Implications for Development. ISBN 92-1-112703-4, New York and Geneva.

UNCTAD - United Nations Conference on Trade and Development (2007). World Investment Report 2007, Transnational Corporations, Extractive Industries and Development. ISBN 978-92-1-112718-8, New York and Geneva.

UNCTAD - United Nations Conference on Trade and Development. (2008). World Investment Report 2008, Transnational Corporations and the Infrastructure Challenge. ISBN 978-92-1-112755-3, New York and Geneva.

UNCTAD - United Nations Conference on Trade and Development (2011) World Investment Report 2011, Non-equity modes of international production and development. ISBN 978-92-1-112828-4, New York and Geneva.

Vaara, E, Tienari, J., Sauri, N. & Bjoerkman, I. (2001). Global Capitalism Meets National Spirit: Discourses in Media Texts on a Cross-Border Acquisition. *Paper presented at the 2nd Critical Studies Conference, Manchester,* 09.11.2004, Available from: http://www.mngt.waikato.ac.nz/ejrot/cmsconference/2001/Papers/Lanaguage%20of%20New%20Capitalism/Vaara.pdf.

Wruuck, P. (2006). *Economic Patriotism – Blind Alley in a Globalized World?* In: *YaleGlobal,* 8. 8. 2006. Accessed 20.07.2008, Available from: http://yaleglobal.yale.edu/article.print?id=7939.

Wymeersch, E. (2008). The Takeover Directive, light and darkness. Financial Law Institute. *Working paper series 2008-01.*

Yased - International Investors Association of Turkey. (2007). *Foreign Direct Investments Report,* 04.02.2009, Available from: http://www.turkey-now.org/db/Docs/YASED_FDIReport-june07.pdf..

Chapter 7

Transboundary Animal Diseases and International Trade

Andrés Cartín-Rojas

Additional information is available at the end of the chapter

http://dx.doi.org/10.5772/48151

1. Introduction

Currently, livestock sector accounts for nearly half of global agricultural economy. Recent animal health emergencies have highlighted the vulnerability of pecuary industry to epizootic episodes caused by infectious diseases. The impact of animal diseases on health and human welfare is being increasingly considered. Sixty percent of emerging diseases that affect humans are zoonoses, most of them (*about 75%*) originate from wildlife. Many of those diseases are common to productive domestic animals, due to the multiple inter-relationships and the ability of many microorganisms to mutate and to colonize new hosts. Therefore, direct impact of Transboundary Animal Diseases in agriculture and public health, constitute a serious limitation to export living animals and their products, as well for international trade. Moreover, seriously compromised food security and causing a high socioeconomic impact on agricultural exporting nations.

During the next 15 to 20 years, the demand for livestock products is considering to double, a process called "*Livestock Revolution*" driven by changing a cereal-based diet to a diet based on proteins. It is estimated that in 2015, 60% of meat and 52% of the milk, will be consumed in developing countries [27]. The increasing globalization markets, facilitates the introduction of transboundary animal disease. Trade in agricultural products is increasingly accepted as an important factor in the strategy to mitigate and reduce poverty. This indicates that developing countries also need more support and sustained efforts to achieve fully integrated within the animal health standards and food safety, since progress in these areas are bound to have a beneficial impact, not only in the ability to participate in foreign trade but also trade locally, allowing integrative markets in the poorest communities. However, is essential to generate a concerted effort to be meeting the basic elements of the Agreement on Sanitary and Phytosanitary. Therefore, recognized international organizations such as FAO, OIE, WTO and WHO recognize the need to change veterinarian's traditional view and focusing animal health services on the early epidemiological investigation and prevention of zoonoses through a holistic and transdiciplinary joint initiative called the "*One Health*".

In this conceptual chapter, topics on emerging and zoonotic diseases origin and dynamics, the importance of transboundary animal diseases for international trade of livestock commodities and possible future solutions among medical and biological disciplines is developed by reviewing relevant literatures, analyzing and exemplifying applicable case studies, identifying current trends and discussing the potential impact on developing and growth of countries' economies. With few studies in this particular area, the author adopts an inductive approach, designed to generate new understanding and propositions for further research.

2. Origins and catalysts of zoonoses and emerging diseases

Food and Agriculture Organization of the United Nations, defines Transboundary Animal Diseases (*TADs*) as: *''Those diseases with an essential impact on the economy, trade and/or food security of a group of countries, which can be easily spread to other countries, reaching epidemic proportions and that require control and eradication cooperation between different nations''* [32].

There are two major types of TADs with an economic impact on international trade: emerging diseases and zoonoses. The World Organization for Animal Health (OIE) defines emerging diseases as: *''Those that are able to expand its epidemiological spectrum, appearing in a not endemic geographic area, affecting new susceptible species; or referring to a completely unknown pathogen which is detected for the first time''*. Zoonoses are: *''Any diseases or infections which are naturally transmissible from animals to humans''* [69]. Zoonotic infections, according to its cycle can be classified as synanthropic when they have an urban cycle or exoanthropic when the cycle is sylvatic [23]. When a zoonotic disease is not well addressed by national or international public or animal health services is known as neglected zoonoses. Newly emerging diseases such as avian influenza, Nipah virus or variants in prionic diseases, also have showed the potential of the domestic productive animals-humans-wildlife interface to develop and transmit new infectious agents.

The human-animal interface is fluid and our interaction with other species, varies in response to anthropogenic factors that favor the potential for transmission of zoonotic agents [12, 77]. For instance, this is extremely important for two pragmatic issues:

1. Pests and animal diseases cause the annual loss of more than 40% in the global food supply [33], causing a direct impact in the agricultural sector, compromising seriously food security, constraint on international trade and export of living animals and their products, and causing an annual high economic impact on agricultural exporting nations.
2. TADs also have an important effect on public health. The disability-adjusted life years (*DALYs*) is a measure of overall disease burden, expressed as the number of years lost due to ill-health, disability or early death [3]. Infectious diseases also lead to compromised health and disability, accounting for nearly 30% of all DALYs worldwide

[36]. Therefore, they contribute to increase the burden of diseases and the subsequent economic loss to governments, due to the associate cost of dead, hospitalization and inabilities. Nowadays it is estimated that about 60% of currently known infectious diseases affecting humans are zoonoses. Nearly three-quarters of them are diseases which have a wild reservoir [22, 54].

Thus, emerging and zoonotic diseases characterizes by having natural nidality (a term proposed by the Russian parasitologist E. N. Pavlosvky in 1939), that means: ''The ability to maintain a dynamic focus and a permanent movement of a pathogen in a wild animal population within a geographic location, contributing to maintain a zoonotic pool''[43]. According to this theory, humans can acquire diseases (zoonoses or emerging diseases) or transmit diseases to susceptible animal populations (antropozoonoses) when the natural balance of the ecological nidus of a particular disease is disrupted. Consequently, any change or alteration affecting the ecology, distribution and abundance of its reservoirs/vectors, significantly alter the disease epidemiology [4]. Most disruptors that alter the dynamic equilibrium and favor the emergence of new pathogens are anthropogenic [24, 74]. In other words, disease emergence is actually a temporal and spatial evolutionary response to different environmental changes caused by humans [39], which has a dual component: a) first, is necessary a colonization and adaptation of a pathogen to its new host (initially the number of pathogens decrease reaching extinction, but some organisms will survive and increase their virulence), this process is called microbial traffic, b) the subsequent spread of the pathogen within the new susceptible population (greatly favored by anthropogenic changes) [84]. Therefore, TADs have a multicasual origin; some factors associated with this process include: a) Trade and international travel (increased frequency and speed of local and international travel, fostered by the globalization process promotes the spread of microorganisms on a global scale), b) Changes agricultural practices (animal domestication was one of the main promoters of microbial evolution by facilitating the availability of new susceptible hosts at high densities, due to the intensification of livestock systems), c) Climate change (which causes changes eco-geographical distribution of vectors), d) Reduction of habitat and increased contact with wild vectors/ reservoirs, and h) Introduction of naïve wild and domestic animals to new geographic areas where the disease is endemic and immunologically unknown for them (increases zoonotic pool within a geographic region) [13, 19, 26].

3. Wildlife and their importance on international trade of livestock's products

The term global express is defined as: ''*The volumes of goods moving globally*'' [12]. The globalization of markets has contributed to the continually increasing of the gross domestic product (*GDP, a modality for measuring economies and development of nations*) in the last two decades. Thus, international trade of livestock products has become an important part of the world economy. Therefore, the current economic trend around market globalization by TADs, the increase in human population and the subsequent increase in food demand (*mainly in developing countries*), the evolution of pathogens and changes in the distribution of vectors as a direct result of climate change, seems to be the biggest challenges in the coming years to the national public and animal health systems, in terms of animal disease control and prevention of emerging zoonoses [66, 90].

Estimating that human population will increase from nearly 7 billion in 2010 to about 9.5 billion in 2050, food supply will increase too with a consequent continually rising social and environmental pressures. For example, it is estimated that by 2015, 60% of meat and 52% of milk will be consumed in developing countries [32]. Since the 1960´s global meat production has more than tripled, milk production has doubled, and egg production has almost fourfold [89]. Global production and consumption of livestock products will likely continue to rise. In Latin America meat productions represented in the 1990 decade, 30% of the entire world production and 22.7% of the exported commodities. Poultry industry grew 8% in Central America with an annual growth rate of 14%. The participation of agricultural exports in gross domestic product in Central America represented 9.7%, 4.8% in the Caribbean region and 2.7% in South America [101]. Interestingly, although developing countries contribute with a large percentage of livestock production and raw materials used in food industry, developed countries that account for only 20% richest in the world; consumes 86% of all goods and services in the world. Instead, the poorest countries in the world (*mostly located in Africa, with the exception of one (Haiti) located in the Latin American region*), ingest only 1.3% of all food world production [102].

Infectious diseases share a common pathophysiology between domestic and wildlife animals. These diseases are not only one of the largest sources of non-tariff barriers to international trade. But also, they affect the dynamism and fluidity of the agronomic input markets, either by creating higher costs of production in industries directly dependent on these inputs, or generating commercial levies to the export country on certain animal products as a direct consequence of a disease epidemic, generating an increase in the complexity of the patterns of consumption and access to competitive global markets. Additionally, are the monumental annual costs that several countries worldwide spend on control and eradication programs of TADs, as well as, the resilient and compensatory payments by governments to livestock sector after a disease outbreak [98]. The Organization of the United Nations Food and Agriculture Organization (FAO), pests and animal diseases cause the loss of more than 40% in the global food supply, being a clear threat to the residual economies of developing countries and food security of its inhabitants [35]. In general livestock´s products have increased their international trade in 4% only in the last two decades [62]. However, as a result of the emergence and re-emergence of various animal diseases, such as bovine spongiform encephalopathy (*BSE*), the annual growth of meat products decreased 2% in the late 1990s [63]. Therefore, the cost of transboundary animal diseases relates to agricultural products, to the country's economy and international markets are monumental. Thus, it is very important to create public policies focused to assure countries' food security (*especially in developing nations*) to avoid negative economic impacts caused by TADs, especially on the more susceptible social stratus.

The World Bank has estimated that zoonotic disease outbreaks in the past 10 years have cost worldwide more than $US200 billion due to loss of trade, tourism and tax revenues [67]. For example, the outbreak on Newcasttle virus in Australia on 1999 costs on trade and export losses was about $15 million [40]. The economic costs of the hog cholera epizooty in the Netherlands in 1997–1998 will approach $US 130 million. The eradication cost of African Swine Fever only in the US on 2000 was calculating on approximately $US 16.2 million [46].

In Canada, the outbreak of BSE detected in 2003 represented a loss of $US 333 million to its livestock industry, imposed a commercial blockade on Canadian beef purchases and generating a decrease of 25% in their meat metric annual tons produced and exported to United States, the main destination market. Later, United States faced a similar problem when there was an outbreak on December 2003. The first reaction of the international meat market was the immediate suspension of U.S. beef purchases, causing a loss of over 2,600 million dollars and a fall of 18% in the American beef commodities export volume only in 2004. Similarly, commercial losses to Argentina and Uruguay, as a result of the same disease were estimated at $US 400 million and $US 150 million, respectively. While the value of trade losses for the english meat industry due to BSE was egregious ($US 9.2 billion) [102].

The 1993 Food and Mouth Disease (*FMD*) outbreak in Italy cost was estimated at $US 120 million. Similarly, FMD diagnosed in Taiwan on 1997 costs approximately $US 15 billion. The outbreak of FMD in China produced a decrease of $US 1600 to 234 million on 1996-1997 in their international market [63]. Average expected annual losses due to FMD epidemics in the Netherlands were also calculated on approximately US$15 million [47]. The FMD outbreak in Korea in 2000 ended its trade with Japan, with an approximate cost of $US 300 million, enabling other exporting countries increase their participation in the Japanese market. The extreme interrelation and importance among wildlife, international trade and agricultural economy of developing countries will be widely exposed with two case studies focused on the ecoepidemiology of some emerging and zoonotic viruses.

3.1. Case study I: Orthomyxoviruses and wild birds

There are several strains types of avian influenza virus, belonging to the Orthomyxovirus genus and commonly isolated from aquatic birds, mainly orders Anseriformes and Charadriiformes. In addition, the highest ecoepidemiological prevalence is observed on migrating birds who feed on the water surface [7]. This is particularly important for Costa Rica, where more than 60% of reported bird species are migratory, found in the wetlands of some important national parks (*Tortuguero, Palo Verde, Isla del Coco and Caño Negro*), which are important wintering sites to stop during migration season, working as nesting shelters [78]. Various studies show the transmission of the influenza virus among wild and domestic birds [15].

The avian influenza virus has managed to avoid animal health barriers imposed by various international territories, expanding by more than 45 countries and causing over 100 deaths, seriously affecting the global poultry system productivity, and also generating to national health services an economic burden associated with a reduction of the workforce; product of death and direct side effects of the disease.

In commercial terms, it is estimated that more than $US200 million animals have died or been slaughtered only in Asia, where economic losses in the poultry sector are estimated in more than $US10 billion. Added to this, uncertainty about the disease spread have created a widespread fear that affects all markets and consumers, caused a decline in poultry marked consumption, and the imposition of sanitary restrictions to poultry commodities. These events led to a decrease of 8% in the international poultry trade in 2004. Nowadays, the American continent has the two biggest exporters worldwide (*Brazil and USA*) for poultry products. In this scenario, preventive measures become urgent, especially when you consider that the restoration of trade flow is slow, due to international trade embargoes which countries are subjected [86]. For example, the United Arab Emirates (*UAE*) is one of the largest importers of poultry products worldwide. In 2004 this country was the seventh largest importer of Brazilian products, corresponding to 122,000 metric tons or 4.6% of total exports for that country. South Africa is also one of the main consumer markets for poultry products in Brazil and is the largest importer in Africa. This country was the sixth largest importer in 2004, corresponding to 6% of the volume of poultry products exported by Brazil in that year. In this context, in the case of an avian flu spread in the Americas its represent a reduction of more than 270,000 metric tons to Brazilian goods [85].

It is estimate that the Latin American poultry industry, representing about 12.7% of all livestock in the region, produces 14 million metric tons of meat and 5 million metric tons of eggs annually [75]. In addition, the sector employs 0.88% of the economically active population in the continent. Therefore, the budget needed by Latin American countries for a possible outbreak of Avian Influenza is $US274 million, of which $US148 million would be to coordinate prevention and surveillance, $US72 million for animal vaccination and $US 54 million used as a compensation fund. The authors estimate that the cost of a pandemic to Latin America ranges between 1% -5% of GDP across the region. Meanwhile, it is estimated that the number of deaths range between 45,000 to 2.2 million people. Currently, is estimated that the economic impact of pandemic avian flu is over $US300 billion worldwide [2]. Therefore ecoepidemiological studies of disease in wild birds in developing nations, by the national public animal health services are of utmost importance for anticipation, monitoring, prevention and preparedness for possible disease outbreaks.

3.2. Case study II: Paramyxovirus and fruit bats

Nipah virus is a neurotropic paramyxovirus first recognized in Malaysia during 1998-1999. Subsequent epidemiological studies demonstrated that fruit bats (*genus Pteropus sp.*), are natural reservoirs and swines acts as amplifiers for humans. The large-scale deforestation occurred in Malaysia and Sumatra together with a large climatic oscillations of the phenomenon of El Niño, a widespread drought during the year 1997 that altered bat migration routes and feeding behavior producing a greater association between bats and pigs, are the main ecological disruptors associated to facilitating for the first time the introduction of this virus in Malaysian pig farms. Added to this, pig farms size and intensive management techniques (*high turnover of piglets*) allowed the virus to circulate within the population, and subsequently infect humans working with them [70].

The outcome of this outbreak can be viewed from two different angles. In terms of public health, a total of 265 cases of viral encephalitis led to 105 human deaths. However, the major implication of this emerging disease was its direct impact on Malaysian goods and livestock trade. For example, to prevent the spread of the outbreak, the local government closed 896 pig farms. The cost was estimated at $US58.3 million for the slaughter of approximately 1.1 million animals and the subsequent financial compensation to pig producers [29]. In addition, the government spent another $US136 million to implement sanitary control programs. Malaysia also lost $US120 million dollars as a direct consequence in the fall of its international markets, $US124 million associated with the pig farmer's financial losses due to a decrease in 80% consumption of pork products by the international public [38]. The Nipah virus outbreak also had a direct impact on the country's workforce with a huge social cost affecting over 12.000 people working on pig farms and related industries [55]. For example, most swine farms changed their business approach to focus on dairy or bovine beef production and many pig farmers are also now employed in palm plantations, where working conditions are not very optimistic [30]. In addition, as Malaysian's livestock sector was markedly decreased, fat and oils industry derived from these animals also suffered losses for $US35 million and other agricultural industries such as production of palm, coconut and tea also suffered an indirect impact due to these crops constitutes an important part of *Pteropus* bat's natural diet. Finally, after the outbreak of Nipah virus, pork consumption was reduced by approximately 30% and Singapore (*previously the largest importer of pork meat products and breeding stock from Malaysia*), banned all imports from this country on 1999. The total cost of national economic damage was estimated at approximately $US541 million [30, 93].

Costa Rica has currently over 110 species of bats reported [56]. Despite that the presence of Nipah virus has been found mainly in the genus *Pteropus* sp., located only in Asia and Africa, scientific reports have identified the presence of antibodies against the virus in insectivorous bats of genus *Myotis* spp [57], of which there are 6 species already reported for Costa Rica (*it is thought that some bat viruses have been co-evolve and coexist with them for thousands of years*). The discovery of new Paramyxovirus and Artrovirus [105-106] (*which are capable of avoiding the species barrier, but its zoonotic potential remains unknown*) remarks the importance of studies ecoepidemiological in neotropical bats, as well as for others wildlife reservoirs of important etiologic agents that can generate a high economic negative impact to the livestock sector, through trade barriers imposition and possible future infectious to humans.

4. Wildlife diseases monitoring systems and their importance for international trade

Avoiding closure of a country commercial borders by the national veterinary services, is accomplish by having an adequate, robust and effective monitoring system, that integrate not only the veterinary practice in the field, but also involving and integrating national public health system and private productive sector with the accredited international bodies' normative. Monitoring systems should base their functionality on the scope of the same system, by studying or evaluating not only traditional animal diseases, but also reporting significant epidemiological events related to neglected zoonoses and emerging diseases; integrating a holistic component based on the ecological understanding of disease dynamics, its transmission routes/sources and its economic impact on the international trade [8, 94]. TADs are a continuous ecological process difficult to eradicate, whose main deficiency lies not in the scarcity of control means, but in the failure of public policies that involves all stakeholders.

Adequate national and international legislation, must focused on actively combat the deliberate or accidental introduction of pathogens and pests to protect the agriculture of the harmful effects of bioterrorism; renounce the mass slaughter as a method of struggle, make the appropriate investments in technology and science within the country to produce shared efforts to facilitate adequate preparation for the government and private sector working together in a process whose costs bear the economic and social impact caused by different diseases; allowing the application of an effective system of surveillance, diagnosis and first response must be applied [11].

There is also a decrease in the infrastructure of health services worldwide. There is also an urgent need to rebuild and expand scientific knowledge and skills in new areas of human and veterinary medicine by integrating them within a global context of health, in which human, animal and ecosystem health are intrinsically linked. According to Brown (2004) [11], "*Despite the twin threats of agroterrorism and emerging diseases ... there is a sharp decline in the number of veterinarians and other health professionals at government level, compared to existing emergency*". Veterinary public health must resurgence, aimed to promoting control and eradication of zoonoses, especially in developing countries that relies its economy in a resilient economic system. Therefore, it is vital to increase the scope of the veterinarian role by generating and stimulating incentives and public policies aimed to controlling transboundary animal diseases and supporting the economy and world trade of livestock inputs [42, 96].

The decision to close the borders to trade when a neighbor country detects a transboundary disease does not appear to be the most appropriate measure for three main reasons:

1. Constitutes a transgression to international law,
2. Causes undue financial loss to other exporter regions within the injury country, that is not affected by the disease and,
3. Because it weakens the enforcement or international normative when an opposite situation is given, since no country is completely safe from pests and diseases due to intense the current trade flows.

Historically, most research efforts of zoonoses and emerging diseases have been focused on human domestic animal species and pecuary production systems, translating biosecurity as a risk analyses concept focused essentially on bio-economic consequences of biological hazards introduction [22, 76]. The competent international body which harmonizes and equates such sanitary measures worldwide in this area is the World Organization for Animal Health (*OIE*). The OIE is an intergovernmental organization created by an international convention on January 25, 1924, signed by 28 countries. In May 2004, the OIE totaled 167 Member Countries. Its headquarters is in Paris, France.

The main functions of the World Organization for Animal Health, include: i) Ensure transparency of the animal health situation in the world, ii) Collection, analysis and dissemination of veterinary scientific information, iii) Offer technical assistance and encourage international solidarity to promote the control and eradication of diseases, iv) Protect the safety of international trade in animals and animal products by harmonized sanitary guidelines and recognized by the World Trade Organization, under the mandate of the OIE in the Agreement on the Application of Sanitary and Phytosanitary Measures (*SPS Agreement*), v) Improving the legal framework and resources of veterinary services, and vi) To ensure better food safety of animal and improve animal welfare by using science-based. In fact, OIE is accepted as the reference standard organization for SPS Agreement on animal health and zoonoses (*SPS Agreement Art. 3, and annex A paragraph 3-b*) [41]. These tasks are achieved through various activities, including the establishment of normative standards, guidelines and recommendations in the field of animal health and its products. The OIE also maintains a list of mandatory reporting diseases of economic importance and the World Animal Health Information System (*WAHIS*), an internet-based computer system that processes data on animal diseases worldwide in real-time and then informs the international community constituting an early epidemiological warning system [97]. WAHIS has a juridical validation for all OIE members and since 2009 wildlife diseases online notification system have been ongoing.

In 2005, the OIE's Terrestrial Code introduced the term of compartmentalization or regionalization, a concept that subsequently has been included on its new versions (*for more information, please see chapter 4.3, OIE Terrestrial Animal Health Code 2011*). This designation also contained in the SPS Agreement has been of great importance for world trade, as it allows flexible trade restrictions arising from the presence of animal diseases. Thus, countries or a group of them may have the opportunity to export from areas that have demonstrated to be free of a particular disease or pest or where disease prevalence is low, even when the disease existed elsewhere in the country/region [14]. Therefore, the International Animal Health Code published by the OIE establish the methodology for quantitative risk analysis associated with trade in living animals and its products, through assessing a potential partner for trade avoiding the imposition of tariff barriers. This method applies in principle to standardize procedures for all countries. However, this does not erase the reality that for some countries the use of these procedures is extremely expensive. Thus, the fundamental importance of regionalization for agricultural exporting countries, efforts in the meetings of the WTO-SPS Agreement should focus on the major challenges:

1. Definition of agency will be responsible for issuing the guidelines containing explicit provisions on the procedures that countries must apply for recognition of disease in other countries and effective enforcement the subsequent incorporation of these guidelines in national legal systems of the members,
2. Promotion of programs of cooperation among members, especially between neighboring countries, for cases in which adjustments are required regulatory or technical training,
3. Provision in international standards of a simpler procedure that allows automatically receives recognition of disease free zone made by international organizations.

Today, it is widely recognized that those countries implementing ecoepidemiologic monitoring programs in wildlife possess significant advantages in the fight against TADs, such as:

1. Improved scientific basis for understanding the epidemiology of certain animal diseases and zoonoses that can have a profound economic and health impact on public health and animal health,
2. Detect the presence of key pathogens, especially those cited in the list of mandatory reporting of the World Organization for Animal Health (*OIE*), which can seriously compromise the perception of "country´*s disease free status*" that a nation possesses,
3. Monitoring programs in wildlife are serving as strategies aimed at integration, both supporting and strengthening the national infrastructure for animal health, and their respective programs preventive epidemiological,
4. Allow for early detection and early emerging and exotic agents with potential economic impact on the livestock sector and international trade of a country [43, 65].
5. Allow the detection, prevention and control of etiologic agents that may reach seriously compromise a country's public health, causing high mortality/morbidity, and
6. Wildlife often serves as a sentinel of various pathogens, enabling effective management and control of diseases in domestic animals.

In Africa, the Wildlife Conservation Society (WCS), OIE, WHO and other NGOs worldwide as IUCM (*The World Conservation Union*) and WWF (*World Wildlife Foundation*), among others, implement a joint initiative called AHEAD (*Animal Health for the Environment and Development*), which conducts research on transboundary animal diseases at the interface-wildlife-human-productive domestic animals in various African nations including Kenya, Zimbabwe, Tanzania, Uganda, Zambia, Namibia, South Africa, Botswana and Mozambique [72]. Another successful examples of wildlife disease monitoring systems are: National Wildlife Disease Program (NWDP) in the Unites States, Canadian Cooperative Wildlife Health Center in Canada (CCWHC), the Instituto de Investigación en Recursos Cinegéticos (IREC) in Spain, and the Réseau National de Surveillance Sanitaire de la Faune Sauvage (SAGIR) in France-Martinique Island.

5. The one health concept: An holistic, integrative and transdisciplinary paradigm for controlling, preventing and monitoring TADs

The term zoonosis was proposed in 1855 by the German scientist Robert Virchow [17]. Virchow was also the first to propose the term one health, emphasizing the importance and interrelationship between human and veterinary medicine for diseases prevention, study and control [71]. Subsequently, the one health concept was internationally distributed by Calvin Schwabe [43] and William Osler [51].

The OIE's strategic plan for the period 2011-2015, seeks to ensure transparency in communication and global spread of animal diseases. One of the primary concepts of the operational plan is to create forums and opportunities for a global strategy for risk management in the interface-wildlife-human-domestic productive animals, and to mitigate the impact of climate change on the distribution and epidemiology of TADs and livestock production systems.

Under the premise that international animal health is a public good, in the last 8 years the term one health has reemerged as an innovate solution to combat TADs. The European Union adopted the following definition for One Health approach: *''The improvement of health and well-being through (i) the prevention of risks and the mitigation of effects of crises that originate at the interface between humans, animals and their various environments, and (ii) promoting a cross-sectoral, collaborative, "whole of society" approach to health hazards, as a systemic change of perspective in the management of risks''*[67]. Additionally, the Executive Summary of the American Veterinary Medical Association (AVMA) One Health Initiative Task Force (OHITF), describes One Health as: *''The integrative effort of multiple disciplines working locally, nationally, and globally to attain optimal health for people, animals, and the environment''* [53].

The one health concept also matches with Conservation Medicine (CM), an emerging veterinary medical discipline. CM links human and animal health within an ecological context, studying the effects of emerging diseases in terrestrial vertebrates and their impact on human health, animal health and direct impact on species conservation [91].

Nowadays, many countries around the world have adopted the initiative One Health initiative, due to the fundamental bases of all health and scientific effort begins with education and collaborative research. Likewise, many internationally renowned organizations such as American Medical Association, American Veterinary Medical Association, Center for Disease Control and Prevention, American Association of Tropical Medicine, World Health Organization, Food and Agriculture Organization, United States Geological Survey National Wildlife Health Center, United States Department of Agriculture, Canadian Cooperative Wildlife Health Center, Laboratoire Nationale de Sante Post of Republic of Congo Brazzaville, IUCN Commission on Environmental Law, Wildlife Trust, The Consortium for Conservation Medicine, and the Wildlife Conservation Society have now taken the initiative and promote this movement [71].For more information please visit: http://www.onehealthinitiative.com. Similarly, the joint strategic framework for reducing risks of infectious diseases at the interface-ecosystems-human-livestock from

United Nations Children's Fund (UNICEF), in conjunction with the World Bank (WB), Organization of the United Nations Food and Agriculture Organization (FAO), World Organization for Animal Health (OIE) and World Health Organization (WHO) [68] seeks to develop this initiative by:

1. Creating integrated systems of public health and animal health in the long term, and consistent with the International Health Regulations of the World Health Organization and the international standards established by the World Organization for Animal Health.
2. Generating better response capabilities within its members, aimed to prevent regional and international crises caused by epizootic diseases outbreaks.
3. Creating partnerships between developed and developing countries (*especially those with low per capita income*), to facilitate the transfer of economic resources and knowledge on animal disease control globally.
4. Promoting a multidisciplinary, multinational and cross actions.
5. Developing programs targeted control and eradication of key diseases.
6. Developing strategies to address emerging diseases that involve the private sector in order to build local capacity and strengthen long-term sustainability.
7. Allowing the development of regional, national and international capacity to control TADs through the use of standards, tools and monitoring procedures.

Then the importance of monitoring programs in passive and active wildlife monitoring system, for controlling and preventing of TADs will be exposed by analyzing the situation of a leader and world famous country on conservation (*Costa Rica*).

5.1. Case study III: Costa Rica´s situation on wildlife transboundary diseases

Costa Rica has historically been and still is a country that bases its economy in a residual agricultural market. It is, that produces mostly for domestic consumption and exports its surplus. Costa Rica's economy is the 11th largest in Latin America, with a nominal GDP of $US 34.564 million (*2010, 84th place worldwide*). The food and livestock industry sectors in Costa Rica are relevant to the national economy, occupying approximately 35% of the national work force in the pecuary sector and 4.2% of total employment in the country. The beef and dairy sub-segments constitute both 26% of the domestic food production. This productive sector occupies (*with 14%*), the second place in the composition of the value of its exports in 2008. Nowadays, Costa Rica is now one of only three Latin American countries in dairy surplus, along with Uruguay and Argentina. For example, over 2.2 million liters of milk are produced per day (*over 60% of that volume is processed industrially*), exporting over 20% of the total national production [45].

Costa Rica has only slightly more than 52,000 km^2 (*about 0.003% of the global area*) and 589,000 km^2 of territorial sea, having approximately 4% of the world total biodiversity [18]. Placing it among the 25 most diverse countries in the world and the first Central American level, although we have only identified about 18% of our flora and fauna, much of them is endemic (*Tables 1 and 2)* [49]. However, in Costa Rica there is a marked lack of *ex-situ* (*free ranging animals*) ecoepidemiological diseases studies from wildlife, even when OIE established in 2007 the need to develop an epidemiological surveillance system in wild animals within its members (*Costa Rica is an OIE member since 1993*) and the Costarrican National Service for Animal Health (*SENASA*) has a national program for *in-situ* (*captive animal populations*) wildlife health monitoring approach ongoing since 2009. This is very important as the majority of emerging diseases originate in wild animals are concentrated in neotropical developing countries [50]. Therefore, Costa Rica`s richness on biodiversity and its unregulated anthropogenic change on landscape constitute an epidemiological risk for a zoonoses high incidence zone. A list of TADs that may be present in Costa Rica and their respective wild reservoirs was carried out, based on the mandatory OIE animal disease notification´s list and the taxonomic basis species of Costa Rica (*Atta*) running by the National Institute of Biodiversity [48] (*Table 3*).

Group	1 place	2 place	3 place	4 place	5 place	Costa Rica
Plants	Brasil 55000	Colombia 50000	China 30000	Indonesia 27500	México 26000	#11 (11467 described species)
Amphybians	Colombia 585	Brasil 502	Ecuador 402	Perú 315	México 290	#13 (189 described species)
Reptils	Australia 867	México 704	Indonesia 511	Colombia 475	Brasil 468	#20 (234 described species)
Mammals	Indonesia 515	México 491	Colombia 453	USA 428	Brasil 421	#32 (described species)
Birds	Colombia 1753	Perú 1678	Brasil 1635	Ecuador 1559	Indonesia 1534	#24 (864 described species)

Table 1. Species diversity on megadiverse nations and Costa Rica´s position.
Source: Taken from [49]

Food security is defined as *´´A situation that exists when all people, at all times, have physical, social and economic access to sufficient, safe and nutritious food that meets their dietary needs and food preferences for an active and healthy life.´´* [31]. Traditionally, evaluations on animal's disease economic impact have focused on decreasing production costs after a disease outbreak and the subsequent costs associated control and eradication measures. Nowadays is broadly recognized the impact that these diseases have on the international markets for livestock commodities, and the importance of reporting systems in protecting food supplies (food security), international commercial relationships and global trade´s fluency [83]. As the impact of TADs is translated into economic losses and costs to production and trade, it's also generate several externalities affecting the differential price between domestic

Group	1992	2002	2007	2008
Virus	125	ND	ND	ND
Monera	213	ND	ND	ND
Fungi	825	2311	2394	3820
Algae	503	564	ND	ND
Plantae	10.000	10.353	11.451	11.453
Protozooa	670	ND	ND	ND
Nematoda	85	88	ND	182
Mollusca	1.050	1.550	ND	ND
Insecta	65.000	66. 265	66. 946	68.494
Peces	916	1.080	ND	1.150
Anfibia	150	175	183	189
Reptiles	215	222	226	234
Birds	850	854	857	864
Mammals	228	234	237	239

Table 2. Species diversity per taxonomic group in de Costa Rica (period 1992-2009)
ND: *not determine.* **Source:** *Modified from* [49].

Disease	Etiology	Wild Reservoir	Referencie
I. Viral diseases			
Vesicular Stomatitis	Rhabdovirus	*Mazama americana, Didelphis marsupialis, Tayassu tajacu*	[5-6, 103]
Foot and Mouth Disease	Picornavirus	*Rattus norvegicus, Tayassu pecari, Tayassu tajacu, Mazama americana*	[82]
Rabies*	Rhabdovirus	*Desmodus rotundus, Eptesicus fuscus, Tadarida brasiliensis*	[10, 88, 95]
East Equine Encephalitis*	Alphavirus	*Desmodus rotundus,*	[20]
West Equine Encephalitis*	Alphavirus	*Desmodus rotundus,*	[20]
Venezuelan Equine Encephalitis*	Alphavirus	*Desmodus rotundus,*	[20]
II. Bacterial diseases			
Brucelloses*	*Brucella abortus*	*Odocoileus virginianus, Didelphis virginiana, Procyon lotor*	[1]
	Brucella suis	*Tayassu tajacu*	[58]
Paratuberculosis*	*Mycobacterium paratuberculosis*	*Odocoileus virginianus*	[79]
Bovine Anaplasmosis	*Anaplasma marginale*	*Odocoileus virginianus*	[60, 64]

Disease	Etiology	Wild Reservoir	Referencie
Bovine Babesiosis	*Babesia bovis*	*Odocoileus virginianus*	[16]
	Babesia bigemina	*Odocoileus virginianus*	[16]
Bovine Tuberculosis *	*Mycobacterium tuberculosis*	*Odocoileus virginianus*	[59]
Leptospirosis*	*Leptospira* spp.	*Tayassu tajacu, Canis latrans, Didelphis marsupialis, Rattus norvegicus, Tayassu pecari*	[21, 37, 92, 99]
III. Parasitic diseases			
Hydatidosis*	*Echinococcus granulosus*	*Canis latrans*	[28]
Dourine	*Trypanosoma equiperdum*	*Desmodus rotundus*	[80]
Surra	*Trypanosoma evansi*	*Desmodus rotundus, Tayassu pecari, Tayassu tajacu*	[44, 81]

Table 3. List for OIE obligatory reporting diseases with wildlife reservoirs in Costa Rica

and imported products, with potential important implications for government policy on biosecurity [100], and also limiting the access to basic food items for poorest people. According to the Economic Commission of the United Nations for Latin America and the Caribbean (ECLAC), the poorest stratus in society, face an inflation rate between 3 and 4 points higher than the general inflation rate for the remainder of the population. Thus, only in Latin America during an important episode of TADs and as result of the subsequent food insecurity, more than 26 million people could fall into poverty and extreme poverty could affect more than 17% of the total Latin America and the Caribbean′s population [34]. In Costa Rica, 16.7% of households are poor, 3.3% are in extreme poverty, 4% of the population is malnourished and the poorest households spend more than 40% of their salaries on food [61]. Thus, infectious diseases play an important role in decreasing food supply globally and nation's economic growth. The imposition of nontariff barriers to Latin American countries like Costa Rica, would force those nations most vulnerable to import their goods as a direct result for the fluctuating food prices, creating a huge economic impact with profound social consequences in terms of food security, especially affecting marginalized social sectors. Additionally, as a direct result for closing international markets to livestock products, countries could present low economic rates, reduced incomes, a rising on internal inflation and therefore increasing also the dependence on commodities imported [73].

The International Organization for Animal Health (OIE) recognizes the improvement of national standards in animal health, should be parallel to the improvement of veterinary services in terms of increasing the capacity of early epidemiological detection, diagnosis and control of TADs [104]. This raises the questions:

1. If Costa Rica is not fully involved in this topic, can continue a free zone diseases without any idea of the epizootiology and ecoepidemiology of wildlife TADs in their territory?,
2. How Costa Rica can deal with the emergence of infectious diseases that impact and directly involve human-animal health, generating an impact on the domestic livestock sector which constitutes an important percentage for costarrican economy annually?.

6. Conclusions

Animal husbandry and secondary production plays a vital role in the economies of developing countries; through providing protein sources, income, employment and foreign exchange. For low income produces, livestock also serve as a store of wealth. Nowadays, several nations worldwide are investing large amounts of money to eradicate and combat animal diseases; due to humans and climate change are creating favorable conditions for the occurrence of animal pests and diseases into new regions, and are also transforming its transmission mechanism, making that developing countries that rely more on stockbreeding are the most vulnerable. Thus, all countries need to know the endemic animal diseases that circulate in its wild populations and have an adequate veterinary infrastructure to enable early detection of a wide range of zoonotic and emerging diseases at the wildlife-domestic animals-human interface [9, 52].

In addition, the biggest challenge for developing countries is to implement and develop actions within a comprehensive framework that considers the different roles on pecuary health and all its actors (*public and private*), facilitating the ability to respond quickly to TADs with adequate official services sustainably, enabling joint actions, elements for an inter-sectorial planning compensation and an adequately addressing of emerging issues. Therefore, it is vital that countries in addition to generating disease monitoring programs also implement alternative population control mechanisms in these animal species. Due to lethal control (*culling or killing animals*) is no longer consider an ethical or decent option for mitigate the transmission of TADs (*mainly on threatened or endangered animal populations*), substitute novel techniques to control and prevent infectious outbreaks with a legal component based on animal welfare such as vaccination, fertility control and strategic contraception should be contemplated.

Considering that the concept of health is inherent to all species on Earth and it provides a unifying principle that sustains life on all levels has a continuing dynamism complex and inextricable interdependence [87], the amalgamation of many sub-disciplines of biology, veterinary and human medicine is critical to understanding multidisciplinary and controlling emerging diseases. Therefore, national public and animal health systems will play a pivotal role to monitor, assess, predict and prevent the movement of TADs in the oncoming decades.

Undoubtedly, in future developed nations will be involved in moral and ethical decisions on how help to mitigate the effects of TADs on developing countries. One Health Initiative through Conservation Medicine as a medical discipline will become the necessary engine for the integration of various scientific sectors to promote holistic, integrative and multidisciplinary research, becoming an indispensable tool of national public health or animal control and early prevention of TADs [25].

Author details

Andrés Cartín-Rojas
Department of Small Animal Sciences, School of Veterinary Medicine,
University of Florida at Gainesville and White Oak Conservation Center Animal Science Building, Yulee, FL, USA

7. References

[1] Acosta-González R, González-Reyes I, Flores-Gutiérrez G (2006) Prevalence of *Brucella abortus* Antibodies in Equines of a Tropical Region of Mexico. Canadian. j. vet. research. 70: 302–304.

[2] Aguirre A (2009) Essential Veterinary Education in Zoological and Wildlife Medicine: a Global Perspective. *Rev. sci. tech. off. int. epiz.* 28: 605-610.

[3] Anand S, Hanson K (1997) Disability-adjusted Life Years: a Critical Review. J. health. econom. 16: 685-702.

[4] Arrivillaga J, Caraballo V (2009) Medicina de la Conservación. Rev. biomed. 20: 55-67.

[5] Arboleda J, Restrepo G, Wolff M, Uribe J, Bedoya H, Quiroz V, Pérez S, Morales L, Piedrahita I, Zuluaga F, Ossa J (2001) Ecoepidemiología de la Estomatitis Vesicular en un Municipio Cafetero de Antioquia. Rev. cololomb. cien. pec. 14: 20-27.

[6] Beldomenico M (2006) Medicina y Animales Silvestres: El Desafío de las Ciencias Veterinarias en el Siglo XXI. Rev. FAVE-cien. vet. 5: 7-20.

[7] Beldomenico P, Uhart M (2008) Ecoepidemiología de los Virus de Influenza Aviar. Rev FAVE-cienc. vet. 7: 25-40.

[8] Bengis R, Kock R, Fischer J (2002) Infectious Animal Disease: the Wildlife/Livestock Interface. Rev. sci. tech. off. int. epiz. 21: 53-65.

[9] Ben Jebara K (2004) Surveillance, Detection and Response: Managing Emerging Diseases at National and International Levels. Rev. sci. tech. off. int. epiz. 23: 709-715.

[10] Bernardi F, Nadin-Davis S, Wandeler A, Armstrong J, Gomes A, Lima F, Nogueira F, Ito F (2005) Antigenic and Genetic Characterization of Rabies Viruses Isolated from Domestic and Wild Animals of Brazil Identifies the Hoary Fox as a Rabies Reservoir. J. gen. virol. 86:3153-3162.

[11] Breeze R (2006) Technology, Public Policy and Control of Transboundary Livestock Diseases in Our Lifetimes. Rev. sci. tech. off. int. epiz. 25: 271-292.

[12] Brown C (2004). Emerging Zoonoses and Pathogens of Public Health Significance-an Overview. Rev. sci. tech. off. int. epiz. 23: 435-442.

[13] Brown C (2010) Emerging Diseases: The Global Express. Vet. pathol. 47: 9-14.

[14] Brückner G (2011) Managing the Risks of Disease Transmission through Trade: a Commodities-Based Approach?. Rev. sci. tech. off. int. epiz. 30: 289-296.

[15] Camacho-Escobar M, Pérez-Lara A, Arroyo-Ledezma E, Sánchez-Bernal J, Jiménez-Galicia E, Marcela M (2009) Guajolotes de Traspatio como Reservorios de Enfermedades de Aves Domésticas y Silvestres en Tres Ecosistemas de la Costa Mexicana. Trop. Subtrop. agroeconomics. 10: 109-115.

[16] Cantu A, Ortega J, García-Vázquez Z, Mosqueda J, Henke E, George E (2009) Epizootiology of *Babesia bovis* and *Babesia bigemina* in Free Ranging White-tailed Deer in Northeastern Mexico. J. parasitol. 95: 536–542.

[17] Cardiff R, Ward J, Barthold S (2008) One Medicine—One Pathology': are Veterinary and Human Pathology Prepared?. Lab. invest. 88: 18–26.

[18] Chen S (2005) Turismo y Ambiente: Un Potencial para el Desarrollo Económico de Costa Rica. Rev. reflex. 84: 25-37.

[19] Chomel B, Belotto A, Meslin F (2007) Wildlife, Exotic Pets, and Emerging Zoonoses. Emerg. infect. dis. 13: 6-11.

[20] Constantine D (2003) Geographic Translocation of Bats: Known and Potential Problems. Emerg. infec. dis. 9: 17-21.

[21] Corn J, Lee R, Erickson G, Murphy C (1987) Serologic Survey for Evidence of Exposure to Vesicular Stomatitis Virus, Pseudorabies Virus, Brucellosis and Leptospirosis in Collared Peccaries from Arizona. J. wildlife dis. 23: 551-557.

[22] Cutler S, Fooks A, Van der Poel W (2010) Public Health Threat of New, Reemerging, and Neglected Zoonoses in the Industrialized World. Emerg. infect. dis. 16: 1-7.

[23] Dabanch J (2003) Zoonosis. Rev. chil. infectol. 20: 47-51.

[24] Daszak P, Cunningham A, Hyatt A (2001) Anthropogenic Environmental Change and the Emergence of Infectious Diseases in Wildlife. Act. trop. 78:103-116.

[25] Daszak P, Tabor G, Kilpatrick M, Epstein J, Plowright R (2004) Conservation Medicine and a New Agenda for Emerging Diseases. Annals. n. y. acad. scien. 1026: 1-11.

[26] Daszack P, Epstein J, Kilpatrick A, Aguirre A, Karesh W, Cunningham A (2007) Collaborative Research Approaches to the Role of Wildlife in Zoonotic Diseases Emergence. Current. top. microbiol. inmunol. 315: 463-475.

[27] Delgado C (2003) Rising Consumption of Meat and Milk in Developing Countries has created a New Food Revolution. J. nutrition. 133: 3907-3910.

[28] Eckert J, Deplazes P (2004) Biological, Epidemiological, and Clinical Aspects of Echinococcosis, a Zoonosis of Increasing Concern. Clin. microbiol rev. 17: 107-135.

[29] Elbers A (2002) Local and Global Impact of Disease Outbreaks. Advan. pork. product. 13: 17-27.

[30] FAO. Animal Production and Health Commission of FAO (2002) Manual on the Diagnosis of Nipah Virus Infection in Animals. Rome: FAO. 90 p.

[31] FAO. Economic and Social Department of FAO (2003) Trade Reforms and Food Security. Conceptualizing Linkages. Rome: FAO. 315 p.

[32] FAO. Food and Agriculture Organization of the United Nations and World Organization for Animal Health (2004) The Global Framework for the Progressive Control of Transboundary Animal Diseases (GF-TADs). Rome: FAO. 40 p.

[33] FAO. Natural Resources Management and Environment Department of FAO. Climate-Related Transboundary Pest and Diseases. Technical Background from the Expert Consultation (2008a). Rome: FAO. 59 p.

[34] FAO. Iniciativa América Latina y Caribe Sin Hambre, a través del Observatorio Regional de Seguridad Alimentaria y Nutricional (2008b). Panorama del hambre en América Latina y el Caribe. Roma: FAO. 64 p.

[35] FAO. Agriculture and Consumer Protection Department of FAO (2009) Livestock's Long Shadow: Environmental Issues and Options. Rome: FAO. 493 p.

[36] Fauci A, Touchette N, Folkers G (2005) Emerging Infectious Diseases: A 10-Year Perspective from the National Institute of Allergy and Infectious Diseases. Emerg. infect. dis. 11: 519-525.

[37] Gese E, Schultz R, Johnson M, Williams E, Crabtree R, Ruff R (1997). Serological Survey for Diseases in Free-Ranging Coyotes *(Canis Latrans)* in Yellowstone National Park, Wyoming. J. wild. dis. 33: 47-56.

[38] González A (2003) Las Enfermedades Virales Emergentes de los Cerdos. Cienc. vet. 9: 197-227.

[39] Greger M (2007) The Human/Animal Interface: Emergence and Resurgence of Zoonotic Infectious Diseases. Crit. rev. microbiol. 33: 243-299.

[40] Hafi A, Reynolds R, Oliver M (1994) Economic Impact of Newcastle Disease on the Australian Poultry Industry. Canberra: Australian Bureau of Agricultural and Resources Economics. 77 p.

[41] Hallet L (2003) Les modes de collaboration entre vétérinaires officiels, vétérinaires privés et organisations d'éleveurs. Rev. sci. tech. off. int. epiz. 22: 523-532.

[42] Heath S (2006) Challenges and Options for Animal and Public Health Services in the Next Two Decade. Rev. sci. tech. off. int. epiz. 25: 403-419.

[43] Herbold J (2005) Emerging Zoonotic Diseases: An Opportunity to Apply the Concepts of Nidality and One-Medicine. Enviro. Health. Prevent. med. 10: 260-262.

[44] Herrera H, Abreu G, Keuroghlian A, Freitas P, Jansen M (2008) The Role Played by Sympatric Collared peccary (*Tayassu tajacu*), White-lipped Peccary (*Tayassu pecari*), and Feral Pig (*Sus scrofa*) as Maintenance Hosts for *Trypanosoma evansi* and *Trypanosoma cruzi* in a Sylvatic Area of Brazil. Parasitol. res. 103: 619-24.

[45] Hidalgo-Nuchera A, Herrera-González R, López-Rodríguez V, Velásquez-López G. (2009) El Sector de la Industria Alimenticia de Costa Rica: Una Perspectiva desde la Cadena de Valor. San José: Editorial Universidad de Costa Rica. 315 p.

[46] Horst S, Huirne R, DLikhuizen A (1997) Risks and Economic Consequences of Introducing Classical Swine Fever into the Netherlands by Feeding Swill to Swine. Rev. sci. tech. off. int. epiz. 16: 207-214.

[47] Horst S, de Vos C, Tomassen F, Stelwagen J (1999) The Economic Evaluation of Control and Eradication of Epidemic Livestock Diseases. Rev. sci. tech. off. int. epiz. 18: 367-379.

[48] INBio, 2012a. Instituto Nacional de Biodiversidad de Costa Rica. Atta (Base de datos de biodiversidad). http://darnis.inbio.ac.cr/ubisen/FMPro?-DB=UBIpub.fp3&-lay=WebAll&-error=norec.html&-Format=default2.htm&-SortField=nombre%20cientifico&-Op=eq&nueva=S&-Max=3&-Find. (Acceded 26-may-2012).

[49] INBio, 2012b. Instituto Nacional de Biodiversidad de Costa Rica: http://www.inbio.ac.cr/en/default.html (Acceded 23-may-2012).

[50] Jones E, Patel N, Levy M, Storeygard A, Balk D, Gittleman J, Daszak P (2008) Global Trends in Emerging Infectious Diseases. Nature. 451: 990-994.

[51] Kahn L, Kaplan B, Steele J (2007) Confronting Zoonosis through Collaboration between Medicine and Veterinary Medicine. Vet Italia. 43: 5-19.

[52] King L, Marano N, Hughes J (2004) Between New Animal Health Partnerships and Public Health Services Agencies. Rev. sci. tech. off. int. epiz. 23: 717-726.

[53] King L, Anderson L, Blackmore C, Blackwell M, Lautner E, Marcus L, Meyer T, Monath T, Nave J, Ohle J, Pappaioanou M, Sobota J, Stokes W, Davis R, Glasser J, Mahr R (2008) Executive summary of the AVMA One Health Initiative Task Force report. J. american. vet. med. assoc. 233: 259-260.

[54] Kruse H, Kirkemo A, Handeland K (2004) Wildlife as Source of Zoonotic Infections. Emerg. infect. dis. 10: 2067-2072.

[55] Lam S (2003) Nipah Virus—a Potential Agent of Bioterrorism?. Ant.res. 57: 113–119.

[56] La Val R, Rodríguez R (2002) Murciélagos de Costa Rica.Heredia: Editorial Instituto Nacional de Biodiversidad. 320 p.

[57] Li Y, Wang J, Hickey A, Zhang Y, Li Y, Wu Y, Zhang H, Yuan J, Han Z, McEachern J, Broder C, Wang L, Shi Z (2008) Antibodies to Nipah or Nipah-like Viruses in Bats, China. Emerg. infect. diseases. 14: 1974–1976.

[58] Lord V, Lord R (1991) *Brucella suis* Infections in Collared Peccaries in Venezuela. J. wild. dis. 27: 477-481.

[59] Lyashchenko K, Greenwald R, Esfandiari J, Chambers M, Vicente J, Gortazar C, Santos N, Correia-Neves M, Buddle B, Jackson R, O'Brien D, Schmitt S, Palmer M, Delahay R, Waters W (2008) Animal-side Serologic Assay for Rapid Detection of *Mycobacterium bovis* Infection in Multiple Species of Free-ranging Wildlife. Vet. microbiol. 132: 283–292.

[60] Maas J, Buening G, Porta W (1981) Serologic Evidence of *Anaplasma marginale* Infection in White-tailed Deer (*Odocoileus virginianus*) in Missouri. J. wild. dis. 17: 45-47.

[61] MEIC. Instituto Nacional de Estadística y Censos (ENIGH) del Ministerio de Economía, Industria y Comercio (2006) Encuesta Nacional de Ingresos y Gastos de los Hogares 2004. Principales resultados. San José: ENIGHP. 259 p.

[62] Morens M, Folkers G, Fauci A (2004). The Challenge of Emerging and Re-emerging Infectious Diseases. Nature. 430: 242-249

[63] Morgan N, Prakash A (2006) International Livestock Markets and the Impact of Animal Disease. Rev. sci. tech. off. int. epiz. 25: 517-528.

[64] Morley R, Hugh-Jones M (1989) Seroepidemiology of *Anaplasma marginale* in White-tailed Deer (*Odocoileus virginianus*) from Louisiana. J. wild. dis. 25: 342-346.

[65] Morner T, Obendorf D, Artois M, Woodford M (2002) Surveillance and Monitoring of Wildlife Diseases. Rev. sci. tech. off. int. epiz. 21: 67-76.

[66] Morse S (2004) Factors and Determinants of Emerging Disease. Rev. sci. tech. off. int. epiz 23: 443-451.

[67] Okello A, Paul E, Gibbs J, Vandersmissen A, Welburn S (2011) One Health and the Neglected Zoonoses: Turning Rhetoric into Reality. Vet Record. 169: 281-285.

[68] OIE, FAO, WHO, UNICEF, WB (2008). A Contribution to ''One World, One Health'', a Strategic Framework to Reduce Risks of Infectious Diseases at the Animal-Human-Ecosystem Interface. Paris: OIE. 68 p.

[69] OIE Terrestrial Code, version 2011: http://www.oie.int/en/international-standard-setting/terrestrial-code/access-online/ (Acceded 23-may-2012).

[70] Olival J, Daszak P (2005). Reviews in NeuroVirology: Emerging Infectious Diseases the Ecology of Emerging Neurotropic Viruses. J. neurovirol, 11: 440–445.

[71] Osburn B, Scott C, Gibbs P (2009) One World – One Medicine – One Health: Emerging Veterinary Challenges and Opportunities. Rev. sci. tech. off. int. epiz. 28: 481-486.

[72] Osofsky S, Cleaveland S, Karesh W, Kock M, Nyhus P, Star L, Yang A (2003) Conservation and Development Interventions at the Wildlife/Livestock Interface. Implications for Wildlife, Livestock and Human Cambridge: IUCN Publications Services Unit. 241 p.

[73] Otte M, Nugent N, McLeod A (2004) Transboundary Animal Diseases: Assessment of Socio-Economic Impacts and Institutional Responses. Rome: FAO. 46 p.

[74] Patz A, Daszak P, Tabor M, Aguirre A, Pearl M, Epstein J, Wolfe D, Kilpatrick A, Foufopoulos J, Molyneux D, Bradley J (2004) Unhealthy Landscapes: Policy Recommendations on Land Use Change and Infectious Disease Emergence. Environment. health. perspect. 112: 1092-1098.

[75] Prat N, Falconi C (2006) Impacto Económico Potencial de la Influenza Aviar en el Sector Avícola de América Latina y el Caribe. Washington: Banco Interamericano de Desarrollo, Serie de informes técnicos del Departamento de Desarrollo Sostenible. 88 p.

[76] Perry B, Grace D (2009) The Impacts of Livestock Diseases and their Control on Growth and Development Processes that are Pro-Poor. Phil. trans. r. soc. b. 364: 2643–2655.

[77] Pike B, Saylors K, Fair J, LeBreton M, Tamoufe U. Djoko C, Rimoin A, Wolfe N (2010) The Origin and Prevention of Pandemics. Clin. infect. dis. 50: 1636–1640.
[78] Quesada G (2006) Reporte Final: Aves Acuáticas en Costa Rica. San José: Departamento de Historia Natural, Museo Nacional de Costa Rica. 77 p.
[79] Quist C, Nettles V, Manning E, Hall D, Gaydos K, Wilmers J, Lopez R (2002) Paratuberculosis in Key Deer (*Odocoileus virginianus clavium*). J. wild. dis. 38: 729–737.
[80] Rodrigues A, Fighera R, Souza T, Schild A, Soares M, Milano J, Barros C (2005) Surtos de tripanossomíase por *Trypanosoma evansi* em eqüinos no Rio Grande do Sul: Aspectos Epidemiológicos, Clínicos, Hematológicos e Patológicos. Pes. vet. bras. 25:239-249.
[81] Rojas A (2005) *Desmodus rotundus* (Chiroptera: Phyllostomidae) Reservorio y Vector Mecánico de *Trypanosoma evansi* y *T. equiperdum* en América Latina. Rev. asoc. vet. v. sil. 1: 10-13.
[82] Rosenberg F (1975) El Conocimiento de la Epidemiología de la Fiebre Aftosa con Particular Referencia Sudamérica. Rio de Jainero: OPS. 55 p.
[83] Rushton J, Upton M (2006) Investment in Preventing and Preparing for Biological Emergencies and Disasters: Social and Economic Costs of Disasters versus Costs of Surveillance and Response Preparedness. Rev. sci. tech. off. int. epiz. 25: 375-388.
[84] Rhyan J, Spraker T (2010) Emergence of Diseases from Wildlife Reservoirs. Vet. pathol. 47: 34-39.
[85] Salles-Almeida J (2006a) La Aplicación de la Regionalización al Comercio de Carnes: ¿A qué Obedece la Reticencia?. Bol. FAL. 241: 1-4.
[86] Salles-Almeida J (2006b) Gripe Aviar: los Impactos Comerciales de las Barreras Sanitarias y los Desafíos para América Latina y el Caribe. Chile: CEPAL-ONU. 55 p.
[87] Santisteban F (2007) Zoonosis Emergentes: Un Reto Interdisciplinar. Gacet. med. bilbao. 107: 7-10.
[88] Schneider M, Romijn P, Uieda W, Tamayo H, Fernandes D, Belotto A, Barbosa J, Leanes L (2009) Rabies Transmitted by Vampire Bats to Humans: An Emerging Zoonotic Disease in Latin America?. Pan. american. j. publ. h. 25: 260-269.
[89] Sherman D (2010) A Global Veterinary Medical Perspective on the Concept of One Health: Focus on Livestock. ILAR. j. 51: 281-287.
[90] Slenning B (2010) Global Climate Change and Implications for Disease Emergence. Vet. pathol. 47: 28-33.
[91] Tabor G (2002) Defining Conservation Medicine. In: Aguirre A, Ostfeld R, Tabor G, Haouse C, Pearl M, editors. Conservation Medicine. New York: Oxford University Press. 407 p.
[92] Tavares T, Keuroghlian A, Eaton D, de Freitas E, Figueiredo A, Nakazato L, de Oliveira J, Miranda F, Paes R, Monteiro L, Lima J, Neto A, Dutra V, de Freitas J (2010) Prevalence of *Leptospira interrogans* Antibodies in Free-ranging *Tayassu pecari* of the Southern

Pantanal, Brazil, an Ecosystem where Wildlife and Cattle Interact. Trop. animal. h. prod. 42: 1695-1703.

[93] Tey S, Suryani D, Emmy F, Illisriyan I (2009) Food Consumption and Expenditures in Singapore: Implications to Malaysia's Agricultural Exports. internt. f. res. j. 16: 119-126.

[94] Thierman A (2004) Emerging Diseases and Implications for Global Trade. Rev. sci. tech. off. int. epiz. 23: 701-708.

[95] Trimarchi C, Debbie J (1977) Naturally Occurring Rabies Virus and Neutralizing Antibody in Two Species of Insectivorous Bats of New York state. J. wild. dis. 13: 366-369.

[96] Vallat. B, Mallet E (2006) Ensuring Good Governance to Address Emerging and Re-emerging Animal Diseases Threat: Supporting the Veterinary Services of Developing Countries to Meet OIE International Standards and Quality. Rev. sci. tech. off. int. epiz. 25: 389-401.

[97] Vallat B, Pinto J, Schudel A (2006) International Organizations and their Role in Helping to Protect the Worldwide Community against Natural and Intentional Biological Disasters. Rev. sci. tech. off. int. epiz. 25: 163-172.

[98] Vandeputte S, Humblet M, Fecher-Bourgeois F, Gosset C, Albert A, Vernaillen F, Saegerman C (2011) Instruments de Gestion Économique des Crises Sanitaires Touchant les Animaux de Production en Europe. Rev. sci. tech. off. int. epiz. 30: 683-701.

[99] Vieira A (2009) Levantamento de *Leptospira* spp. en Animais Silvestres do Pantanal Sul-Matto-Grosense, por Meio de Técnicasa Sorologicas e Moleculares. Brazil: Universidade Federal de Matto Grosso do Sul. 83 p.

[100] Waage J, Mumford J (2008) Agricultural Biosecurity. *Phil. trans. r. soc. b.* 363: 863–876.

[101] Walker W (1998) Taller sobre Inocuidad de los Alimentos en el Comercio Agropecuario Internacional. México, D.F: Instituto Interamericano de Cooperación para la Agricultura (IICA) 9 p.

[102] Wilson T, Logan-Henfrey L, Weller R, Kellman B (2000) Agroterrorism, Biological Crimes, and Biological Warfare Targeting Animal Agriculture. In: Brown C, Bolin C editors. Emerging Diseases of Animals. Washington: ASM Press. 310 p.

[103] Wilson A, Araínga M, Gálvez H, Manchego A, Rivera H (2005) Anticuerpos Contra el Virus de la Estomatitis Vesicular en Sajinos (*Tayassu tajacu*) de Zoocriaderos de Iquitos y Pucallpa. Rev. invest. vet. Perú. 16: 180-183.

[104] Woodford J (2004) Synergies between Veterinarians and Para-professionals in the Public and Private Sectors: Organizational and Institutional Relationships that Facilitate the Process of Privatizing Animal Health Services in Developing Countries. Rev. sci. tech. off. int. epiz. 23: 115-135.

[105] Yaiw K, Bingham J, Crameri G, Mungall B, Hyatt A, Yu M, Eaton B, Shamala D, Wang L, Thong K. 2008. Tioman Virus, a Paramyxovirus of Bat Origin, Causes Mild Disease in Pigs and has a Predilection for Lymphoid Tissues. J. virol. 82: 565–568.

[106] Zhu H, Chu D, Liu W, Dong B, Zhan S, Zhang J, Li L, Vijaykrishna D, Smith G, Chen H, Poon L, Peiris J, Guan Y (2009) Detection of Diverse Astroviruses from Bats in China. J. gen. virol. 90: 883-887.

Chapter 8

International Trade Promotion in Southern Africa: Challenges and Lessons

Mercy Mpinganjira

Additional information is available at the end of the chapter

http://dx.doi.org/10.5772/50096

1. Introduction

World Trade Organisation (WTO) driven agreements, specifically those involving reduction in tariff and non-tariff barriers in world markets, have created a framework for an open trading system worldwide. More open trading systems have also been created by reforms that most countries have taken on their own or as part of bilateral or regional agreements. In most sub-Saharan African countries, opening up of markets to international players come into significant prominence in the early 1980's due to the implementation of World Bank led structural adjustment and market liberalization policies. According to Kherallah et a.l (2000) as well as Crawford (1997) many African countries were in the late 1970s hit by prolonged economic crisis caused by continuous decline in industrial production and commodity prices as well as stagnating agricultural sectors, the main stay of most of the economies. This resulted in persistent deterioration of balance of payment accounts. Crawford (1997) observed that many governments during this time reacted to the situation by implementing measures that ended up fuelling rather than solving the problem. He outlined some of the measures taken which included increased import tariffs, restricting access to foreign exchange, increased control of imports through licensing requirements as well as extension of price controls.

By the early 1980's it was clear that the future economic growth potential of most African countries was under severe threat. This forced most of them to accept World Bank sponsored structural adjustment and market liberalization policies which were specifically aimed at reversing balance of payments deficits and declining economic growth rates. This entailed a reversal of most of the initial measures taken to deal with the problem. New measures included elimination of government control over input and output marketing as well as prices and reduction in foreign exchange controls (Kherallah et al. 2000). According to Crawford (1997), structural adjustment programs were also aimed at broadening of the economic base of the countries. It was noticed at the time that many African countries were over dependent on a few agricultural commodities for their export trade. Diversification of the economic base was seen as a way of ensuring that the economies would in future be able to withstand external shocks such as sharp falls in world prices of commodities and adverse weather conditions.

Increased forces of globalisation over the years have resulted in intensified efforts aimed at increasing their participation and competitiveness in the world markets. A lot of policies and programs have been formulated specifically aimed at international trade promotion. Most of the countries actively participate in the shaping of world trade systems through their membership to the World Trade Organisation.

2. Research problem and objectives

Although many countries in Africa have over the years actively pursued efforts aimed at growing their countries involvement in international trade there is a general lack of studies aimed at examining how the countries' have faired and the reasons behind their performance. There is also lack of sufficient studies on trade promotion efforts pursued over the years.

This chapter aims at examining international trade promotion efforts in Africa with a special focus on countries in the Southern Africa Development Community (SADC) regional group. The group was established in 1992. SADC was preceded by the Southern Africa Development Coordination Conference (SADC) which was formed in 1980. SADC is made up of 15 Southern Africa countries namely Angola, Botswana, Democratic Republic of Congo, Lesotho, Madagascar, Malawi, Mauritius, Mozambique, Namibia, Seychelles, South Africa, Swaziland, Tanzania, Zambia and Zimbabwe. The specific objectives of the chapter are to (a) examine global, regional and country trends in import and export trade (b) investigate export promotion efforts in the SADC region (c) understand export promotion challenges in the region and (d) provide recommendations on how best to manage the challenges.

3. Methodology

This study involved a review of secondary sources of information and analysis of secondary data. A number of sources were used in the analysis including publications by governments as well as regional and international bodies such as the World Bank, World Trade Organization and SADC secretariat. Use of multiples sources of information and data is highly recommended in desk research as it helps in ensuring the reliability and validity of the findings. Malhotra (2007) noted that use of multiple sources of information also helps in making it easy to assess validity of each source by comparing it with other sources covering the same issue. The World Development Indicators and Global Development Finance database of World Bank was the main source of statistical information used in the trend analysis of imports and exports. The database was chosen mainly because of its comprehensiveness and in order to avoid difficulties associated with use of non-standardised data, especially data from different countries that may be reported in different currencies which make comparisons difficult.

The rest of the chapter has been divided into four main sections. The first section looks at the importance of exports particularly in the context of SADC countries. This is followed by a discussion of export promotion efforts in the region. The third section provides a trend analysis of exports and imports at global and regional level as well as at SADC member country level. The fourth section looks at export promotion challenges in the region and suggests ways in which governments can manage these challenges. The chapter concludes by providing a summary of the key observations made in the analysis. It is important to note that the focus of this chapter is more at the macro-level and not at individual business level.

4. Importance of exports in the SADC region

The fifteen member countries making up the Southern Africa Development Community are all developing economies. According to the World Bank classification of countries, 8 of the 15 members countries are classified as least developed countries. These are Angola, Democratic Republic of Congo, Lesotho, Madagascar, Malawi, Mozambique, Tanzania and Zambia. The United Nations (2005) least developed countries are countries characterised by three main things namely low gross national income (GNI), weak human assets and high degree of economic vulnerability. Maringwa (2009) observed that as undeveloped economies most SADC member countries see trade as an important instrument for economic growth. There are many ways in which international trade and exports in particular can help in economic development of the member countries. These include generation of foreign exchange reserves, improving individual country's competitiveness internationally, as well as in creation of employment.

4.1. Generation of foreign exchange

SADC member countries rely on export earnings for their foreign exchange reserves. These reserves are critical to financing imports and improving a country's balance of payment. One important characteristic of SADC countries is that most of them are dependent on primary products for their exports. The production of these primary products often requires machinery and other inputs that are not manufactured domestically. Generation of foreign reserves thus enable member countries pay for their imports some of which are critical to the generation of exports.

Gunsel et al (2010) observed that countries get concerned with deterioration in balance of payments because it often results in loss of currency value. Although in theory devaluation of a currency is supposed to help in improving the competitiveness of a country's exports by making locally produced goods cheaper, for countries that are heavily dependent on imports to produce their exports as is the case with most SADC countries, devaluation of currency does not always have the desired positive effect.

4.2. Improving international competitiveness

Exports help in promoting international competitiveness through, among other things, improved production efficiencies that are made possible by increased opportunities to exploit larger economies of scale (Ahmed et al. 2008). Exploitation of economies of scale is often a major problem in most SADC countries due to the small sizes of their industries and low purchasing power. Table 1 provides statistics on the size of each SADC member country in terms of total population and total GDP at current prices. As can be seen from the statistics except for South Africa, the GDP at current prices of all SADC countries has for the past three decades remained below the US$100 billion. Thus despite most of the countries having high population figures, their output as reflected by GDP is very low. The low GDP at current prices are indicative of low purchasing power of the people in general. At regional level, Table 1 shows that the GDP at current prices for the whole of Sub-Saharan Africa is less than a quarter of GDP for developing countries from East Asia and the Pacific as well as Latin America and the Caribbean.

Country	Country Size (Sq km)	2010 Total Population (millions)	GDP current US$ (billions)		
			1990	2000	2010
Angola	1,246,700	19.1	10.3	9.1	84.9
Botswana	581,730	2	3.8	5.6	14.9
Democratic Republic of Congo	2,344,858	66.0	9.3	4.3	13.1
Lesotho	30,355	2.2	0.54	0.75	2.2
Madagascar	587,041	20.7	3.1	8.5	8.7
Malawi	118,484	14.9	1.9	1.7	5.1
Mauritius	2,040	1.3	2.7	4.6	9.7
Mozambique	799,380	23.4	2.5	4.2	9.6
Namibia	824,292	2.3	2.4	3.9	12.2
Seychelles	455	0.09	0.37	0.61	0.94
South Africa	1,219,090	50.0	112.0	132.9	363.9
Swaziland	17,364	1.1	1.1	1.5	3.7
Tanzania	947,300	44.8	4.3	10.2	22.9
Zambia	752,618	12.9	3.3	3.2	16.2
Zimbabwe	390,757	12.6	8.8	6.7	7.5
Sub-Saharan Africa	-	854	301.4	343.8	1,123.6
Developing countries - Latin America and the Caribbean	-	583	1,159.5	2,137.98	5,123.2
Developing countries – East Asia and the Pacific	-	1,962	670.8	1,727.2	7,630.5
World Average	-	7,021.8	21,921.24	32,249.68	63,256.97

Sources: World Bank (2012). World Development Indicators and Global Development Finance, CIA (2012) World Fact Book.

Table 1. Size, Population and Basic Economic Indicators of SADC Economies

Rapid growth in exports compared to imports also helps in ensuring economic stability of a country and building international investors' confidence. In SADC countries such investment is needed in order to finance more large scale production activities most of whose output is often sold in international markets. Growth in exports has thus the ability to trigger more investment in a country which can create more exports in an upward spiral cycle. Bothma (2011) further observed that export marketing brings with it opportunities for technology transfer through exposure in targeted international markets to new technologies, new designs and new products. All this helps to improve the competitiveness of a country's output.

4.3. Employment generation

In promoting exports, SADC countries are also interested in ensuring that export growth is accompanied with improved structural transformations including growth in employment levels. Exports directly contribute to job generation through high volumes often associated with export orders. Production of large volumes will often entail the need to expand the labour force. Exporting also contributes indirectly to job generation through creation of backward and forward business linkages. Increased export production volumes result in increased purchase of raw materials used in production. If the suppliers of the raw materials are based in the domestic market, this will also often entail the need for them to increase their labour force in order to cater for increased demand for their products. It is for this reason that exports are linked not only to growth in national output but also improvements in standards of living.

There are thus many benefits associated with increased export activity at country level especially in relation to its potential to enhance society's well being. It is therefore not surprising that export development is at the centre of growth and development deliberations of SADC countries. Member countries have in place policies and programs aimed at stimulating export growth. The section below outlines some of the initiatives being undertaken in order to boost SADC member countries' involvement in international trade through growth of exports.

5. Export promotion programs in the SADC region

According to Seringhaus (1986) export promotion refers to all public policy measures that actually or potentially enhance exporting activity from a national, industry or firm perspective. Mpinganjira (2004) noted that there are three main ways in which governments promote exports. These are through economic cooperation with other nations; pursuing business-friendly fiscal measures and through provision of export assistance programs.

5.1. Economic cooperation

Trade agreements are part of almost all economic cooperation initiatives that countries enter into at both bilateral and multilateral level. As an intergovernmental organization responsible for ensuring deeper integration of member countries, SADC realises the importance of enhancing cross border trade and investment in the realisation of its objectives. The SADC protocol on trade signed in 1996 sets among its objectives to further liberalise intra-regional trade in goods and services; contribute towards improvement of the climate for domestic, cross-border and foreign investment as well as the establishment of a Free Trade Area in the region (SADC, 1996). In order to achieve the set objectives SADC countries specifically committed themselves to easing tariff and non-tariff barriers to trade between them. For example, under the protocol member states are not allowed to apply export duties on goods to other member states. Member states also agreed under the protocol on a phased reduction and eventual elimination of import duties for goods and services originating from member countries.

Apart from the SADC grouping many member countries have preferential access to other markets through their membership to other regional agreements. For example Botswana, Lesotho, Namibia, Swaziland and South Africa are all members of the Southern Africa Customs Union (SACU). Established in 1910, the five members of SACU form a common customs area in which tariff and non-tariff barriers are removed on trade in products originating from member countries and a common external tariff is applied to non-members (SACU, 2007). Tanzania is a member of East African Community (EAC) which has five member countries in it including Burundi, Kenya, Rwanda and Uganda. The treaty for establishment of EAC was signed in 1999. Its main objective is to widen and deepen co-operation among member states and to this extent EAC countries established a customs union in 2005 and a common market in 2010 (EAC, 2012). The Democratic Republic of Congo, Madagascar, Malawi, Mauritius, Seychelles, Swaziland, Zambia and Zimbabwe are members of the Common Market for Eastern and Southern Africa (COMESA), a grouping of currently 19 member states. The other members of COMESA are Burundi, Comoros, Djibouti, Egypt, Eritrea, Ethiopia, Kenya, Libya, Rwanda, Sudan and Unganda (COMESA 2012). Formed in 1994, COMESA is a large economic trading unit working diligently on, among other things, elimination of tariff and non tariff barriers for products originating from member states. At the time of its establishment COMESA preplaced the Preferential Trade Area which was established in 1981. 14 of its current members are part of the COMESA free trade area which started with 9 members in the year 2000 (Ndiho, 2011). From this, one can see that each SADC member country is part of at least one other regional grouping whose aims include promotion of international trade.

SADC member countries also have bilateral and multilateral trade agreements with other groupings and individual countries such as the European Union and USA. Some of the agreements included the 'Everything But Arms' initiative and the African Growth Opportunity Act (AGOA) respectively. Under the 'Everything But Arms' initiative which was adopted in 2001, products from Least Developed Countries (LCDs) except arms and ammunitions are granted duty free access to the EU market (European Commission [EC], 2012). Under AGOA which was signed into law in 2000, beneficiary countries in sub-Saharan Africa are provided with the 'most liberal access to the US market available to any country or region with which they do not have a Free Trade Agreement with' (ITA, 2012). Economic cooperation and integration have thus been actively used by SADC countries for the purposes of promoting its exports.

5.2. Fiscal policy measures

Fiscal policy measures including policies on exchange rates and tax can significantly impact on export success. When it comes to exchange rates, the major concerns are the value and volatility of currency relative to currencies of major trading partners. While some countries work hard to reduce the value of their currencies in order to make their exports competitive on the international market and make imports expensive, for most SADC countries the major concern is ensuring that there is relative stability in exchange rates. This is due to the heavy reliance on imports such as fertilizers to produce exports. Devaluation in exchange rates is such cases does not produce desires positive effects on exports. It is for this reason that countries in the region are increasingly using the ability to open foreign dominated accounts as an incentive targeted at exporters. Under this incentive exporters are allowed to retain a specified percentage of their export earnings in a foreign dominated account which they can use to finance their imports. In terms of tax incentives, duty drawback schemes on imports used to generate export sales are the commonly used incentive by member countries. The scope for targeting tax incentives to exporters in the region is however constrained by WTO Agreements on Subsidies and Countervailing measures (Masters, 2006).

5.3. Export assistance programs

Export Assistance Programmes are mainly targeted directly at individual firm level. They include export service and market development programs (Kotabe and Czinkota, 1992). Diamantopoulos et al. (1993) noted that export marketing assistance is mostly provided in the form of information in order to reduce uncertainty in the process of decision making. Each of the SADC countries has a dedicated government unit or government supported organisation whose main responsibility is to work with the business community in provision of export assistance services and implementation of the country's export policy. Examples of such organisations are the Botswana Export Development and Investment Authority, the Malawi Export Promotion Council, the Mauritius Export Development and Investment Authority and the Instituto para a Promoção de Exportações (IPEX) in Mozambique. Common services provided by such organisations include export training and counselling services targeted at both exporters and non-exporters, dissemination of international sales leads, provision of assistance with representation on their country's business community at international trade fairs, as well as collecting and making available to businesses market access information including details relating to documentation needed for exporting.

Each year, Southern African governments are investing a lot both financially and non financially in export promotion programs. The extent to which such investments are yielding benefits can only be known through a detailed analysis of international trade activities. The section below provides such an analysis by firstly looking at developments at both the global and regional level as well as at country level.

6. Export and imports – A trend analysis

Discussed in this section are trends over time in member countries' export earnings; export products including the share of manufacture to total merchandise exports as well as destinations of exported products. According to World Bank (2012) the total value of world merchandise exports was at 3.4 trillion US dollars in 1990. World merchandise trade statistics as presented in table 1 show that efforts to promote international trade globally have been bearing a lot of fruit. According to the statistics the total value of world exports reached 5.17 trillion US$ in the year 2000 and 15.21 trillion US$ in 2010. This represents 338 percentage growth in export value over the past two decades. Trade statistics for Sub-Saharan Africa show a significant upward trend in export earnings over the years. The level of growth in earnings is actually higher than the world average. For example, at 343,155 million US$, Africa's export earnings in 2010 were 402 percent higher than in 1990. In terms of its share of world trade, the figure is however only 2.25 percent in 2010 which is marginally higher than its share of 1.97 in 1990. According to table 1, the statistics show a decline in level of contribution of developed countries to world merchandise trade. According to the statistics, at US$2,440,032 million in 1990, developed countries contributed 70 percent to world trade. At US$ 7,997,507 in 2010, developed countries contributed 53 percent to world merchandise export trade.

World Trade Statistics at country level, show that despite some fluctuations in export earnings, all countries in the region have on average been in the last two decades on a general upward path in their export earnings. Statistics however show clear continued domination of a few countries in SADC's export earnings. For example, at 81,821 million US $ in 2010, South Africa export earnings represent 47.3 percent of SADC's total export earnings. The top five exporting countries in 2010 as measured by export earnings in the SADC region were South Africa; Angola; Zambia; Democratic Republic of Congo and Botswana. One common characteristic of SADC top export earning countries is that they all have significant mineral/oil reserves in them.

Presented in table 2 are also import trade statistics. From the statistics it is clear that except for the top exporting countries, international trade in the majority of SADC countries is characterised by persistent negative trade balances. Of more concern is the widening of trade deficits in most of the countries registering persistent trade deficits.

Export diversification has been one of the major trade goals of Africa. For a long time a African countries have recognised the need to diversify their exports particularly into manufactured products. Growth in manufactured products presents a good opportunity for African countries to significantly raise their export earnings. This is because primary exports unlike manufactured products are associated with slow growth in global demand as well as relatively low elasticity of demand. There is thus always concern that an increase in supply of primary commodities will result in a decline in export prices. Table 3 presents statistics on the contribution of manufactured exports to total trade in the years 1990 and 2010 as well as information on the top export products. Table 3 shows that 69 percent of world merchandise exports in 2010 were manufactured products. The figure for Sub-Saharan Africa in 2010 was 30.8 percent. This means that about 70 percent of merchandise exports from Sub Saharan Africa are primary commodities. In general, Sub-Saharan African countries and indeed SADC countries have not managed over time to significantly transform the structure of their exports from primary to manufactured products. It should however be noted that countries such as Botswana, Lesotho, Madagascar, Mauritius ad South Africa had 45 percent or more of their merchandise exports as manufactured goods. Despite this the concern with most of these SADC countries is the heavy reliance on export earnings coming from a few products. For example, statistics shows that in 2010 about 80% of Botswana export earnings in 2010 came from diamond and nickel while 62.2% of Lesothos' export earnings came from footwear and clothing. Of more concern are countries such as Malawi, Mozambique, Namibia and Seychelles who had in 2010 less than 10 percent of export earnings coming from manufactured products.

		1990	1995	2000	2005	2010
World Exports	Exports	3,473,231	5,171,030	6,456,422	10,489,632	15,211,311
Developed countries % of world exports	Exports	2,440,032 70%	3,561,498 69%	4,129,803 64%	6,149,288 59%	7,997,507 53%
Sub-Saharan Africa	Exports Imports	68,368 57,641	76,681 78,497	94,489 81,808	199,158 173,195	343,155 308,353
Angola	Exports Imports	3,910 1,578	3,642 1,468	7,921 3,040	24,109 8,353	53,500 21,500
Botswana	Exports Imports	1,784 1946	2,142 1,911	2,675 2,081	4,425 3,161	**4,693** 5,657
Democratic Republic of Congo	Exports Imports	2,326 1,739	1,563 871	807 683	**2,403** 2,690	5,300 4,500
Lesotho	Exports Imports	**62** 672	**160** 1,107	**220** 809	**651** 1,410	**820** 2,200
Madagascar	Exports Imports	**319** 651	**507** 628	**824** 1,097	**855** 1,706	**1,090** 2,650
Malawi	Exports Imports	**417** 575	**405** 475	**379** 532	**508** 1,165	**1,066** 1,900
Mauritius	Exports Imports	**1,194** 1,618	**1,538** 1,976	**1,557** 2,093	**2,143** 3,157	**2,239** 4,402
Mozambique	Exports Imports	**126** 878	**168** 704	**364** 1,158	**1,783** 2,408	**3,200** 4,500
Namibia	Exports Imports	**1,085** 1,163	**1,409** 1,616	**1,320** 1,550	**2,070** 2,577	**4,052** 5,360
Seychelles	Exports Imports	**56** 186	**52** 233	**194** 342	**340** 675	**400** 650
South Africa	Exports Imports	23,549 18,399	**27,853** 30,546	29,983 29,695	**51,626** 62,304	**81,821** 94,040
Swaziland	Exports Imports	**556** 663	**866** 1,008	**910** 1,046	**1,770** 1,900	**1,550** 1,700
Tanzania	Exports Imports	**331** 1,027	**682** 1,675	**734** 1,524	**1,679** 3,287	**3,687** 7,830
Zambia	Exports Imports	1,309 1,220	1,040 700	892 888	**1,810** 2,558	7,200 5,321
Zimbabwe	Exports Imports	**1,726** 1,847	**2,118** 2,660	1,925 1,863	**1,850** 2,350	**2,500** 3,800

Sources: World Bank (2012). World Development Indicators and Global Development Finance, IMF (1997, 2011). International Trade Statistics Year book.

Table 2. World Merchandise Trade: Imports and Exports a trend analysis

	Share of manufactures to total merchandise exports			Major export commodities
	1990	2000	2010	2010
World Exports	72.3	74.5	69.0	
Sub-Saharan Africa	-	30.7	30.8	
Angola	0.1	0.02	-	Petroleum products and diamond (80%), coffee, sisal, fish, timber, cotton.
Botswana	-	89.6	79.5	Diamonds (68.4%), nickel (10.9%), meat and edible meat offal's (3.4%), ores, slag and ash (2.3%)
Democratic Republic of Congo	-	-	-	Diamonds, gold, copper, cobalt, wood products, crude oil
Lesotho	-	94.9	-	Foot wear, articles of apparel and clothing (62.2%), electrical machinery, equipment and parts (16.4%) Beverages, spirits and vinegar (5.2%)
Madagascar	14.4	52.2	48.2	Coffee, Vanilla, Shell fish, Sugar, textile, Chromate
Malawi	5.1	7.4	9.0	Tobacco (53%), uranium, tea, sugar, cotton, coffee, peanuts
Mauritius	65.8	80.8	60.2	Clothing and textiles, sugar, cut flower, molasses, fish
Mozambique	-	6.7	2.0	Aluminium, prawns, cashews, cotton, sugar, citrus,
Namibia	-	6.7	2.0	Diamonds (25.5%), Ores, slag and ash (16.3%), fish and crustaceans (13.7%), meat, edible offal and live animals (6.1%) Vehicles (6%), Zinc and articles thereof (4.9%),
Seychelles	0.2	5.0	-	Canned tuna, frozen fish, cinnamon bark, copra
South Africa	-	53.8	46.6	Gold, diamonds, platinum, other metals and minerals, machinery and equipment, fruits and nuts.
Swaziland	-	54.4	-	Soft drink concentrates, sugar, wood pulp, cotton yarn,
Tanzania	-	19.6	24.1	Gold, coffee, cashew nuts,
Zambia	-	10.7	6.3	Copper/cobalt (64%), electricity, tobacco, flowers
Zimbabwe	30.9	28.1	36.4	Platinum, cotton, tobacco, gold, ferroalloys, textiles and clothing.

Sources: Complied using mainly data from World Bank, CIA – world Fact Book, SACU and IMF

Table 3. International Merchandise Trade: Export Composition

In general the high levels of dependence of most SADC countries on a few export products or for many of them on primary products is that it increases the vulnerability of countries to shocks arising from volatile international prices.

Country/ Region	Destination	1990	2010	2010 Top export destinations
Angola	High income economies Sub-Saharan Africa	90.4 0.5	42.1 3.7	China (42.8%), USA (23%), India (9.5%), France (4%).
Botswana	High income economies Sub-Saharan Africa	- -	73.1 18.8	UK (55%), South Africa (12.9%), Norway (9.3%)
Democratic Republic of Congo	High income economies Sub-Saharan Africa	87.3 7.1	25.8 25.7	China (46.9%) Zambia (23.3%), USA (10.4%), Belgium (4.2%)
Lesotho	High income economies Sub-Saharan Africa	-	-	South Africa (48.9%), USA (31.8%), Canada (15.1%) - 2009
Madagascar	High income economies Sub-Saharan Africa	88.1 4.9	72.1 5.3	France, USA, Germany, China, UK.
Malawi	High income economies Sub-Saharan Africa	76.8 15.0	49.1 22.3	Belgium Canada, Egypt, Germany, USA,
Mauritius	High income economies Sub-Saharan Africa	95.6 2.2	80.8 14.6	UK, France, USA, Madagascar, Italy
Mozambique	High income economies Sub-Saharan Africa	71.4 3.0	64.0 25.9	Netherlands (52.7%), South Africa, Portugal, China, Zimbabwe
Namibia	High income economies Sub-Saharan Africa	-	-	South Africa, UK, Angola
Seychelles	High income economies Sub-Saharan Africa	96.0 1.2	71.6 10.0	Saudi Arabia, France, UK, Italy, Germany
South Africa	High income economies Sub-Saharan Africa	89.0 6.5	56.1 14.9	China, USA, Japan, Germany, UK, India

Country/ Region	Destination	1990	2010	2010 Top export destinations
Swaziland	High income economies Sub-Saharan Africa	-	-	South Africa (56.7%), USA (6.8%) and Mozambique (3.9%)
Tanzania	High income economies Sub-Saharan Africa	64.6 7.8	38.4 19.6	Switzerland, China, South Africa,
Zambia	High income economies Sub-Saharan Africa	72.0 7.8	59.4 19.1	Switzerland, China, South Africa, DRC
Zimbabwe	High income economies Sub-Saharan Africa	62.0 31.7	29.4 47.3	South Africa, Netherlands, Switzerland
Sub-Saharan Africa	Sub-Saharan Africa	7.2	12.2*	
Developing Asia	**Developing Asia**	**33.3**	**37.6**	
Advanced economies	**Advanced economies**	**76.3**	**66.4**	

Sources: Complied using mainly data from World Bank, CIA – world Fact Book, SACU and IMF

Table 4. Export Destination Percentage of the Region/Country Total Trade

Table 4 presents details relating to analysis of destination of exports from the SADC region. The results show that developed economies are the major export markets for the SADC region. The results also show an expansion over the years in Intra-Sub-Saharan Africa trade. As noted before, promotion of regional trade is one of the priority goals of the region. Intra-Africa trade is particularly attractive to many of the smaller land locked economies in the SADC region mainly because of the tremendous challenges that they face in trading at inter-continental level.

It should however be pointed out that at 7.2 percent in 2010 intra- Sub Saharan trade is significantly lower that that of many other regional economic groupings. According to table 4 intra-regional trade in 2010 among developing counties in Asia was at 37.6% while that for advanced economies was 66.6 percent. The table also shows heavy dependence of many SADC countries on a few countries for the export trade. For example in 2010 over 40 percent of exports from Angola, Botswana, Democratic Republic of Congo, Lesotho, Mozambique and Swaziland went to a single country.

The analysis above shows that SADC countries have only marginally benefited from the massive growth in exports that the world as a whole has experienced over the past twenty to thirty years. A number of challenges face SADC's ability to significantly grow its export earnings. The section below outlines some of these challenges and provides suggestions on how the region can deal with them in order to grow its share in world export earnings.

7. Challenges and recommendations to export promotion in the SADC

7.1. Region

There are many challenges to export promotion in the SADC region. In order to effectively deal with them, it is important for countries to focus on the whole value chain associated with exporting. It is for this reason that this section looks at the challenges by focusing on what happens from the production side to the demand side of export products.

7.1.1. Production related challenges and recommendations

Of particular concern when it comes to production related challenges are issues relating to production capacity and diversification. Mpinganjira (2004) noted that many firms in Africa shun away from international markets. Some of the major reasons found for doing so were lack of capacity to produce the large quantities often demanded in international trade and inability to produce products of export quality. Governments need to critically look at ways of enhancing production capacity within their countries by among other things providing strategic support to industries targeting export markets such as having earmarked financial support investments in export related production activities. Governments in the region also need to pay particular attention to ensuring access to technologies critical for quality assurance purposes.

On the production side, there is also need for SADC countries to critically look at ways in which they can diversify their exports. Programs that support industrialisation of the economies can go a long way in growing SADC countries share of manufactured products to its total export trade. It should however be acknowledged that for many SADC countries, industrialisation may take long to realise. Thus while pursuing this strategy, countries need to also look at ways of diversifying their primary exports to avoid over dependence on a few commodities. The argument put forward is that any form of diversification in SADC exports is likely to provide them with a better shield against fluctuations in commodity prices on the international market.

7.1.2. Demand related challenges and recommendations

On the demand side, the challenges are mainly related to finding ways of diversifying target markets for exports as well as assisting companies with identifying buyers internationally. African countries have for long relied on Western countries, in particular European countries as their major export markets. Afari-Gyan (2010) noted that Africa's dependence on Europe can be traced back to colonial days when the structure of Africa trade was determined by the need for raw materials to supply the manufacturing sector in the colonising countries. Decades after independence, Africa has not significantly changed the composition of its exports. The economic crisis experienced by European countries has resulted in increased calls for Africa to diversify its markets and avoid the pitfalls associated with overreliance on a few markets. China and India are increasingly being looked at as alternative markets to be aggressively pursued. China in particular has demonstrated a lot of interest in Africa by significantly growing its investments and ties in the continent over the past five years. It is however important to note that just like Europe, China and India's interest in Africa is on its natural resources and not manufactured products. Nevertheless Africa needs to take advantage of the demand coming from these countries in order to not only grow demand for its exports but also diversify its markets. One way in which it can do this is by negotiating preferential trade agreements with the new major trading partners.

SADC governments need to also realise that it will take more than negotiation of preferential trade agreements for actual demand to be created. One thing that needs to be critically looked at are ways of assisting local companies get a foothold in the targeted markets. While provision of information including trade leads cannot be discounted, governments need to invest in international buyer-seller meetings. Such meetings assist companies develop close working and personal relationships with international business partners. Close personal relationships established during such meetings can go a long way in helping secure ongoing business deals.

7.1.3. Trade related infrastructure challenges and recommendations

Well functioning infrastructure system including a good road, railway and air networks are essential for trade facilitation. According to Mbekeani (2007) poor infrastructure significantly adds to making exports from many African countries uncompetitive on the international market by adding to costs and time taken to move goods to target markets. The UN Economic Commission Report (2012) reported that less than 25 percent of African roads are paved. The report further states that Africa's maritime ports productivity is only 30 percent of the international norm and that costs are high. The Economic Times (2012) reported that poor infrastructure make transport costs in Africa 60 percent higher on average than the average for developed countries.

With over 90 percent of the volume of cargo in the SADC region transported by road and a good number of its members being land locked countries a good road infrastructure is essential. Thus efforts to grow Africa's exports need to include major infrastructural developments with the countries as well as improving on efficiencies in the region's major ports. Unless these issues are addressed SADC countries will continue to face high costs of production for their exports thus making it hard for the region to compete and grow its export earnings.

7.1.4. Effective export assistance programs

While the improvements in the macro-economic environment are essential in establishing a conducive environment for international trade participation, improvements in this area will be meaningless if individual firms are not persuaded to take up exporting. Effective export assistance programs thus become essential as they can help deal with issues affecting firms at the individual firm level. Past studies on export assistance programs however often report that most firms find export assistance programs provided by government or its agencies not be very useful to their needs. Mpinganjira (2004) noted that most export promotion bodies in Africa suffer from poor funding and that this limits their ability to help businesses. It is important for government to strengthen the area of export assistance programs in their export development strategies. They need to not only ensure that export promotion bodies are well supported but also that they are taken to task to show returns on investment. This will also help in minimising wasted expenditures on their part.

Export promotion bodies need to realise that firms can only make use of their services if they perceive them to be useful. It is thus important that export promotion programs are developed based on a good understanding of the needs of the business community. In doing so export promotion bodies need to bear in mind that firms go through different stages in the internationalisation process. The needs of firms at different stages are likely to be different. Assistance programs have to take this into consideration.

8. Conclusion

The focus of this chapter is on international trade promotion efforts in countries making up the Southern Africa Development Community (SADC). As developing countries, the promotion of international trade, exports in particular, is regarded as one of the main ways in which SADC countries can ensure sustained economic growth. This is because through international trade these countries earn much needed foreign exchange necessary for them to finance their imports. Exports are also an effective way in which the countries can improve their production efficiencies, generate employment and grow investors' confidence and ensuring economic stability.

Preferential trade agreements, pursuance of business friendly fiscal measures as well as provision of export assistance services are the key measures taken by SADC countries in order to improve on their chances of realising the many benefits associated with international trade. An analysis of changes in SADC member countries involvement in international trade shows that the measures taken have yielded some benefits. Of particular note is the growth in export earnings experienced by all SADC countries over the past two decades. It is however important to note that there are still many areas of concern when one looks at SADC's export performance. Some of these concerns relate to the fact that the level of growth in export earnings in most of the member countries is far below the world average and the average for developing economies in general. Many countries in the region continue to experience persistent trade deficits, the region in general has not registered much success in export diversification both in terms of range products exported as well as major markets for export products. Of much concern in this regard is the fact that many SADC countries have not managed to significantly grow their share of exports of manufactured products.

Continued efforts to grow SADC's international trade performance need to address a number of challenges facing export promotion in the region. Specifically governments need to find ways of diversifying their export products by providing strategic support to export production activities in non-traditional products; take measures aimed at ensuring that firms have easy access to technologies necessary for quality control; invest more in assisting companies identify buyers in not only the current major export markets but also exploring demand in new markets. Governments have to also work towards investing a lot in improving trade related infrastructures including transport networks and ensuring adequate funding of export assistance programs while at the same time demanding returns on investments from the export promotion bodies.

Changes in SADC's trade performance heavily depend on a better understanding of the current trade situation and taking measures to address any challenges. The analysis provided in this chapter has assisted in providing a better picture of the situation. Lastly, the chapter has also provided some recommendations on what needs to be done in order to improve on SADC's international Trade Performance.

Author details

Mercy Mpinganjira
University of Johannesburg, South Africa

9. References

Afari-Gyani, N (2010). Transforming Africa's structure and composition of Trade after the global economic crisis. [Online] Last accessed http://www.globaltradealert.org/sites/default/files/GTA5_afari-gyan.pdf Last accessed 20th April 2012

Ahmed, A. Cheng, E. Messinis, G. (2008). The role of exports, FDI and imports in development: New evidence from Sub-Saharan African countries. Working paper no. 3. Center for Strategic Economic Studies, Victoria University, Australia

Bothma C (2011) Introduction to International Marketing *in* Bothma, C and Burges, S International Marketing 2nd Edition. Oxford University Press: Cape Town, South Africa

CIA (2012) The World Fact Book. [Online] Available at https://www.cia.gov/contact-cia/index.html. Last accessed on 12th May 2012.

COMESA (2012). Common Market for Eastern and Southern Africa: About COMESA. [Online] Available at: http://about.comesa.int/index.php?option=com_content&view=article&id=75&Itemid=106, Last accessed on 8th April 2012

Crawford, IM (1997). Agricultural and food marketing management. Food and Agriculture Organisation of the United Nations. FAO: Agriculture and Consumer Protection, Rome.

Diamantopoulos, A., Schlegelmilch, B.B. and Tse, K. (1993), 'Understanding the Role of Export Marketing Assistance: Empirical Evidence and Research Needs', *European Journal of Marketing,* Vol. 27 No. 4, pp. 5-18.

EAC (2012) East Africa Community: About EAC. [Online] Available at: http://www.eac.int/about-eac.html. Last accessed on 10th April 2012.

EC (2012) Generalised System of Preferences: Everything But Arms. European Commission [Online] Available at http://ec.europa.eu/trade/wider-agenda/development/generalised-system-of-preferences/everything-but-arms/ Last accessed 15th April 2012

Economic Commission for Africa (2010) Trade Facilitation and intra African Trade. Briefing No. 15 [Online] Available at http://www.uneca.org/atpc/Briefing_papers/15.pdf Last Accessed on 9th April 2012.

Economic Times (2012) Africa losing out billions in trade. [Online] Available at: http://economictimes.indiatimes.com/news/international-business/ Last accessed 10th April 2012.

Gunsel, N. Turoy, T and Rjoub, H. (2010). An empirical analysis of currency crises: Fundamentals and Speculative Pressure. Africa Journal of Business Management 4(6): 972-978.

IMF (2011; 1997), *Directions of Trade Statistics Year Book,* IMF Publications, Washington, DC.

ITA (2012) International Trade Administration: Frequently asked questions about AGOA. [Online] Available at: http://www.agoa.gov/faq/index.asp#P18_1079 Last accessed on 15th April 2012.

Kherallah, M. Delgado, C. Gabre-Madhin, E. Minot, N. Johnson, M. (2000). The road half travelled: Agricultural market reform in Sub-Saharan Africa. International Food Policy, Washington, USA.

Kotabe, M. and Czinkota, M.R. (1992), 'State Government Promotion of Manufacturing Exports: A Gap Analysis', *Journal of International Business Studies,* Vol. 23 No. 4, pp. 637-58.

Malhotra, N.K. (2007). Marketing research: an applied orientation. New York: Prentice Hall International

Maringwa, J (2009). SADC Regional Integration: What role has bilateral trade agreements played in promoting intra-regional trade? AusAid, Australian Government.

Mbekeani, K. (2007). The role of infrastructure in determining export competitiveness: Framework paper. Working paper No. ESWP_05. Africa Economic Research Consortium, Nairobi, Kenya

McCombie, J.S.L., and A.P. Thirlwall. *Economic Growth and the Balance-of-Payments Constraint.* New York: St. Martin's, 1994.

Mpinganjira (2004). The determinants of export involvement in small and medium sized businesses: The case of Malawi. Thesis submitted in fulfilment of the requirements of Doctor of Philosophy Degree, University of Newcastle, Australia.

Ndiho, P (2011). COMESA open for business. [Online] Available at http://www.vipiafrica.com/2011/08/comesa-open-for-business.html; Last accessed 6th April 2012

United Nations (2005) The Criteria for the identification of Least Developed Countries. United Nations, New York, USA

SADC (1996). Southern Africa Development Community Protocol on Trade. [Online] available at http://www.sadcstan.co.za/protocol.html. Last accessed 12th May 2012

SACU (2007). What is SACU. [Online] available at http://www.sacu.int/main.php?id=471. Last accessed 10th April 2012.

Seringhaus, R.F.H. (1986), 'The Impact of Government Export Marketing Assistance', *International Marketing Review,* Vol. 3 No. 2, pp. 55-66.

World Bank (2012) World Development Indicators and Global Finance [Online] Available at: http://databank.worldbank.org/ddp/home.do?CNO=2&Step=12&id=4; Last accessed 10th May 2012.

Chapter 9

Technical Barriers to Trade of Leather and Footwear: Impacts and Challenges Posed by International Standards, Regulations and Market Requirements in Brazil

Mauro Silva Ruiz, Alexandre de Oliveira e Aguiar,
Pedro Luiz Cortez, Cláudia Echevenguá Teixeira
and Gustavo Silveira Graudenz

Additional information is available at the end of the chapter

http://dx.doi.org/10.5772/50575

1. Introduction

A technical barrier is a type of non-tariff barrier related to a technical standard, regulation or a market requirement applicable to features of industrial products, processes or methods of production aiming at protecting the environment and consumers. In this case it relates to restrictions imposed by international directives, standards and regulations, and market requirements regarding the presence of a number of chemical substances in leather (wet blue stage) and footwear, as well as physical and mechanical characteristics of soles and heels.

As the market globalization became more evident right after the Uruguay Round organized by World Trade Organization (WTO), several technical barriers showed up in the market of many products, most of them imposed by European countries. At first, these barriers were seen as protectionist measures most of them taking an environmental issue as some sort of appeal. One question frequently asked in the early nineties was: can an increase in the international trade result in more environmental degradation?

Although it is not quite clear in the surveyed literature, obstacles that in previous decades were seen as protectionist measures are being more and more seen as opportunities for companies and corporations that have been incorporating environmental management as a competitive advantage in their strategies. In fact, this issue is somewhat related to the controversial relationship between trade and development (Philip; Jeanet & Finn, 2009).

Braga and Miranda (2002) refers to Porter hypothesis that emphasizes the synergy effects between environmental regulation and competitiveness (Porter and Van der Linde, 1995). It means that the more companies go beyond the basic standards, improving their own environmental control and monitoring, the better their competitiveness in the marketplace.

The technical barriers with "green roots" in general have their birth in countries and economic blocks where the awareness of society of sustainable consumption started several years ago. Usually, the presence of the economic benefits of environmental regulations such as better distribution of natural resources or avoiding public health issues has already been perceived in these countries. Thus, the demand for environmentally friendly products and goods pushed regulations forward in these places firstly and in the countries from where they have been importing afterwards.

International trade is currently regulated by World Trade Organization. More than 150 state members are involved in the liberalization of international trade, particularly in the removal of unnecessary barriers to international trade and in the solution of disputes. Technical barriers are also discussed in this context.

One important aspect of directives that establish technical or environmental standards is that at first they violate two basic principles of the Technical Barriers to Trade (TBT) as it concerns to "no discrimination" and "harmonization of rules regulations and procedures". The first principle is violated particularly when a rule, regulation or a technical procedure is required to be followed by an exporting one that is less developed than the importing one. If violation can be proved by the reclaiming country, a round of negotiation will be settled by WTO to resolve the matter.

Fornasari Filho and Coelho (2002) point out that the WTO has been concerned with detecting, characterizing and eliminating restrictions or distortions of an environmental nature that can result in barriers to trade.

Presently there is a growing concern for environmental issues and the associated barriers to international trade in products coming from industrial sectors located in developing countries that could be affecting the environment. This is the case of the leather and footwear sector that can potentially have a heavy impact the environment due to a number of chemical substances used in the treatment of the hide and skin into processed leather.

Progressively, regulatory pressures coming from new rules and regulations resulting from both the international and domestic market forced the leather and footwear companies to introduce continuous improvements in their production processes reducing pollution at its source and also aggregating new technologies in the tanning process. On the other hand, footwear consumers worldwide are becoming aware of the environmental and health effects of the chemical substances used in leather processing. This has led to a more effective monitoring of the environmental effects caused by the leather and footwear industry especially in developed countries.

Public pressure on tanneries and all industries that are leather users, including footwear factories, furniture, cars and clothes, has been intensified requiring them to use leather having reduced levels of hazardous substances.

One assumption of this chapter is that international standards, regulations and market requirements tend to pose constraints to the exports of leather and footwear in developing countries (e.g. Brazil) in the short-run, but in the mid to long run their negative effects tend to be attenuated and become beneficial to the productive chain as a whole. In this regard, the research question pursued was the following: *what are the impacts and challenges posed by current international standards, regulations and market requirements that can be seen as technical barriers to trade of leather and footwear produced in developing countries such as Brazil?*

Based on this question, two following objectives were designed to guide the research: (i) to analyze and discuss to what extent the international standards and regulations, and technical requirements can effectively be considered technical barriers to trade of leather and footwear; and (ii) to assess qualitatively the impacts and challenges posed by these standards, regulations, and technical requirements to the Brazilian industry in the short, mid and the long-run.

The research methodology to carry out this study consisted of (i) literature review - including documents, websites, papers, dissertations and reports; (ii) interviews with Brazilian professionals from private companies, universities and research institutions, and (iii) a brainwriting session with experts in the leather and footwear industry. The interviews were supported by open-ended questionnaires and the brainwriting session was carried out with fifteen experts from the industry, academia and research institutions.

2. Literature review

Technical barriers to trade have deserved attention in the areas of economic policy, industrial and foreign trade, and environmental studies. WTO defines technical barriers as trade barriers arising from the use of standards or technical regulations that are not transparent or not based on internationally accepted standards. These barriers can also result from the adoption of conformity assessment procedures that are not transparent and/or are too expensive to exporting companies and countries. In addition, they can derive from excessively stringent inspections resulting either from the standards set by the signatory countries or the harmonization of standards worldwide (Instituto Nacional de Metrologia, Normalização e Qualidade Industrial, 2005).

Prazeres (2003) argues that technical barriers are restrictions on the flow of international trade based on requirements related to the characteristics of the goods to be imported. These requirements can either refer to the content of the product or the tests showing that a product meets the relevant specifications imposed by the importer.

According to Perina; Machado & Miranda (2003), the technical standard is characterized as a non-tariff barrier when there is:

a. An imposition of cultural and technological standards incompatible with the exporting country, implying major changes in the production process, increasing costs without technical justification;
b. Discrimination against imported products;
c. Discrimination of input use, especially for agricultural products under the unproven allegation of damage to health and the environment;
d. Lack of clear disclosure about the technical requirements.

According to the Brazilian Ministry of Development, Industry and Foreign Trade, the growing complexity of international relations coupled with the evolution of society have led to the establishment of environmental and social requirements that traditionally had not been covered in trade negotiations (Ministério do Desenvolvimento, Indústria e Comércio Exterior, 2002). According to Castro et al. (2003), it is difficult for negotiators of international agreements to differentiate between those measures required by importers that are really necessary and legitimate for environmental protection required from those that have a protectionist character. In the short run, this leads to an increase in the costs of production and price of the product affecting its competitiveness in the exporting market, as the adaptation to new requirements is necessary.

Procópio Filho (1994) calls this eco-protectionism, an assignment to the use of environmental policies that restrict international trade. In order to deal with this challenge, at the commencement of the Doha Development Round in November 2001, a group was formed to analyze the insertion of multilateral environmental agreements in trade negotiations.

It is important to remark that establishing objective criteria for environmental, social and sustainability issues is a hard task due to a) scientific uncertainties regarding quantitative issues; b) lack of acceptable short-term or long-range risk levels for each of these issues; and c) lack of a general consensus on how to effectively pursue sustainability when the international trade is the subject matter.

The Brazilian Ministry of Development, Industry and Foreign Trade points out that the technical regulations are promulgated by the government. Such regulations impose technical requirements that are mandatory for all products they encompass or establish rules for the corresponding conformity assessment procedures applicable in these cases (Ministério do Desenvolvimento, Indústria e Comércio Exterior, 2002).

However, there are some barriers that are not based on measures established by the State. In this case, it is the market that sets them up either by practice or tradition. In specific cases, they can also be established by "technical habits", technical requirements, or even by reasons specified by clients regarding the quality of the demanded product or service. Thus, these requirements may end up as being technical barriers, especially when they differ from those valid for countries to which exports of goods and services will be made.

Garrido (2004) considers that the legitimacy of the barriers in these cases should not be questioned because any importer may establish requirements as it deems necessary to meet its needs. This author argues that technical barriers, broadly speaking, have always existed, although its importance has increased due to the continuous decrease in tariffs in recent years. According to him, many of these barriers were not noticed before because of the existence of high tariffs which made them somewhat invisible. He also adds that from the point of view of competitiveness of the countries involved, as most markets require different technical requirements for the same products or services, this multiplicity of demands results in rising costs posing serious difficulties for them. Prazeres (2003) considers that the developing countries tend to be the losers in this case because of the impacts of the requirements on exports.

3. An overview of the leather and footwear industry

For the purpose of this chapter, the leather and footwear industry can be divided into two major areas: leather processing and leather products manufacturing. However, it has important interfaces with other sectors, such as chemistry, footwear components production, machines and tooling, packaging, among others (Instituto de Pesquisas Tecnológicas, 2006).

In recent decades the spatial distribution of this industry has been changing worldwide and also at the regional level. Internationalization of production and industrial relocation towards less developed countries, regions and states with less stringent environmental regulations and cheaper labor are among the major factors responsible for this change. In this new geographical scenario, Eastern European countries have increased their wet-blue leather production (Santos et al., 2002), and China and India have turned into the biggest leather and footwear suppliers. Brazil still remains as an important footwear producer and exporter due to its comparative advantages of having the biggest cattle herd of the world. Other than being an important leather exporter, Brazil has also exported qualified labor to China and India (Santos et al., 2002). USA, Germany and other European countries are major leather importers (Saravanabhavan, 2005) turning part of the imports into high quality finished leather and footwear for export (Instituto de Pesquisas Tecnológicas, 2006). Italy is known to be benchmark for high-quality finished leather, and uses this to keep a position in the fashion and design market (Santos et al 2002).

In the early 1990s India was the eighth largest footwear producer (Desai, 1995), but its performance in the international market has been changing rapidly through the removal of restrictions to the international trade. Although its economy is still relatively protected, government has been cutting tariffs and non-tariff barriers, phasing out quantitative restrictions and removing other limitations to foreign investments. Progressive liberalization has produced remarkable results (World Bank, 2008) pointing out that the country has the potential to become an important player in the international market in several industrial areas, including footwear.

The role of Brazil as an important leather exporter started in the 1990s. However, it has historically exported mainly low-value contents leather, in the wet-blue stage. Only recently the finished product exports surpassed 50% of the total amount as shown in Figure 1.

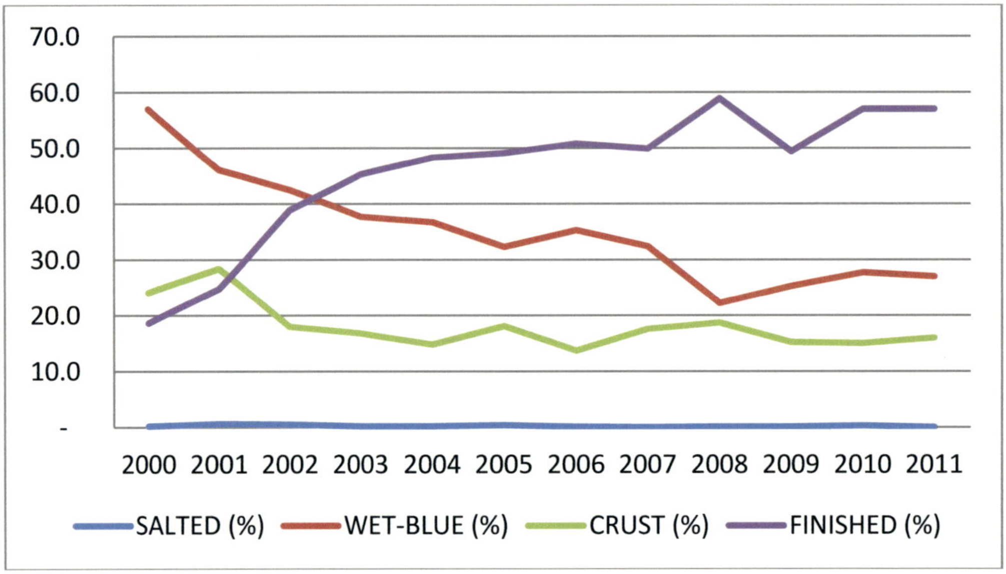

Figure 1. Brazilian exports by leather type

Source: Agência Brasileira de Promoção de Exportação e Investimentos (2012)

According to Fernandes (2004), leather and footwear supply chain is key to the Brazilian economy. By moving around US$ 21 billion annually, from which US$ 3.5 billion have been exporting of leather and footwear in 2010, it can significantly affect internal and external markets, and generate many job positions.

Brazil also moves intense trade in the footwear market. It is a traditional producer and exporter of leather shoes, and now also plays a role in importing sports footwear from Asian countries. Table 1 and figures 2, 3 and 4 summarize key information on this.

Description		2008	2009	2010	%2010/09	%2010/08
Production	Pairs (millions)	816.0	813.6	893.9	9.9%	9.6%
	Value (US$ millions)	10,233.2	9,454.6	12,34 0.4	30.5%	20.6%
Exportation	Pairs (millions)	165.8	126.6	143.0	12.9%	-13.8%
	Value (US$ millions)	1,881.3	1,360.0	1,487. 0	9.3%	-21.0%
Importation	Pairs (millions)	39.3	30.4	28.7	-5.5%	-27.1%
	Value (US$ millions)	307.5	296.5	304.6	2.7%	-0.9%

Source: Associação Brasileira das Indústrias de Calçados (2011)

Table 1. Brazilian footwear industry in numbers

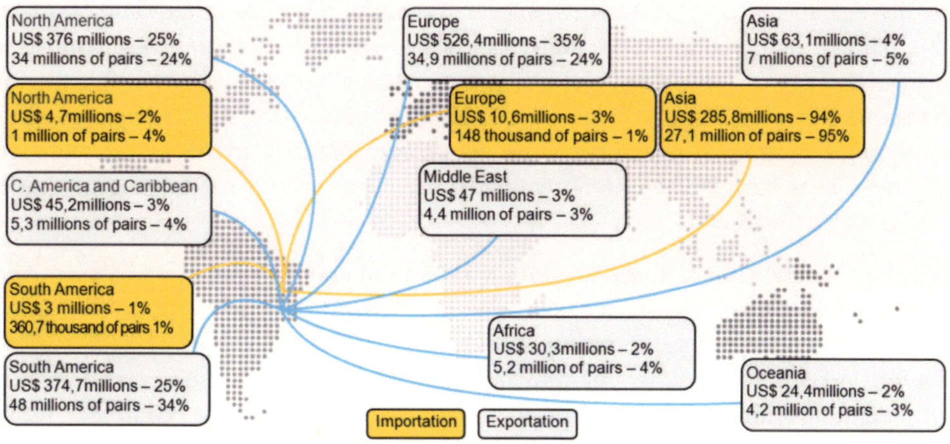

Source: Associação Brasileira das Indústrias de Calçados (2011)

Figure 2. Brazilian footwear imports and exports (2010)

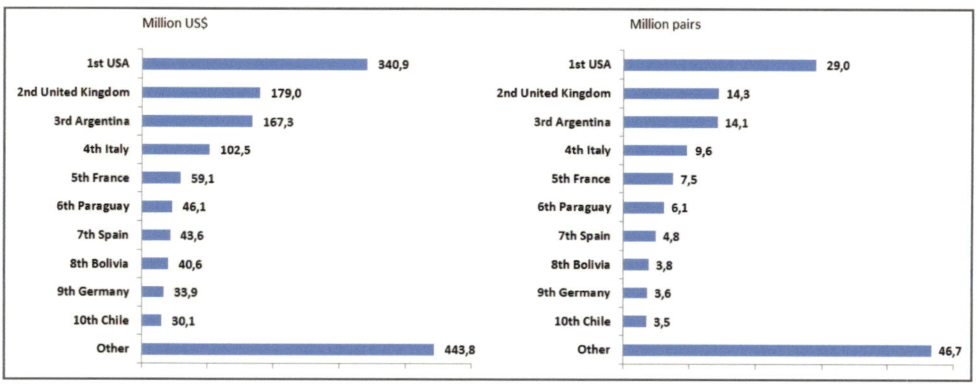

Source: Associação Brasileira das Indústrias de Calçados (2011)

Figure 3. Brazilian shoes industry – exports by destination (2010)

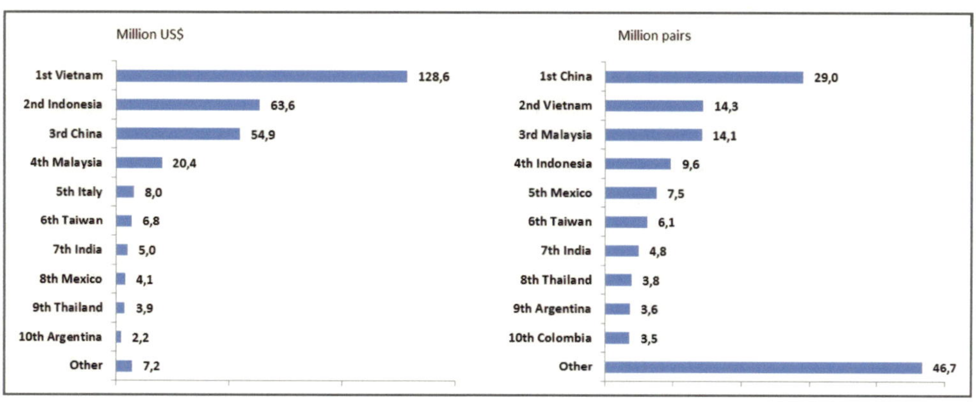

Source: Associação Brasileira das Indústrias de Calçados (2011)

Figure 4. Brazilian shoes industry – imports by origin (2010)

Originally leather industry in Brazil was located mainly in both Southern and Southeastern regions. However, the cattle have significantly grown in the Central-west region, where companies that produce meat are also in the wet-blue leather business. Their location is due to cost reduction opportunities (Santos et al., 2002). Gaspar (2006) argues that this change is a consequence of unfavorable currency taxes, closure of some markets and more intense competition. Less stringent environmental requirements and lower labor costs have also been reasons for the moves.

Footwear production went through similar migration moves countrywide. According to Rosa and Corrêa (2006), this started in the early 1990s. At that time production conditions and competition changed and the companies moved from the South and Southeast states to Northeast, looking for cheaper manpower, local government incentives and to a better geographical position to export. These advantages surpassed the complete industrial integration in the traditional Southern production centers, e.g. Sinos River Valley (Gorini & Siqueira, 2002).

In Brazil, most of the leather processing industries and leather artifacts industry are small and medium sized companies that are still owned and managed by families (Campos, 2006). Small enterprises focus on internal market, and typically use processes with low level of automation ("artisans") and have no or scarce knowledge of the requirements and limits for the use of certain substances and processes in the external market. Only a few medium companies are prepared for exports.

These companies are facing pressures due to competition coming from foreign countries where an ongoing fast technological development is taking place (e.g. China and India) and also from other regions in Brazil where local government are providing incentives for new companies.

3.1. Leather processing and environmental issues

Leather processing plays a key role in several countries all over the world. Food and Agriculture Organization (2011) estimates that 1.67 billion of square meters of leather are produced annually worldwide. The complete processing for the leather production, from raw skins up to completely finished leather can be summarized as follows:

a. Cleaning and preservation after abatement: basic cleaning and care to preserve skin/hides to processing;
b. Pre-tanning: elimination of certain parts such as meat, fat and hairs;
c. Tanning: chemical treatment to make leather stable and non-putrescible; and
d. Finishing: operations to give leather specific features such as color, softness, waterproofing, among others.

Approximately 90% of pollution loads comes from pre-tanning and tanning. Tanneries are generally under pressure to minimize final pollution loads (Saravanabhavan et al., 2005; Ramasami et al., 1999). Box 1 summarizes the main environmental issues of leather processing.

Environmental aspects	Features	Comments
Use of azo dyes	Chemical gives color to leather	
Use of formaldehyde	Used for tanning	Tanning material, hardener and fastness (Wolf e Schuck, 2003)
Use of chemicals - Hexavalent chromium	Used for tanning. Heavy metals can contaminate water, bringing risk of deseases such as neural and cancer in some cases, and can be cumulative in the live organisms.	Substitutes such as Zr, Al, Ti and vegetable tannins are not effective for all applications Hoinacki, Moreira & Kiefer (1994); Sousa (2006) Risks of spontaneous oxidization of CrIII to CrVI in the open-air dumps as well as the possible risks of wearing bad quality shoes, in which the chromium content is not controlled (Kolomaznika, 2008)
Solid Waste	Significant amount of trimmings, degraded hide, lime sludge, flesh and hair from beamhouse processes. Depending on the stage can contain Hexavalent chromium Production wastes containing hexavalent chromium can be characterized as hazardous waste according to Brazilian regulations (Sousa, 2006)	Can represent 70% in weight of original hides (World Bank, 1999)
Effluents	Off-neutral pH, lime, sulfides, hexavalent chromium (Contador Junior, 2004)	Azo dyes are also present
	Organic matter	Mainly proteins (Sousa, 2006)
	Salinity (Contador Junior, 2004; Sousa, 2006)	
Air emissions of toxic or odor substances	Ammonia	Released during deliming (World Bank, 1999)
	Hydrogen sulplhide	Released during mixing of dehairing and pickling wastewater (World Bank, 1999)
Air emissions of fuels (Contador Junior, 2004)		
Wastewater treatment Sludge	Coming from tanning and chromium-treatment (Contador Junior, 2004)	Chromium levels in untreated tannery wastewater are typically 100–400 mg/L, while the international standard for chromium bearing discharges is less than 2 mg/L (World Bank 1999; Buljan 1996; Saravanabhavan et al., 2005)

Table 2. Major environmental issues of leather processing

Today, the main environmental concerns of this industry focus on the disposal of the large volumes of potentially hazardous wastes. Due to their degree of risks to human beings they should be disposed of in landfills, recycled or treated via an environmentally sound process. However, it is remarkable the amount of small tanneries in the interior of Brazil that are operating with low technological conditions and far from the environmental agency's eyes. Although in theory the existing environmental regulations are able to deal with them, it is almost impossible to assure that their waste disposal is always carried out following adequate technical procedures. The main wastes are chips, shreds, crumbs, sander dust and mud of both chromium and re-tanning.

As for wastewater, concerns focus on the large volumes with high salt concentration (sulfides, sulfates, chlorides) and high toxicity, especially due to the mineral chromium tanning and various azo dyes from the dyeing. Requirements of the European directive on these dyes from February 24, 1994 applicable to articles of clothing and artifacts of leather producers deserve the special attention of labs providing chemical analysis for the leather and footwear industry at the country level.

On one hand, tanning industry can be seen as an important way to deal with wastes coming from the meat industry. On the other side, data provided by Kolomaznika (2008) show that it is both a low eco-efficient and a serious pollutant industry, as follows:

a. Final leather product yield is 200 kg/ ton of raw hides;
b. Waste generation is around 250 kg of non-tanned solid waste and 200 kg of tanned waste containing 3 kg of chromium per ton of raw hide;
c. Wastewater generation is around 50 m3 / ton of raw hide, containing approximately 5 kg of chromium;
d. More than 60% of originally used chromium is lost in the wastes and wastewater.

Additionally, it is estimated that each footwear production leads to the generation of 220 g of total wastes. According to Centro Tecnológico do Couro (as cited in Companhia de Tecnologia Ambiental de São Paulo, 2011) the generation of wastewater in Brazil is around 25-30 m3/ ton of salted skin. In order to facing environmental, regulations and productivity challenges, the leather industry is internalizing a number of technological changes in its production processes, as follows:

a. Use of enzymes in the tanning process as substitutes of chemicals (Gutterres, 2005);
b. Use of enzymes to treat waste and wastewater (Saravanabhavan et al., 2005);
c. Minimization of use of hexavalent chromium, azo dyes and formaldehyde due to regulations in several countries, particularly in Europe.

Considering that in several countries the leather industry is still at lower technological stages, many companies will have to invest in modernization, including machining, layouts, wastewater treatment systems, automation and process controls (Gutterres, 2005).

3.2. Environmental management in the leather industry

International pressures coming from technical barriers to trade are pushing footwear manufacturers that are involved in exports to follow the requirements to reduce the level of hazardous substances in these products. Backward in the supply chain, these manufacturers push the leather processors that ultimately push the tanneries in this regard. As a response, only the most organized tanneries tend to effectively reduce the use of chemicals that pose risks to human health. A number of them are not capitalized enough to meet all the requirements. This tends to create two different industries, just like two different worlds: the world of the companies that export, and the world of the companies that only meet the demand of the domestic market. In general, the latter is small sized ones that use traditional technology, this way barely meeting the requirements of the local regulations or being completely invisible to environmental agencies.

CETESB, the environmental agency of Sao Paulo State, coordinates an environmental chamber with the participation of leather companies to discuss environmental issues. A recent agreement of this chamber resulted in a procedure for an environmentally sound destination of powder and trimming wastes containing hexavalent chromium (Companhia de Tecnologia Ambiental, 2011).

Currently, the environmental management practices are key to companies that intend to achieve International Standardization Organization – ISO 14001 management systems certification. Such practices are also important to improve employees′ awareness, enhance productivity, reduce loss, minimize accidents, and improve the organization as a whole.

According to International Standardization Organization (2011), there was 440 plants in the leather and leather products sector that were ISO 14001 certified in 2010. Similar statistics were not found in Brazil.

Implementation of environmental management actions in the leather and footwear sector is important based upon a series of issues that the sector faces, such as presence of heavy metals in effluents, air emissions from glues and solvents that can have negative impacts on workers in the internal environment. Among other relevant issues are the financial resources that have to be spent on water and electricity, risks that are associated with chemicals handling and storage, and odor that is generated by tanning.

3.3. Issues involving leather products

In the case of finished footwear, the European ecological label scheme establishes a maximum of 150 ppm of formaldehyde in the leather. Equivalent Japanese standard limits formaldehyde to 112 ppm (Glasspool, 2006).

Wolf e Schuck (2003) reported an increase in positive results for CrVI in the analysis. According to them this increase can be related to both lack of previous attention given by leather producers to the restrictions and the increase in the chemical analysis demanded by importing countries. They emphasized that excessively high pH, ammonia and use of fish-oil based greasing agents should be avoided in tanning to minimize CrVI presence.

Even considering that presently several tanneries are not intentionally using CrVI compound, there has been a few cases in which a high concentration of this element was found in their exported leather products to European and Asian countries (Sousa 2006). In this regard, Dexheimer (2006) states that this CrVI can result from a cumulative process derived from one or more processing steps or as impurities of chemicals used in the "wet" stages of tanning, re-tanning and finishing.

4. International standards, regulations and market requirements on leather and footwear

This section covers the major technical regulations and market requirements given special attention to the EC directives, as follows: 76/769/EEC that sets up limits to market insertion of leather products and also to the use of hazardous chemical substances and preparations; 2002/231/EEC that refers to ecological criteria for attribution of community ecological labels to shoes; and 2004/21/EC that sets up limits to market insertion of leather products and also to the use of azo dye.

The EC directives dealing with restrictive substances in products are imposed by the EU technical regulations whose compliance is mandatory. These directives give priority to the safety of the user in respect of any products or chemicals in products as well as with respect to physical well-being.

The European legislation, which tends to establish general standards for global mandatory restrictions, restricts the use of certain chemicals and these should be in accordance with the goods traded within the EU. Most restrictions are amendments to the directive 76/769/EEC which governs individually all aspects of production, sale and use of chemicals.

The directive 76/769/EEC was adopted on July 27, 1976 aimed at limiting the concentration of hazardous substances to human health and the environment. Over the years, it had twenty-nine amendments and adaptations. Its last revision occurred on January 18, 2006 and was published as directive 2005/90/EC.

A very significant directive for the leather and footwear industry was approved by Decision of the Commission of European Communities and published on March 18, 2002. This policy established revised ecological criteria for the award of community eco-label to footwear. It applies to footwear and its production process, including processing of leather, as considered in the life cycle approach. The main criteria considered in the policy and standards aim to:

a. Limiting the levels of toxic waste;
b. Limiting emissions of volatile organic compounds (VOC);
c. Promoting a more durable product.

The criteria for obtaining the eco-label are:

a. The concentration of toxic substances in the final product, especially the hexavalent chromium content that must not exceed 10 mg/kg; in addition, heavy metals such as arsenic, cadmium, and lead are not expected to be detected at all;
b. The concentration of free and partially hydrolysable formaldehyde expected in the textile components of the footwear must not exceed 75 ppm; the amount of these compounds present in the leather components must not also exceed 150 ppm;
c. Emissions from the footwear manufacture (priority given to wastewater), which must have after due treatment in individual or collective stations, a chemical oxygen demand (COD) reduction of at least 85% related to raw wastewater and total chromium concentration less than 5 ppm;
d. Footwear must not contain harmful substances such as pentachlorophenol (PCP), tetrachlorophenol (TCP) and their salts and esters. The threshold values are 0.05 ppm for textile components and 5.0 ppm for leather components;
e. Azo dyes that can be decomposed into a series of aromatic amines may not be used; tolerable limits are 30 ppm for textiles and leather;
f. The rubber used in footwear manufacturing must not contain a series of N-nitrosamines;
g. Chloroalkanes (C10-C13) must not be used in components of leather, textile or rubber;
h. Volatile organic compounds (VOC) must not be used in the assembly;
i. Footwear shall not contain polyvinyl chloride (PVC), except when this compound is recycled in soles and is not employed in preparing some phthalates;
j. Providing information, on a voluntary basis, on energy consumption per pair of shoes;
k. Footwear shall not contain electric and electronic components;
l. Final packaging of footwear must contain at least 80% recycled material, statement of use, and information making it clear that a shoe was manufactured within the standards established in the directive;
m. Adoption of environmental management systems such as ISO 14001 is not mandatory but recommended (Comissão das Comunidades Europeias, 2002).

An example is the New Zealand criteria for ecolabelling of leather products. The criteria establish a limit of 3 ppm of CrVI in the leather products and a maximum of 1 ppm of CrVI in the treated effluent (The New Zealand Eco-labeling Trust, 2006). This is more stringent than the European criteria and shows that the lack of consensus in risk perception can lead to different technical criteria and therefore to technical barriers.

The European directive 2004/21/EC, established in January 1, 2005 is another policy that affects the leather and footwear industry. Its purpose is to protect the health of the population, limiting the insertion of finished goods in the European market of textile and/or leather in any parts dyed with azo dyes; the major concern is that a person under a prolonged exposure to these substances may become susceptible to cancer (Comissão das Comunidades Europeias, 2002).

According to this policy, by reductive cleavage of one or more azo groups (-N=N-), the dyes may release one or more of aromatic amines, detectable at concentrations above 30 ppm as the test methods set forth. This is a significant topic supported by the following information supplied by Clariant Brazil (2006):

a. 90-95% of leather produced worldwide is dyed with azo dyes;
b. 50-60% of all produced leather is dyed in black;
c. There is a high demand for dyed through leather;
d. There is an increasing demand for strong re-tanned and strongly dyed leather for shoes manufacturing;
e. There has been an increase in the production of leather upholstery, especially in Brazil;
f. Continuous growth in solidity requirements and internationally normalized resistance;
g. Enhancement of the human ecology concept, restricting the use of substances classified as hazardous to the consumers′ health and welfare.

According to Inmetro – Instituto Nacional de Metrologia, Normalização e Qualidade Industrial (2005), monitoring for compliance of products with the requirements of the referred directive is carried out by sampling of products found in the consumer market and not at the borders. The Brazilian Association of the Textile and Clothing (ABIT) concerned with possible harm to Brazilian exporters, asked the companies producing dyes and pigments countrywide a statement of compliance to the directive 2004/21 as it concerns to manufacturing and marketing of dyes for textiles and leather.

Currently labeling is also a topic addressed in technical rules notified by the countries at the WTO, especially as a justification for imposing technical requirements. According to Castro, Castillo, and Miranda (2004), the eco-labels are seals that are intended to inform the consumer about some characteristics of the product. Environmental labels are often known as Green Seal, Environmental Seal or Eco-label. Presently there are many different labeling programs that can be classified into two groups as follows: those adopted and implemented by the manufacturer of the products, and those named third party labeling, conducted by an independent manufacturer.

The European label was created in 1992 by decision of the European Parliament, implemented by the EU Council in the following years, and finally named Ecolabel. It is voluntary, but required for imported products, taking into account the life cycle of each product. This is the first seal to be adopted both regionally and transnationally (Ecoetiqueta Europea para el Calzado, 2006).

The European Eco-label distinguishes the products of high standards of performance and environmental quality. Every product awarded the European Eco-label is subject to rigorous environmental testing by independent organisms. To obtain the seal the following measures should be adopted:

i. Large part of manufactured packaging has to come from recycled material;
ii. Water consumption during production has to be limited;
iii. The amount of chemical residues has to be limited;

iv. Non-recyclable plastics are prohibited;
v. Use of certain categories of dangerous chemicals is also prohibited;

In addition to all these measures, the footwear must comply with the flexural strength, tear strength and abrasion as well as the accession of the sole to the top. Other countries also have created regulations on leather and footwear that sometimes can be seen as technical barriers to trade. In the USA, for instance, concerns seem to be more focused on physical and mechanical properties of materials used in soles and heels than properly on chemical hazardous substances. Schneider (2006) argues the American rules' flexibility as compared to the EU ones is related to the USA dependence on the China's footwear production. According to him, being the USA the largest consumer of footwear worldwide, it would not be wise to counter an industrial power like China, which provides the basic day to day articles to that country, especially for lower income people.

Japan requirements on leather and footwear are similar to the imposed by The European Directives. This happens because the exports are made via European trading companies that receive the shipments in Rotterdam sending them to Japan afterwards.

Due to the increasing awareness of society, corporations such as Adidas, Nike, Clarks, Reebok and Ralph Lauren are also imposing stringent technical requirements for both suppliers of raw materials (leather, plastics, adhesives, glues etc.) and finished products (artifacts in leather and textiles) so as to ensure end-user safety and environmental protection. This also happens with footwear that has been sent to popular mega stores such as Wal-Mart in the USA and Bic in Germany. These demands on imported footwear are forcing producers in developing countries to attend these requirements. Since trading companies export to a number of countries which adopt different rules, tanneries in the domestic market are being forced to meet most of these requirements.

The most important restrictions focus on heavy metals and azo dye on input suppliers or finished products. In addition, some physical and mechanical requirements usually related to soles and heels are also made by these companies.

5. Impacts and challenges posed by international directives and regulations

In the short-run, specialists consider that the high costs of chemical analysis demanded by the EC directives to adjust products and production to the requirements of the foreign market as a negative impact. Small tanneries are the ones having their competitiveness affected as a result of this economic impact on leather processing. On the other hand, some specialists also mentioned that adoption of clean technology, labor qualification, and selection of better qualified raw material suppliers are the positive impacts of the EC directives in the referred sector. This way, the assessment of the impacts depends on the perspective of analysis and also in the time horizon taken into consideration.

Girolla (2006) states that the certification of the leather and footwear supply chain is something to be expected in the coming years as the market and regulatory pressures for cleaner production grows up. He emphasizes that the whole process has to be supported by labs that need to be recognized, certified or accredited by importing countries. In this regard, it is important to highlight the high costs of maintenance of a lab quality system as required to the Brazilian Technical Norms known as ABNT NBR 17025 series.

A positive impact of the EC directive mentioned by Schneider (2006) is the periodic visit of international auditors in the Rockport office at Campo Bom – RS to assess whether industries manufacturing footwear is adequately following the international rules and technical requirements on both environmental and social issues. As for social issues the major concerns focus on child labor and the working conditions in the footwear factories.

Another positive impact of the EC directives is that initiatives similar to the ecological footwear, originally developed in Europe, are being spread around the world. This type of footwear is customized and manufactured with biodegradable materials.

In Brazil, the Footwear Division of the National Service of Industrial Learning (Senai of Novo Hamburgo – RS has developed an ecological footwear with leather tanned with organic products and other non-hazardous substances. In addition, the soles were made with natural rubber, adhesives prepared without organic solvents, foams manufactured without toxic, flammable or corrosive substances, and packaging made of recycled material. Also the manufacturing process resulted in a reduction of water consumption and waste generation (Girolla, 2006).

According to the interviewed specialists, the major challenges posed by the EC directives that need to be overcome by developing countries in the mid to long-run are the following:

a. Development of new tanning processes and products, and definition of productive strategies as to prevent the formation of CrVI during the tanning process.
b. Lab improvements as it concerns to infrastructure and methodologies, metrological updates, accreditation, and organizations of inter-lab programs.
c. At scale production of ecological footwear will depend on changes of current production processes as to allow the introduction of new tanning materials less harmful to the environment than the traditional ones.
d. Problems related to sample heterogeneity and differences in assay results are expected to be subject of future insurance (legal barriers) to be covered by the leather and footwear industry.

6. Discussion of major findings

At the global level, the most common technical barriers on leather and footwear are related to rules and regulations posed by economic blocks (e.g. European Community) or developed countries such as Japan, Korea, USA and Canada. The EC directives are the major example as they set up limits to toxic wastes in leather and footwear aiming to promote more durable products based on international standards. Since these directives define the methods or analytical procedures for conformity assessment, in some aspects they have been considered technical barriers to trade; this is the case when the exporting countries are not able to meet the required standards due to technological limitations in the production processes or in the lab infrastructure.

Differences in fixing specific limits for hazardous substances as well uncertainties regarding the presence of some of them in leather can also be subject of controversy as it concerns to technical barriers. For instance, while German regulation sets 3 ppm as the tolerable limit for CrVI, the European legislation sets it at 10 ppm. It is worth mentioning, however, that both methods are debatable, since it has been argued that a formation and subsequent detection of CrVI could occur when the chemical analysis is being performed. In this context, one of the major concerns of the leading leather and footwear producing countries today is that these limits and the required conformity assessment tests do not result in unjustified discrimination or arbitrary restrictions to international trade of these products.

As to preventing problems related to CrVI, both automobile and furniture companies all over the world are increasingly demanding mineral tanned (titanium-based) leather.

According to some interviewed specialists, the adequacy of this sector to the new market conditions will require a considerable amount of investment and also a new management perspective. Some tanneries in Southern Brazil are already adapting their production processes to the ISO 14.001 standards.

Also in response to the global market pressures, some multinationals (e.g. Colorobbia, Clariant) have already developed specific lines of natural dyes to meet the growing demand for products with lower content of potentially harmful chemical substances (Souza, 2006).

In Brazil and other Latin American countries there is no specific legislation limiting the level of toxic waste in leather and footwear. Since technical barriers affecting this industry are growing up in importance worldwide, some concerns expressed in the international directives are expected to be internalized in the Brazilian environmental regulation in the coming years.

Considering also that most of the rules and regulations that impose restrictions on the marketing of hides and artifacts requires proof of compliance (e.g. via conformity assessment, including certification), targeted actions for lab training to issue certificates and to participate in certification programs countrywide should be part of a specific public policy in Brazil. One important step in this direction is to make the Brazilian NBR norms compatible to the European ISO norms. The expansion of interlab programs nationwide is also becoming more evident to attend chemical analysis and mechanical tests demanded by the leather and footwear sector and others.

7. Conclusions

The final remarks are focused on what extent the analyzed technical standards and regulations (including the EC directives) and the market requirements that can be considered technical barriers to trade, and also on some suggestions to face them. Two aspects were considered relevant in this regard: (i) the time frame between the promulgation of an international regulation and its applications in the leather and footwear industries worldwide, and (ii) the resulting impacts of this regulation at both the industry and lab infrastructure levels in Brazil. For instance, the EC directives can be considered informal technical barriers in the short-run (right after promulgation by EC and imposed on developing countries exporting to Europe) as they directly affect the industries´ production costs and competitiveness. Although WTO recognizes the right of the developing countries to have enough time to adequate their industries to meet the requirements of these regulations, EU countries tend not to pay attention to this right after the directives promulgation. EC directives only become formal technical barriers to trade by the time they are recognized by the WTO as accepted technical regulations. Since the technical requirements posed by corporations are not accepted as technical regulation by the WTO, they are considered informal technical barriers to trade.

However, it was realized that there is a controversy among specialist on what is a form (legitimate) or informal (illegitimate) technical barrier to trade. While some consider that a technical requirement can be seen as a technical barrier only if it is demanded by a country, others argue that they can also be required by a corporation, especially if it can influence the global market of the leather and footwear, for instance. In the latter, it has been argued that in some cases corporations are adopting different specifications for a unique type of product, for instance, only as a business strategy to acquire products at relatively lower prices. One could argue that it is a discriminatory procedure and, this way, the corporation would be introducing a technical barrier to trade.

Another important aspect to be pointed out is that the introduction of new technologies in the developed countries tends to be less difficult than in developing ones creating a technological asymmetry that can result in technical barriers to trade. This happens because even when the rules and technical requirements are formal, the developing countries face difficulties to follow them. In this case, it should be remembered that the GATT recognizes the right of developing countries to introduce technical standards according to their level of development and have a longer time to adapt to the requirements of international standards.

A service named "Alerta Exportador" provided by Inmetro (Brazilian focal point), has helped domestic small and medium size exporting companies to identify and inform technical barriers.

Also it is possible to conclude that the international market for leather and footwear has forced environmental improvements in the Brazilian supply chain of leather and footwear. However, oeHoconsidering that the stage of technological development of tanneries is higher in the southern states than in the ones located in the northern states, it cannot be expected that all the country´s production is environmentally sound.

Some specialist argument that these technical barriers affect the exports of the developing countries in the short-run, but in the mid to the long-run they have a positive effect both in the qualification of all firms in the footwear and leather productive chain and in the competitiveness of the exporting ones. However, it is not easy to perform a cost–benefit balance on that or, the other way, to say who gained or who lost in this two side polemic issue.

As it refers to laboratory infrastructure, one can say that several Brazilian labs need to improve their infrastructure to attend the demand for chemical analyses on restrictive substances required by the EC directives. The ones that are better qualified to attend this demand are located in both Rio Grande do Sul e Sao Paulo states, but they still need to be both recognized and accredited abroad.

A strategy previously adopted by both India and China that could be also adopted in Brazil is the attraction of labs that perform analyzes and tests that are recognized worldwide. In addition, our country could also make the accreditation of national labs by Inmetro and also by international organizations, such as Satra, Bureau Veritas and others. Finally, we suggest that the Brazilian Ministry of Development, Industry and Foreign Trade provide funds for a study to quantify both the positive and negative impacts of technical barriers in the leather and footwear sector. The results of this study can provide relevant data and information to support a public policy to help tanneries, labs and leather using companies to overcome some negative impacts and also to improve exports. This policy could make a difference considering that the market for leather and footwear is becoming even more competitive with the emergence of China and India as major exporters.

Author details

Mauro Silva Ruiz and Cláudia Echevenguá Teixeira
Nove de Julho University – Uninove, Brazil
Institute for Technological Research of Sao Paulo State – IP, Brazil

Alexandre de Oliveira e Aguiar and Gustavo Silveira Graudenz
Nove de Julho University – Uninove, Brazil

Pedro Luiz Cortez
Nove de Julho University – Uninove, Brazil
University of Sao Paulo – USP, Brazil

8. References

Agência Brasileira de Promoção de Exportação e Investimentos. (2012). *Estatísticas gerais 2010/2012.* Available from: http://www.brazilianleather.com.br/index.php?option=com_content&view=article&id=166&Itemid=101. Access in May 3, 2012.

Associação Brasileira das Indústrias de Calçados. (2011a). *Cartilha - Indústria de Calçados do Brasil 2011.* Abicalçados, São Paulo. Access in March 3, 2012, Available from: <http://www.brazilianfootwear.com.br/relatorios/exibe/219840>

Braga, S. A., Miranda, L. C. (Eds.). (2002). *Comércio e meio ambiente: uma agenda positiva para o desenvolvimento sustentável*. Ministério de Meio Ambiente, Brasília.

Buljan, J. (1996). Pollution limits for discharge of tannery effluent in water bodies and sewers. *World Leather November*: 65.

Campos, S. H. (2006). *A indústria de couros no Brasil: desempenho superior ao da indústria calçadista em 2006*. Porto Alegre: Fundação de Economia e Estatística, 2006. Access in October 13, 2006. Available from: <http://www.fee.tche.br/sitefee/download/indicadores/34_02/6_parte.pdf#search=%22cinco%20paises%20produtores%20couro%202004%202005%22>

Castro, D. et al. (2003). *O comércio e meio ambiente - as diversas faces desse binômio*. Centro de Estudos Avançados em Economia Aplicada, Piracicaba.

Castro, D., Castilho, S. & Miranda, S.(2004). A *rotulagem ambiental no contexto de comércio internacional*. Centro de Estudos Avançados em Economia Aplicada, Piracicaba.

Clariant do Brasil. (2006). *Tingimento: aspectos atuais*. São Paulo.

Comissão das Comunidades Europeias. (2002). Decisão da comissão de 18 de março de 2002 que estabelece critérios ecológicos revistos para a atribuição do rótulo ecológico comunitário ao calçado e que altera a Decisão 1999/179/CE. *Jornal Oficial das Comunidades Europeias*, 20 mar.

Companhia de Tecnologia Ambiental de São Paulo. (2011). *Câmara ambiental da indústria de couros, peles, assemelhados e calçados*. Access in April 23, 2012, Available from: <http://www.cetesb.sp.gov.br/tecnologia-ambiental/cas-em-atividade/44-camara-ambiental-da-industria-de-couros--peles--assemelhados-e-calcados>

Contador Junior, O. (2004). *Tecnologia e proteção ambiental nas indústrias do couro e calçados na região de Jaú-SP*. Dissertação (Mestrado) - Centro Universitário de Araraquara, Araraquara. 163p.

Desai, P. N. (1995). Technology assessment in the Indian footwear sector. *Technological Forecasting and Social Change*, Vol. 48, No 2, pp. 177-187, ISSN 0040-1625.

Dexheimer, M. A. (2006). Riscos do cromo hexavalente no couro. *Revista do Couro*, Estância Velha, ed. 186, pp.102-104.

Ecoetiqueta Europea Para el Calzado. (2006). *Ficha resumen*. Access in March 30, 2012, Available from: <http://www.life-ecofoot.inescop.es/>

Food and Agriculture Organization. (2001). *World statistical compendium for raw hides and skins, leather and leather footwear 1982–2000*. Rome: Food and Agriculture Organization of the United Nations.

Fernandes, A. P. Política industrial trava a cadeia produtiva do couro. (2004). *Couro News*, July 7, 2004. Access in July 18, 2006. Available from: <http://www.couro.news.com.br/Perfil%20do%20Setor/view.htm?id=217304&ca_id=19>

Fornasari Filho, N., Coelho, L. R. (2002). *Aspectos ambientais do comércio internacional*. Federação das Indústrias de São Paulo, São Paulo.

Garrido, A. E. (2004). *As barreiras técnicas ao comércio internacional*. Instituto Nacional de Metrologia, Normalização e Qualidade Industrial, Rio de Janeiro. Access in March 31, 2005, Available from: <http://www.inmetro.gov.br/infotec/artigos/docs/51.pdf>

Gaspar, L. G. (2006). *Ciesp - Centro das Indústrias do Estado de São Paulo Regional Franca*. May 3, 2006. Interviewed by Alexandre Bos, Mauro Silva Ruiz, Regina Nagamine e Luis Carlos Faleiros.

Girolla F. (2006). *SENAI - Centro Tecnológico do Calçado*. Novo Hamburgo, April, 4, 2006. Interviewed by Alexandre Bos, Mauro Silva Ruiz, Regina Nagamine e Luis Carlos Faleiros.

Glasspool, J. (2006). Substâncias nocivas: atualização quanto à comercialização e usos. *Revista Tecnicouro*, Novo Hamburgo, Vol. 27, No. 8, pp.68-71.

Gorini, A. P. F., Siqueira, S. H. G. (2002). Complexo coureiro – calçadista. *Comércio Ext*erior. Access in May 1, 2012. Available from:
http://www.bndes.gov.br/SiteBNDES/export/sites/default/bndes_pt/Galerias/Arquivos/conhecimento/bnset/bsespcal.pdf

Gutterres, M. (2005). *Tendências emergentes da indústria do couro*. Porto Alegre: UFRGS, Access in October 13, 2006. Available from:
<http://www.enq.ufrgs.br/pos/projetos/curtumes/Arqs/WPM$6F4A.pdf#search=%22tabela%20produ%C3%A7%C3%A3o%20mundial%20couro%22/>

Hoinacki, E.; Moreira, M. V. & Kiefer, C. G. *Manual básico de processamento do couro*. Porto Alegre: Senai, 1994. 402p.

Instituto de Pesquisas Tecnológicas. (2006). *Observatório de tecnologia e inovação (OTI): barreiras ao comércio internacional de couros e calçados – desafios para o enfrentamento das barreiras técnicas atuais e futuras*. Relatório técnico. IPT, São Paulo. Vol. 2.

Instituto Nacional de Metrologia, Normalização e Qualidade Industrial. (2005). *Barreiras técnicas às exportações: o que são e como superá-las*. Inmetro, Rio de Janeiro. Access in April 9, 2012, Available from: <http://www.inmetro.gov.br/barreiras técnicas>

International Standardization Organization. (2011). *ISO Survey of certifications 2010*. Geneve: ISO, [CD-ROM].

Kolomaznika, K.,Adameka, M., Andelb I.& Uhlirova, M. (2008). Leather waste - Potential threat to human health, and a new technology of its treatment. *Journal of Hazardous Materials*. Elsevier. 160, pp. 514–520.

Ministério do Desenvolvimento, Indústria e Comércio Exterior. (2002). *Barreiras técnicas: conceitos e informações sobre como superá-la*s. Confederação Nacional da Indústria, Brasília.

Perina, M. A., Machado, R. Q. & Miranda, S. H. G. (2003). *As notificações do Brasil no acordo TBT e a importância das normas técnicas no comércio internacional*. Centro de Estudos Avançados em Economia Aplicada, Piracicaba.

Philip, A., Jeanet, B. & Finn, T. (2009). Trade and development: lessons from Vietnam's past trade agreements. *World Development*, Vol. 37, No. 2, pp. 341–353, ISSN 0305-750X.

Porter, M. E., Van Der Linde, C. (1995). Green and competitive: ending the stalemate. *Harvard Business Rev*iew. Boston: Sep./Oct. 1995. Vol. 73, ISS. 5b; pp. 120 – 134.

Prazeres, T. L. (2003). *Comércio internacional e protecionismo: as barreiras técnicas na OMC*. Aduaneiras, São Paulo.

Procópio Filho, A. (1994). Ecoprotecionismo: comércio internacional, agricultura e meio ambiente. *Instituto de Pesquisa Econômica Aplicada*, Brasília.

Ramasami, T. et al. (1999) Beamhouse and tanning operations: process chemistry revisited. J. *Soc. Leather Technol. Chem.* 83:39.

Rosa, S. E. S., Corrêa, A. R. *A indústria calçadista no Brasil.* Rio de Janeiro: BNDES, 2006. 4p. (Informe Setorial). Access in October 10, 2006, Available from: <http://www.bndes.gov.br/conhecimento/setorial/informe-01AI.pdf>.

Santos A. M. M. M. et al. (2002). Panorama do setor de couro no Brasil. *BNDES Setorial,* Rio de Janeiro, No. 16, pp. 57-84.

Saravanabhavan, S. et al. (2005). A source reduction approach: Integrated bio-based tanning methods and the role of enzymes in dehairing and fibre opening. *Clean Technologies and Environmental Policy,* Vol. 7, No 1, pp.3–14, ISSN 1618-9558.

Schneider, F. (2006). *Rockport Brasil.* Campo Bom, 05 abr. 2006. Interviewed by Alexandre Bos, Mauro Silva Ruiz, Regina Nagamine e Luis Carlos Faleiros.

Sousa, J. D. F.(2006). *Peles, couros e resíduos.* São Paulo: Edgard Blucher.

The New Zealand Ecolabelling Trust (2006). *EC-31-06 License criteria for textiles, skins and leather.* Auckland, Access in April 2, 2012, Available from: <http://www.environmentalchoice.org.nz/docs/products_services/textiles_skins_leather/ec3106textilesskinsleather.pdf>

Wolf, G.; Schuck, F. (2003). Substâncias nocivas no couro - um panorama atual. *XVI Congresso Nacional da ABQTIC,* 16, Foz do Iguaçu, Anais...Foz do Iguaçu: ABQTIC.

World Bank.(1999). Tanning and leather finishing. In: Pollution *prevention and abatement handbook 1998,* Washington, D.C.: World Bank Group, p 404.

Section 4

Business Perspective of International Trade

Chapter 10

A Perspective on Remanufacturing Business: Issues and Opportunities

Mosè Gallo, Elpidio Romano and Liberatina Carmela Santillo

Additional information is available at the end of the chapter

http://dx.doi.org/10.5772/48103

1. Introduction

Nowadays, the continuous technological innovations and the growing consumerism accelerate the rate at which products are replaced, causing the exponential increase in the production of waste and landfills' saturation. The production processes of many products, however, requires a large amount of non-renewable resources and of substances that represents a potential threat to environment and human health if those products are not recovered or disposed of properly. This situation has turned on the environmental awareness of consumers and sensitized legislator from different countries to enact and implement specific laws and directives for the management of the end of the life cycle of products and to regulate the employment of hazardous materials. However, although disposed product represent a threat, they represent, also, a resource for companies that have to manage them, more if the recovery activities are properly integrated into the product' design phase and manufacturing activities. In fact this situation is pushing toward new profit models, based on an integrated product life cycle management. The innovative policies oriented to recover disposed products on the one hand improve the efficiency in natural resources consumption, but on the other hand show new business opportunities to original equipment manufacturers and third-party companies. Among the different recovery options, remanufacturing is an important and interesting one. The aim of this chapter is to increase the wealth of technical/managerial ability to integrate the production cycle of new manufactured products with the recovery of discarded products In particular the multifaceted field of remanufacturing will be targeted identifying those strategic factors making the remanufacturing business sustainable from an economic point of view. In the second section the various models for an integrated product life cycle management will be presented together with the several recovery options. A brief discussion will be conducted on the impact of these choices on configuring a reverse logistics network. In the third section a profile of the remanufacturing industry has been drafted considering in particular its model of business. In fact, factors that have led various OEMs to undertake remanufacturing programs on their products are different and in many cases dependent on actors' geographic location and the product category. Although many companies have started this activity as a mere compliance against increasingly compelling regulations aimed at products recovery, the empirical evidence shows that in the most successful cases companies simply tried to seize business opportunities already identified on that market. Companies designing remanufacturing programs within an integrated business model, with the aim to build a durable competitive advantage, put profit before legislative requirements and incentives. The purpose of this section, then, is to dissect the business of remanufacturing in order to highlight their strengths and weaknesses, its opportunities and its dangers. In the forth section we sum up some results of this study and future possible developments.

2. The recovery of the product at the end of life phase

The recovery of the product ,as an alternative to traditional disposal, is a response to environmental damage caused by the disposal of end of life products. Product recovery, in fact, minimizes the demand for energy and raw materials and the environmental impact of waste, and also provides the opportunity to start a profitable business. Therefore, environmental issues, eco-sustainability and production cost aspects are linked together.

Product recovery implies reviewing the management logic of product lifecycle, from an "open" production system to a "closed" one of variable length [1]. In the open loop logic, the process starts by taking resources from the ecosystem, when raw materials and energy are channeled into the transformation process, and ends with landfill disposal or incineration process. This situation is sustainable only if the natural resources consumption is lower than eco-system's ability to regenerate them.

On the other hand, in a closed loop supply chain some recovery activities delay the product disposal by starting new production cycles on the product, its part and components or raw materials. The adjective "closed", however, should not suggest a completely self-sufficient system, since the use of new resources is almost always necessary at each new cycle and it is related with the recovery option considered. Undoubtedly such a new approach to product lifecycle management improves the efficiency of the exploitation of natural resources and opens, at the same time, new business opportunities. The end of life phase is transformed into a testing time, to establish the most suitable recovery option to extend the product's useful life. (Figure 1).

Products at final stage of their lifecycle, can be recovered in many ways and with different levels of efficiency in exploiting natural resources. In literature, these recovery options can be found (Figure 2):

- reuse;
- restoration;
- refurbishing;
- remanufacturing;
- cannibalization;
- recycling.

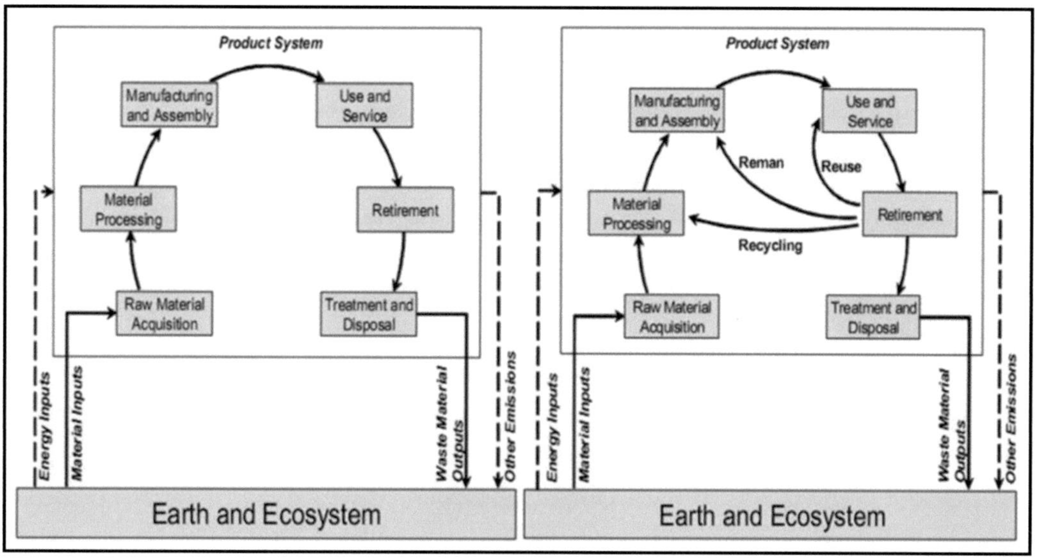

Figure 1. Open loop and closed loop supply chains [1]

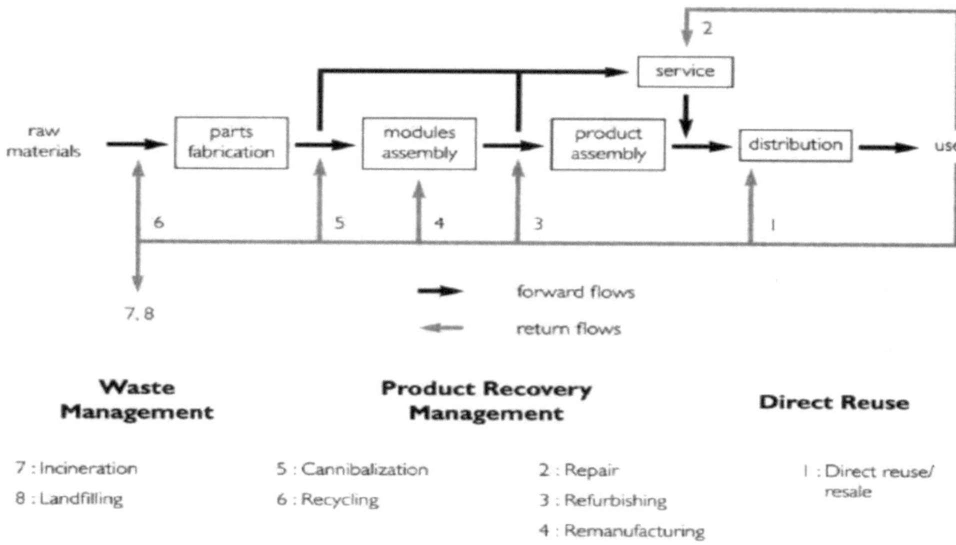

Figure 2. Recovery options in a closed loop supply chain [2]

The recycling process is at the lowest level of recovery efficiency, it allows to recover only raw materials but not the added value of production cycle. Higher efficiency options, where the whole product, part or components are recovered, are reconditioning, remanufacturing and cannibalization. Intermediate options, are repair and reuse. A closed loop system consists of distribution, product recovery and waste management. The products and/or components, that come back through the reverse logistics channels, can be directly sold, recovered or disposed off.

2.1. Remanufacturing

The original definition of the remanufacturing concept is due to Robert Lund, professor at Boston University, a luminary in the study of this sector. His contribution paved the way for a systematic study of this recovery option. In literature there are many definitions of the remanufacturing concept [3,4] and a meaningful one is: "....remanufacturing is an industrial process whereby products referred as cores are restored to useful life. During this process the core pass through a number of remanufacturing steps, e.g. inspection, disassembly, part replacement/refurbishment, cleaning, reassembly, and testing to ensure it meets the desired product standards" [5].

The previous definition clearly refers to remanufacturing as a process, a set of linked activities, rather than a single step aimed at restoring the performance of a product. The same cannot be said, for example, for repair or reuse, which are simply defined as an activity.

This option is applied firstly to electronic and mechanical products and components, as they maintain, when recovered, a relatively high added value with respect to the market evaluation or to their original cost [6]. Gaudette and Giuntini consider this practice as the most evolved form of recycling: "...It Conserves not only the raw material content but also much of the value added during the processes required to manufacture new products " [7]. In fact, the energy used to remanufacture a product, basing on a study of Lund, is, on average approximately 20-25% of that required for an ex-novo manufacture, while the remanufacture cost is equal to about 60% of the original [8,9].

In Figure 3, the fundamental differences between the options of remanufacturing, reconditioning and repair are depicted, basing on three dimensions: warranty, product performance and content of work needed.

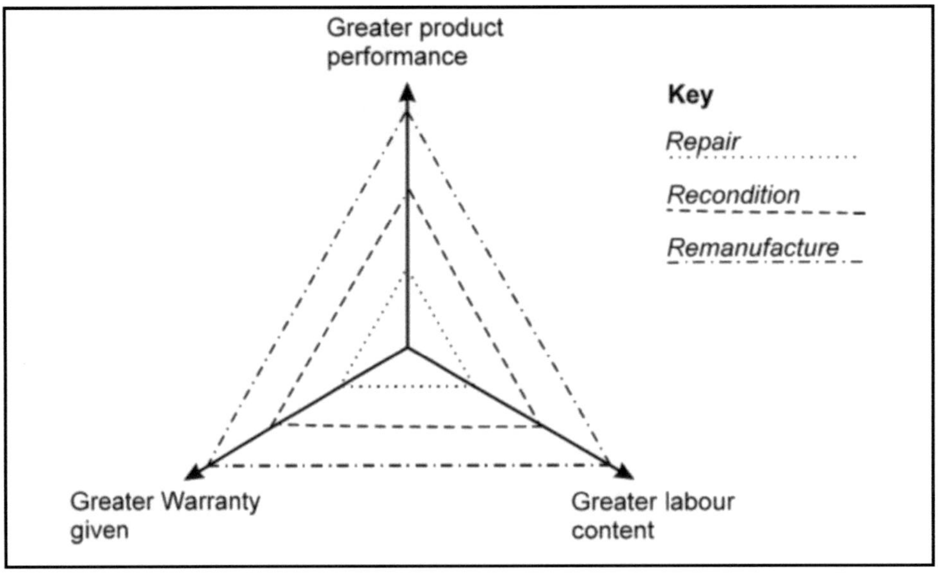

Figure 3. Hierarchy of recovery processes of a product intended for a secondary market [10]

The entire remanufacturing process can be decomposed in three sequential sub processes: disassembly, overhaul, reassembly. "The coordination of these sub-systems is key for a successful production planning and control system" [11].

2.2. Analysis of the remanufacturing process

According to Steinhilper [12] and Sundin [5] the activities composing a remanufacturing process can be divided into (Figure 4):

- disassembly;
- inspection;
- sorting;
- cleaning;
- reprocessing;
- reassembly;
- checking and testing.

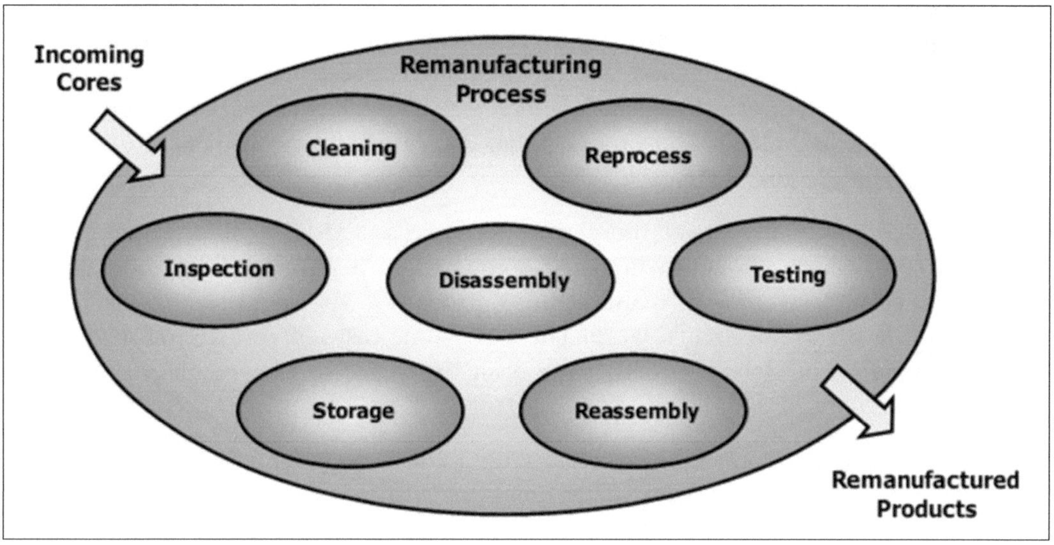

Figure 4. A generic remanufacturing process [5]

Empirical evidence shows that companies, involved in remanufacturing activities, organize their processes in different ways. Although the sequence disassembly -restore-assembly appears to be a fixed point, activities such as inspection, cleaning or testing have not an unique position into the process. The sequence, therefore, must be chosen considering the recovery process, the characteristics of the product, and the technology available for treatment.

The disassembly activity is located upstream of the entire process and it is extremely critical, since its implementation directly affects the quality of recovered material for successive activities. This step plays a central role in preserving the value of recovered cores. The main reasons for that are high incidence of manual labor, necessity of specialized equipment or time required. These issues are directly influenced by the design quality and its capability to respond not only to customer requirements but also to recovery necessity with higher environmental-friendly criteria. Several researches report that this phase is mainly carried out in a manual way, while the use of automation occurs only in case of large batches of standardized products [13]. The disassembly activity could be more complicated, if conducted by a third-party operator as it must develop a reverse engineering, rarely having access to OEM specifications.

The inspection and sorting phases are closely related: the second activity can be seen as the completion of the first one. The result is the sorting of cores into three subgroups:

- "as is" reusable cores without need of revision;
- Recoverable cores, for which a refurbish activity is necessity;
- Not recoverable cores.

After inspection and sorting, it is possible to proceed to the cleaning phase of recovered parts. Cleaning goes beyond the elimination of dust and dirt from components [12]. Many cleaning processes cannot derive from the common ones of manufacturing processes. Therefore, the development of new ad-hoc solutions is necessary. As new methods are developed, they are more and more environmental friendly. It is crucial to implement such an operation with techniques and products that do not affect the component quality and combine a low environmental impact.

Reprocessing activities involve all those operations necessary to the component to provide a planned performance (or even higher if compared to new ones). The technical tools normally used are the same of manufacturing processes. The small size of batches can lead to the prevalence of manual work. There are some cases in which production lines, used for manufacture new products, have been "updated" to remanufacture recovered products.

The reconditioned components represent a large part of the remanufactured product. In order to limit the use of new parts, many times, the number of disassembled units can be increased if compared with the units to be re-assembled with the aim to recover enough parts from the cores.

The reassembly is the final phase to obtain remanufactured products. The greatest difficulty arises from ensuring a continuous flow, quantitatively and qualitatively adequate, in order to avoid blocks or slowdowns, inevitably resulting in higher costs and lower profits. The reassembly operation can be carried out with reprocessed or reused components, with new components or with cannibalized components. A monitoring problem arises as it is impossible to know in advance how many components can be reused or reprocessed. A possible solution is to purchase and store new components in case of need. However, this solution is not always suitable, because it increases the inventory level and obsolescence problems. It can be difficult to coordinate the reassembly of the various parts, if the reprocessing lead-times are uneven.

At the end of the whole process, there is a testing phase to ensure the achievement of quality standard set for this kind of products. Testing in remanufacturing contexts affects all products and is more rigorous than the random sampling in new products case.

2.3. Managerial issues of the remanufacturing process

Remanufacturing systems have a high level of uncertainty and complexity if compared to the traditional production systems. The management of these aspects makes the role of planning and control systems critical .In fact, companies, involved in remanufacturing activities, have to face a series of problems that limit the efficiency of their production process. These problems are typical of this sector and cannot be addressed by the traditional tools of planning and control. In literature, several technical and management issues have been identified [14]:

- difficulties in disassembly of the product;
- uncertainty about the quality of returns;
- difficulties in matching of the parts;
- uncertainty in working cycles and processing times;
- the lack of correlation between returns and demand;
- uncertainty in quantities and timing of returns;
- configuring and managing a reverse logistics network.

From the Table 1 it can be argued that these features impact at various levels on the management of remanufacturing systems and in particular on the planning and production control activities.

Complicating characteristic	Production planning and control activity			
	Forecasting	Logistics	Scheduling/shop floor control	Inventory control and management
(1) The uncertain timing and quality of returns	✓	✓	✓	✓
(2) The need to balance returns with demands				✓
(3) The disassembly of returned products			✓	✓
(4) The uncertainty in materials recovered from returned items			✓	✓
(5) The requirement for a reverse logistics network		✓		✓
(6) The complication of materials matching restriction			✓	
(7) The problems of stochastic routings for materials and highly variable processing times			✓	

Table 1. Relationship between production planning and control activities and the characteristics of a remanufacturing system [14]

3. Remanufacturing as a business sector

3.1. Features of a remanufacturable product

Virtually every manufactured product may be remanufactured at the end of its life cycle. However, aspects such as the business model or product's design makes remanufacturing a certain product more profitable than others, or in some cases totally not convenient. Literature has tried to trace the profile of a remanufacturable item, using some parameters.

The main orientation of the research activities on this subject has been, not only to evaluate the "remanufacturability" from a strictly technical point of view, but also to verify the conditions that allow a sustainable business for the company. Parker identifies three key parameters for remanufacturable products [15]:

- the intrinsic value, the market value of the product being reprocessed;
- the re-constructability, the ease of disassembly a product and then its assembly at the end of recovery process;
- the evolution rate, the speed at which new variants of the product are launched on the market.

Basing on these parameters, Parker recommends a legislative intervention intended to allow the reuse of components into new products, investments in research to develop the Design for Remanufacturing (DfRem) and the development of a system of services to extend product's lifecycle and, if possible, to update it from a stylistic and functional point of view [15].

Robert Lund identified 75 categories of remanufacturable products and developed reference criteria also confirmed by subsequent research [6].

These criteria are:

- the product is durable;
- the product has only failed in its functionality;
- the product is standardized and consists of interchangeable parts;
- the added value at end of life, is high;
- the cost to obtain the core is low if compared with the remaining intrinsic value;
- the product's technology is relatively stable over a period of time that exceeds the single lifecycle;
- the consumer should be informed about the availability of remanufactured products, so to create an adequate demand on the market;
- a technology exists to remove parts from products without damaging them and to restore the product.

Sundin identifies in a empirical way four relevant characteristics of product/component to simplify the implementation of activities required in a process of remanufacturing [5]:

- wear resistant;
- easy to identify;
- easy to remove;
- easy to be reprocessed.

These analysis provide a valuable support to identify those concerns during the design phase to facilitate a proper and simple reprocessing at the end of life.

In the current scenario, there is also the additional requirement of a minimum market value for certain categories of products, to secure a profit at the end of reprocessing. In fact, only on this condition, today, remanufacturing may be considered as an attractive business and not only conceived for environmental issues, but physiologically in loss. The low profit margin is due to the high labor cost involved in the various recovery options. This, however, should become secondary in the future thanks to the increased volumes of products to be treated with positive implications on economies of scale and experience, as well as the degree of automation in the process [16].

3.2. Remanufacturing business figures

The remanufacturing business was born in United States during the Great Depression of the'30s and achieved the final consecration during the Second World War, when the plants were converted to military commitments. Most of the available resources were reserved for war needs, while those for civilian use were very low. In this context, to balance the decreasing in supply of new products, used products were reprocessed extending their useful life.

This recovery option is currently used for several categories of products among which:

- Aerospace and aeronautical;
- Automotive ;
- Industrial machinery;
- gaming machines;
- data communication systems;
- robot;
- electrical and electronic equipment with high residual value ;
- compressors;
- office supplies;
- copiers;
- printer cartridges;
- musical instruments;
- refrigeration appliances;
- ATMs.

As it can be seen from the above list, the remanufacturing field mainly concerns consumer and durables goods for professional use. This recovery option has had, until today, a little impact on consumer goods. On these products, in fact, aspects such as fashion design or status, have a strong relevance on the purchase decision.

Today, remanufacturing is widespread in the sector of high value and high technology products. In addition, this recovery option thrives in those sectors that have adopted the concept of Product Service Systems (PSS), the costumer has access to the service provided by the product, without having the property of it. In this case, when the product is no longer able to deliver its performance, it is recovered to be used by other costumers, satisfying shared goals of longevity, durability and performance.

The remanufacturing industry is defined by Lund as an "hidden giant", in fact many companies operating in this sector is not devoted exclusively to remanufacturing activities, but practice them as an aftermarket service.

Data on the remanufacturing sector are rather difficult to find, because of the overlapping between Original Equipment Manufacturers and remanufacturers, among which there are OEM and "third party" operators, independent or working on commission. However, the potential growth of this business is very high, especially in new sectors and in the EU market, where it has so far been undervalued.

Industry Sector	Products	Firms in the Database	Estimated firms not in Database	Total
Automotive	Alternators, Starter Motors, Water Pumps, Clutches and Engines	4 536	46 000	50 536
Compressors & Refrigeration	Air conditioner and Refrigerator Compress.	55	100	155
Electrical Apparatus	Transformers, Electrical Mot--ors and Switch gear	2 231	11 000	13 231
Machinery	Machinery and Equipment for various industries	90	30	120
Office Furniture	Desks, Files and Partitions	220	500	720
Tires, retreaded	Truck, Auto and Off-road Tires	1 210	180	1 390
Toner Cartridges	Laser toner cartridges Ink jet cartridges	1 401	5 100	6 501
Valves, industrial	Control & Relief valves	110	300	410
Other	Diverse	50	200	250
Totals		9 903	63 410	73 313

Table 2. Distribution of companies engaged in remanufacturing by industry sector [17]

Basing on the research of Lund [17] the majority of companies engaged in this activity are independent actors with OEMs playing a restrained role. From Table II. 1 it can be argued that most of the US remanufacturers operate in the automotive sector, about 70% of the total. No coincidence that the automotive industry has a long tradition in the recovery of engines, but also of other vehicle parts, which can be used in several lifecycles before the final disposal. However, Table II 1 refers to data older than ten years. Today it is estimated that the weight of the automotive sector has been reduced in favor of other product categories such as office supplies or photography.

Turning to specific examples there are independent firms such as Flextronics, a US firm, with an international vocation and a comprehensive know-how to recover printers, PDAs, cell phones, medical equipment, notebooks and desktops.

About the OEMs, Xerox is a global leader in the remanufacturing of photocopiers and other office equipment, whose return is secured by lease sales [18]. The greatest obstacle to the success of remanufacturing program, according to officials, has been the spread of the idea among some customers that products containing some used parts, may be less in terms of performance to products consisting exclusively of new parts. The unique process, the technologies used and the product's warranty should ensure that all products regardless of the presence of remanufactured parts, have the same quality standards, the same performance and the same reliability. Other companies like Kodak and Fuji normally practice this option on disposable cameras returning for the development of films. Caterpillar, involved in this business from 1972, recorded in 2005 for "Remanufacturing Division a revenue of $ 1bn. Other well-known brands involved in this field are General Electric, Boeing, Deere, Navistar, HP and Pitney Bowes. In the U.S., however, the larger re-manufacturer still remains the Department of Defense.

Basing on these data it can be noted an intense activity, which, however, is still restricted within specific business ambits. Only in particular cases and conditions, products are recovered on a large scale. However the remanufacturing process has difficulty to come out these limited areas and it is struggling to establish itself as an industrial application on a large scale, beyond the traditional sectors in a consumer goods application.

3.3. Business model

3.3.1. Value proposition

Remanufacturing companies tend to frame the satisfaction of customers' need by placing on the market a product that optimizes also its life-cycle costs. More than through the selling activity, they try to create value providing a service through the product in a Product Service System concept, "a system of products, services, infrastructure and support network designed to be competitive, satisfy customers and have a lower environmental impact than a traditional business model" [19].

This business model has a central focus on customer satisfaction and value creation, keeping in mind that these results are not achieved only through technological development, but also emphasizing the contribution of intangible assets such as intellectual property, image, brand, design or style. These aspects, in fact, help the company to differentiate its products from the competition, improving the degree of "customization" of supply and strengthening the relationship between supplier and consumer.

The PSS model is widespread in various business sectors, where the relationship between consumers and companies can be articulated according to the three main approaches in Figure 5 [20]:

- product orientation, where the product sale is also associated with additional services such as maintenance contracts and end-of-life repurchase agreements to ensure the functionality and the conservation of the product;
- user orientation, where the product still remains central in the relationship but the service provider has the property of the product, that is available to consumers through various contractual arrangements such as leasing etc.;
- result orientation , where the supplier and the consumer agree on a service delivery (without specifying a particular product).

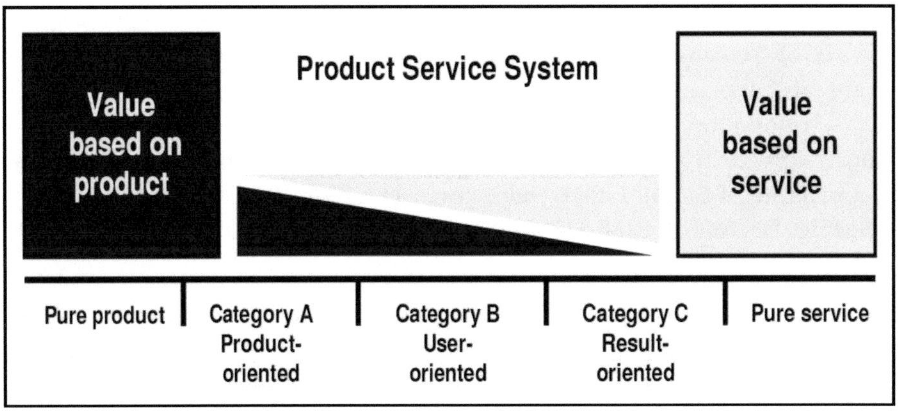

Figure 5. The product-service concept [21]

Whatever is the orientation of the company, in general the value proposition relies on a combination of product and service with different weights. "The *orientation to result*, however, is the most popular definition and the most sophisticated interpretation, and with the greatest potential for a PSS model" [22].

In remanufacturing case, the value proposition is based more on a performance value than on product's property. Corresponding to low economic sacrifices there are functional and psycho-social benefits. A PSS model emphasizes the de-materialization of the offer and the strict relationship with the consumer. The company's competitive vision moves towards a product life-cycle perspective that starts from the product development and production, passes through additional services delivery, and ends up with product recovery or final disposal [23]. In addition, a co-creating value process is highlighted: the end user is requested to work together and more closely to the supplier, moving from a logic of satisfaction based on property of the product to one based on access to benefits deriving from its functionalities [24].

Those producers, providing a combination product / service through the remanufacturing option, focus, of course, on the product's use and on end of life phases aiming at a cost reduction. In this perspective, in fact, many levers of profit for a traditional business (i.e. supply of spare parts and maintenance service) are transformed into additional costs that the company must internalize. Considering that a product will have multiple life cycles, a correct life cycle cost/benefit analysis must take into account not only the initial cost (to which apply the markup), but also those costs related to the whole useful life of the product and the corresponding revenues. The pricing strategy, in particular, will be evaluated according to criteria of multiperiod choice.

The relationship between customer and company becomes very strong. In a traditional business model the profits to companies derive from the costs incurred by customers (e.g. price of the product, cost of spare parts, etc..). The transition to a PSS model, however, distributes these benefits among the actors of the economic system. Both the company and the consumer obtain benefits, creating conditions for a win-win situation.

3.3.2. Players

Remanufacturing business can involve OEMs, which remanufacture their own returned products, independent remanufacturers working on products from various producers, and committed, when OEMs decide to outsource remanufacturing activities. OEMs could face a great difficulty in controlling the entire product's value chain and this can create the conditions for market entry of independent remanufacturers. In this case, the end of life products are remanufactured by small independent companies, faster to take market opportunities than the large ones. However, when the OEM itself chooses to rely on these independent remanufactures, as in the automotive sector, contracts on orders are developed.

OEMs are becoming increasingly aware of the opportunities offered by remanufacturing. Beyond the possible profits, it offers feedbacks on failure modes and duration of the products, moreover controlling the remanufacturing process allows companies to maintain a good reputation of their brand.

However, for different reasons not always managers have had a positive attitude towards this type of activity. Primarily they raise the problem of cannibalization between new and remanufactured products. "...Cannibalism occurs when the sale of some of a company's portfolio of products reduces the sale level of one or more products in the company's portfolio of products" [25].

Although in literature the issue of cannibalization between products has been treated from different point of view, there is not an organic study concerning the cannibalization of new products by the remanufactured ones. However, that is to be considered desirable if it allows to maintain company's market share [26]. In fact, the incertitude of an OEM may represent a business opportunity for independent remanufacturers, but also for direct competitors.

Even if Linton verifies, for an OEM introducing on the market a remanufactured version of its product, a decrease, in relative terms, in profitability, considering all the market this trend is not so obvious [27]. An increasing in sales of remanufactured products could be accompanied by a lower decrease in sales of new products, perhaps because a diversification of the offer reaches customers who would never have bought new products, or because this move would make the remanufacturing business less attractive to independent actors with a consequent decrease in their competitive intensity. So, there are many good reasons to believe that a certain type of cannibalization can increase the overall level of sales, especially under two conditions:

- the remanufactured product, if sold at a lower price, could be used in alternative ways;
- the product could be offered to market segments very sensitive to price

The importance of the participation of an OEM to the remanufacturing process causes usually a positive effect on return rate and quality of cores (intermediaries, engaged in the collection of cores, may retain only those of higher quality). However, third parties cannot have the same economies of scale of an OEM and compensate this weakness with a wide freedom of movement both from a strategic point of view (an independent remanufacturer can treat cores of different brands) and technological.

The use of outsourcing for remanufacturing activities can be a complicating factor in this context. Toffel, in fact, recognizes a trade-off between internalization and outsourcing [28]. According to this author, an OEM should consider a vertical integration (or even a joint venture), rather than relying on independent companies, when tacit knowledge, confidential information related to the design, engineering and production phase, are involved. Moreover, this choice should be made when there is a risk of becoming dependent on third-party because of components becoming rare.

So, a competitive or collaborative relationship may develop between the players of this business. The competition may concern both the final market and the procurement market of cores. For this reason, there are various deterring actions for new incomings. They range from legal restrictions (which prohibits a third party to remanufacture products) to technological or economic restrictions, such as encrypted code known only by OEMs or prohibitive tariffs on relicensing software, in order to discourage or, at least, make the process more expensive.

The possible collaboration relationships may be work on commission or full outsourcing. In some cases the practice of de-branding could occur, i.e., the OEM requires that its products, entering a secondary market through third parties, have a different look, in particular, the original brand is removed. However, this operation requires additional work and may be expensive [29]. It is also possible to find cases of *coopetition*, where two or more independent producers agrees to develop a specific partnership, while maintaining a competitive relationship in other areas.

3.3.3. Value system

The system value of a remanufacturing process is depicted in figure 6. From this figure it can be argued that the value systems of direct production and remanufacturing are strictly integrated, sharing some upstream stages (on the supply side) and some downstream (on the distribution side). There is a very little difference if an OEM or an independent remanufacturer is involved in the remanufacturing process, in fact the current trend for OEMs is to devote different facilities to manufacturing and remanufacturing activities. In some cases they employ hybrid systems rather than fully integrated production systems because of the specificity and uncertainty characterizing the remanufacturing process. The trend is to configure two different networks for forward and reverse flows.

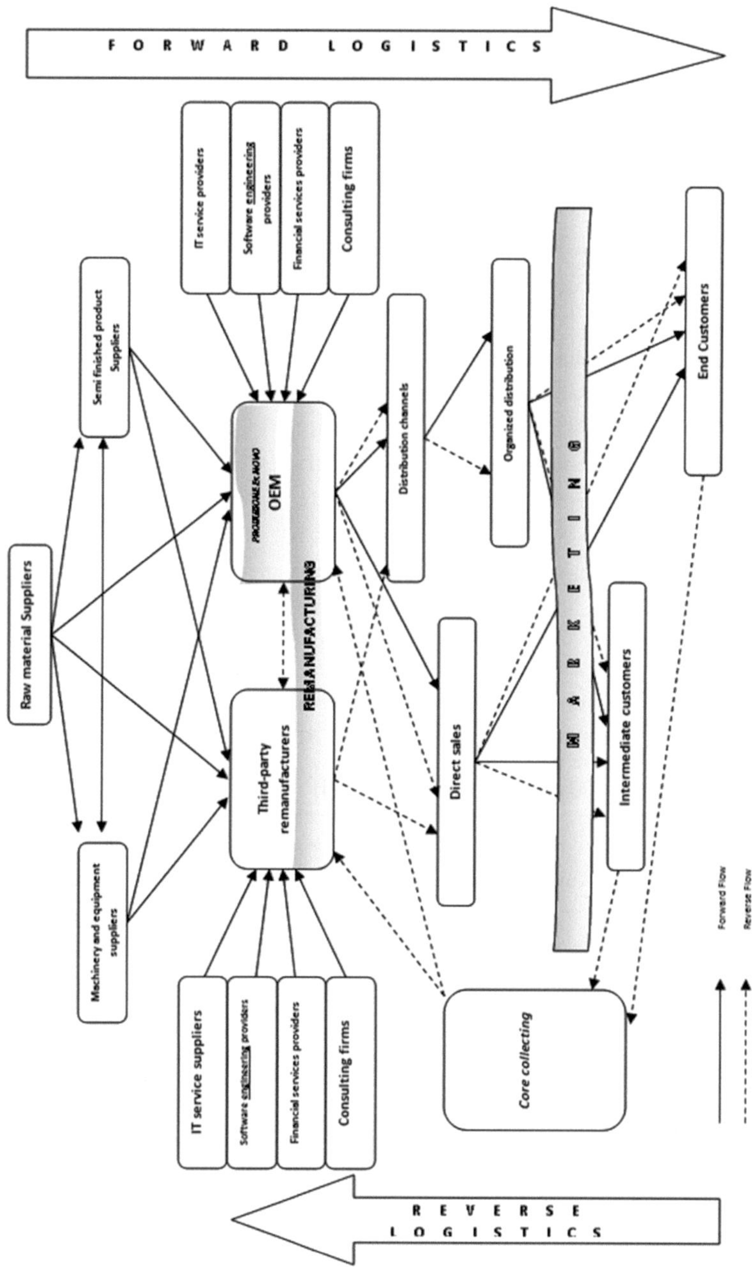

Figure 6. Value System of remanufacturing The role of information is crucial in influencing consumer's behaviour. Unfortunately there is not a systematic study on this subject. Nevertheless, basing on [30], it is possible to make some considerations on the relationship between customer and company, in the remanufacturing case. It is no coincidence that the most difficult obstacle in this business has been and is the prejudices of the market towards this category of products. As a remanufactured product is by definition not new, many consumers associate to it a judgment of low quality. This implies a low WTP, but it may be increased by working on communication.

What distinguishes the *value configuration* of a remanufacturing process is the creation of a reverse logistics system supporting the direct one to ensure the return of end of life products as input for the remanufacturing process. Actually, at network level the reverse channel can be seen as a further lengthening of the direct one. In this model, in fact, the use phase is not the final phase of life cycle, but rather an intermediate phase, to which the collecting phase follows to close the loop.

This model of value creation integrates the end customer, not only, as a player in the use phase, but also as a potential supplier of products to recover. The customer becomes a node of the network and with his behaviour impacts on the effectiveness of reverse logistics. If consumers does not return back their end of life products, there is a lacking of raw material to remanufacture. The reverse logistics system creates physical flows of products, but also intangible flows of information. So, the remanufacturing player bets on a collaborative attitude of consumers, moreover it work to formulate specific policies to facilitate it. Remanufacturers rely on networks allowing to save resources and to spread fixed costs over more use cycles of products, whit physical return flows supporting feedback on products' performance and on market evolution in terms of requirements.

3.3.4. Customer relationship

Consumers' behavior is particularly complex to analyze with reference to the remanufacturing business, since they can cover two potential roles:

- purchaser of a product (new or remanufactured);
- supplier of a core.

According to a microeconomic approach the preferences of a consumer can be analyzed through the "Willingness to Pay", the maximum price he are willing to pay for a certain good. This parameter can be measured through questionnaires, games, auction mechanisms, etc.. Camacho et al. studied the willingness to pay for an environmentally friendly product using surveys and economic experiments [30].

An interesting aspect of this study is that the participants said they were willing to pay for a product improvement in an ecological sense, but this inclination was not related to the magnitude of improvements made. This situation has important implications for corporate strategy, because the company could benefit from a rise in consumer WTP only marginally improving product's environmental performance. Therefore, it depends much on the marketing policy adopted, than on the actual environmental performance delivered. Needless to say that situations which may lend themselves to abuse must be faced.

An index to monitor the behaviour of the consumer as a supplier of used products may be the "Willingness to Receive" (WTR:), the minimum price at which a person is willing to make his product available to supply a reverse logistics program. In this situation, the customer must be encouraged to return its product through specific policies (e.g., repurchase price, leasing, buy-back transactions, etc.).

The WTR is, also, influenced by the exchange of information between the parties. With other conditions being equal, we can expect a high WTR if the company organizes an effective collecting system for end of life products, because this can be interpreted by customers as the demonstration of company's interest towards the product.

On the contrary, if the collecting phase is conducted by a no profit organization the WTR lowers significantly and philanthropic purposes take over. Contracts, linking enterprise and consumer, may be critical: in a leasing case, in fact, the company don't have to push the consumer to return the product back. Moreover, it is important how the consumer perceives the value of used products. The remanufacturing is focused on preserving the added value of products, but in many cases the consumer is not aware of it [31].

It must be also considered the fact that, although European legislation is based on maximum transparency in order to promote an informed purchase, in many countries, especially developing ones, there is no obligation to communicate to consumers the status (remanufactured or not) of a certain product. In these cases firms may exploit the information asymmetry to their advantage, keeping silent about product's nature. In contrast to it, there could be an information campaign with emphasis on the value proposition, namely low economic sacrifices to get the product in exchange for high returns for consumers in both functional (performance is comparable or higher of new products) and psycho-social (think about the value of environmental benefits for ecologically sensitive subjects). In many cases the result of information campaigns has been to overcome the distrust of the market, especially if it starts from a proper definition of the target customer profile.

3.3.5. Target market

The potential market consists of consumers and businesses. The drivers, that may spark interest for a remanufactured product, environmental sensibility, or in the case of durable goods, product's features that discourage or not allow access to a new one. In a vertically segmented market, a company may choose to serve two different target customers with the same product, using variables such as price and quality. So, on the same iso-value line, it is possible to locate "the primary market" and "the secondary market". The two offers are the same in relative terms, but different in absolute terms.

On the primary market the value proposition concerns the best quality products sold at a high price, on the secondary market, on the contrary, are sold low quality products sold at a lower price. The product's quality refers not only to functional aspects but also to product's image and its perception by the customer himself. In fact, many remanufactured products are sold at a lower price than the new ones, even if they have similar characteristics, due to its perception by the consumer, who associates the concept of remanufactured product with that of used product.

The different perception linked to new and remanufactured products is closely related to the philosophy of product recovery and not only to the specific required remanufacturing activities. Some firms, for example, might sell new products at a certain price and remanufactured products (or *as-is* or repaired / refurbished products) at a lower price. Others, however, could sell remanufactured or returned products as new ones on the primary market.

The type of products (new, remanufactured or refurbished) sold in the primary market, depends on the specific situation considered. Primary and secondary markets are generally separated from a geographical point of view, but this is not always true because in some cases they can even overlap. This is the case of offers devoted to consumers sensitive to the environmental impact of purchasing decisions, to the less affluent social groups most sensitive to price or, in general, to consumers of products with very high price elasticity (i.e. office consumables materials).

However, in these evaluations are also involved aspects such as product's characteristics, its intrinsic value or its propensity to technological obsolescence, brand policy, characteristics of the target market. For example, primary and secondary markets, which tend to be separated in the case of mobile phones, overlap when automotive components and industrial machinery are considered. The concept of primary and secondary markets are connected to the several possibilities of product recovery and to different prices of recovered products.

The development of secondary markets, especially for Electric and Electronic Appliances, is strongly linked to growth in demand for these products in developing countries. It is easy to understand how these markets are definitely the most attractive to businesses. In areas like Latin America or Equatorial Africa, in fact, demand for these products is growing at two-digit rates. For example in Nigeria that, from 2000 to 2006, there has been an increasing number of mobile lines (from one to about 25 million). Because of the economic conditions of that population, a significant share of this demand was satisfied with mobile phones and accessories (210,000 used cell phones imported only in 2005) used or remanufactured imported from more developed countries.

In Nigeria there is a high rate of repair and reuse of mobile phones. This extends their life from about 18 months in developed countries to approximately 7 years. A further aspect that encourages the use of remanufactured products is the high availability of cores, especially in developed countries.

In addition to Nigeria and other African countries, a significant demand also comes from countries of South America and Asia, particularly from Brazil and China. It has been estimated that the demand for second hand mobile phones is still higher than their availability [32].

Offering a remanufactured product can increase the usefulness perceived by the consumer, whose willingness to pay for products in like-new conditions should increase with respect to second hand products. Meanwhile the manufacturer can increase its profits leveraging on products that can become attractive after appropriate transformations. Therefore, changes on the demand level and price could occur [33].

The importance of secondary markets for companies is demonstrated, also, by the fact that often a product not having demand in the primary market, could still have a certain attractiveness in secondary markets. For mobile phones, for example, the secondary market cannibalizes less than 1% of sales of new products [29]. Another type of secondary market is that of components. For example, computer chips may have an alternative use in devices simpler from a technological point of view, like toys etc..

3.4. Benefits of remanufacturing

3.4.1. Environmental returns

A remanufacturing process can allow an higher saving of natural resources if compared to other forms of reuse. According to the Energy Systems Division of Argonne National Laboratory, through this type of product recovery the equivalent of $422 * 10^{21}$J of energy per year can be saved. This energy would be used to satisfy the need of new components, that in the remanufacturing case is reduced of about 80%.

The energy saving is associated with lower emissions of carbon dioxide in the atmosphere for 800.000 t. In a long term perspective if everything would be recovered from returned products, a closed loop cycle for management of products / wastes could occur eliminating the use of landfill.

Waste form electronic and electric appliances, in particular, can cause serious health damage, since they contain a wide range of hazardous substances such as cadmium, chromium or mercury. For these reasons, the legislation from several countries in the world have been improved several times to ensure a correct management of potentially dangerous products during their lifecycle.

However from an environmental point of view it is important to check the opportunity of prolonging the life of a product, especially if potentially obsolete or polluting. In fact, that the impact of many products is higher during the use phase than in the disposal one [34].

Therefore even the best environmental intentions can lead to product take-back regulations counterproductive if not coordinated with the type of materials resulting from the recovery process. This lack coupled with the breakthrough role of technology has created a strange situation that still does not find solution.

3.4.2. Economic aspects of remanufacturing business

The product recovery can be a profitable business, in fact a remanufacturing process can allow a general price reduction of 35% - 40% with an average margin of 20% [16]. Furthermore, the reuse allows saving in raw materials and energy, avoiding the disposal costs that OEM by law have to support.

The cost reduction is at the base of profitability of this business and can ensure appropriate returns on investment. This will benefit the competitive position of the company that can share these benefit with its customers.

In a multi period perspective, the cost reductions do not affect only remanufactured products, but also the new ones. The pricing policy, in fact, has to take into account that many of the costs incurred ,during first production cycle, can also be amortized in the following remanufacturing cycles. Often, recovery programs are not started fearing for the negative effect on sales of new products. This is a *push* view of business, that does not consider the profile of the target market and competitive intensity. Actually, nothing ensures that the condition of maximum profit passes necessarily through a new release of product. The company can profit from new products on the primary market and from remanufactured ones on the secondary one, and if these markets are separated, there is no risk of demand substitution.

Moreover, the strong tensions on market prices of materials, due to the rapid growth of some developing countries, are making the direct costs of materials an increasingly important factor of business profitability, as the labour costs. "…As valuable resources become scarcer and more expensive, companies managing their resources efficiently are likely to gain a competitive advantage" [31].

In many cases, strategies aimed at exploiting the added value of the product, as a policy of relocation, could be source of competitive advantage. Therefore, the profitability of this business is more pronounced if the incidence of raw materials, on the full cost of the product, is high.

Among the benefits of a remanufacturing program we can find the achievement of economies of scale and experience. The increase of production size allows to spread fixed costs over a higher volume of output. However, the economies of experience allow to maximize the overall efficiency of the process optimizing the use of variable factors and the time required for operations. For example, the benefits may relate to aspects such as quality of recovered materials, waste reduction, processes organization. In this case tacit knowledge is very important. It becomes crucial how this resource is managed by the organization to allow a wide spread use and exploitation, through various stages of socialization, externalization, combination and internalization in order to create explicit knowledge [35].

Ferrer and Guide argue that ethical and environmental reasons alone are not sufficient to justify a remanufacturing program [36]. Each firm to produce profits focuses on core activities and outsources the others. Eco-friendly production logic and principles of CSR (Corporate Social Responsibility) follow this approach.

In the US the business of product recovery and remanufacturing, has not developed only for regulation reasons or environmental awareness. Legislative obligations, incentives and taxes intended to address the problem, were not the key determinants for the emergence of this industry. This is also testified by the fact that the remanufacturing business was already established in different sectors before the concepts of EPR or Product Stewardship, grow up. The determining factor turns to be the business profitability, beyond environmental aspects or taxes.

3.4.3. Business strategy motivations

The aspects related to policy and corporate strategy, although not directly related to the purpose of profit, could be particularly important for OEMs in starting remanufacturing activities. Among these there are the connotation of brand, the corporate image, the aftermarket coverage, feedback on sold products.

The image is a very critical factor in a successful business because it can only be built through a shrewd marketing policy and substantial investment diluted in time. Products devoted to remanufacturing activities, if not consistent with market expectations, could significantly damage the relationship between consumer and OEM regardless of who has carried out the remanufacturing activities.

For this reason it is crucial for an OEM to be interested in these activities. The purpose may be to stop any remanufacturing activity on its products, preventing others players from exploiting its brand image and possibly causing unwanted effects through lock-out systems, or to manage remanufacturing activities on its products.

As regards the implications of building a strong brand image, the company that enhances, in the public eye, its focus on the environmental problems by means of a suitable marketing strategy, can create an *environment friendly* image. The key element to have an environment friendly approach rewarded by the market, is its correct presentation highlighting the commitment made by the company and providing data that spell out the benefits obtained by consumers and all stakeholders.

The information used can be of two types: associated with the lower environmental impact of products and / or related to its higher performance. These two types are not mutually exclusive, rather, from their synergy the company can get the best results in terms of image return.

The first type of information is intended to highlight the aspect of product such as reduced use of resources, greater durability, the reduced number of components, the absence of environmentally hazardous materials in the product or its production process. The latter, instead, aims to highlight the performance which consumers can expect using it as, for example, greater accuracy, increased flexibility, modularity, etc.. The latter, instead, aim to highlight the performance which consumers can expect using it as, for example, greater accuracy, increased flexibility, modularity, etc.. All these information are intended to influence judgments and feelings of consumers, to amplify the potential value of the offer, working on those aspects to which the target market is more sensitive.

For an OEM collecting used components and products from its customers allows to preside over the aftermarket. In many cases this market turns out to be very profitable even more the main one. Recovery activities through the collection of end of life products is a way to preserve the aftermarket by competitors or potential players. The take-back activity represents an opportunity to maintain and increase the value of customer relationships. The product return represents a moment of interaction with customer with the chance to establish a new relationship. Hence the importance of policies aimed at valuing this phase, perhaps through an incentive system that motivates the customer to return the product. Business models like "System Lock-In, Competitor Lock-Out" oriented to a "Restricted Access" can limit the opportunities for contact between the customer and competitors preventing new consumer experiences, and comparisons of several offers. The complementary aspects of the offer and the economies of the system should be taken into account, considering also those systems that allows the multi-period use of products [37].

Conversely, avoiding to consider this option, means not to cover a market opportunity, waiving a retention action, and, yielding to competitors. A evidence of that is represented by the statements of a German manager of the automotive industry: "officially a remanufactured engine can be purchased only if a core is returned. But if a customer provides the core without buying a remanufactured product , we tend to buy it anyway, because otherwise it could become "food" for competitors "(Seitz, 2007).

The remanufacturing process allows to extend the offer and introducing also low-cost options, to conquer new market spaces. This could be particularly important when spaces are not relevant [38]. Moreover, for products with a very long life-cycle, remanufacturing represents the only option to ensure replacement parts, because it is very difficult that companies provide new manufactured parts beyond a certain period of time. Remanufacturing activities allow a continuous monitoring of customer needs and conditions of installed products. Basing on these information, companies may decide reformulate its offer in a proactive way. Information highlighting the strengths and weaknesses of products can be collected as an input for the design phase of the product. In particular, the most critical data are the deterioration under the actual operating conditions, since many information are impossible to anticipate or difficult to simulate during experiments.

4. Conclusion and future developments

There are several reasons for considering remanufacturing as a business opportunity very attractive in a competitive advantage view. Savings in terms of natural resources through remanufacturing may be viewed as a reduction of the transactions between the actors involved in order to improve the overall efficiency of the economic system.

However, this improvement should be not considered only from an environmental and sustainability point of view, as produces lower production costs for companies. In fact they limit the purchase of raw materials and maximize the added value of their products with the additional benefits of feedback on products, image, customer relationships, and diversification.

A virtuous business, recovery-oriented, requires the transition from an industrial economy to an access economy, where services and the dematerialization are predominant. Hence, the most advanced form of value proposition based on a remanufactured product is represented by a result-oriented positioning, where there is an agreement contract with the customer based on target performance.

However, not always the relationship between customer and producer has evolved into a pure access one for several reasons: a marked relationship with the ownership of the product still remains for certain categories of products; the companies have not been able to promote correctly their value proposal to the market; the market is not ready yet for this kind of experience.

The criticality of technical, technological and design aspects in remanufacturing, shows that the value system of a remanufactured product goes towards a situation where the presence of independent actors decreases in favor of OEMs, who should overcome, therefore, fears of a possible substitution effect of remanufactured products with new ones.

A future development of this study could be, as a preliminary activity to any remanufacturing program, the development of a logical model for the evaluation of remanufacturability a generic product taking into account logistics, demand and technology aspects of the recovery process.

Author details

Mosè Gallo, Elpidio Romano and Liberatina Carmela Santillo
Department of Materials Engineering and Operations Management,
University of Naples "Federico II", Naples, Italy

5. References

[1] Nasr N., Thurston M., *Remanufacturing: A Key Enabler to Sustainable Product Systems.* Rochester, NY-USA: Rochester Institute of Technology, 2006.

[2] Thierry, M., Salomon, M., Van Nunen, J., Van Wassenhove, L. 1995. "Strategic Issues in Product Recovery Management". Californian Management Review. Graduate Schools of Business Administration, University of California, 1995, Vol. 37, 2, pp. 114-135.

[3] Lund R.T., Remanufacturing, *Technology Review.* MIT, 1984, Vol. 87, 2, pp. 18-23

[4] Agudo Dominguez E., Boosting Remanufacturing Industry: Looking for a Change in the Remanufacturing Paradigm. A Case Study in UK Automotive Sector. MSc Thesis. Cranfield University, United Kingdom, 2005.

[5] Sundin E., Product and Process Design for Successful Remanufacturing, *in Production Systems Dissertation,* Department of Mechanical Engineering, Linköping University, Linköping, Sweden, 2004.

[6] Lund R.T., Remanufacturing: The Experience of the United States and Implications for Developing Countries, World Bank Technical Paper, 1985, Vol. 31, ISBN 0821300776.

[7] Giuntini R., Gaudette K., Remanufacturing: The Next Great Opportunity for Boosting US Productivity, *Business Horizons*, 2003, November-December, pp.41-48

[8] Lund R.T., Remanufacturing: An American resource, *Proceedings of the Fifth International Congress Environmentally Conscious Design and Manufacturing.* Rochester, NY, USA: Rochester Institute of Technology, 1998.

[9] Mitra S., Webster S., Competitive Strategy in Remanufacturing and the Impact of Take-Back Laws, *Journal of Operations Management.* Elsevier Science, 2007, Vol. 25, 6.

[10] Ijomah W. 2002. A Model-Based Definition of the Generic Remanufacturing Business Process, doctoral thesis, University of Plymouth.

[11] Guide V.D.R, Jayaraman V., Srivastava R., Production Planning and Control for Remanufacturing: A State-of-the-Art Survey, *Robotics and Computer Integrated Manufacturing,* 1999, 15, pp. 221-230.

[12] Steinhilper R., *Remanufacturing: The Ultimate Form of Recycling,* Stuttgart: Frauenhofer IRB Verlag, 1998.

[13] Clegg A., Williams R., The Strategic and Competitive Implications of Recycling and Design for Disassembly in the Electronics Industry, *Proceeding of IEEE International Symposium on Electronics and the Environment,* San Francisco, California, 1994.

[14] Guide Jr. V.D.R.,. Production planning and control for remanufacturing: Industry practice and research needs, *Journal of Operations Management,* Vol. 18, No.4, 2000, pp. 467–483

[15] Parker D., *Remanufacturing in the UK: A Significant Contributor to Sustainable Development?,* Oakdene Hollins, Aylesbury,UK, 2003.

[16] Nasr, N., Hughson, C., Varel, E., Bauer, R. 1998. "State of the Art Assessment of Remanufacturing Technology" . Draft Document. Rochester NY : Rochester Institute of Technology, 1998.

[17] Lund R.T.. 1996. "The Remanufacturing Industry: Hidden Giant". Boston, Massachusetts: Boston University, 1996.

[18] Guide V.D.R., Jayaraman V., Linton J.D., Building Contingency Planning for Closed-Loop Supply Chains with Product Recovery, *Journal of Operations Management,* 2003, Vol. 21, 3, pp. 259-279

[19] Williams A., The Strategic Management of Product Service Systems, *Working Paper.* Cardiff, UK: The Centre For Business Relationships, Accountability, Sustainability and Society. Cardiff University, 2005. 28. ISBN 1904393608

[20] Behrend S., Firzner R., Hrauda G., Jasch, C., Kortmap J., Velte D.,*Eco-Service Development. Reinventing Supply and Demand in the European Union.* Sheffield, Greenleaf, 2003. ISBN 1874719446.

[21] Sundin E., Ostlin J., Ronnback A.O., Lindahl M., Sandstrom G.O., Remanufacturing of Products Used in Product Service System Offerings, *Manufacturing Systems and Technologies for the New Frontier.* Springer, 2008, 14, pp. 537-542.

[22] Baines TS., Lightfoot H.W., Evans S., Neely A., Greenough R., Peppard J., Roy R., Shehab E., Braganza A., Tiwari A., Alcock J.R., Angus J.P, Bastl M., Cousens A., Irving P., Johnson M., Kingston J., Lockett H., Martinez V., Michele P., State of the Art in

Product-*Service Systems, Journal of Engineering Manufacture. 2007, Vol. 221, 10, pp.1543-1552.*

[23] Lindahl M., Olundh G., Ostlin J., Ronnback A.O., Sundin, E., Integrated Product and Service Engineering, *Proceedings of Changes to Sustainable Consumption. Workshop of the Sustainable Consumption Research Exchange. Copenhagen, 2006.*

[24] Prahalad C. K., Ramaswamy V., *Il Futuro della Competizione. Co-creare Valore Eccezionale per i Clienti,* Il Sole24Ore, Roma, 2004, ISBN 8883635558.

[25] Taylor M.B., Cannibalism in Multibrand Firms, *Journal of Consumer Marketing. Emerald, 1986, Vol. 3, 2, pp. 69–75.*

[26] Chandy R.K., Tellis, G.J., Organizing for Radical Product Innovation: The Overlooked Role of Willingness to Cannibalize, *Journal of Marketing Research. American Marketing Association, 1998, Vol. 35, 4, pp. 474–487.*

[27] Linton, J.D., (2008). Assessing the Economic Rationality of Remanufacturing Products. Journal of Product Innovation Management. 25(3), p. 287-302.

[28] Toffel, 2004 M.W. Toffel, *Strategic management of product recovery Californian Management Review*, 46/2 (2004), pp. 120–141

[29] Neira J., Favret L., Fuji M., Miller R., Mahadavi S., Blass V.D., *End of life management of cell phones in the United States, Final Group Project* Report in the Master's of Environmental Science and Management of the University of California Santa Barbara, Santa Barbra, California, U.S.A., 2006

[30] Camacho, E., Gallego, A.G., Georgantzis, N., Sabater Grande, G, 2002, An experimental validation of hypothetical WTP for a recyclable product, Working Paper, 34/02, LINEEX, Universitat Jaume I, Castellon, Spain.

[31] Michaud C., Llerena, D., *An economic perspective on remanufactured products: industrial and consumption challenges for life cycle engineering,* Proceedings of the 13th CIRP International Conference on Life Cycle Engineering, Leuven, Belgium, 2006, pp. 543-548.

[32] Osibanjo O., Nnrom I.C., Material Flows of Mobile Phones and Accessories in Nigeria: Environmental Implications and Sound End-of-Life Management Options, *Environmental Impact Assessment Review*, Elsevier, 2008, 28, pp. 198-213.

[33] Robotis A., Bhattacharya S., Van Wassenhove L., The effect of remanufacturing on procurement decisions for resellers in secondary markets, *European Journal of Operational Research*, Vol.163, No.3, 2005, pp. 688-705

[34] Bras B., Hammond R., *Design for Remanufacturing Metrics*, Proceedings of First International Working Seminar on Reuse. Eindhoven, The Netherlands, 1996. pp. 35-51.

[35] Nonaka I., Takeuchi H., The *Knowledge-Creating Company: How Japanese Companies Create the Dynamics of Innovation*, Oxford University Press, New York, 1995.

[36] Ferrer G., Guide V.D.R., *Remanufacturing Cases and State of the Art*, In Ayres R.U., Ayres L.W., The Handbook of Industrial Ecology, Elgar Academic Publishers, 2002.

[37] Hax A.C., Wilde D.L., *The Delta Project: Discovering New Sources of Profitability in a Networked Economy*, MacMillan, London, 2001.

[38] Seitz M.A., A Critical Assessment of Motives for Product Recovery: the Case of Engine Remanufacturing, *Journal of Cleaner Production*. Elsevier, 2007, Vol. 15, 11-12, pp. 1147-1157.

Chapter 11

Optimizing Global Value Chain Activities by Diagonal Cumulation of Origin

Romana Korez-Vide

Additional information is available at the end of the chapter

http://dx.doi.org/10.5772/46535

1. Introduction

The pace and scale of contemporary globalisation is unprecedented. One reason for the speeding-up of the globalisation process is the emergence of global value chains (GVCs). First theoretical aspect, important for our research in this paper, is *the framework of GVCs analysis.* One of the four dimensions that are being explored by GVCs methodology is *the institutional context*[1] in which the industry value chain is embedded [1]; the institutional context identifies how local, national and international conditions and policies shape the globalization in each stage of the value chain. The second important theoretical aspect for our research is *the institution-based view of international business strategy (IBS),* which is argued to be, besides industry- and resource-based views, one of the three leading perspectives in international business strategy [2]. According to the institution-based view of IBS, which has been influenced by the North's [3] metaphor on institutions as being the "rules of the game", the researchers explore the topics, such as entry decisions, foreign direct investment strategies and diversification decisions. The third important theoretical aspect for our research is the Dunning's [4] *OLI paradigm* of a firm's international expansion. According to this paradigm, besides ownership-specific and internalisation advantages, the international expansion of a firm and its competitive performance are based also on exploitation of *the location-specific advantages.* The location-specific advantages affect the attractiveness of a given country or region for companies either in the role of the host or home location for their activities. As part of the institutional context and the specific location advantages are also institutional incentives of regional economic integrations.

[1] The other three dimensions are: (1) an input-output structure, which describes the process of transforming raw materials into final products; (2) a geographical consideration and (3) a governance structure, which explains how the value chain is controlled [1].

1.1. Research aims and methodology

In dynamic international business context market knowledge is viewed as a key ingredient of companies' competence to effectively manage their international operations. As key knowledge is usually experiential in its nature, firms differ in their capabilities regarding the understanding and application of this knowledge in their business processes and operational procedures [5, 6]. As note Kogut and Zander [7], a key added value of knowledge for firms is derived from the proper alignment of their strategic and operational activities with contextual and institutional requirements in each country market in which they operate. Transaction costs optimization resulting from the utilization of location specific advantages is seen as companies' important competitive driving-force for their internationalization processes. Exploiting various institutional incentive mechanisms in their strategies can be thus an important step for strengthening their competitiveness, when the value of such institutional initiatives for their competitive positions and business performances is properly recognized by managers and then integrated into their strategic and operational decisions.

In this paper we explore how companies could take advantage of *the SAP+ diagonal cumulation of origin* as a supranational institutional mechanism – European Union's (EU's) Common Commercial Policy instrument - in order to improve their business performance. We show how they could optimize their cost structure by integrating this form of cumulation of origin into their strategies for GVC configuration. In the theoretical part we discuss the concept and economic effects of Rules of Origin (RoO), the characteristics of diagonal cumulation of origin schemes in the EU, the importance of SAP+ diagonal cumulation of origin for foreign investors and trade growth of Western Balkan Countries (WBCs) and introduce the origin management as a part of companies' strategic and operational decisions in designing and implementing their cross-border business operation. In the second part we analyse the existent trade patterns in the proposed SAP+ diagonal cumulation zone with the emphasis on the EU-WBCs trade. In the third part we present the possible effects of the SAP+ diagonal cumulation on company's performance by a case study approach. The latter comprises the calculations of the effect of import duty allowances on export prices for two selected products of a Slovenian company's production programme in its affiliation in Serbia. On the basis of summaries of these calculations we present the importance of RoO for cost optimization of companies' GVC activities and the necessity to conduct *the trade intelligence database and origin management* to enjoy the advantages of this institutional mechanism.

1.2. The hypotheses

Our research is based on two hypotheses:

H_1: In order to exploit available institutional incentive mechanisms the optimization of company's business performance should be put into a proper institutional context of a specific country or region as it is dependent on strategies for product components physical flows optimization.

H2: The diagonal cumulation of origin is an important institutional incentive mechanism that drives company's transaction cost optimization when the origin management is conducted in the company.

The basic assumption of our research is that company can optimize processes and cost structures of its GVCs, if managers know and understand how the diagonal cumulation of origin as the institutional incentive can affect the company's business activities and respond properly.

2. Theoretical backgrounds

2.1. Institutional perspective and value chain optimization

With increased dynamics of international business environment strategic and operational aspects of company's international operations have been broadened, as crafting an effective strategy for world markets requires a better understanding of how far a firm can effectively leverage its domestic advantages for developing a strong competitive position in international markets [8]. A company should continuously align its internationalization strategy in order to optimize the use of its key sources for achieving competitive advantage and optimize its performance in variety institutional settings. For achieving a sustainable competitive advantage, a company should carefully design its geographic scope of operations as the spatial configuration of its assets, capabilities, and resources together with the ability to effectively manage them is a key part of its global strategy. International business performance of a company should be observed on an integrative way by considering institutional perspective of its international business activities together with the industry to which a firm belongs and resource-based perspective. According to the institutional view of international business, institutional factors affect the attractiveness of a given country or region for a company [4] in its dual role, either as a host country or a home location for its business activities. Since company's capabilities are seen as a dynamic concept based on processes that are embedded in a firm [9], a company could take advantage of, for example, opportunities of offered duty reductions, if managers will be able to align the operational *processes* and *procedures* in a way, that the firm will be awarded a status of eligible beneficiary of such institutional incentives. To develop a proper business context by which a company will be able to provide all necessary evidence of its eligibility status, both, objective and experiential knowledge are required.

With such perspective we broaden a traditional institutional view of international business, based on company's effort to comply with institutional restrictions and barriers in a foreign country with the option that it may also take advantage of institutional incentives that are available in foreign countries.

2.2. The concept of Rules of Origin

The concept of rules of origin (RoO) is one of the building blocks of implementing the foreign trade policy provisions of any regional economic integration (REI). Based on the origin of goods, products being traded with non-member countries remain subject to a preferential or non-preferential treatment when entering REI. The goods with preferential origin can benefit from a reduction or exemption of customs duties and, eventually, they can enter a REI without non-tariff barriers. The goods with non-preferential origin, however, are subject to tariffs and non-tariff barriers.

Rules of origin specify that only products entirely produced in one country, using only materials from that country, or products, which have been treated in a regulated way in that country, can be regarded as originating products [10]. These products are eligible to benefit from preferential treatment under a free trade agreement (FTA) or under the General System of Preferences (GSP) (autonomously granted preferences). Such goods (components, parts, final products) must fulfil the relevant conditions laid down in the origin protocol to the FTA or in the rules of origin of the autonomous arrangements. They must either (1) be manufactured from raw materials or components which have been produced in the beneficiary country or, alternatively, (2) undergo a certain amount of working or processing in the beneficiary country. Explicit rules of origin set out the least amount of working or processing required on non-originating materials in order for the resulting goods to obtain the originating status.

For a better comprehension of the mechanism of RoO and its form "cumulation of origin", we make a practical explanation of their significance and impacts. The rules of origin set in a FTA between A and B are designed to prevent trade deflection, which would happen if, for example, the third party (C) would try to export to B via A, since A implements lower tariffs. Therefore, the exporters to A and B need to prove intra-FTA originating status in order to obtain a reduced or free customs duty access to each other's market. If, for example, A and C sign a similar FTA as do countries A and B, both goods – goods originating in B and goods originating in C would have preferential access to country A. However, goods produced in B, using intermediates from C, which do not meet the rules granting originating status for exporters from B (according to the rules applied between A and B), would then be subject to non-preferential status when exported to A. Hence, goods directly exported from C to A would be granted preferential access, but goods exported from B using intermediates from C in this case would not be granted preferential access [11]. A means of overcoming this is to allow for cumulation of the use of materials or processes across countries with parallel or overlapping FTAs. *Cumulation of origin* therefore exists in order to encourage the use of materials and processing within the FTAs while maintaining a common standard for treating third country non-preferential inputs (identical protocols on rules of origin). Three types of cumulation are identified in the literature: bilateral cumulation (between any pair of countries or a single FTA), diagonal cumulation (between three or more countries or several FTAs with interlinked trading agreements), and full cumulation (the same as diagonal cumulation, but involving more flexibility than with diagonal cumulation).

Several empirical studies confirm that RoO have an important impact on trade flows and that diagonal cumulation of RoO can enhance trade. Gasiorek [12] shows that in the European trade context, RoO serve to restrict trade flows with non-cumulating countries, and trade with those countries could be lower by up to 50 percent. Woolcock [13] finds that incompatible RoO in different preferential trade agreements (PTAs) are the antithesis of trade facilitation. The latter is particularly important in the context of GVCs, which, through trade in intermediate goods, involve two or more countries in the production of a single final product. Furthermore, as the number of concluded FTAs increases, different RoO in multiple, overlapping FTAs can pose an additional burden on firms. This phenomenon is referred to as the »spaghetti bowl« of trade deals [14].

Thus, the mechanism of RoO may greatly limit the expected economic benefits of REI, or may cause distortions in favour of the partner who has been able to negotiate RoO which match the capacity of domestic industries.

2.3. Trade intelligence and origin management

In order to make informed decisions regarding origin matters, the decision makers need to have access to data up to date *Trade intelligence (TI)*. TI is defined as the sum of all legislation and market information needed to make informed decisions with regard to FTAs [15]. TI provides the exporter and importer with the ability to assess whether or not preferential claims can be made, what the country of origin is, and what the duty rate implications are. TI includes the rules of origin, compliance requirements, documentation, (future) duty rates, and insight into FTA and industry developments. These data are required in an organized/structured format that allows the importer and exporter to make (long-term) business decisions. The publication of TI is dispersed across a variety of sources. A step further is to integrate the TI in the Enterprise Resource Planning (ERP) system. Feeding the TI into such a system increases the transparency of the decision-making process regarding origin issues, as now all relevant intelligence is in a single central location. The challenge with TI is the "freshness" – the information must be updated continuously and immediately available to decision makers. This ties into the decision to outsource or collect TI in-house. Either way, that decision needs to include a review of the sources and the capabilities to provide data on time and in the format in which the data can be provided.

Origin management is the holistic approach toward the creation of a single, auditable, and global platform that enables companies to successfully claim preferential origin, sustain, review, and audit preferential claims [15]. A well-run origin management program can provide several advantages: an internal knowledge centre that collects and distributes relevant information and makes origin matters transparent for all parties involved (such as logistics, purchasing, finance, legal, customs/compliance), a clear overview of the duty rate benefits associated with preferential programs on the relevant trade lanes, capacity to identify the most beneficial production location from a duty rate perspective, functionality to automatically generate the necessary documents that will need to accompany the shipments to claim preferential treatment, possibility to determine the non-preferential country of origin, ensuring that for each shipment the FTA eligibility is determined and the calculations, documentation, etc., are properly stored to sustain the preferential claims, creation of a platform/portal where suppliers can submit origin information, capability to run "what-if" scenarios and to identify risks with regard to eligibility, for example, associated with exchange rate fluctuations, dual sourced goods, or supplier price changes and an opportunity to add new preferential programs within the same framework of compliance, i.e., no excessive costs associated with setting up new programs based on either new trade lanes or newly available FTAs.

2.4. The characteristics of diagonal cumulation of origin schemes in the European Union

The Pan-European diagonal cumulation, which was introduced between the EU and European Free Trade Association (EFTA) member states in 1997[2], evolved in 2005 into the Pan-Euro-Mediterranean (PEM) diagonal cumulation of origin [16][3]. In 2007 it was decided to include countries participating in the Stabilization and Association Process (SAP)[4] (WBCs) with the EU into the PEM diagonal cumulation [18, 19][5]. It was also agreed to start the drafting of a single regional Convention on preferential RoO for the PEM area in order to facilitate the application of identical rules of origin[6] for the purpose of diagonal cumulation of origin for goods traded in the PEM cumulation zone. In 2009 it was supported the conclusion of the regional Convention on Pan-Euro-Mediterranean preferential RoO (PEM RoO) [22, 23] and in 2011 the Council of the EU has decided to sign it [24]. The Convention was open for signature on 15 June 2011 [25].

The study on the economic integration of the Euro-Med region [26] which is based on the survey of government and business representatives in the EU and in 5 Euro-Med countries (MED5) – Egypt, Israel, Jordan, Morocco and Tunisia –, has shown that among the MED5 the percent of companies, that have benefited from this system, changed from sector to sector. Although it is difficult to generalize, in some sectors the rate of utilization of the PEM diagonal cumulation of origin was as high as 70 percent of exports, however, the industries with high level of vertical integration, i.e. textiles, automobiles, electronics, found these RoO out of date and very strict. On their opinion, they do not recognize the "division" of labour and hence the exporters cannot benefit from this mechanism. On the other hand, since the

---

[2] The Turkey was included in the Pan-European diagonal cumulation of origin in 1999.

[3] PEM comprised the EU and EFTA member states, Turkey, Faroe Islands and the southern Mediterranean countries participating in the "Barcelona Declaration". This decision aimed at replacing the network of some 60 bilateral protocols on RoO among the countries or territories of the Euro-Med zone.

[4] The Stabilisation and Association Process (SAP), as the framework for EU negotiations with Western Balkan Countries (WBCs) has three main aims: firstly, stabilising the countries and encouraging their swift transition to a market economy, secondly, promoting regional cooperation, and thirdly, eventual membership in the EU. The countries covered by the SAP are Albania, Bosnia and Herzegovina, Croatia, Macedonia, Montenegro and Serbia, including Kosovo as defined in UN Security Council Resolution 1244/99 [17].

[5] The Salzburg European Commission Communication from 2006 [20] establishes a two-step approach to extend diagonal cumulation to the WBCs: (1) a new cumulation zone should be established between all Western Balkan countries and territories and the EC, known as SAP diagonal cumulation of origin between the EU, WBCs and Turkey) (for manufactured goods only) (see [21]); (2) WBCs should be included in the Pan-Euro-Med zone of diagonal cumulation.

[6] This decision aimed at replacing the network of some 60 bilateral protocols on RoO among the countries or territories of the Euro-Med zone.

MED5 is beginning to be more and more integrated with Asia, several respondents reported these RoO would not allow inputs from certain countries.

The decision of Euro-Med trade ministers to include WBCs into the PEM diagonal cumulation of origin was related to the fact that the bilateral cumulation of origin, enabled by the Stabilisation Association Agreements (SAAs) signed between EU and WBCs (except Serbia and Kosovo), failed to effectively promote mutual trade within broader region. Bilateral cumulation of origin in trade with the EU discouraged firms from the WBCs from developing mutual production links oriented toward supplying EU markets, because inputs from other WBCs countries were treated as "external" imports. Another consequence of bilateral cumulation of origin was that it erected a barrier to the development of trade, based on fragmentation of production, i.e., moving across border various fragments of a supply chain. These arrangements thus prevented companies from establishing production networks across WBCs. Since the Common Commercial Policy (CCP) of the EU has a central role in the SAP, the inclusion of WBCs in the PEM cumulation of origin is the EU's strategic aim [27, 18].

2.5. Western Balkan countries and the concept of SAP+ diagonal cumulation of origin

Trade flows analyses [28] have shown that PEM diagonal cumulation of origin for WBCs has a rather limited impact on long-term trade and economic growth prospects. These assessments are based on the limited trade relations between the WBCs and the potential partners in the Mediterranean region. It is therefore questionable whether the WBCs could make effective use of diagonal cumulation with Mediterranean business partners in the long run. The inclusion of the WBCs in the PEM cumulation of origin has also proved to be a long lasting process as existing procedural and implementing dilemmas have to be solved in the first place [28]. The main dilemma is related to the lengthy preparation and implementation of the decision on amending the protocols on origin of WBCs, which should be harmonized with all PEM countries. Another dilemma is related to the proposed technical amendments to the PEM protocol, which implies the use of EUR-MED certificates in trade between the EU and the WBCs. This would complicate existing trade between the EU and the WBCs because of the double certification (movement certificates EUR1 and EUR-MED).

Therefore, four forms of rules of origin, which could be used for the WBCs in the meantime, have been presented by the European Commission in 2007 [28]. Amongst them the form of *SAP+ diagonal cumulation of origin*[7], which would create diagonal cumulation zone between the EU, EFTA, WBCs (CEFTA 2006)[8] and Turkey, would be the most justified from the point of view of existing business ties between these partners. Introduction of SAP+ cumulation is seen as a practical, fast and procedurally straightforward solution that includes powerful tools to prevent some of the negative effects that arise from the current lack of diagonal

[7] SAP stands for Stabilization Association Process, and + is because the idea includes Turkey and EFTA beside EU.

[8] As of 1 May 2007, members of CEFTA are: Albania, Bosnia and Herzegovina, Croatia, Macedonia, Montenegro, Moldova, Serbia and Kosovo (under UN Security Council Resolution 1244/99). Moldova is not covered by the SAP. For CEFTA 2006 impacts and problems see Kumar [29].

cumulation, in particular trade suppression and trade diversion effects [28-30]. Spreading the free trade zone by SAP+ diagonal cumulation would serve the foreign companies which are ready to invest in the WBCs, but are hindered by the limiting rules of origin. Greater attractiveness of the WBCs as areas for foreign direct investment (FDI) would be an incentive for foreign companies to invest and establish production networks across the WBCs region. At the same time, the companies which are active in this region could reduce the unnecessary costs related to customs barriers and consequently increase competitiveness. The removal of technical barriers would give impetus to increased trade in intermediate goods, based on fragmentation of production, and accordingly, the share of intra-industry trade would also increase. According to some theoretical explanations [see 11], the form of diagonal cumulation of origin leads to three positive effects – trade creation, trade reorientation and trade expansion – and the negative effect of trade diversion. The latter might occur if some of the imported goods from the most efficient suppliers in certain segments from the rest of the world would be redirected towards the less efficient partners in the system of cumulation. Since the overwhelming share of WBCs' trade is already taking place with the partners in the prospective SAP+ zone (see the subsequent Chapter), there is little scope for trade diversion to occur.

3. Empirical research

3.1. Trade flows between prospective partner countries in SAP+ diagonal cumulation zone

With the aim of justifying SAP+ diagonal cumulation of origin the actual trade flows between prospective partner countries of this form of cumulation were analyzed. The important indicator of existing trade linkages within this region is EU-extra trade in goods with EFTA member states, WBCs, and Turkey, that was, in 2010, comparable with EU-extra trade in goods with its main trading partners – China and USA (Table 1). In the same period, the extra-EU trade in goods with WBCs represented 0.9 and 2.0 %, respectively, in extra EU-trade in goods with the world.

	Imports	Exports	Imports + Exports
World	100.0	100.0	100.0
Main trading partner	18.8 (China)	17.9 (USA)	14.4 (USA)
EFTA	11.1	11.1	11.1
Turkey	2.8	4.5	3.6
WBCs	0.9	2.0	1.4
EFTA + WBCs + Turkey	14.8	17.6	16.1

Table 1. Extra EU-trade in goods with EFTA, WBCs and Turkey (2010, in %).
Source: [25].

It is evident from Table 2 that the importance of trade in goods with prospective partner countries from the SAP+ diagonal cumulation zone is much higher for WBCs: WBCs trade in goods with these countries amounts 68.5 % of all trade with the world.

	Imports	Exports	Imports + Exports
World	100.0	100.0	100.0
Main trading partner	63.7 (EU27)	64.5 (EU27)	64.0 (EU27)
EFTA	1.6	1.0	1.4
Turkey	3.9	1.6	3.1
EU27 + EFTA +Turkey	69.2	67.1	68.5

Table 2. WBCs trade in goods with EU27, EFTA and Turkey (2010, in %).
Source: [25].

The average annual growth in the EUs' trade with WBCs amounted to 13.2 % in the period from 2004-2008, which was higher than its average growth rate with the rest of the world, over the same period (9.7 %) [31]. The average annual growth of WBCs trade with the EU was lower during the same period (1.1 %), however, a growth in WBCs exports to the EU achieved almost the same growth rate (5.7 %) as the whole of WBCs exports (6 %). International economic crisis, however, left the consequences also in the trade between the EU and WBCs and vice versa: in the period from 2006-2010 the average annual growth in the EU's trade with the WBCs amounted only 2.5 % and was lower than its average growth rate with the rest of the world (3.3 %) [25]. Substantially lower growth levels achieved also the trade between the WBCs and the EU during the same period: average annual growth of WBCs trade with the EU achieved negative level (-5.5 %) and was lower than the level of WBCs growth of trade with the rest of the world (-2.9 %). The decrease in FDI affected the entire region and represented the first mean through which the crisis was transmitted from Western Europe countries to the Western Balkans. The need for foreign direct investment becomes more important to make national economies rescue their previous paths of growth.

In times of economic crisis, regional cooperation may represent a crucial instrument in order to avoid unilateral policies and manoeuvres that could result in a general deterioration of the economic environment in WBCs. Enhancing the region's economic cooperation requires not only political will, but also substantial investment in better regional inter-connections, for instance improved infrastructure and cross-country networks. Transports, energy, environment are all fields that ask for regional cooperation and needs a coordination of policies and strategies in order to get international donors' and investors' support.

Data [25] also show that the average share of exports to WBCs within the total EU-27s' exports (2.0 %) is higher than the average share of imports from WBCs in the total EU-27s' imports (0.9 %), whereby the highest shares belong to the export of textiles (6.2 %) and import of iron and steel (4.4 %) (Table 3).

Within the EU-27 exports to WBCs, as well as within the EU-27 imports from WBCs, the highest shares belong to machinery and transport equipment as they climbed to 27.8 % and 18.3 %, respectively. The structure of trade between the EU-27 and the WBCs shows that the larger parts of WBCs exports to EU27 are represented by goods with low value-added.

Product Groups	EU27 Exports to WBCs	Share of total EU27 Exports	EU27 Imports from WBCs	Share of total EU27 Imports
Total	100.0	2.0	100.0	0.9
Primary products	23.4	3.0	32.2	0.8
- Agricultural products	11.3	3.0	13.0	1.6
- Fuels and mining products	12.2	2.9	19.2	0.6
Manufactures	75.2	1.8	67.0	1.0
- Iron and steel	4.1	3.1	8.3	4.4
- Chemicals	16.3	1.8	7.8	0.8
- Other semi-manufactures	12.3	3.2	9.9	1.9
- Machinery and transport equipment	27.8	1.3	18.3	0.6
- Office and telecommunication equipment	5.0	1.7	1.7	0.1
- Transport equipment	9.1	1.1	4.5	0.6
- Other machinery	13.7	1.3	12.1	1.2
- Textiles	3.6	6.2	1.2	0.8
- Clothing	2.7	4.2	9.4	2.0
- Other manufactures	8.4	1.8	12.1	1.2
Other products	0.6	0.4	0.6	0.3

Table 3. Structure of EU27 trade with WBCs by product grouping (2010, in %).
Source: [25].

Other empirical analyses, based on gravity model estimations [32, 33], have shown that the trade potential between the EU member states and WBCs is not fully utilized, since trade flows between the two remain at 2 to 3 times below their potential level. Hence, there are great opportunities for EU companies to increase their sales within this region. In addition to trade potential, for a detailed evaluation of trade between particular countries/regions it is necessary to examine the qualitative aspects of mutual trade flows and the integration potential of a country/region, respectively. One of the main indicators is the share of intra-industry trade within the total trade of the country/region, being the prevailing type of specialization regarding trade among developed countries. Recent analysis [34] has shown that the share of intra-industry trade within the total trade of WBCs with the EU is relatively low. When analyzed at the total trade level, Croatia has the highest level of intra-industry trade, slightly exceeding 30 percent of trade with the EU in 2004. This is a relatively low-level when considering that, for developed countries the level of this type of trade usually exceeds 70 %, and may indicate low-levels of interaction among firms operating in the same networks of production and distribution as the suppliers of parts and components, as well as limited utilization of economies of scale during the production of parts and components.

Lacking product differentiation through international trade may be the consequence of such a trading pattern.

The low level of intra-industry trade within the WBCs' trade with the EU suggests that trade among WBCs and the EU is driven by differences in factor endowments rather than by the utilization of economies of scale associated with supplying a larger market, and that firms from the WBCs mainly rely on their strategies for price/cost competitiveness. This fact is confirmed by those calculations revealing the comparative advantage indices of WBCs regarding trade with the EU [35], showing the comparative advantages of WBCs in those industries that are relatively intensive in the use of unskilled labour and raw materials.

3.2. Simulations of value-chain optimization via SAP+ diagonal cumulation of origin

This paper presents a case study approach for simulating the effects of SAP+ diagonal cumulation of origin on business performance at the company level. On the basis of calculated summaries regarding export prices for two selected products from a company's production program at its subsidiary in Serbia, the importance of the concept of origin of goods and the consequences of accepting SAP+ diagonal cumulation of origin are presented. These calculations are relevant for the simulations of three possible scenarios concerning the origin of goods [5, 6].

It is obvious from Tables 4 and 5, that conditions for acquiring the status of preferential origin (according to Article 15 of the Protocol on origin [36] that defines exemption from customs duties) for the two observed products, with the intention to export them from Serbia to the EU, have been fulfilled.

	Euros	% (in EXW price)	% (in material)
Value of material	112.38	74%	100%
- Material with preferential origin	106.90	71%	
EU preferential origin	83.34	55%	74%
RS preferential origin	23.56	16%	21%
- Material without preferential origin	5.48	4%	5%
Labour, profit and others	39.12	26%	
EXW price at WBC »X«	151.50	100%	
Transport, insurance and other costs	3.50		
CIP consignee WBC	155.00		

Table 4. The structure of EXW and CIP export price of deep freezers.
Source: own calculations of company's data.
Note: RS – Republic of Serbia.

This is because during the production of these two products more materials with preferential origin than with non-preferential origin are used – 95 % and 75 % respectively (the necessary condition is 50 % of the total value of the used materials), less than 40 % of materials without origin are used – 4 % and 20 %, respectively, and, according to company's data, less than 10 % of materials without origin from the same tariff number as the products are used (2 % and 5 %, respectively).

	Euros	% (in EXW price)	% (in material)
Value of material	98.28	81%	100%
- Material with preferential origin	74.31	61%	
EU preferential origin	56.38	46%	57%
RS preferential origin	17.93	15%	18%
- Material without preferential origin	23.97	20%	24%
Labour, profit and others	23.22	19%	
EXW price at WBC »X«	121.50	100%	
Transport, insurance and other costs	4.50		
CIP consignee in the EU country	126.00		

Table 5. The structure of EXW and CIP export price of refrigerators.
Source: own calculations of company's data.
Note: RS – Republic of Serbia.

When studying the exports of the Serbian subsidiary of household appliance producer, it can be concluded that, from 1st February 2010 onwards, when the Interim Agreement between EU and Serbia on trade and trade related matters entered into force [37], the conditions for the Serbian products to acquire the status of preferential origin (the importing country is exempted from the import tariffs on the basis of the movement certificate EUR.1 or on the basis of the statement on the invoice) are fulfilled, not only for member states of EU and EFTA, but also for member states of CEFTA 2006 and Turkey.

In the present situation, this subsidiary uses mainly materials with the European origin (50 %) for its production, whilst the share of materials from Serbia amounts to approximately 15 %. It is obvious from Table 6 that from the perspective of present position in the market, and before the Interim Agreement between EU and Serbia has entered into force, the subsidiary had to bear extremely high tariff costs on all of the WBCs markets, where the actual sales potential is the highest.

Before the above-mentioned agreement has entered into force, for the local subsidiary of a Slovenian firm high customs expenses per year had been incurred and this amount did not include the possible savings, if it could import raw materials from the CEFTA 2006, EFTA and Turkey, instead from China, South Korea and other countries. If these funds were invested in product and technological development, they would result in production increase, decreased production expenses, cheaper products, and better position for the firm vis-à-vis European competitors. From the documentation performance point of view regarding the import process, this subsidiary implemented "customs procedures with an economic impact"[9] which allow for refunding the duties that were paid on imports of goods once these goods have been exported.

	Quantity (pcs)	Value (Euros)	Tariff costs (Euros)	Export price (Euros)	Tariff costs per piece (Euros)	Tariff (%)
Bosnia and Herzegovina	25257	3.518.470	351.847	139.00	13.9	10.0
Croatia	30444	4.255.390	313.998	140.00	10.3	7.4
Kosovo	7151	1.082.650	108.265	151.00	15.1	10.0
Macedonia	4218	628.540	33.861	149.00	8.0	5.4
Montenegro	5278	710.296	69.531	135.00	13.2	9.8
Average export price				142.80		
Average tariff costs per unit					12.1	
Average tariff						8.5
Moldova	38	7.073	379	186	10.0	5.4
Turkey	1036	156.623	3.461	151	3.3	2.2

Table 6. Company's exports and tariffs in selected WBCs, Moldova and Turkey.
Sources: [38] and own calculations.

Consequently, subsidiary avoided payment of import duties for materials from third countries. The calculations show that a greater part of the tariff costs belong to import tariffs for products sold to other WBCs. After the agreement has entered into force, the products being sold to Croatia are cheaper, on average, by approximately 10 €, whilst the products being sold to Bosnia and Herzegovina, and Kosovo are cheaper, on average, by about 14 € and 15 €, respectively. According to the company's estimation of yearly sales volume to other WBCs, the absolute figure for additional costs regarding import duties had amounted to 1.000.000 € per year. This amount is considerably higher than the cumulative amount of additional costs regarding import tariffs for materials being used in the production of products for the Serbian market (the cost of import tariff amounted, on average, to 6 €/product unit).

On the basis of these calculations subsidiary has developed three business scenarios in relation to its eligibility for using origin of goods in its import/export transactions:

1. In the period until the bilateral acceptance of SAA between EU-Serbia, the subsidiary postponed the payment of import duties in the import transactions, on the basis of the duty relief scheme "customs procedures with an economic impact". In the export

[9] Specific form of customs duty relief known as 'drawback' allows to companies to refund the import duties once the goods have been exported [39].

transactions with other WBCs, however, subsidiary paid, on average, 12.1 € tariff duty/product unit, since it did not comply with the conditions for issuing the Movement Certificate EUR.1.

2. In the period after the acceptance of SAA between EU and Serbia, the subsidiary abandons the scheme "customs procedures with an economic impact" in its import transactions and pays import tariff duties on materials to be used in production in the Serbian subsidiary (the average import tariff duty for Serbian market amounts to 5.6 %), whilst in export transactions with other WBCs, it issues the Movement Certificate EUR.1.
3. In the period after the possible enforcement of SAP+ diagonal cumulation of origin the subsidiary would postpone the payment of import tariff duties (only for materials without origin and not for all imported materials), whilst in export transactions to the countries of SAP+ diagonal cumulation of origin (despite Article 15 of the Protocol on origin [36]) it would issue Movement Certificate EUR.1. If the origin of those materials, used in production in the Serbian subsidiary, would be exclusively from the EU, Serbia and other countries of the SAP+ diagonal cumulation of origin, the subsidiary would not pay the tariff duties, neither on these materials nor for final products being exported to the countries of this cumulation zone.

4. Discussion of research results

Our empirical research has shown that the volume of actual trade between the EU and prospective partner countries in the SAP+ diagonal cumulation of origin zone is comparable with the volume of actual trade between the EU and its main trading partners. However, the share of the WBCs and Turkey in the whole of the EU's extra trade is moderate, in spite of existing FTAs (SAAs) between the EU and CEFTA 2006 member countries, and the customs union between the EU and Turkey (see Table 1). The share of the WBCs' trade with the prospective SAP+ diagonal cumulation of origin zone is much higher, whereby the trade of WBCs with EFTA and Turkey lags behind the trade of WBCs with the EU-27, considerably (see Table 2). One reason for such a situation undoubtedly relates to the fact that WBCs are not part of the proper diagonal cumulation zone, which would take into consideration geographically dispersed value-chain activities and would enable less costly trade inside broader region of the WBCs, EU, EFTA and Turkey. WBCs have been under-performing relative to their potential with respect to the magnitude and quality of trade flows with the EU, and intra-regionally as well. WBCs' trade is characterized by a low share of intra-industry trade and specialization in unskilled labour and natural resource intensive industries with low technological inputs. The rules of origin, allowing only for bilateral cumulation of origin in trade with the EU, offers limited advantages for firms from the WBCs and discourages intra-regional trade. According to the trade flows analysis [28], that has shown the limited trade relations between the WBCs and the potential partners in the Mediterranean, the long-term trade effects of the decision of Euro-Med trade ministers to include WBCs into the PEM diagonal cumulation of origin are, however, questionable.

Our case study analysis has shown that the subsidiary of the Slovenian household appliance producer in Serbia was, before the Interim Agreement has entered into force, confronted with additional costs regarding levied customs duties during the processes of sourcing and selling its products within the broader region. It is evident from various sources (see [28]) that comprehensive difficulties existed for exporters from the EU to the WBCs. These studies show that when the exported products mostly contained components or raw materials originating from EFTA countries they could not benefit from the status of preferential origin at the WBCs' markets. Such a situation also complicated the firm's foreign direct investment decisions as it was difficult to assess whether a specific location truly offers adequate institutional advantages as a main argument for investment. The discussed subsidiary has elaborated three possible business scenarios in relation to its import and export operational procedures. Implementation of the third discussed scenario is obviously the best option for cost optimization of the firm's value chain activities.

In regard to those EU companies already operating in the WBCs, SAP+ diagonal cumulation of origin would result in a simplification of those procedures relating to the determination of origin of goods and a simplification of trade operations because of the extended possibilities regarding usage of materials, and the possibilities of preferential treatment for goods. This would lead to reduced costs and lower prices, which would finally result in improved business performance. This zone of cumulation would also increase the attractiveness of the region as an export destination and as a location for FDI and, at the same time, it would encourage companies from the WBCs to develop mutual production links and other complex types of cooperation among firms, leading towards a higher potential for trade and investment at an international level.

5. Conclusions

The rapid growth of number and variety of free trade agreements (FTAs) lead to a "spaghetti bowl" phenomenon [14], where crisscrossing RoO impose higher transaction costs to industries and distort trade and investment flows. Such situation has called for more systematic approach towards projecting company's global value chain activities.

The research in our paper is based on the institutional perspective of international business strategy: while projecting their global value chain activities, companies should consider available institutional incentives for international trade and business promotion. Due to dynamic and transitional nature of such incentives – they may be introduced for a limited time period, and after their purposes have been achieved, they may be changed or abolished – the companies have to be constantly informed of changes in this field. Changing contextual circumstances are thus part of companies' business reality, which forces them to often change their strategies in the midst of their implementation because the institutional rules of the game have been changed either by a host country government, or by supranational institutions. Dynamic capabilities are seen as process embedded in firms, and, thus, a firm will be able to take advantage of, for example, opportunities of offered duty reductions, if managers will be able to align their firm operational processes and procedures in a way, that the firm will be awarded a status of eligible beneficiary of such institutional incentives. With the aim of using FTAs to their benefit and to establish new competitive advantages, companies should assure trade intelligence database and perform origin management. The integration of trade intelligence in the Enterprise Resource Planning system increases the transparency of the decision-making process regarding origin issues and enables companies to successfully claim preferential origin and sustain, review, and audit preferential claims.

At its conceptual level, the cumulation of origin institutional incentive mechanism is seen as a comprehensive framework for promoting a dynamic growth of trade flows among signatory countries. The mechanism is viewed also as a driver of transaction cost lowering, which may be achieved through a proper spatial configuration of MNEs' operations for product component assembly inside the diagonal cumulation zone [4, 5]. Our research has revealed also some drawbacks of such incentive tool that do not fully support our first hypothesis: the partial implementation of this incentive mechanism (bilateral cumulation of origin between EU and WBCs and prospective inclusion of WBCs into Pan-Euro-Med diagonal cumulation of origin) does not contribute to the optimal business performance of the companies in the region and does not have considerable effects on the trade growth within the region.

Based on the empirical validation of the benefits of the proposed SAP+ diagonal cumulation of origin mechanism and by simulating different scenarios on companies' dealing with existent RoO and their effects on the transaction cost structure, we concluded that diagonal cumulation of origin is an important institutional incentive mechanism that drives firm transaction cost optimization when it is considered in relation to the proper spatial configuration of the global value chain activities. To achieve this, the company has to conduct the origin management. Thus, our second hypothesis was fully supported.

Despite the limitations of the empirical research on a case study of one company in a household appliance production industry and with a company's specific heritage of its cost structure, market position and a portfolio of international operations, our study offers several issues that have important implications for policy makers, managers, and for future academic research.

To optimize their value adding activities and improve competitiveness, managers should seek to develop a proper understanding of existing institutional mechanisms (barriers, restrictions, and incentives) as a starting point in developing their firm internationalization strategy for the selected country markets [5]. In this process, they should consider strategic options that would enable their firms to optimize their goods flows, properly align the value-adding processes, and cost structure of their products in a broader geographic and institutional setting. With properly designed strategies, firms may comply with existing institutional barriers to international trade, and take, at the same time, advantage of institutional incentive mechanisms (import duty allowances, etc.) that are offered by local or supranational institutional actors.

Managers should be alert on changes in institutional framework of the EU (and of other regional economic integrations) in order to timely assess the implications of such institutional change for strategies and performance of their firms. Then they have to act accordingly with the aim to take advantage of offered incentives that may improve the business performance of their firms in selected foreign countries. With proper configuration of the value adding processes in their supply chains, managers can improve business performance of their firms by reaping additional cost savings in their cross-border goods flows and transactions. During this process, both objective and experiential knowledge are required by a firm in order to develop a proper organizational context, i. e. transform its strategic decisions into efficient operational procedures, activities, and routines in such a way that it would comply with the prescribed institutional requirements (formal condition) for achieving the status of eligible entity for utilizing available institutional incentives. The consideration of such requirements should be made very early in the business process planning, preferably during the phase of a firm's international expansion strategy formation, in order to properly integrate them with its foreign market entry mode decisions and with its evolving operational business framework (organization, processes, etc.). The firm's direct exposure to local institutional context should provide managers with relevant experiential knowledge for developing and cultivating relationships with key partners in its supply-chain network and framing a consistent and efficient international assembly network. This effort should lead toward the providing of such flows of supplied components and semi-finished assemblies that will enable the firm to comply with all required formal provisions, prescribed by the institutional incentive package.

Further research could address the feasibility and costs of tracking of origin of goods for a firm, in comparison to the effects of the incentive mechanism presented in the paper, which would allow for obtaining an insight into 'the whole picture' regarding its benefits for a specific firm. Also a detailed comparative analysis of different cost structures of firms operating in different industries might reveal the effects of the transaction cost lowering on their overall business performance. Such analyses may also show the relative strategic importance of firm's operations adjusting with the RoO in comparison with other strategic options (outsourcing, licensing, etc.). A more longitudinal study would be also useful in order to check the effects of discussed incentive mechanism from a dynamic perspective and firms' market knowledge accumulation.

Author details

Romana Korez-Vide
University of Maribor, Faculty of Economics and Business, Maribor, Slovenia

6. References

[1] Gereffi G. Global Value Chains in a post crisis world: A development perspective. Washington: World Bank; 2010.
[2] Peng MW. Global Business. Cincinnati: South Western Cengage Learning; 2009.

[3] North D. Institutions, Institutional Change, and Economic Performance. Cambridge, MA: Harvard University Press; 1990.

[4] Dunning JH, Lundan SM. Multinational Enterprises and the Global Economy. Cheltenham: Edward Elgar; 2008.

[5] Jurše M, Logožar K, Korez-Vide R. Diagonal cumulation of origin as the EU's institutional incentive mechanism for promoting international trade and business. Zbornik radova Ekonomskog fakulteta u Rijeci 2010; 28 (2) 221-250.

[6] Jurše M, Logožar K, Ključevšek M, Korez-Vide R. Diagonal cumulation of origin as an institutional incentive mechanism for cost optimisation in contemporary international business. Acta oeconomica 2011; 61 (2) 165-191.

[7] Kogut B, Zander U. Knowledge of the Firm and the Evolutionary Theory of the Multinational Corporation. Journal of International Business Studies 1993; 24 (4) 625-645.

[8] Craig S, Douglas S. Managing the Transnational Value Chain – Strategies for Firms from Emerging Markets. Journal of International Marketing 1997; 5 (3) 71-84.

[9] Eisenhardt K, Jeffrey MA. Dynamic Capabilities: What are they? Strategic Management Journal 2000; 21 (10-11) 1105-1121.

[10] Inama S. Rules of Origin in International Trade. UK: Cambridge University Press; 2011.

[11] Augier P, Gasiorek M, Lai Tong C. The impact of rules of origin on trade flows. Economic Policy 2005; 20 (43) 567-624.

[12] Gasiorek M. The impact of the diagonal cumulation of RoO in the context of Euro-med integration. http://www.femise.org/PDF/ci2006/FEM31-13.pdf (accessed 23 November 2009).

[13] Woolcock S. European Union Policy towards Free Trade Agreements. ECIPE Working Paper No. 03/2007. Available from: http://www.ecipe.org/publications/ecipe-working-papers/european-union-policy-towards-free-trade-agreements/PDF (accessed 2 January 2010).

[14] Bhagwati J. Termits in the Trading System: How Preferential Agreements undermine Free Trade. New York: Oxford University Press; 2008.

[15] Van de Heetkamp A, Tusveld R. Origin Management: Rules of Origin in Free Trade Agreements. Berlin, Heidelberg: Springer; 2011.

[16] European Commission. Taxation and Customs Union, System of Pan-Euro-Mediterranean cumulation. http://ec.europa.eu (accessed 5 January 2009).

[17] European Commission. The Stabilisation and Association Process. http://ec.europa.eu/enlargement/enlargement_process/accession_process/how_does_a_country_join_the_eu/sap/index_en.htm (accessed 27 November 2009).

[18] European Commission. Communication from the Commission to the European Parliament and the Council – COM (2008)127 final, Western Balkans: Enhancing the European perspective. http://ec.europa.eu/enlargement/pdf/balkans_communication/western_balkans_communication_050308_en.pdf (accessed 12 November 2009).

[19] European Commission. The Thessaloniki Agenda for the Western Balkans. http://ec.europa.eu/enlargement/enlargement_process/accession_process/how_does_a_country_join_the_eu/sap/thessaloniki_agenda_en.htm (accessed 16 November 2009).
[20] European Commission. Communication from the European Commission COM (2006) 27 final The Western Balkans on the road to the EU: consolidating stability and raising prosperity.http://eur-lex.europa.eu/LexUriServ/LexUriServ.do?uri=COM:2006:0027:FIN:EN:PDF (accessed 13 November 2009).
[21] HM Revenue & Customs. Tariff Preference: Cumulation of Origin – EC and the WBCs. http://www.hmrc.gov.uk/jccc/cips/2009/cip-09-69.pdf (accessed 10 November 2009).
[22] European Union & United Nations Partnership in Action, 8th Union for the Mediterranean Ministerial Conference. Conclusions from the 8th Euromed Trade Ministerial Conference. http://www.europa-eu-un.org/articles/en/article_9301_en.htm (accessed 21 December 2009).
[23] Council of the EU. Regional Convention on Pan-Euro-Mediterranean preferential rules of origin. http://register.consilium.europa.eu/pdf/en/10/st09/st09/st09429.en10.pdf (accessed 12 November 2011).
[24] Council of the EU. Council Decision on the signing, on behalf of the EU, of the Regional Convention on pan-Euro-Mediterranean preferential rules of origin. http://register.consilium.europa.eu/pdf/en/10/st09/st09124-re03.en10.pdf (accessed 12 November 2011).
[25] European Commission. Western Balkan Countries, Main Economic Indicators. http://trade.ec.europa.eu/doclib/docs/2006/september/tradoc_113477.pdf (accessed 30 March 2012)
[26] Centre for Social and Economic Research. Economic Integration in the Euro-Mediterranean Region. Final Report. http://trade.ec.europa.eu/doclib/docs/2009/october/tradoc_145214.pdf (accessed 21 December 2009).
[27] European Commission. News about Western Balkans. http://ec.europa.eu/enlargemet/press_corner/whatsnew/western-balkans_en.htm (accessed 2 February 2010).
[28] Centre for European Perspective. Movement of goods in the area of the EU, EFTA, Turkey and CEFTA: Facilitation of Cooperation Potential, Seminar Report. Ljubljana: CEP; 2008.
[29] Kumar A. EU Trade Policy and Western Balkan Countries – A Way to regional trade growth. In: Zalokar M., Ferle T., Dolničar Jeraj, A. (eds.) Movement of goods in the area of the EU, EFTA, Turkey and CEFTA: Facilitation of Cooperation Potential. Ljubljana, Slovenija: Centre for European Perspective; 2008. p99–115.
[30] Kumar A, Kandžija V. Theory of trade and integration applied for trade perspectives in the area of western Balkans. In: Kumar A, Kandžija V. (eds.) 7th International Conference Economic Integration, Competition and Cooperation, 2-3 April 2009, Opatija, Croatia. Rijeka: Ekonomski fakultet; 2009.
[31] European Commission. Bilateral Relations Statistics. http://ec.europa.eu/trade/creating-opportunities/bilateral-relations/statistics (Accessed 15 November 2009).

[32] Montanari M. EU trade with the Balkans. Large Room for Growth? Eastern European Economics 2005; 43 (1) 59-81.
[33] Bussière M, Fidrmuc J, Schnatz B. EU Enlargement and Trade Integration: Lessons from a Gravity Model. Review of Development Economics 2008; 12 (3) 562-576.
[34] Škuflić L, Botrić V. Analysis of the Cohesive Trade Elements between the European Union and the SEEC-7. Eastern European Economics 2008; 46 (1) 6-23.
[35] Zajc Kejžar K. Ideas for EU extended support for trade growth in the Western Balkan Countries: Diagonal versus bilateral cumulation of origin. In: Zalokar M, Ferle T, Dolničar A. (eds.) Movement of goods in the area of the EU, EFTA, Turkey and CEFTA: Facilitation of Cooperation Potential, Ljubljana, Slovenia: Centre for European Perspective; 2008. p117-131.
[36] European Commission. A User's Handbook to the Rules of Preferential Origin used in trade between the European Community, other European Countries and the countries participating to the Euro Mediterranean Partnership. http://ec.europa.eu/ taxation_customs/ resources/documents/handbook_en.pdf (accessed 21 December 2009).
[37] European Commission. Proposal for a Council Decision concerning the signing and conclusion of the Interim Agreement on trade and trade-related matters between the European Community, of the one part, and the Republic of Serbia, of the other part COM(2007)744 final. http://eur-lex.europa.eu/LexUriServ/site/en/com/2007/com2007_ 0744en01_01.doc (accessed 12 November 2009).
[38] European Commission. Western Balkan Countries. http://trade.ec.europa.eu/doclib/ docs/2006/september/tradoc_113477.pdf (accessed 15 November 2009).
[39] World Bank. Duty and Tax Relief and Suspension Schemes. Improving Export Competitiveness. http://siteresources.worldbank.org/INTEXPCOMNET/Resources/ duty_and_tax_toolkit_pub_screen_2009.pdf (accessed 14 December 2009).